D1189575

BEYOND
NAIVE
BELIEF

BEYOND NAIVE BELIEF

The Bible and Adult Catholic Faith

PAUL E. DINTER

CROSSROAD • NEW YORK

DB # 1212345

1994

The Crossroad Publishing Company
370 Lexington Avenue, New York, NY 10017

Printed in the United States of America

Library of Congress Cataloging-in-Publication Data

Dinter, Paul E. (Paul Edward)
    Beyond naive belief : the Bible and adult Catholic faith / Paul E. Dinter.
        p.   cm.
    Includes bibliographical references and indexes.
    ISBN 0-8245-1421-1
    1. Catholic Church—Doctrines. 2. Faith and reason. 3. Bible—Hermeneutics. 4. Vatican Council (2nd : 1962–1965) 5. Catholic Church—Apologetic works.   I. Title.
BX1751.2.D532 1994
230'.2—dc20   94-1498
                                                                          CIP

BX
1751.2
.D532
1994

In gratitude to
Joe and Michele
Doug and Susan
Marilyn, Caitlin, and Tara

Let it be recognized that all the faithful, clerical and lay,
possess a lawful freedom of inquiry and of thought,
and the freedom to express their minds humbly
and courageously about those matters
in which they enjoy competence.

—Pastoral Constitution on the Church in the Modern World,
Second Vatican Council

Contents

Acknowledgments

My interest in biblical and doctrinal hermeneutics began under the tutelage of Joseph A. Komonchak (Catholic University of America), Richard E. Dillon (Fordham University), and James A. Sanders (Ancient Biblical Manuscript Center, Claremont, California). A year's sabbatical granted by Cardinal John O'Connor while I was still a member of the clergy allowed me to begin work on this book, and the hospitality of the Collegio Maryknoll in Rome provided a most congenial setting for it. My thanks to Peggy and Peter Steinfels, Daniel and Sidney Callahan, and John and Regina Garvey, who read an early version of the initial chapter and provided good advice and encouragement. In addition, I would like to thank Richard Billow, Curt Cadorette, Marie Giblin, and Jack Ratschmitt for their advice on different chapters. My onetime editor at Crossroad, Frank Oveis, was an invaluable help. A final and thorough once-over by my old-new colleague Chuck Antony helped make many rough ways smooth. Lastly, the friends to whom I have dedicated this book know how much I owe them.

Introduction

Living with the Aftershocks of Vatican II

This book began its long gestation period during a sabbatical year I spent *ad limina apostolorum*, "on the doorstep of the apostles," in Rome. For fifteen years before that sojourn, I had ministered at a major secular university, known to Catholics as the spawning ground of Thomas Merton's conversion. As he found it in 1936, so Columbia has remained: a bastion of academic rationality with all the thrills and ills of a large "factory." Working as a chaplain with religious and secular Jews, with liberal Protestants as well as evangelicals, with medievalists and molecular biologists, with historians who doubled as activists, with feminists seeking to move mountains of masculine prerogative, and with unnumbered earnest, bright, and high-achieving students contributed greatly to my own spiritual and emotional life.

My Columbia experience also gave me a perspective that, when I was in Rome, made me increasingly uncomfortable with the way Roman ecclesiastics continue to formulate, promulgate, and enforce Catholic truth claims. As a result, I have increasingly found myself questioning, not the Catholic faith as such, but the hierarchy's mode of proclaiming that faith today. In this work, then, I have tried to puzzle through the historical clash between biblical faith (as it continues to be handed on — the act of *traditio* — in the Catholic Church) and its antagonist Reason. I explore two very different ways of knowing and expressing human experience: the world of the Bible, the mythopoetic realm of thought, and that of the modern mindset we call critical rationality. I also ask how these two worlds can encounter each other afresh.

Until recently, the task of handing on the Bible's message was not thought to be so problematic. It had taken the form of identifying the "timeless truths" of the Bible and of expressing them in a permanent idiom that reflected the permanence of "the True Faith." But the Second Vatican Council (1962–65) enormously complicated this task when it explicitly accepted historical change as the normative context for understanding and appropriating the ancient faith of the church: henceforth

1

even the notions of "timeless truth" and "perennial philosophy" had themselves to be interpreted within the historical context in which they were formulated.

With Vatican II, Catholics turned a corner on the past. We admitted, unknowingly for the most part, that we have a history. Because of *historical consciousness,* we think differently about ourselves than people in former eras did. The past is available to us only through critical study of its evidentiary traces, and our own contemporary history is at least partly the result of the way we have constructed the past. Historical consciousness reveals, further, that at some point Christians stopped seeing themselves as participants in a sacred drama and found themselves sitting in the audience as spectators.

Before the advent of historical consciousness, people naturally paid attention to eternal values and changeless truths; they had a sense that "things don't change." But beginning with the Renaissance and continuing through the Reformation to the Enlightenment and the scientific revolution, every society affected by modernity has slowly had to admit that things have changed. History has a real claim on us, because we live in a world different from that of St. Paul when he wrote to the church at Corinth that "the shape of this world is passing away" (1 Cor 7:31). Contemporary believers know that the world has *not* passed away, nor do most believe it will do so soon — but the world *has* changed greatly. Having a history indelibly marks our way of thinking about everything, not just about the past, for history demands that we constantly reevaluate the past; and when we do, our own present context changes also.

Even before the Second Vatican Council, the Catholicism shaped in the era after the Council of Trent (1545–63) had begun to accept many of the habits of modernity, at least in northern Europe and North America. Yet much of the way Catholic faith was practiced continued to flout the notion of historical change, holding to a standard of orthodoxy that saw itself reflected in the mirror of eternity. When the council was meeting, it intuitively engaged in a formidable balancing act. Council documents affirmed continuity with the mythopoetic world of the Bible and with the dogmatic and moral tradition shaped by it; tensions between the biblical tradition itself and the philosophical and legal habits that had come to dominate Catholic faith expression generally went unnoticed. But, at the same time, the council documents broke with this complex past, accepting some of the Reformation's program, employing historical-critical perspectives, and admitting the reality of progress, development, and pluralism — all "social science" perspectives — as it proceeded to make new applications of the tradition.

During the council, the friction inherent in these diverse perspectives was lost on most participants in their acceptance of the groundbreaking nature of their work. Thirty years later, that friction has become harder to live with and the balancing act is tougher to sustain. More than the council fathers could have envisioned, their bold acceptance of the critical rationality of the Enlightenment has irretrievably changed the moral and spiritual world that the church inhabits. No longer is the church challenged by outside secular or political forces. The crisis we have been enduring (at least since 1968) has been, to the chagrin of many at both ends of ideological spectrum, internally generated.

Like two great plates shifting beneath the earth, the council's two tensive modes of affirmation, representing historically diverse ways of understanding and speaking about belief, have begun to produce significant shockwaves throughout the household of faith. The equilibrium struck by Vatican II (and purposely maintained in the documents of the Extraordinary Synod of 1985) has become unsteady both in ordinary settings of church life and in settings where centralized Roman authority makes itself felt. Tensions have been building for people on either side of the fault line: for the average layperson constantly torn between the hierarchy's teaching and a host of modern attitudes; for parents smarting over the different treatment the church affords their male and female children; for women angry with the hierarchy's uncompromising stands; for curial and chancery officials who feel responsibility for guiding the body of believers; for theologians wary of censorious authority; for educational administrators on notice against unacceptable speakers and teachers; for bishops afraid of appearing weak or unorthodox.

So much energy is required to balance the tensive forms of expressing Catholic belief and so intense has the friction become that there are parishes, faculties, and dioceses beginning to split apart, attitudinally if not organizationally. In the rough seas created by these seismic rumblings, the pope and the Curia have grabbed at the rudder to steer the Bark of Peter in the direction of "church tradition" (the *tradita,* the concrete faith expressions of the past) at the expense of "new applications" (the ongoing process of *traditio*). But other crew members — and many passengers — want to set a course in a new direction lest tradition petrify and theological plurality be prevented from expressing the full range of cultures that encompasss global Catholicism today.

The council's momentary reconciliation of worldviews was inspired and truly historic, but also adventuresome. As I hope to show, Vatican II began to heal a rift in Western culture and history that had alienated religious faith from humanist endeavor for centuries. The council was the kind of great historical event whose repercussions are felt long after it met. But it acted intuitively; it did not work out any long-term reconciliation between two very different ways of talking about God the creator and us, God's creatures. Throughout this inquiry I will use the terms "naive" and "critical" as shorthand ways of referring to the different worldviews that the council juxtaposed. But because these mentalities are not so easily balanced over time and because Catholic theology has not worked through a way of moving beyond the differences between them, I fear that we face a prolonged conflict between their proponents. Tragically, this would appear to many to repeat the eighteenth-century battle of revelation vs. reason, or the religion vs. science (fideist vs. rationalist) debate of the nineteenth century, or, worst of all, the modernist vs. integralist struggle of the early twentieth century.

Rather than choose either right or left, orthodoxy or orthopraxis, conservatism or liberalism, I wish to explore the actual way that faith in the Christ event is developing as a result of Catholicism's newfound historicity. This study, then, will try to stage a conversation between a *naively expressed revelation* and a *critically shaped culture* that seems to have repudiated its naive, mythopoetical base. I wish to suggest that when we look at the roots of both mythopoetic antiquity and critical modernity from a genuinely postcritical perspective, we have the wherewithal to transcend the naive-vs.-critical impasse. In other words, a new conversation between the two, when expanded to take our basic modes of knowing into account, yields a common shape, a parallel morphology between human culture and religious faith.

Changes in the form faith has taken and the languages it has used follow a pattern similar to the changes Western religion and culture have undergone and that we as developing human beings also necessarily undergo. When we correlate these patterns we can perhaps see better that the risk the Second Vatican Council took was truly inspired. As a result, what the church believes and how we affirm that belief can continue to develop, first, by appropriating the critical rationality of the Enlightenment and, second, in a move beyond critical autonomy, by arriving at a postcritical belief. But this can happen only when Catholic faith accommodates itself to the legitimate demands of critical rationality, beyond its mythopoetic matrix. Rather than resisting these demands, faith affirmation can learn from them; and by attending more deeply to its own inner sources of identity, faith can grow, through a process of critical judgment that arrives at postcritical affirmation.

The current work begins by exploring how the Bible's first reading of God's relationship to the world exemplifies the naive understanding that arises in the mythopoetic origins of all human knowledge; "in the beginning" symbolic formulations are inevitable and represent a necessarily naive level of apprehension (chapter 1). Chapter 2 will show how both philosophical interpretation and law-keeping enactment of the Bible's mythic perspectives conditioned and conceptually nuanced, but did not question, the basic shape of naive belief. The accommodations made by both Jewish and Christian interpreters of mythopoetic texts in fact resemble the accommodations between intellectual and affective areas of development that preadolescents make in the period known as latency.

In chapters 3 and 4 I will then draw a parallel between the loss of the mythopoetic worldview at the hands of the Enlightenment's rationalist agenda and the critical moment in individual development when adolescence begins the journey to adulthood. Chapter 5 will argue that the critical rejection of naive religious consciousness has been undermined by its own inability to dispel the unconscious or metarational aspects of the way the world impinges on human experience. This discovery will allow me to suggest that reappropriating meaning (and faith) on a deeper level can occur through a postcritical, mature recovery that reincorporates the mythopoetic elements of the scriptures (and the self) in a chastened but truthful fashion. I will argue that reintegrating the personal unconscious in mature individuals approximates the dynamics involved in working out a mature (canonical) hermeneutics of the Bible (chapter 6). Analogously, in chapter 7 I will parallel another aspect of maturity, the ability to mourn the past, with faith affirmation's capacity to repent of historical attitudes that have left us guilty, submissive, and childish in the kind of faith that we profess.

In chapters 8 though 10 I will sketch the various forms of faith affirmation across a spectrum that examines the way each stage looks at specific modern doctrinal formulations: natural law, papal infallibility, the Immaculate Conception, and the Assumption of Mary. A comparative reading of these doctrines will show the extent to which Catholic faith in the modern era has been formulated too narrowly in reaction to rationalism and historicism. A defensive quest for unity of faith has led to a stunting of doctrinal understanding, secured by oaths and enforced by ideological watchdogs who are convinced only one kind of faith affirmation is adequate to express that living relationship between believer and Revealer which is the gift and response of faith.

In opposition to this perspective, I will argue that naive, critical, and mature believers all worship the object of their faith and live their response legitimately within a range available in the metaphorical indeterminacy of faith and morals. Finally, *what* doctrine affirms is not independent from but a correlate of *how* it is affirmed. Ultimately, mature faith is authorized by an encounter with the living and self-revealing Mystery of God, not by recourse to authoritative teaching that grasps to control what is ineffable. Grace abounds, no matter the circumstances of our personal or historical development: the accommodating womb of God's mercy provides shelter for the various forms of belief we find ourselves professing.

Bibliographical Essay

(In acknowledgment of the authors whose written works I have consulted, the sources of quotations will be cited in end notes, and other contributions will be credited in the bibliographical essays that follow each chapter.)

Thomas Merton's *The Seven Storey Mountain* (New York: Harcourt, Brace, 1948) describes his experience extensively, but introduces it in this way:

Now I come to speak of the real part Columbia seems to have been destined to play in my life in the providential designs of God. Poor Columbia! It was founded by sincere Protestants as a college predominantly religious.... Yet, strangely enough, it was on this big factory of a campus that the Holy Ghost was waiting to show me the light, in His own light. And one of the chief means He used...was human friendship. (177)

I have found persuasive the work of Peter Gay, whose *The Enlightenment — An Interpretation: The Rise of Modern Paganism* (New York: Random House, 1966) details

the great discovery of Enlightenment historiography, a discovery for which writers of our time have found more precise language: that there are, generally speaking, two ways in which men confront themselves, their experience, their fate, and that these are summed up in the mythopoeic and the critical mentality. (89)

On doing critical theology: David Tracy's *The Analogical Imagination: Christian Theology and the Culture of Pluralism* (New York: Crossroad, 1986) describes theology as the effort to "reinterpret or retrieve classical resources of the church tradition in genuinely new applications for the present day" (340). In his *Plurality and Ambiguity: Hermeneutics, Religion, Hope* (San Francisco: Harper & Row, 1987) he characterizes the attitude of today's intransigents in the church in this way: "We true believers, and we alone, have not ceded to the demands of cultural change. We alone have remained pure and innocent, treating modernity with the contempt it deserves. We are the tradition and the tradition is pure" (101). I have found in both of these works analyses of our present situation that undergird my own attempts to stage conversations both between faith and reason and between faith and history. Sandra M. Schneiders's *The Revelatory Text: Interpreting the New Testament as Sacred Scripture* (San Francisco: HarperSanFrancisco, 1991) presents a careful attempt at formulating a hermeneutical method for Catholic scriptural interpretation. The present work encompasses her concerns, especially the results of our "effective historical consciousness," but seeks to work out some of the implications of these results for the church's faith. Unlike James W. Fowler's *Stages of Faith: The Psychology of Human Development and the Quest for Meaning* (San Francisco: Harper & Row, 1981), which protests the "shallowing of faith" involved in reducing "belief" to adherence to creedal statements and distinguishes between "faith" and "belief" (14), I will not surrender to the reduction and will continue to use the words synonymously. I use "faith affirmation" throughout to speak of both the praxis of believing and the reasoned attempt to make sense of an experience of revelation.

Adela Y. Collins adumbrates the framework of this present work in her *Crisis and Catharsis: The Power of the Apocalypse* (Philadelphia: Westminster Press, 1984), where she affirms that "every text can be read in three different ways: precritically, critically, and postcritically." Her work, benefiting (as does Schneiders's) from the interpretation theory of Paul Ricoeur, seeks to "explore the possibilities for a postcritical reading of Revelation" (22).

On the impact and outcome of Vatican II and the postconciliar setting: Walter Ong, S.J., in his *Fighting for Life: Contest, Sexuality and Consciousness* (Amherst: University of Massachusetts Press, 1989), locates an underlying male-female dialectic not only in all Catholic theology but particularly in Vatican II's change from an "agonistic" and polemical (masculine) manner of self-affirmation to a nonagonistic (feminine) one (170). Because he affirms that this is part of a feminine change in consciousness away from the contest orientation of earlier periods, it means that male-female issues were bound to become the most neuralgic in the postconciliar period. John W. O'Malley, S.J., argues in *Tradition and Transition: Historical Perspectives on Vatican II* (Wilmington: Michael Glazier, 1989) that Vatican II's idea of *aggiornamento* was "a revolution in the history of the idea of reform" in that it brought modernity's "historical consciousness" directly to bear in Catholicism, bringing about a shift in Catholic consciousness. Vatican II thus constitutes a "great reformation" in the church and not just a "reform" movement (107–8). Xavier Rynne's *John Paul's Extraordinary Synod: A Collegial Achievement* (Wilmington, Del.: Michael Glazier, 1986) notes that the "issue of the comprehension of love in communion of the church hierarchical as well as parochial had been cavalierly avoided by the synodal participants" (104).

Frans Jozef van Beeck, S.J., in his *Catholic Identity after Vatican II: Three Types of Faith in the One Church* (Chicago: Loyola University Press, 1985), writes of three levels of faith experience but distinguishes his efforts from those of Erik Erikson and James Fowler, because they can create "the impression that growth in the spirit is a function of human perfection" (80). The older approach van Beeck seeks to revive is that of the Alexandrian and medieval writers who proposed categories like natural, psychic, and spiritual understanding or the purgative, illuminative, and unitive ways to perfection. The present work seeks to combine the insights of developmental psychology with the theological tradition of *how* grace "elevates and perfects" not static but dynamic natural forms of understanding.

Chapter 1

In the Beginning Was the Image

Once upon a Time

Anyone wishing to trace the tangle of Christian imagination as it flows through history must return to its source in the two-testament Bible. Though other tributaries have fed Christianity's self-identity, the Bible's worldview remains foundational. Even at the end of the twentieth century, the Bible's naive first reading of the world, as it appeared once upon a time and as it appears to the eye of the naive beholder today, pervades our consciousness. Its pictures of the world, which we ingested early on, are embedded in our imaginations.

In the first chapter of Genesis, God calls light into being to fill the void where yet there was nothing. Because light exists even when the sun is not shining (both before dawn and on a completely cloudy day), the prescientific author does not see a cause and effect relationship between light and its physical source: the sun is created three days after the light! Only on the fourth day does God create sun and moon and give them authority over day and night. But daylight is merely ruled by the sun, not caused by it. This text of Genesis, then, is a good example of a primarily naive understanding of the world. It represents a first reading of the *text* of the cosmos, which results in a narrative text whose simple, mythopoetical picture of the world reflects the author's (and readers') primarily naive understanding. Ironically, the author's ignorance of physics allowed "light" to expand symbolically. By analogy with the way it replaces darkness, light became a metaphor for awakening, for understanding, for illustrating and celebrating the growth of knowledge, for the moral opposition of good to evil, and for a host of "illuminating" human experiences. Hence, light is a symbol, properly speaking, whose surplus or excess of meaning cannot be exhausted by a single determinant. Yet its excess of meaning does not diminish or obscure its ability to name the physical reality itself. Rather, its symbolic quality encompasses all the physical properties that scientific investigation has discovered (including its speed, which opens up new possibilities for its metaphorical use). As has been noted in fields from theology to politics, symbols function. They mean more than can be easily described.[1]

Physically sensuous modes of perception underlie all naive understandings of our world. But when I speak of naive understanding or primary naivete, I do not intend a pejorative, hypercritical, or condescending attitude toward this mode of knowing. Nor do I argue for the quaintness, the superiority, or the radically chic nature of primary naivete. Rather, I am trying to read the Bible on its own terms before asking how we continue to be affected by its worldview, by its preference for metaphor, for poetic and symbolic expression, rather than literal, factual description. To do this fairly, it will help to take into account other settings in which events and ideas are metaphorically or symbolically presented.

Mythic versions of national dramas are the common stock of popular culture. They become the stuff of story books, novels, films, and, more problematically, political campaigns as well. An eclectic version or text of a familiar myth runs something like this:

I believe that God put this great land here between the ocean seas so that it could be discovered by people who were longing to be free. They came here and settled this uninhabited wilderness, clearing the land with their bare hands, working from dawn till dusk on their farms and in their cities. When necessary, they were willing, although reluctant, to take up weapons to ensure their freedom and their independence. And in the wake of these pioneers came shiploads of the tired, poor, and oppressed people from the old world who were welcomed to these shores and given their rightful place in a productive economy so that they too could, within a generation, enjoy the blessings of life, liberty, and the pursuit of happiness. Twice within this century the brave people of this land have gone to the rescue of the countries they themselves had fled to win a similar liberty for their cousins whom they had left behind. We truly are "the land of the free and the home of the brave," willing to bear any burden and pay any price to keep the torch of liberty glowing in a world threatened with tyrannical darkness.

This not unfamiliar recital of the American myth is primitive or naive because of the simplicity of its outlook: it summarizes a complex historical phenomenon in uncomplicated terms. Hardly by chance, it ignores whole groups who don't fit its premises (Native Americans, black Africans) and overlooks ambiguous chapters (exclusion of ethnic minorities) that might interrupt the smooth and poetic feel of the whole. Phrases such as "uninhabited wilderness," "brave people," and "bare hands" are evocative and suggestive (if not as symbolic as "torch of liberty"), and the use of phrases from foundational documents and national poetry casts a certain pall of sacrality over the whole text.

From a critical or seriously reflective point of view, this myth is spurious, false, and dishonest. One hopes that no one older than a sixth grader would harbor such a view of the events in U.S. history and that contemporary textbooks avoid presenting it in this light. Nevertheless, we know that when recited in political speeches or debates the myth still has great effect. Politicians who engage in such simplifications are not hooted from the stage or driven from the public arena. Behind a seeming lack of accuracy lies a technical, even cynical, sophistication about symbolic communication, and people who comprehend this mythic text naively will show hostility to a critical perspective that challenges their worldview. But those with a critical worldview normally express hostility to such a myth and its symbols that can obfuscate and distort facts, maintain prejudice, and promote injustice. Such differences between a naive or mythopoetic worldview and a critical perspective on the world — along with conflicts that arise because of them — set the stage for all that follows.

Both the Genesis creation of light and our myth-making politician's tale encourage a primary-naivete perspective on one's mental and imaginative world and hence promote or encourage a first reading not only of texts but of the world around us. While late twentieth-century Western culture prides itself on being scientific in its worldview and self-understanding, our very sophistication can, in turn, make us blind to the enduring impact of the prerational, symbolic aspect of things. Critical pundits shake their heads in disbelief at the endurance into the present of political strife and armed conflict among groups with different religious or symbolic systems. But they ignore what's at work when people in our own society organize their lives around a favorite sports team's schedule, or a ritually repeated leisure-time activity, or a manic garnering of sex partners — all prerational activities symbolic in their enactment, with real implications for the way people live their lives.

For though we live in a society structured by linear time measured in nanoseconds, our imagination still operates *mythically* wherever "once upon a time" still predominates. Mythic events do not require date or place in order to be understood. In fact, we are attracted to the timelessness of mythic recitals because, unlike our day-to-day, businesslike orientation to hours and minutes, the atemporal touches our underlying desire to escape that most abstract, yet real, constraint that we call time. Hence, mythic time (*kairos*) predominates when a professedly critical perspective on the past (*chronos*) does not serve us well in social, political, or religious discourse. An example might make this point more clearly.

In every individual's memory there reside early foundational images of grandparents, parents, and others who surrounded us in our earliest years and made up our immediate world. In most cases, we retain these images in our preconscious awareness, and we need only the right setting, such as a holiday family gathering, for them to spring into life.

Enshrined in familiar stories, these images (or ideals) tend to be mythic principally because they are put together uncritically and, though event-oriented ("Remember the time Mama forgot to cook the turkey..."), they retain an aura of the vague past not unlike the dream time of aboriginal peoples. In fact, the member of the family who claims to be able to pin down mythic events exactly ("It was Thanksgiving 1958") is generally understood to be a bore!

Christmas around the tree and other family gatherings are often remembered in primarily naive terms with a certain mythic glow that obscures the darker elements of what might really have happened. Our mythic memory often transforms a precious gift, a special trip, a favorite place into a symbol that embraces a whole era in our life or an entire skein of formative relationships. Again, the accuracy of such symbolized memories is clearly *a subsequent issue* — our first reading of the text of our lives has a primordial hold on us. Reality is rarely as simple as first readings present it; but first readings and naive understandings preserve elements of truth (unless we're dealing with conscious or unconscious idealizations) that should not be dismissed as simple, silly, or worthless ("naive" in the everyday sense). If we can see how the Bible does on a grand scale something that is characteristic of all human awareness, we may more fairly judge the problems and possibilities of a religious faith anchored in, but not limited to, the worldview of the scriptures.

Paleological Knowledge

Unlike Venus, who sprang full-grown from the brow of Zeus, human awareness had more childlike beginnings. Primitive human thought is said to have grown in stages like those that every human infant undergoes, first in the womb and then outside it. Conscious awareness had a long gestation and, even when "humans" appeared, had not fully developed. Similarly, babies are expelled from the womb before they get too large to pass down the birth canal and out the vulva, not because they are ready to deal consciously with life outside the womb. Some theorists even speak of birth trauma to describe the harsh transition from the unitive state of the womb to the dualistic world of self and other. With its unlooked-for expulsion, a newborn's undetached awareness of the world and the self goes in a short period of time from being at one with its world to being challenged by separateness.

In its earliest stages, the separate awareness of the neonate is rudimentary, for the child is totally dependent on its parental matrix. Slowly, the infant begins to awaken and take on the unique character that we call personality. But this awakening does not occur as a mental act of self-reflection; it arises with the infant's spontaneous awareness of its own essential extrauterine needs. These needs, expressed as instincts, are the body's dawning desire for nourishment, care, relationship, knowledge, love, and life itself. This is the stage of development where *primary narcissism* pertains: newborn does not easily distinguish between its body and its mother's, between inside and outside. The way a child's world treats these primary needs will continue to affect how the child-become-adult imagines, thinks, and understands itself, others, the world — and God as well.[2]

The human infant provides us with an analogy for understanding the earliest stages of human consciousness. Consciousness warmed in the womb of humanity's ancestors as a growing potential for knowing itself as *at one with* and as *separate from* its world. Primitive awareness, like a normal baby, came into the world instinctually preconditioned to know and to be known. *Homo* began to be *sapiens* when pure instinctual awareness, such as every newborn possesses, entertained an original interplay of elements of self and other in a way that the fusion of the two strengthened each to become distinct from the other. Poetically, the first chapter of Genesis captured the significance of this original unity in distinction when it portrayed God as creating light by *separating* it from darkness. Similarly, God created male and female as at one with though separate from each other and from the divine imager. What each had in common was as significant as what separated each from the other. Wholeness was more than the sum of the parts because contrast and unity were not conceived as divergent.

But an infant's ability to make sense of itself and the world develops slowly, in stages that reflect an increasing awareness of self and other. Sights, sounds, smells, tactile objects, cutaneous sensations all intrude upon the infant recently exiled from the womb. But instinctual awareness distinguishes self from the other, paradoxically, by *putting together* meanings in primitive acts of awareness that little by little resemble understanding. As the instincts of growing infants become more refined and their awareness engages in its most basic activity, they preverbally *symbolize* the interaction of the self and the world.[3] For instance, the mother's breast is put together with the child's experience of hunger being satisfied; the child preconceptually and preverbally symbolizes goodness, pleasure, and survival by associating them with its experience of the breast. For the suckling infant, this feedback from the environment begins to shape a primitive representational model of what the world is like. The baby internalizes an image of the breast as a functioning symbol of the world's bounty and care. This becomes the earliest or *paleological* knowledge of the infant. By internalizing an original experience of meaning, the infant develops from a simple reflex stage to a more complex stage of organization. Further along in the process, a baby primitively recognizes facial features, then distinguishes different faces, and so increases its ability to discriminate sensory input by putting together physical experiences with interiorized representations in what we rightly call *symbolic* or *preconceptual thought.* The infant knows intuitively or instinctually whether the care-giver (particularly its mother) is present or absent, though no concept of presence or absence is yet explicitly formed. In all animals, instinctive behavior yields to primitive awareness, but it achieves self-consciousness in humans only through the more developed behavioral systems in which humans learn and integrate everything though their further instinct for model-building or symbolic activity.[4]

Instinct here is different from animal instinctuality. It is our basically human, psychic apparatus precisely in its ability to entertain both ideas and affects. Instinct, then, *puts together* our body-mind unity and, as what Harry Stack Sullivan called *paleologic,* it underlies all abstract, rational thinking. Consequently, as we develop, we continue to differentiate the self and the world through a further interiorization of what is outside of us by representing it symbolically in our mind's eye. What is more, we bridge all subsequent gaps in our understanding by putting together objects, events, sensations, or concrete particulars with what they mean — what value they have, what ideals they bespeak. This link between basic instinctual awareness and our ability to symbolize all of reality undergirds the Aristotelian/Thomistic premise that "all our knowing begins from the senses."[5] In other words, nothing becomes part of human awareness, positively or negatively, without being put together as a sensed or (as it becomes familiar) a known symbol or image — and all of this is true long before we begin to take words or language into account.

Symbols, then, are the mind's earliest way of imaginatively putting together meaning. Our earliest conceptualizations consist of representational models by which subjective phenomena (such as hunger and satiety) interact with the world outside to create networks of associations that underlie all cognition. These model-objects help human consciousness to hold its world together. They function throughout our lives as we struggle to manage, as one theorist has put it, "the strain of relating inner and outer reality."[6]

Infant symbolizing takes on added importance because, as outside stimulations increase and sensations multiply, a baby's developing apparatus cannot consciously take in many ideas, affects, or their immediate associations. As the infant grows into childhood, the overflow is unconsciously catalogued and stored away via symbolic memory. Perhaps the best example of this phenomenon involves the smells that our sensitive, unforgetting olfactory nerves store away in memory cells. Smells act like sensory images that can be recalled years later, recreating an entire scene or environment long lost from consciousness. Sensory impressions of all sorts either remain unconscious, creating strange feelings or distracting ideas in the adult, or they rise to consciousness and reconnect previously unremembered associations with their originating event or persons. These images in the memory sleep, like the princess in *Sleeping Beauty,* waiting to be reawakened. Or they jut up into consciousness, bobbing like so many iceberg tips in the primal sea of the mind, as the self and its world become increasingly differentiated and consciously organized.

Because this process of symbolizing lies at the heart of awareness and of our conscious and unconscious memory, human beings generally begin to understand themselves as separate from and connected to others on the basis of this reservoir of internal or physic images long before they become capable of language or abstract thought. How extensive this psychic reservoir is — whose is it, and where it comes from — are questions still debated and cannot be solved here.[7] But evidence for this image-oriented, symbolic quality of primal awareness comes from the range of daydreams, fantasies, and dream imagery that accompany humans into advanced old age. Both as infants and later, we understand ourselves and our connectedness with (or disconnectedness from) the world first through images, through nonverbal thought. So basic is it to our mind/body functioning that we suppress our capacity and need for it at the price of our mental and emotional health. What is at stake is nothing less than both our sense of being and our sense of being a self.

Coming back to our analogy between individual development and aboriginal human experience, we can suppose that when the earliest humans began to use language, they would have resembled physically mature infants. Both historically and individually, before humans used language explicitly, our awareness was and is instinctually oriented through impressions made on the template of our senses. These sensory images are then primitively assembled into cognitive maps or working models that shape awareness and actions preverbally and prereflectively. This pictorial or image-orientation of our human paleologic creates a predisposition within us for symbolic understanding about ourselves, others, and the world. Before thinking is able to mature and be abstract, schematized, or properly reflective, it is instinctual.

Just as important, this preverbal and technically preratiocinative awareness survives into adulthood alongside, or beneath, linguistic ability and personal self-awareness. Consequently, it affects our fundamental understanding of ourselves, our world, and our personal interactions — both consciously and unconsciously. In Christian anthropology, this depth level of awareness has been generally underestimated, if not blamed on outside forces such as tempters or demons, because of a bias toward viewing humans as *rational* animals, essentially different from all purely instinctive ones. The explicit view of the human mind as essentially spiritual and not material has led the theological tradition to underestimate the paleological (and prerational) basis of all human awareness and understanding. By starting with the instinctual and sensory basis of all human thought "in the beginning," I am seeking to establish how all human knowing is deeply grounded in the seedbed of our mind/body unity, in what may still be called the soul or the psyche. We human beings — for better or worse — *know* ourselves and our world long before we can *reflect upon* either, before we are tuned to explicit, rational thinking, or abstract ideas. Because we develop slowly, our early sense experiences create the very ground of ongoing human awareness and remain embedded there.

Conceptual knowledge follows as we grow, reaching its full potential during late adolescence. But it can never discard the working models we learned as young children. Those preconceptual pictures or cognitive maps determine to a large extent our self-images, our ability to articulate perspectives, even our basic cognitive and moral orientation toward the world around us. This perspective on the prereflective stage of human knowing results from the discoveries made in the last century by the biological and psychological sciences (catalyzed by psychoanalysis). It frankly represents a fundamental challenge to the mentalist tradition that Christian thought took over from classical culture, which held that the mind is distinct from and above the body.

In the past we have underestimated the significance of the body and its instinctual behavior in our evaluation of both mental capacity and moral functioning. A newer scientific view of the organic basis of human feeling and thinking may help us recover a better understanding of the unitary nature of our body-minds. Both as children and as adults, our facial expressions, hand gestures, body postures, and unconscious thoughts all encode messages about the way we see ourselves in relation to the world. Inevitably, we enact those messages symbolically. Before we speak our first word or entertain a conscious thought, images have been at work in us. The language we use is a necessary catalyst for our conscious understanding, but words fail in many situations because human awareness from the start has a preverbal basis that is aboriginally image-oriented and symbolic in its structure and operation. Early humans, much like infants (the word means "nonspeakers") not yet capable of reflective thinking, mapped their world in images, in unconscious impressions, because they were instinctually adept in the basic stuff of symbolic formation long before their mythopoeic imaginations achieved any form of speech.[8]

Language Born of Images

But eventually, as the human desire and capacity for intersubjectivity grows, nonverbal symbols slowly reach a critical mass. The uniquely human propensity to put together a more adequate relationship with the world, to act upon the environment and interact with it, reaches out via complex verbal expression. Yet the process is not automatic. It depends greatly on the total environment as well as the potential speaker's native capacities. According to language theorists, a human child comes to self-consciousness and learns language simultaneously. This means that a maturing child learns to correlate significant persons, things, and actions with overheard signs or words, not through individual conscious acts but instinctually, through the everyday practices that make up the public world of the child. Sounds develop meaning as they are used because of what has been called the pictorality of thought. We do not *name* reality by tagging it with syllables, words, sentences, or propositions. Rather, our conscious minds operate in continuity with earlier symbolizing. As language users, increasingly capable of explicit thinking or reasoning, we project a mental picture through the sounds that we have learned to be adequate for what we are interiorly imaging. Language is not something artificially invented to express knowledge already treasured in the mind; we practice language in order to live in society because society itself depends on language games to understand its own forms of life. The babble of infants, which represents their earliest form of language, is actual practice that allows them to experiment with a range of sounds. Eventually, through trial and error, the sounds become complex and children learn words. Thus, words and the concepts they will eventually express make sense only as part of the stream of life in which language-users participate as so many actual players. Lacking the opportunity to trade in pictures of shared reality, a child will not develop well and may always lack a capacity for language and a conscious self-presence. Even when we become sophisticated language users, we continue to transact reality by shaping, refining, hinting at, or playing with words against the background of the shifting pictorial and imaginative template of the mind, by which alone we can relate inner and outer reality.[9]

Like it or not, from childhood on we must learn to deal with the frustration of having more images or ideas than we will ever have adequate words to express. We can dream an entire drama in an instant but never find the right words to tell the tale. We instantly see complicated scenarios in our mind's eye, but only the best authors develop the skill to make literature of them. We feel the complex web of our emotional connections to those we love, need, or desire, but we struggle for the words to express what we feel. There has to be more to language than naming because there is so much more that cannot be said in any exact way.

This brings us back to the phenomenon of bridging the gap that underlies language. Human beings grow in their ability to bridge gaps between inner and outer reality and to connect the worlds that different individuals experience by *symbolizing*. This basic capacity underlies all our attempts to fashion meaning imaginatively and linguistically; yet because symbolizing engages imagination more basically than words can, language alone has a hard time expressing what the imagination, in its multileveled playfulness, does quite naturally. This is why a picture is worth a thousand words. Pictorial, poetic, or artistic creations do something for us because they function symbolically. They shape material objects (including musical sounds) in a way that defies simple denotation. Paintings, photography, poetry, music, and sculptures never possess merely a simple sense or have only one meaning. They always encapsulate multiple references or complex meanings.

It follows that all genuine symbols possess an excess of meaning that guarantees they will say something beyond the immediate setting or circumstance of their construction. In symbolic expression, more is always imagined than is said, more is seen than can be portrayed, more is encountered than can be expressed, more is transacted between people than can be described. As is said of the incarnate Word in the fourth gospel, "the whole world could not contain the books that would be written" if all that Jesus manifested were put into words (Jn 21:25). All profound moments of human communion are similar. The human imagination constantly incarnates its primary encounters with reality in literary, visual, musical, architectural, or plastic form and will never run out of ways to shape these often inchoate meanings. Some efforts achieve classic or canonical status, but, even so, we will never succeed in saying all there is to say, in understanding all there is to understand, in bridging absolutely the gaps we experience between the past and present, the inner and the outer, the temporal and the eternal. Indeed, it seems that we are not meant to close such gaps, but merely to bridge them over and over in the only way that we can do so — symbolically.

Symbols, Metaphors, and Models

Because my primary interest here is the way the Bible mediates faith affirmation and gives rise to a secondary tradition of symbolic enactment, it will be helpful to examine the way language mediates the symbolic before comparing linguistic and nonlinguistic symbols.

All words have a very general or diffuse symbolic character, but most words are simple designators and function, when read or heard, customarily or conventionally. Hence, words commonly act denotatively, even if most common expressions or colloquialisms regularly depend on an element of connotation. ("I'm sorry, Mr. M's tied up right now," would denote a form of bondage were its conventional sense not understood connotatively.) Most verbal speech operates at a low level of symbolization. The majority of words, in their everyday use, are linguistic signs or denominators and do not require interpretation in any proper sense, for we communicate instinctively or habitually in much of our linguistic activity.

At the same time, words with a customary meaning can be imbued with a formidable new significance that raises their symbolic temperature. Take, for instance, the social, sexual, and political significance recently attached to the word "gay." The word not only connotes far more than it denotes but has acquired a decidedly *symbolic* reference. For advocates of the normalcy of the homosexual condition, "gay" puts together or bridges a gap between a psychosexual condition and its social validation, so that people will regard homosexuality in a very different manner than has been the case in Western society. In general, common speech in the stream of life tends to recycle customary words and infuse them with special significance in order to meet new demands for meaning in ever-changing social situations. These new meanings then become more customary and conventional, and novel metaphors (see below) or symbolic terms spring up to bridge even newer gaps in social meaning.

On a somewhat more regular level of signifying, we use words or phrases in highly conventional configurations that clearly express what they stand for to someone aware of the configuration. The best example of this conventional configuration or stenosign is traffic or directional signs such as the ubiquitous STOP or ONE WAY signs. Here, the sign literally denotes what it means. One author describes the stenosign or index in this way: "there is usually a straightforward, one-to-one correspondence; the task of decoding, when giver and receiver belong to the same stable community, represents few difficulties."[10] The same is true of the "signal" (e.g., S-O-S in Morse Code), which is an example of simple correspondence and not symbolic in any genuine sense. Although in colloquial speech people tend to use "sign" and "symbol" synonymously, there is much to be gained by recognizing the specificity of a properly symbolic level of awareness and communication. The symbolic deserves to be both specified more exactly and examined more closely to determine what it reveals about consciousness in the act of knowing and in communicating what it knows. This is especially true about matters of love and faith, for when we need to communicate more deeply, transact an intimate relationship, or make a statement of greater personal and social significance than a direction, we use symbols proper. Symbols always operate on a higher order of signifying and have a more complex structure. Here is where the excess of meaning latent in all symbolization is most strictly found.

Symbols, properly speaking, always possess multiple meaning; the primary meaning (the plain sense of the symbol, linguistic or pictorial) intentionally involves us in a secondary (latent) meaning. In this understanding, the symbol proper always involves a tension between the first or plain meaning and a second or hidden meaning. Symbols express something about reality, not by naming or describing it directly, but by taking a detour and naming or picturing something else. They always signify an implied negation, a "whispered no" that helps to make a positive but complex affirmation.[11]

An example may help make the point. The linguistic symbol "kingdom of God," central to the synoptic gospels' framing of Jesus' message, depends for its positive sense on a *tension* between the plain (royal and political) meaning of "kingdom" and the meaning of "of God" (not of any human king). This tension between the plain sense of kingdom and its resignified meaning is heightened by the way Jesus employs "kingdom" in the parables and in his proclamatory and proverbial sayings as well. As in all symbols, the tension must remain unresolved in order to avoid reducing the symbol to a cliché. Without two levels of meaning rubbing against each other tensively, there would be no spark struck, no new meaning announced. Without tension between an apparent meaning and a latent one, it would be impossible for us to penetrate beyond appearances into the depths of human experience. Symbols exist because the imagination needs to be spurred to grasp the more than ordinary and other than obvious elements of what reality presents to us.[12]

This also means that symbols proper are more complex than either allegory or analogy. In allegory, what is lacking is the tension proper to symbolic expression. One reference merely replaces another and remains interchangeable with it. Levels of allegory can be multiple; as in Spenser's *Faerie Queen,* one character can stand for a philosophical or moral virtue and a narrative figure at the same time. The point of allegory is transparency, either artful or otherwise.

Like allegory, analogy involves, not a necessary tension between two different meanings, but rather a discovery of similarity or likeness in dissimilarity. Often a primary analogue provides the basis for stretching one term to fit a pluriform reality. For example, "law" is used to describe the consistent results of empirical observations, moral obligations, and legislative statutes. The differences between these various phenomena are major, but they all share some qualities of a primary analogate, a reasoned order for the common good. Analogy may be present in symbolic expression, as when a physical term (e.g.,"stain") represents moral guilt, but an analogy essentially observes similarities in the world around us irrespective of any tensive relationship in the analogues. For example, a STOP sign and a red light resemble each other only in their common use of a color, but that color, in analogous configurations, denotes something similar in many different traffic situations. A traveler may not know the literal meaning of the various words *Arrêt, Alt,* or *Stop,* but their display on similar looking red signs allows the speaker of only one language to understand, by analogy, the meaning of the direction.

Philosophical theology uses analogy deductively (the "analogy of being") to reason to the similarity between the creator and all creatures, despite the different levels of being that the divine and human occupy. But scientists also use analogy, though inductively, as when they shape hypotheses based on what they have observed and apply the principles to similar settings that they then seek to test. But analogy, by relying on comparison in contrast, does not normally bridge gaps or leap chasms as much as it maps out highways across rugged or even hostile terrain. Emphasizing the significance of analogy in a culture fascinated by pluralistic possibilities, David Tracy has made a case for analogy as a major paradigm for cross-cultural understanding by asserting, "We understand one another, if at all, only through analogies."[13] In general, then, analogy is both a rational principle and an aesthetic canon as well. Analogies can be simple, even banal, or exciting and dynamic. When analogies expand into the realm of metaphor (below), they can have unexpected effects on those venturing them. This is because when the similar and dissimilar are rubbed together rather than just juxtaposed, the tension introduced tends to change the chemistry at work.

In contrast to allegory and analogy, metaphors participate in the dynamic of symbols because they introduce new information beyond the normal meaning of the two terms juxtaposed in the metaphorical utterance. True metaphors are not merely stylistic. Instead, the metaphor expresses a semantic operation: it affects the meaning, and not just the style, of a statement or proposition. Like symbols, metaphors involve tension and, when they are true metaphors, create new extensions of the meaning that words take on in the stream of life. Metaphorical phrases such as "a cold hell" or "worldly piety" exploit our capacity to entertain logical absurdity and open our conscious minds to realms they do not normally inhabit. Thus, metaphorical expressions testify to the inadequacy of the normal range of words to represent the depth and breadth of our imaging of the world and our involvement in all that is real for us. They bridge a gap between ordinary experience and intuitions of the extraordinary, not simply but in a paradoxical fashion. As Paul Ricoeur has expressed it, "Metaphor is nothing other than the application of a familiar label to a new object which first resists and then surrenders to its application. ... Literal falsity is thus an ingredient of metaphorical truth."[14]

Similarly poetical expression involves the comprehensive use of metaphors in which consciously produced tension between significations gives rise to a new vision of reality that is resisted by the ordinary way that we use words. While the conventions of poetry are multiple, the dense use of metaphor is perhaps the most constant feature of poetical expression. Poetry sets human language the task of getting beneath surface appearances and dealing with the deeper realities that we intuit our lives are really about but can never demonstrate conclusively. It seeks new and fresh relationships between images and words and is the primary example of the special sort of discourse that we use in situations where more than ordinary reality is what interests us. It is the kind of "discourse [that] thickens meaning found in reality and then increments that meaning with style. People do this sort of thing when statements of mere fact fail due to the complexity of what the statement needs to express."[15]

Further into the realm of the symbolic, myth, both as it is used in ordinary language and as it has been used in history, religion, and literature, tends to be understood negatively. Technically, myth refers to the dreamlike and imaginative elements in narratives of the origins, progress, or final accomplishment envisioned by an imaginative (often religious) symbol system. Though it has come to connote "unreal," "false," or "purely imaginary," the term denotes something very real. But rather than swim upstream against an almost universally negative connotation, I have adopted the adjective "mythopoetic" to describe the dreamlike and highly symbolic aspects of much of biblical narrative and its underlying worldview. As an adjective, "mythopoetic" refers to real meaning in the same way that our accounts of dreams are about real, if nonhistorical, events. Dreams signify nonrationally the way that dreamers deeply and unconsciously understand events, persons, or crises in their lives. In the same way, mythopoetic events are ones whose narrative or poetic form imbues the events behind the narrative with a more than literal, polyvalent significance.

Full-blown myths are complex in the same way that symbols are: they combine diverse elements tensively and weave together various levels of fact and interpretation. Myths couch themselves in symbolic language to create meaningful discourse because human beings have never been content with "just the facts" but have always created ways of valorizing certain persons, events, and ideas with other than ordinary significance. Mythopoetic texts are often indications that some real event, person, or experience has become a catalyst for a community's self-understanding. This, in turn, opens the way for later interpreters to renew their community's self-understanding through an appropriation of the myth for their own time. Just as symbols contain an excess of meaning, so mythopoetic sayings, narratives, and poems possess a thickness that can continue to be mined or unpacked by and for later generations.

In this work I will refer to *mythos* to label the whole complex of wondrous events that comprise the narrative element of mythopoetic texts. In the Bible, this refers specifically to the great works of God or *magnalia Dei* (the creation of the world, the exodus and feeding in the desert, the incarnation and miracles of Jesus, the resurrection accounts, the renewal of creation in various apocalyptic texts) that tell of the presence and activity of more-than-human actors in more-than-historical events. *Mythos* or "gospel story" represents the biblical material that portrays the story of God's deeds and differs in emphasis from *ethos* or "laws/ ethics," the obedience or lifestyle response to what God has done for us. Like the lists of laws and cultic regulations in Exodus, Leviticus, Numbers, and Deuteronomy, the wisdom books also emphasize *ethos* in their emphasis on right action. But *mythos,* or the story aspect of the Bible imaginatively and poetically presented and resignified, also differs in emphasis from *logos,* or the verbal-message, covenant-stipulating aspect of the written scriptures that calls forth *ethos.* Ultimately, both *mythos* and *logos* (e.g., as vision and word in the prophets, miracle and teaching in the gospels) comprise the biblical material. Too much emphasis on the one to the exclusion of the other makes for an imbalanced understanding of the whole. Though both *ethos* and *logos* have conditioned the mythopoetic outlook and presentation of the biblical material from the beginning, attempts to suppress the mythopoetic as out-of-date, and to extract the literal or ethical as the perennial element always runs the danger of distorting the message.

The mythopoetic, then, shares a metaphorical, poetic orientation with the symbolic because, as expressive of the origin and ultimate shape of things, it expresses the meaning of events beyond what is obvious or literally recorded about the past (or presaged for the future). A prime example is Paul's reminder to the Corinthians of the events of the Exodus (1 Cor 10:1–4):

I do not want you to be ignorant, brethren, that our ancestors were all under the cloud and all passed through the sea, and all of them were baptized into Moses and in the sea. All ate the same spiritual food, and all drank the same spiritual drink (for they drink from a spiritual rock that followed them, and the rock was Christ).

Above, I described the metaphorical, poetic, and mythic as symbolic because they all contain a surplus of meaning resulting from the rubbing together of literal elements and extended references. In this example from Paul's writing, "baptized into Moses and the sea," as well as "spiritual food," "spiritual drink," and "spiritual rock" are all *symbolic* of a whole new reality (communion in the death and resurrection of Jesus) that the original elements (sea, manna, and water from the rock) do not literally express. At the same time, the sea, the food, and the drink of the original narrative were already part of a wondrous, mythopoetic account of Israel's liberation from Egypt and its salvation in the wilderness. The character of the original helps to create the conditions for their reworking into a specifically Christian myth, but this is not necessary. While for literalists this only compounds the felony, for students of the renewable meaning of events it reveals something ineradicable in the human imagination. Attempts to reduce the mythopoetic to underlying *bruta facta* always and everywhere result in a shriveling of people's imaginative participation in fuller relationships and deeper levels of understanding.

Earlier, I suggested that the source of this excess or tension between words and their extended meanings resides in the nature of humans as symbol makers and, particularly, in our preverbal history of imaging at the root of our awareness of our self and our world.[16] The priority I am giving to mythopoetic expression is an attempt to ground reflection on the human condition in general and on faith-affirmation in particular in the age-old symbolic and mythopoetic activity of cultural and religious tradents, the original symbol makers and interpreters of the biblical tradition. My attempt to give a primacy to the symbolic in the structures of meaning that Western religion and culture have traditionally depended upon is also an attempt to understand Catholic dogmatic theology in other than the dialectics of rational argument that have predominated for so long. The dialectical method operates on a notion of truth that looks mainly for victory over the foe, for the dominance of one set of ideas over competing conceptualizations, the typically agonistic ritual of male combat and theological disputation. By contrast, the theological method I wish to use looks first to the founding visions and intuitions that manifest truth in a primordial fashion before they are systematized in second-order or analytical concepts. These secondary processes have often yielded to a narrow scholasticism that does not respect either the surplus of meaning present in symbolic language or the priority of *mythos* to the *logos* that seeks to sort it out. As we shall see, attempts to rediscover truth as manifestation grants a "primary role to symbol in all discourse" without needing to disparage concepts, or "second-order thought."[17] Before examining the relationship of first-order, experiential, symbolic expression and second-order, conceptual, or abstract interpretation of the symbolic, I wish to look at a final category of symbols proper to fill out even more the role of the symbolic in our everyday appropriation of reality.

Unlike most expressions of metaphor, in poetry and myth, models are not primarily verbal or literary in nature. Models refer to structures along a spectrum from internal cognitive plans and extramental scientific gadgets to complex theories by which unobservable processes are either mathematically or theoretically represented. Earlier, we saw how behavioral biology characterizes the mental systems by which animals and humans learn to deal with their environment as cognitive maps. These are interior images, patterns, and representations that imprint themselves in a neonate's mental apparatus. By means of such models, young children, from about nine months, can seek out an absent mother. These then represent true symbolic or preconceptual thought because they are working models by which infants receive feedback, readjust to new circumstances and patterns, and respond — all before they can verbalize or think in any explicit way. These models are real metaphors in the sense that they exist as actual patterns of neural connections in the brain. As part of our cognitive apparatus, a model is like "a toy that is not yet a tool, an imitation world, which we can manipulate in the way that will suit us best, and so find out how to manipulate the real world, which it is supposed to represent."[18]

When scientists construct working models on various scales as experimental or demonstration models of the way that macro- or microorganisms function, they are operating on analogy with the way our brain functions. They can be said to be employing models as *heuristic symbols*, for they are seeking to discover the operations of the system that they are explaining. When they do so, they are only extending the same adaptive mechanism familiar to us from infancy as we drew on working models of our world, often experimenting as we became more familiar with our surroundings. Though language and abstract thinking allow us to refine our operative working models, they never replace or render obsolete the more primitive symbolic structures that imprint themselves deeply in the brain and hence in our psyche as well. If models describe internal symbolic structures at the base of human cognition, then we can say that, at a primordial level, *we understand ourselves and our world most basically through symbols*. Often we do not consciously attend to the pervasive nature of the way in which we interact symbolically because so much symbolic transaction takes place on the preconscious or unconscious level. When asked to engage in some thoroughly symbolic activity — writing a poem or sharing in a sacrament — we often seize up and think too hard about what we are supposed to be doing or feeling. This secondary, ratiocinative reflex then takes over and we shut off the wellsprings of imagination where the symbolic level of expression naturally dwells.

As I indicated above, models share in the dynamics of symbols because, like mythopoetic narratives, they are heuristic in nature. This means that they invite us to seek to discover something about the nature of reality by accepting, rather than resolving, the tension between the model itself and what is being modeled. Even in the case of scientific models, where a one-to-one correlation of modeled to model is required for it to function properly, there is a tension between the model as it is perceived (its appearance) and all that it refers to in reality (its meaning to the observer). When we see a model of the double helix, it helps us bridge the gap between the model and what it says about the actual structures of the chromosomes. In this case, we comprehend, not because we commit the model to memory as fact, but because the picture that the model projects interacts with the other pictures already in our awareness. These pictures can be said then to merge or refine each other to provide a new and fuller understanding.

When external models adequately picture reality, they enable our internal cognitive representations or models to adjust accordingly. This suggests that models, precisely as symbols, are critical to the whole human process of understanding. Once again, thinking, before it becomes logical thought (*logos*) is pictorial and shares in the primordial capacity of the mind for *mythos*. At its most fundamental level, human understanding mixes and matches pictures of reality. Even a text, though composed of words, has the overall effect of presenting itself as a picture to our understanding. Our mental horizon is said to fuse with that of the world of the text as the picture being presented interacts with the patterns that are inscribed in our cognitive apparatus. Reflection can refine or question these pictures, and abstract (logical) concepts, such as the principal of noncontradiction, can expose some of these new horizons as wishful thinking, but these second-order operations can never replace our organic, first-order symbolization.[19]

At the same time, our internal models or cognitive maps do not just mediate external reality to our inquisitive minds. They also describe some of the earliest subjective phenomena in an infant's life, as the growing child feels its way from models to concepts. These phenomena can be objects, words, even songs or persons that provide a child with a neutral area of experience that will not be challenged and that guarantees some security in its experience of being one with and separate from its maternal matrix. At some point in their early development, infants begin to use something that is called a "first not-me possession." In object-relations theory, these are also real metaphors that represent the child's externalizing of the internal process of modeling, its first use of symbols and an archetypical experience of play. D. W. Winnicott described these *transitional objects* as follows:

The object is a symbol of the union of the baby and the mother (or part of the mother). This symbol can be located. It is at the place in space and time where and when the mother is in transition from being (in the baby's mind) merged in with the infant and alternatively being experienced as an object to be perceived rather than conceived of. The use of an object symbolizes the union of two now separate things, baby and mother, at the point in time and space of the initiation of their state of separateness.[20]

In this neutral and privileged area of experience, the child entertains the illusion that allows it to relate inner and outer reality, but also to begin to separate the two. Winnicott understands this intermediate area of experience to underlie an adult's capacity for artistic creativity, as well as for cultural and religious expression, because "there is a direct development from transitional phenomena to playing, and from playing to shared playing, and from this to cultural experience."[21] Similar connections of symbols to infant play, and of infant play to adult artistic, cultural, and religious activity are made today by writers in the areas of biology, cognitive psychology, epistemology, interpretation theory, and theology, who have all recently paid more attention to the symbolic transaction of reality and its importance in both cognitive and affective human development. Today we have become aware that play adumbrates the entire field of culture in which the interaction between originality and the acceptance of tradition becomes the way we continue to perform the basic human task of managing the interplay between separation and union.

As adults we continue to operate, intellectually and affectively, via similar playful transpositions. Works of literature, art, cinema, or music present us with so many heuristic fictions that, even while fictional, can reveal something true precisely because they engage us in play. Even as adults, we understand by being dispossessed of mastery over the meaning of things, by opening ourselves up to new worlds of meaning. In other words, understanding is quite the opposite of achieving mastery — at least with matters of the heart. Here, real comprehension occurs when one is undone in the encounter with a good piece of writing, a symphony, or a play (in the theater). For enjoying a masterpiece and playing a game have something in common with reading a symbolic text: in all of them we are invited to lose our self-centeredness and be freed up to discover something unexpected, to achieve a new sense of what is true beyond any narrow subjectivity.[22] The priority of symbolism and the pervasive nature of symbolic play has raised a host of issues that cannot be dealt with adequately yet. But I hope I have begun to show how the phenomenon of the symbolic pervades the way that we apprehend and communicate throughout our lives.

Mythos and *Logos* in the Bible and in Life

The priority and pervasiveness of images and symbols does not mean that primary naivete, first readings, or mythopoetry are today adequate for faith affirmation. Naivete about injury or untruth received often leads to injury or untruth handed on. The issue then of the relationship of *mythos* (in the sense of dream, poetic expression, symbol) and *logos* (a word or clear message) is central to our fuller understanding of an adequate model of faith. Symbolic thought does not exist in a vacuum, nor is it self-sufficient or self-interpreting. It always tends toward articulated meaning because our imaging capacity registers the impact of the world around us only so that we can understand and negotiate it better. Pictures are pictures and not words. Words are needed to convey what pictures are about, even though pictures are not reducible to their verbal explanations.

As I traced above, preverbal mental development eventually reaches the point where it becomes capable of shared language and abstract thought. *Logos* complements symbol and allows for the primarily naive world of the infant to be shared, then thought about, and even further to be abstractly judged and dealt with on the level of rational possibility and logical cogency. But the acquisition of the capacity for language, abstract thought, logical deduction, or scientific reason does not, in itself, exclude or cancel out the mind's prior capacity for, and attraction to, preverbal symbols and mythopoetic images. In the life of children it is vital for healthy growth and development that both mythopoetic and logical expression coexist and interact. A child whose imaginative capacities are handicapped in its early development will develop serious inhibitions in its emotional life, suffering from such handicaps as lack of object constancy or other personality disorders. Contrarily, a child incapable of communicating its inner life is literally trapped in the self, a victim of autism. In other words, the healthy development of pre-pubertal children results from the coexistence of, and balance between, their capacity for *mythos* and *logos,* the symbolic and the rational.

This coexistence has had its counterpart in the historical development of the religious culture of the West. Pagan, Jewish, and Christian thought each grew in the course of history through later rational interpretation of an earlier mythopoetic substratum. For many centuries, the various logocentric understandings of mythopoetry were more or less balanced as myth received new life and wealth from language, and language from myth, in various interpenetrations and interactions that founded much of Western culture. In the next chapter, I will explore the way *mythos* and *logos* were balanced in the period up through the Reformation, so that we can better understand the impact of their unbalancing, a state of disequilibrium that we are still struggling to survive.

Bibliographical Essay

On the biology of symbolization: The work of J. Bowlby, in his *Attachment and Loss,* vol. 1. *Attachment* (Harmondsworth: Penguin, 1987) and *The Making and Breaking of Affectional Bonds* (London: Tavistock Publications, 1987), has informed my perspective on both phylogenetic and ontogenetic development of human behavioral equipment. His approach combines a behavioral (not behaviorist) biological perspective with the cognitive psychology of Jean Piaget in describing how humans build working models of reality as the basis of their characteristic behavior. I have also spelled out some of the implications of the early connection of cognitive and affective development in dependence on the work of D. W. Winnicott, whose *Playing and Reality* (London: Tavistock Publications, 1971) gave the specific name "transitional objects" to what Bowlby calls "representational models." Though Bowlby is critical of Winnicott's category of transitional objects and adopts a more "parsimonious way of looking at the role of these inanimate objects," i.e., as purely substitutionary (*Attachment*, 1:312, 361), he admits that there is real overlap in Winnicott's notion of play and his concept of exploratory behavior. In later chapters, Alice Miller's *Thou Shalt Not Be Aware: Society's Betrayal of the Child* (New York: New American Library, 1986) and *The Drama of the Gifted Child: The Search for the True Self* (New York: Basic Books, 1981) will figure centrally in developing the implications of symbolic development. Erik Erikson in *Childhood and Society* (London: Paladin, 1987) proposes "the theory that the child's play is the infantile form of the human ability to deal with experience by creating model situations and to master reality by experiment and planning" (199). The biologist Stephen J. Gould (*An Urchin in the Storm: Essays about Books and Ideas* [New York: W. W. Norton, 1987], 63) says: "I believe the analogy between childhood wonder and adult creativity is good biology, not metaphor."

On symbol and language: Paul Ricoeur's work on hermeneutics — in "Biblical Hermeneutics," *Semeia* 4 (1975): 29–145; *Freud and Philosophy: An Essay on Interpretation,* trans. Denis Savage (New Haven: Yale University Press, 1970); *Paul Ricoeur: Hermeneutics and the Human Sciences,* ed. and trans. John B. Thompson (Cambridge: Cambridge University Press, 1981); and *Essays on Biblical Interpretation,* ed. Lewis S. Mudge (Philadelphia: Fortress, 1980) — have influenced my understanding of the role of symbols. Janet Martin Soskice (*Metaphor and Religious Language* [Oxford: Clarendon, 1985], 21) is critical of Ricoeur's tensive theory of metaphor based on a metaphor's dual reference, but she agrees that "each metaphor involves at least two different networks of associations" (49) so that, as Dr. Johnson said, in a metaphor we get "two ideas for one" (53). Ricoeur (*Freud and Philosophy,* 527) sums up his early work *The Symbolism of Evil* on the primacy of the symbolic in this way: "All symbols give rise to thought, but the symbols of evil show in an exemplary way that there is always more in myths and symbols than in all of our philosophy, and that a philosophical interpretation of symbols will never become absolute knowledge."

On the differences between analogy, allegory, metaphors, and symbols: See Soskice (*Metaphor and Religious Language,* 64–66). Hans Urs von Balthasar (*The Glory of the Lord: A Theological Aesthetics,* vol. 1, *Seeing the Form,* trans. Erasmo Leiva-Merikakis [New York: Crossroad, 1982], 20; cf. fn. 1) says that when Plato reduced the original to the status of derivative, he "became the father of all who put allegory (i.e., discourse about something else) in the place of symbol (i.e., a true sign)." Equally, C. S. Lewis (*The Allegory of Love: A Study in Medieval Tradition* [Oxford: Oxford University Press, 1958], 48) distinguishes between the two in this way: "Symbolism is a mode of thought, but allegory is a mode of expression."

Chapter 2

Growth in Thinking and Acting

Just as the individual mind commingles mythopoetic and rational elements, so Western culture and religion demonstrate that *mythos* is never without *logos*. Both the Hellenic and the Hebraic traditions brought *logos,* or reason, to bear on their respective *mythoi*. Though the patterns of interaction are different, both affected how Christianity developed. Looking briefly at the ways that Aristotle and Plato viewed *mythos* will help us see that, even today, people tend to affirm faith in either categories of those ancient thinkers. A complementary look at the alternative way that rabbinic Judaism interpreted its dominant *mythos* will form the backdrop for our looking more closely at the impact of both philosophical traditions and of the Jewish covenantal tradition on Christianity from the patristic period until the period when all Christian forms of interpretation began to be challenged.

The *Iliad,* the *Odyssey,* and the early religious dramas recorded the mythopoetic substratum of the culture and religion of classical Greece. This unofficial canon was filled out by a literature of philosophical reflection that remains basic, even today, to all Western metaphysical thought. The Hebrew canon developed somewhat similarly as its founding visions and images, first transmitted orally, were committed to writing. What eventually became the Torah and the early prophets (the historical books) was then filled out by a literature of prophetic critique or commentary, as well as ritual legislation. Prophecy stressed right action based on a more integrated understanding of the mythic tradition; law stressed the right response to these traditions in moral and religious deeds. In Greek religion and culture, the propensity for thinking prevailed, while in Jewish religion and culture, the habit of doing predominated.

What we find historically are cultural and religious analogues of the endowments with which human beings complement their earliest images of the world and themselves: cognitive reflection and independent action. As in a child's early life, philosophical thinking and moral/legal doing develop alongside the mythic substratum — but only up to a point. In the individual, that point is loosely called adolescence. In Western culture, it is called the Enlightenment, which ushered in modernity's challenge to the world of *mythos* and to faith affirmation's naive attachment to it. By comparing the different ways in which Hellenic and Hebraic *logos* interacted with their founding *mythoi* we will be better able to measure the impact of the Enlightenment on naively conceived Christian belief.

Realism or Idealism

From the sixth century B.C.E., philosophy, the organized reflection on the world and on the nature of human rationality, developed among various Hellenic cultural groups. Though Greek in language, culture, and religion, philosophy flowered in Asia Minor, Southern Italy, and Sicily, as well as in mainland Greece. Its roots lay in the cosmological speculation of the pre-Socratics, who attempted to categorize the essential elements of the physical world. These early Greek natural philosophers represent a reflective, even critical, distancing from the poetry and myth of earlier epics. In the fifth century, the dramatists Sophocles and Euripedes created a dramatic tradition in which gods, demigods, and legendary figures appeared on the same stage — though normally on different levels. The dramatists, though accepting the parameters of the myths, provided their own ethical or philosophical reflection on how fate affected both gods and humans. According to Plato, Greek literature grew out of an "ancient quarrel between poetry and philosophy" (*Republic* 607B).

While Socrates' life and career (d. 399) is indicative of a new mode of dialectical reflection, it is with Plato (d. 347?) and Aristotle (d. 322) that two schools and two different approaches toward nature and toward criticism of the mythopoetic texts of ancient Greece formed. A third school, that of Zeno (d. c. 264) and the Stoics, took an eclectic approach that had a lasting impact, particularly in the field of natural science and natural morality. Its influence has been more covert and will be illuminated when it concerns the shape of religious belief. But first, a brief sketch of the major schools will help us account for the attitudes that most of Western culture and religion have taken on the literal and the symbolic aspects of reality.

We will look first at Aristotle, the founder of realist epistemology, who understood language to be the vehicle of thinking about and expressing the objective categories of extramental reality. Accordingly, he distinguished *logos* (rational argument), which was educational, from *mythos,* which he understood as appropriate for the religious and ethical instruction of the masses. He propounded a logical and ontological theory of univocity in which one interpreted how words have *one* meaning and *one* meaning only. In his treatment of poetics, he asserted that only in the case of tragedy, which leads a person to engage in imitation of the good, is myth ennobling. As part of the genre of comedy, with its inversion of reality and double entendres, myth is a "species of the ugly." At best, myth is a preliminary stage of philosophy; at worst, it is made up of tricks. Because he emphasized what was correct and clear, he rejected the irrational or magical powers of poetic language, insisting that metaphor belonged to prose writing, where its purpose is to clarify as well as adorn.[1]

Aristotle's emphasis on the superiority of *logos* to *mythos* is said to have founded objectivist criticism or the realist tradition. Positively, his confidence that words referred to extramental reality opened the way for the entire tradition of analogy and analogical thinking that underlies all realist metaphysics, aesthetics, and physical science. Negatively, his preference for the univocal sense of words gave rise to a suspicion of the poetic and the imaginative as adequate instruments for speaking of what is real.

By contrast, Plato looked on myth and symbolism as an enigma or puzzle that actually provoked deeper understanding. In his approach, symbols and myth represent flexible elements of reality because myth was capable of carrying *logos* beyond the frontiers of mere sensible knowledge. In his metaphysics, the proper objects of our understanding are the ideal "forms" that are unknowable by sense. One's higher, rational understanding crossed the divide between the sensible and the ideal by being provoked to remember the absolute via shadowy sense-experiences of what was, in ideal reality, unchangeable. Mythopoetry, then, created privileged opportunities to interpret eternal realities in everyday, sensible language. For Plato, the poet or the seer was capable of inspired visions or pronouncements that the wise man or the prophet interpreted.[2]

Plato's dualistic philosophy and aesthetics sharply distinguished understanding from sensation, the soul from the body, the ideal from the real, the rational from the appetitive. He interpreted *mythos* by distinguishing what was physically (or sensibly) written in the text from what was ideally (or spiritually) meant. Known as allegory, this interpretation had a profound influence on the Stoics, on Second Temple Jewish interpretation of the scriptures, on the Christian school of biblical interpretation associated with Clement and Origen, on patristic exegesis well into the Middle Ages, and on early vernacular or romantic literature. While both schools of philosophy spawned traditions of criticism that sought to discover more lasting meaning in mythopoetic images, their significance for us is found in their impact on those Christian interpreters of the naive worldview of the Bible who shaped Christianity before the Enlightenment.

Christian writers as different as Origen and Augustine engaged in the allegorical or spiritual interpretation of the Bible because, like their Alexandrian Jewish forebears, they understood *The Book* to be a sacred medium by which they were given access to a world beyond the senses. In their worldview, the sensible was only apparently real; all sensible, material, and mortal objects pointed to unseen, immaterial, and immortal ones. Thus the believer's studious or prayerful immersion in the Bible promised to establish, maintain, or heighten (depending on the reader's spiritual state) an immediate relationship with God that had been attenuated by humanity's state of alienation. Suprasensible knowledge, available beyond what mere words conveyed, allowed for an intellectual and affective grasp of truth and for personal communion with God because the *mythos* (revelation) was available behind the *logos* (written text) of the scriptures.

Unlike the modern tendency to distrust intuitive (nonscientific) methods, patristic and much medieval exegesis required them because truth could not be logically deduced. More intuitive methods had to be employed. Extremes in exegesis or spirituality were held in check via the rule of faith (*regula fidei*). This meant that interpretations had to accord with the larger framework of Christian belief. As with the rabbis, when they contemporized the law of Moses, imagination did not just run riot; there were rules (*middot*) that kept their imaginative forays tied to a response of faith. In general, then, the Christian neo-Platonic tradition understood the Bible as a divine artifact where God, who had created the world of sense, implanted enigmas for drawing humans up from the sensible to the spiritual.

In effect, the Platonic disjunction between the ways things appear and the way things really are became a fulcrum to propel interpreters beyond their own time and place. It made the entire contents of the Bible a series of heuristic fictions that revealed the eternal order of things. But neo-Platonic metaphysics never challenged the Bible's naive view that the Creator and the creation were related as direct cause and effect, even if the intermediate distance between the spiritual realms and the material world was considerably lengthened. Human sinfulness and materiality attenuated the connection between God and humanity but never severed it. In other words, neo-Platonism accepted the primarily naive understanding of God and the world in much the same way that, in preadolescence, children become increasingly capable of rational abstraction without losing their basically naive worldview.

Here, then, is a further analogy in the developmental parallel introduced earlier. As infancy and early childhood resemble the earliest stages of human consciousness up through the acquisition of language, so later childhood (the period known as latency) parallels Western culture and religion's use of philosophical abstraction and organized reflection in its developing theology. Self-conscious ratiocination, in either a neo-Platonic or a literalist vein, did not change the sense of the immediacy or availability of revelation. The Bible remained a medium offering direct communion with the divine for those who would spiritually interpret it. This led Augustine to dislike bald statement in the Bible. He preferred to read its signs as provocative of a spiritual journey beyond the sensible to the eternal.

By contrast, Christian Aristotelian literalism sought univocity or lack of ambiguity in its interpretation of the Bible. Scholars associated with the city of Antioch established a school of biblical exposition that sought to refute allegorical interpretation and establish the superiority of their historical or narrative reading of the biblical material. Writers such as Theodore of Mopsuestia and Diodore of Tarsus explained the more-than-literal texts of scripture, especially prophetic passages, based on their notion of *theoria*, or foresight (which the prophet had of the later event and which the text foretold). So concerned was Theodore that the truths of scripture be grounded only in what could be literally predicated of their words that he was willing to declare that Job and the Song of Songs (which he likened to Plato's *Symposium*) were not inspired scripture. To Augustine's annoyance, Jerome was so influenced by his study with the rabbis that he accepted "Hebrew truth" (*hebraica veritas*) as the literal standard for the text of the Old, or the First, Testament. For this early philologist, no spiritual understanding of the text could contradict its literal sense but had to be based upon it.

Still, for all the heat these ancient controversies engendered, the Alexandrian and Antiochean traditions of interpretation were not so very different in result. Each was principally concerned with extracting from the sacred text an inspired meaning for its own day. The Alexandrian tradition did this by its imputation of multiple spiritual senses that allowed for imaginative adaptation and encouraged investigation of enigmatic passages. The Antiocheans narrowed the scope of their interpretation, choosing to work mainly with passages that evidenced textual correspondences in both testaments. This similarity in difference was clear by the high Middle Ages, as is evident in the writings of Thomas Aquinas, whom it is admitted today "both Antioch and Alexandria can claim as heir."[3] But by his time a shift had occurred that requires us to classify him more as a dogmatic theologian than a biblical exegete. In fact, today's distinction between scriptural and dogmatic theology exists, to a great extent, because of Aquinas's efforts to remove theology from its role as an interpretive undertaking and to give it its own rational footing. In order to preserve the apologetical uses of scripture for rational argument, he imbued scriptural interpretation with Aristotelian principles, expressing a preference for literalness that matched the rationalism characteristic of his theological summaries.

Thomas distinguished holy scripture from every other *scientia* or form of knowledge by its manner of speech: "in one and the same sentence, while it describes a fact, it reveals a mystery." He attributed this plural signification to the authorship of scripture by God and called the spiritual sense of the Bible that particular property by which "the things signified by the words have themselves a signification." Thus his theory revived the Alexandrian premise that the *logos* of scripture is linked to a *mythos,* a meaning transcending the literal that is cued by the letter and dependent upon it. But Aquinas's Aristotelianism insisted on correlating one word with one thing; he therefore asserted that the figurative (metaphorical) uses of words of scripture belonged to their literal sense. Hence Thomas accepted an allegorical or spiritual sense of the Bible, based not on the intuition of spiritual realities hidden behind the words but on the analogical properties of language. "Spiritual intelligence is not an interpretation of the text but rather of that which the text refers to."[4]

Let us examine for a moment some of the premises behind this objectivist position. Thomas needed to establish a narrow base of the meaning of scripture out of fear that equivocation would impugn the authority of the Bible. Though theology was founded on the revelatory word of scripture (with its double signification of fact and mystery), it must proceed as a deductive, rational activity (*scientia*) so that what was necessary to faith could be proved to anyone with an inquisitive, but not necessarily speculative, mind. This is the reason that, in the medieval schools, dogmatic tractates began to take the place of scriptural commentaries. For the mind (or "soul," understood mentally) achieved the end for which God created it through rational activity. This was his standard until shortly before he died, when he had an experience while saying Mass and wrote no more, declaring, "All I have written seems to me like so much straw compared with what I have seen and with what has been revealed to me."[5]

Although Thomas ended his life with a direct experience of the immediate presence of God, he bequeathed to Western Christianity the tools of Aristotelian rationalism developed by Arab and Jewish philosophers. Chief among these were the principles of analogy and instrumentality. Analogy, or the principle of proportional likeness, allowed one to speak of both God and creatures because they occupied similar but different levels of being. Instrumentality meant that, though God was ultimately the cause of all things that existed (as prime mover or final cause), change in the world of nature and in human society was effected via instrumental or secondary causality. Thus Thomas preserved continuity with the mythopoetic world of the Bible by allowing for the symbols of the Bible to refer literally, but analogously, to God and to the world. But he also departed from the premises of the Bible by separating theology from physics or natural causes and setting them on their own autonomous course. The instability in his thought system (unresolved when he died at forty-nine) would be fully exploited by his successors, some of whom we will encounter later.

In opposition to Thomas's more rationalist approach, the Franciscan Bonaventure maintained a more Augustinian, affective, and Platonic mode of interpreting the scriptures. Seeing the created world itself as the footprints of the creator, Bonaventure saw the mind's journey to God as passing through stages until all logical contradictions and categories were overcome and knowledge was subsumed in love.[6] Both thinkers died in 1274. Soon their Franciscan and Dominican followers became immersed in a struggle between two different philosophical schools of interpretation. The centrality of the *sacra pagina* as well as its interpretation, by which Christians had variously sought for over a millennium to understand God, gave way to scholasticism. Shortly, philosophy developed a preference for univocal meanings and denotative references that words can *name* (hence, nominalism); this so dominated the universities that scholasticism in general abandoned the interpretation of the Bible.

When the schools replaced the monasteries as the focal centers of Christian religious culture, the *mythos* of the scriptures became subordinate to the *logos*, now conceived as reason (*ratio*). In turn, reason had begun to follow the course carved out by scholars like the Oxford Franciscan Roger Bacon (d. 1294), who pioneered the study of mathematics and natural science. Scientific rationalism continued to grow during the Renaissance, but during the Reformation its theological counterpart was rejected as a method of doing theology. Hence, when Protestants turned to the scriptures as the sole principle of religious authority, they concentrated on its power as *logos,* not *mythos.* They stressed how God's will was literally revealed in the Bible, paradoxically exalting *logos* in a way that contributed to the growth of both theological and scientific rationalism in the following centuries.

This is the story that I will take up in chapter 3: in the wake of the Reformation and the Counter-Reformation, autonomous or independent reason rose up against all revealed religion and took the realist/idealist argument in different directions. Before this occurred, fifteen hundred years of interpreting scripture according to Platonic or Aristotelian methods still had not shaken the premises of the naive, mythopoetical world that the Bible took for granted. Neither of the two traditions I have traced, for all their differences, had significantly departed from the worldview of the biblical authors. But as we shall see, history, like biology, has a way of undermining primary naivete. Both philosophical idealism and realism soon became divorced from theology, turned their backs on their original mythopoetic matrix, sought to become independent, and followed their own autonomous course.

Keeping the Covenant

Jewish covenantal nomism represents a different reaction to its founding vision than we find in either Platonic or Aristotelian Catholicism or in Protestant biblicism.[7] Unlike Christian attempts to see in or beyond its mythic substrate and establish a renewed *mythos*, Jewish faith-response is more an attraction toward its underlying symbolism (hence, an *ethos*). Rabbinic Judaism sought to make the images and signs of its mythopoetic narrative real in deeds and in lifestyle: to do or realize its symbols in ritual and law. Hence, it is realist in a very different sense from philosophical realism.

In the Hebrew scriptures, the justification for specifically ritual action as a response to the mythopoetic recital of the deeds of God is explicit in Deuteronomy 26:5–10:

Then you shall declare before the Lord your God,

"My father was a wandering Aramean who went down to Egypt with a small household and lived there as an alien. But there he became a nation great, strong and numerous. When the Egyptians maltreated and oppressed us, imposing hard labor upon us, we cried to the Lord, the God of our fathers, and he heard our cry and saw our affliction, our toil and our oppression. He brought us out of Egypt with his strong hand and outstretched arm, with terrifying power, with signs and wonders; bringing us into this land flowing with milk and honey. Therefore, I have now brought you the first fruits of the products of the soil which you, O Lord, have given me."

And having set them before the Lord, your God, you shall bow down in his presence.

The sacrifice of the first fruits of the harvest is here commanded as a ritual response to an act of God, accomplished generations before and remembered since in this cultic recital. God's "strong hand and outstretched arm ... terrifying power ... signs and wonders" are all mythopoetic expressions that are unrecoverable in any literal or historical fashion. Both the story in Genesis of Israel's descent into Egypt and the longer story in Exodus through Joshua contain many instances of the same combination: mythic statement of God's acts and the requirement of a ritual response (e.g., the covenant with Noah and his sons in Gen 9:1–17; the command and promise to Abraham in Gen 12:1–9; the delivery of the Decalogue in Exod 20:1–26).[8] In other words, fixed in the very bedrock of the Jewish tradition is the concrete notion that the adherent is not expected to reflect on this tradition, or to speculate about the relationship of the myths to ethical conduct, or in any way to abstract from the images and signs in which God has revealed the law. Rather, the response required is set out in the scene where Moses reads the book of the covenant to the people and they answer, "All that the Lord has said, we will heed and do" (Exod 24:7).[9]

Similarly, the key credo recital of God's oneness and of the obligation of the people to love God above all (Deut 6:4–5) calls for an act of appropriation, not merely intellectual adherence: "Take to heart these words.... Bind them at your wrist as a sign and let them be as a pendent on your forehead. Write them on the doorposts of your houses and on your gates" (6:6–9). The key words expressing the essential mythos of Israel's chosenness and the first commandment of its entire ethos here became a *mitzvah* or command to be acted upon, not thought about or abstracted from. This translation of the mythopoetic into law is carried through with great thoroughness in rabbinic Judaism, with its principle of "building a fence around the Torah," or erecting other laws to safeguard the actual 613 commands in the five books of Moses. In the centuries between the destruction of the First Temple (587 B.C.E.) and of the Second (70 C.E.), law-keeping had grown to complement the sacrificial cult of the Jerusalem Temple (itself based on a image revealed to Moses during one of his mythic sojourns on the mountain, Exod 25:9). No less was it the theme of the prophets' preaching with their demands for greater covenant fidelity (which did not always mean ritualized deeds; see Isa 58:1–14). Keeping the commandments was fundamental in Ezekiel's visionary prophecy of national renewal, in Daniel's revelatory dreams about the salvation to come, in the messianic interpretation of scripture at Qumran.[10]

When the Temple, the state, and the restoration hopes of Judaism passed away, the doing of the law (though deprived of sacrifices) as the essential modality of keeping the covenant did not pass away. Observant Judaism into the modern era became a sophisticated system of legal (*halakhic*) interpretation and requirement. At the same time, it engendered a tremendous respect for and promotion of learning. Through it all, its *mythos* remained frozen and unchangeable until the Messiah should come. Judaism changed and developed through the development of its law keeping *ethos*. It retained its naive and mythopoetic worldview by acting upon the covenant stipulations, but in a way that allowed for changes in its program of obedience after both its sacrificial cult and its political center in Jerusalem were destroyed.

Judaism in the diaspora achieved a secure identity in continuity with its mythopoetic matrix because of its ability to act upon its sages' interpretation of the Torah. They articulated a religious system of covenantal law keeping for Israel no less cogent than the religious system of belief and worship for the nations that Christian patristic writers produced. Both covenantal deed and evangelical word were equally, if divergently, founded upon the underlying mythopoetic substratum of the Bible. Even though each community's Bible was of a different length, and even though their methods of actualizing the *mythos* differed, neither community experienced a crisis of confidence in its primarily naive reception of their founding visions until the dawn of the modern era. Hazans removed the Torah scroll from its ark and then chanted from it in their synagogues. In much the same way, deacons carried the bejeweled lectionary in procession and chanted from it in their churches. Both scroll and book contained their respective core myths of God's saving deeds. Both were words of life. Both commanded responses of obedient faith. Both communities developed extensive bodies of interpretation of the written word and rituals for overcoming the alienating impact of covenant transgressions. Both saw enthusiastic and heretical movements come and go, and both — but the Jewish people in particular — weathered their experiences of suffering, persecution, defeat, and revival in continuity with their founding mythopoetic vision. For more than a millennium and a half after Christianity and Judaism had parted company, both had still retained their primary naivete alongside and up against each other. But only up to a point.

For both Christianity and Judaism, that point arrived during the Enlightenment. Up until then, most of their premises about God, the world, and the human being's role in it had remained more or less the same as those of the Bible during the millennium in which it was formed. In the pre-Enlightenment period, traditional religious faith resembled a youth's developing awareness: a naive worldview, or first reading of the way things are, had survived the acquisition of verbal and mental skills, the beginnings of abstract thought, and the developed capacity for both intellectual analysis and purposive action. Because this interplay of *mythos* and *logos* is similar to the interplay that shaped the Bible's sense of things, the parallel has some potential for revealing the shape of the forms that faith affirmation takes in a religious world still struggling with the impact of the Enlightenment.

Growth and Interplay

I wish now to pick up the threads of my sketch of developing awareness from its birth in early instinctual behavior and the beginnings of verbalizing, at the stage when the young infant begins to interact consciously with its environment. The way a child's environment provides for it, both quantitatively and qualitatively, profoundly affects its ongoing development. We saw above that early feelings can be understood as phases of an individual's intuitive appraisals of the world and that our earliest ideas are like working models or cognitive maps. This means that the early encounters between the child and its environment shape its conscious and unconscious repertoire of preverbal images and that these remain the building blocks of knowledge all throughout life. As I claimed above, this is a significant development upon the principle that all knowledge is dependent upon sensation, not upon spiritual illumination. In this realist and now scientific perspective, every child's specifically human awareness involves intersubjectivity from the start of life. Hence, the environment of an infant crucially affects the growing child's affective and intellectual development.

As we saw, an infant makes sense of itself and the objects in its environment by taking in images of the world, by mapping them, and by playing in the intermediate or tensive area between subject and object that is filled by symbolic transactions. Hence, the *symbolizing of reality* arises out of the naturally instinctual behavior of the human organism.[11] The child's ability to put together sounds and images, to experience constancy in the objects and persons in its world, to arrange things in a sensible and orderly way, making of its world a safe and stable place, all depend upon a good enough environment and a native ability to operate in the realm of the symbolic. If the child lacks either the basic psychic energy (as seems to be the case of children born addicted to drugs) or experiences the frustration of basic needs (as happens with starved or abused infants), it will be either affectively or intellectually impaired from very early in life. What is more, the child will suffer a definite symbolic deprivation — an inability to hold itself and its world together, to put together meanings and comprehend changes in relationships, or to act from a sense of its own self-sameness. In other words, primary symbolization underlies a child's perception of its place in the world (hence, its affective self-awareness) just as its capacity for abstraction underlies its ability to solve objective problems. The interplay of these capacities in the individual resembles the way early religious culture interacted with philosophical reflection and ethical action.

This analogy argues for a parallel between two related phenomena: (1) a child's primitive symbolization of the world, which forms the basis of a secondary stage of reflection and action, when symbolism is complemented by discursive thought and symbolic behavior becomes self-conscious, and (2) Western culture and religion's primitive symbolization, which formed the basis of a secondary stage of philosophical-theological reflection and developed religious-moral codes. This parallel allows me to propose my own heuristic model of the early relationship of *mythos* and *logos*. It is constructed from a contemporary (scientific) picture of the dynamics of early childhood development and an equally contemporary historical understanding of the ways that both the Greeks and the Jews dealt with their common mythopoetically conceived world. As children grow, they continue to retain their earliest picture-awareness of the world and of the significant adults who populate it, at the same time that they become capable of speaking, spelling, reading, reasoning, and even operating computers — all by the age of five! The interpenetration involved attests to the unity of the mental principle from which both myth and language spring and to the necessary interplay between conscious and unconscious that gives meaning to our life for as long as we live.[12]

Similarly, in the philosophical academies of the Hellenistic world, in the rabbinical academies of Judaism, in the catechetical schools of the patristic era, as well as in the scriptoria of monasteries and the aulas of medieval universities, intellectual activity retained the received mythopoetic images of the cosmos and the major symbols of the Bible at the same time that scholars interpreted, questioned, and rearranged those early pictures of the world. There was always some tension between the basic biblical image of God's creation as "very good" and the reality of evil, plague, and war. But no essential contradiction between later reflection and early mythopoetic image took hold except in dualist heresies. Augustine argued that one cannot identify the *pax terrena* of Christianized Rome with the City of God. God's providence operates by its own sovereign standards, no matter how disobedient and contrary humanity acts. Similarly, Maimonides taught the immutability of the Torah but held that the law's perfection allowed for its adaptation in changed circumstances. And so both Christian and Jewish thinkers learned to accommodate history and its vicissitudes to their primarily naive view of God the creator of the world. When this changed and rational human nature was set in opposition to mythopoetic worldviews, everything changed.[13]

But before this occurred, Western religious culture was in a position analogous to the preadolescent stage of early childhood that we call *latency*. With all children, a primary, image-oriented, and affective capacity undergirds but coexists with a complementary intellectual ability. At the same time, it is not uncommon for the intellect, once operative, to become the predominant partner. Instead of being seen as a complementary development of symbolic understanding, intellectual ability often tends to supplant one's ability to respond symbolically or affectively to one's environment. As soon as children become capable of abstract, rational operations, they are expected to act out of their understanding rather than their affectivity. Likewise, we make the mistake of believing that philosophical reflection is superior to symbolic awareness because it is a more consciously intellectual activity — the same mistake that parents are tempted to make when their children's intellectual capacity becomes prominent. They demand that children grow up because they can understand harsh realities, ignoring how affective perceptions and needs always underlie abstract thinking and concrete action and that a growing person is always engaged with the interplay between them. When primary naivete (our first reading of the self and the world) is judged inadequate before its time or is disparaged or abused by the onrush of a critical perspective, it will normally go underground (be repressed), to emerge at a time when it is a less convenient or appropriate response to ongoing change. Primary naivete cannot simply be replaced, because it is as fundamental to the individual's perception as it was to the development of Western civilization itself.

It takes years for children to understand whether their parents are poor or well-off, have problems with addiction, are working long hours and are unavailable. But early on, they know far more than they can put into thoughts or words. The way their mother looks at them, how warm her greeting is, what their father's hug feels like, the tone of his voice, his absence or his stern presence all become part of a child's growing awareness. This initial, intuitive knowledge registers at the deepest level of self-awareness. Abstract intellect is crucial for a child to be able to obey instructions, to know what time it is, to perform well in preschool, but it cannot replace an understanding of the world rooted in a child's affectivity. Before ideas ever achieve any independent or truly abstract status, they preexist as symbols or images in the child's affective knowledge of the way the world is and how he or she fits into it. The primacy of this knowing, though scientifically established today, still makes counterintuitive demands on us. Despite all the evidence amassed to support the special developmental needs of infants and children, society prefers a commonsense approach that continues, as in ages past, to treat children like miniature adults.

Adults in general and parents in particular (ex-children though we are) often seem determined to deny the primacy of a child's affective world. That world is best described mythopoetically: it is made up of omnipotent parents who provide everything a child needs; it is filled with threatening adults, comforting teddys, sounds of indeterminate origin, darkness and its attendant threat of absence, even abandonment. It is not fanciful to say that children inhabit this magic world in some of the same ways that early humans inhabited a world of mysterious unknowns, uncharted spaces, and uncontrollable forces. This world shapes a child's affective life before he or she becomes capable of thinking about it. Yet parents, often in the name of sophistication, impose burdens on their children that they are not emotionally capable of bearing. Adults often use the intellectual cleverness of children as an excuse to treat them in ways that correspond more to parental needs than to a child's.

While parents seem to think that their rational understanding of a situation will somehow communicate itself to the child (even without any serious attempt to explain), the child's affective understanding registers only rejection and lack of love. Parental preference for intellectual understanding over affective knowledge results from the way success at cognitive tasks has become a socially desirable goal. This, in turn, has led parents to adopt patterns of child-rearing that promote mastery of cognitive skills, even to the extent of discouraging play as not serious. We have evidence of the enormous cost of imposing an artificial level of abstract intellectual demands on children whose world is based in more affective needs. Abuse of these needs prevents a child's developing the desired integration or balance between its own needs and others'. In addition, children are constantly presented with out-of-balance adults as normal or as role models in public life. When the interplay between affective and cognitive abilities is disregarded, the results can only be detrimental for a person's overall sense of what is good and bad, right or wrong. The lack of internalized values that results is today responsible for our full-to-overflowing jails and the amorality rampant in both the public and private sectors. The problem does not occur just in the frac-tured families who supposedly produce our society's criminal underclass; it is evident at all socioeconomic levels. Integrating values into one's per-sonal life requires that children be given access to an affective knowledge of their world, to the truth that they are centers of well-being, and that their way of putting together a first reading of things merits respect.

For first readings of situations (mostly more intuitive than rational) are more accurate than they seem. Naive understanding often intuits reality more accurately than abstract intellectual readings of the world around us. A whole range of sayings in the gospels on rebirth, on becom-ing a little child, on the kingdom belonging to "such as these [children]" refers to this recognition that primary naivete has a grasp of primal truths that the "learned and the clever" easily misconstrue (Matt 11:25). "Merest children" possess strengths that jaded adults have often ratio-nalized away. Naivete also has its weaknesses, and in due course, we will examine them. But at this stage of our conversation we are only exam-ining the extent to which the interplay of symbolic and rational aspects still constitutes the way many adults continue to view the self, the world, God, and the church. Reviewing some of these mixed notions will also reveal how unresolved conflicts between *mythos* and *logos* have been aggravated by modernity.

Mixed Understanding

Because primarily naive forms of thinking are universal and inevitable, they tell us something about how we acquired the basic elements of our personal and religious worldview. By looking at some examples of the way naive belief construes its worldview, we can understand better what is at stake when we consider the role and scope of the critical moment in the development of faith-affirmation.

Self

At any time, the self is an amalgam of stratified images, concepts, mem-ories, and experiences that prove notoriously difficult to integrate, even when we are in touch with them. Ideally, children are still at one with their primarily naive notions about themselves. The tragedy of abused children resides in the lie at the heart of their naivete: they can pretend the world is simple only because they are forced to repress the violence experienced at the hands of the adults who should be care providers. Unlike children and adolescents (a time of life we will investigate separately), adults who cling to their naive self-understanding are either seriously immature or neurotic, even if they are intellectually very sophisticated.[14] Still, all adults carry around vestiges of childhood within their conscious or unconscious self-awareness. They are still shaped (sometimes quite literally) by their naive understanding of the interaction between their historical child-self and the world around them. Again, the term "naive understanding" does not suggest any immediate judgment about facticity; it refers to the way primal images of the self become the building blocks of the later self. One example of how later personality stems from unconscious retention of childhood images shows up in the dialectic of grandiosity/depression that afflicts certain high-achieving adults. A child who is raised by a parent who needs the child to fill his or her own emptiness will most often repeat the pattern as an adult. As a result, the child's sense of self is bound up with how well it meets the parent's expectations. Its self-image will be symbolically grounded in the looks or words it takes in, based on whether it is pleasing the omnipotent care-provider. Being "Mommy's Little Angel" or "Daddy's Little Girl" refers precisely to an early, unconscious image that is bound to have an impact in adult life.

At the same time, not everything one retains of early naivete has negative results. Often, adult career or marriage choices, the way grown-ups care for children (their own and others'), or the way they play have a compensatory character and seek to make up for what adults were denied as children. The more conscious adults are of this compensation, the more creatively they can become individuals in their own right. The less conscious they are, the more likely they will engage in repetition compulsion, a pattern that clearly affects the children of alcoholics, child abusers (who were once abused), and others. Still, childhood dreams, memories of dead parents and loved ones, images of what brought happiness and what caused sadness in childhood continue to play a formative role in adult lives. The unique and unrepeatable circumstances of childhood remain the personal storehouse of symbolic memories out of which adult identity continues to renew itself. This is true whether the events of childhood call for celebration or for mourning. In either case, childhood symbols account for all first readings of the text of our lives and have an impact on determining who we are throughout life. Of course, no naive self-understanding is adequate once time and biology move us beyond childhood. Because growing up encourages us to rationalize our primarily symbolic understanding (and also to repress or censor the pictures that go along with it), we consciously lose touch with a good deal of our naive understanding of our selves. The trauma of adolescence further distances us from them. Afterward, we cannot reappropriate them in wholesale fashion, or uncritically, any more. They are past even though they remain with us. The interplay of unconscious past and conscious present, when not critiqued or made clear, causes the confusion about the self with which most adults live painfully. The same goes for our tendency to understand our world, for it is partner to the self in all understandings of identity.

World

"World" refers, first, to the mental pictures of our homes, neighborhoods, life-settings, and work experiences, of television, movie images, and travel memories, before it takes planet Earth into account. The term "worldview," by which social scientists describe the cultural, educational, political, and social aspects of people's life-setting, captures the importance of the symbols that make up our individual and collective worlds.

Life in the late twentieth century is strikingly characterized by the interplay of naive, prescientific pictures with critical, technological views of today's life-world. Despite overwhelming evidence from biogenetics to astrophysics that an evolutionary process has been responsible for all known life-forms, a significant portion of the populace (even in Western society) refuses to accept the evidence that humankind evolved from species more primitive than itself. While arguments rage among scientists over Darwinian orthodoxy, and various subforms of evolutionary biology vie for professional acceptance, creationists continue to offer their alternative, pseudoscientific theories, launching suits against the teaching of evolution in schools and scoring occasional victories against secular humanism and its message of evolution.

Fundamentalism is best understood as a social and religious protest against the scientific worldview that displaces traditional religious authority with secular rationality, a religious counterideology to modernism.[15] In fundamentalist perspective, God is not only the primary cause, the prime mover of Thomas Aquinas, the ultimate or final cause of physical creation; God also functions as the instrumental cause of everything that happens in the world. God not only brings about the rising and setting of the sun and watches over weather patterns but determines whether Aunt Sadie is going to remember to go to the drug store to renew her prescription. Paradoxically, creationism and the whole fundamentalist worldview is propagated by some of the most technologically sophisticated telecommunications networks on earth — evidence that naive worldviews continue to organize people's lives even while they participate in a scientific culture whose conclusions they refuse to accept. Here we have a classic case of unconscious interplay of naive and rational (though still precritical) perspectives. Unlike groups such as the Amish and the Hutterites, who maintain a consistent premodern worldview and eschew most technical conveniences developed by science, biblical fundamentalists split off their naive world from their casual acceptance of the benefits of technology and, by asserting the priority of the religious, subordinate the scientific worldview to it.

Naive perspectives also endure in the political life of both developed and developing societies, especially when political choices are correlated with the importance of what pollsters call the "feel good" index. Because naive understanding is rooted in an early, prerational, image-conscious awareness, it also connects us to those earliest instinctual needs for warmth, comfort, nourishment, and care that we call primary narcissism. We have primordial needs to feel good about ourselves and the world, and politicians who know how to exploit such needs (or to summon up fears that can be assuaged) will prosper in a country where sophisticated, critical analysis is relegated to universities, think tanks, the scientific establishment, and the advertising industry. Of these, only Madison Avenue loses no opportunity to use the most sophisticated market analysis techniques to exploit the populace's naive view of their real needs. Primary naivete is uniquely susceptible to being manipulated not only in children but also in adults who, though supposedly more rational, are never very far removed from their primordial needs. Though both politically and personally critical rationality has exercised a significant attraction in the opposite direction, the renewed popularity of plain and simple understandings of complex social and political changes confirms even more that rationality remains unstably engaged with basically naive understanding in many crucial areas of the modern life-world. The result is that most adults today continue to live out of a precritical sense of why things happen in our political, social, and personal worlds.

God

A first reading of the symbol *God* begins when we take into account that no other three-letter word in English except "Mom" and "Dad" has such potential for turning on or putting off its users.[16] In popular speech, the word tends to be flattened or banalized and given an indistinct meaning ("God bless you" after a sneeze). Still, *God* retains evocative qualities that most people learned at their mother's breast or their father's knee. "God knows" or "God forbid" or "Kiss it up to God" (not to mention the angry "goddam") generally have the same sense of *God* as "act of God" does: personified nature. These expressions invoke the presumed force or power beyond our ordinary experience that acts as a nonobvious or hidden cause. Thus in many people's minds, sickness is somehow connected with God — much more than healing is — because despite great epidemiological advances in medical science, most lay people experience a gap in their understanding of how this illness has happened to them. People insert the unsophisticated, amorphous notion *God* into the gap, but often with no more reflection or conviction than is reflected in the apostrophe "My God!" used instead of "Holy Cow!" Naive understanding is not normally an indication of banality, but in the use of the divine name, the general rule is often broken.

Despite this, *God* also names the first cause of the physical universe, whose magnificence, power, and splendor continue to awe all of us from the backyard gardener to the astrophysicist using Hawaii's new Keck telescope. Linking our wonder at the beauty of creation with a figure or force responsible for it (who is also someone in some way like ourselves) creates the magic in *God* as a personal name. Derivative polytheists as they were, the ancient Romans knew that, when you were really serious, you didn't talk about the "immortal gods," the *dei immortales;* you invoked "Almighty God," *Deus Omnipotens,* who as a power undergirded the whole universe and whose majesty demanded conscientious attention.

Still, a naive apprehension of *God,* for all its sincerity, tends to operate within an enchanted, magical framework. Again, this does not imply an immediately negative judgment. A magical notion of the universe represents an original nondualistic understanding in which matter and spirit, life and death (as afterlife), and even good and evil are not yet well differentiated. As we saw earlier, an infant naturally thinks magically because precise imaging, let alone abstract rationality, is beyond its abilities. In like fashion, primitive religions made little distinction between the spiritual and the natural and clung to a primarily naive religious cosmology predating the dualism that sets people against themselves (body vs. soul) or encourages group enmity or sexual antagonism. These naive religious expressions stress immanence (the *God* present in the world) rather than transcendence (the *God* beyond) and use ways of addressing and relating to *God,* or spirits, or saints that are familiar rather than formal. In this prereflective mentality, *God* is easily domesticated and made a spiritual conversation-partner, a naive adult's imaginary playmate. This *God* is understood as present or manifested directly in daily events, in coincidences, at roadway shrines, through miraculous images, in mantic persons.

These primitive ways of imaging God underlay the various Hebrew names for *El,* the common Semitic term for God. Thus in the Hebrew Bible, *El Shaddai,* which was translated (and conceptualized) by the Greek title "God Almighty," originally referred to a tribal god of the mountains who was powerfully manifested in the storm systems that swept through and left the earth changed in their wake. *El Elyon,* the high God of Caananite and Jebusite Jerusalem, was merely added to the litany of names that the ancestral God of the Hebrews acquired as they extended their sway in the eleventh century B.C.E. In similar fashion, the Hebrew God was understood as acting anthropomorphically. When God was angry, God was "hot in the nose" (Num 25:4: "the fierce anger of the LORD"). God's salvific activity, as we saw above in Deuteronomy 26:8, is expressed as the activity of "his strong hand and outstretched arm." When Solomon prayed for mercy, he used the plural (*rachamim*) of the term for the female womb (*rechem*, 1 Kings 8:50). When the God of Abraham, Isaac, and Jacob revealed his name, the mysterious *Yahweh,* we clearly move away from immanence toward transcendence in the way God is (not) pictured among the Hebrews.

Properly abstract thinking and theological reflection on the nature of God have interacted with primary images of God, not dispensed with them. Prophetic and wisdom writers, the rabbis, the authors of the New Testament, and the Christian fathers all sought to schematize belief in the deity beyond a primitive level of mythopoetic awareness, but their reflections amounted to accommodated interplay with the Bible's *mythos* of God. Like the Greek philosophers before them, they adjusted their rational thinking or they became skeptics. Only a few early rationalists like Lucretius and Lucian refused to entertain philosophy and the gods simultaneously.[17] As we saw, scholastic theologians accommodated the biblical God to the prime mover of Aristotelian physics in various systems of cause and effect, introducing the very significant distinction between primary and secondary causality. None of these efforts lacked analytical skill, and it is ignorant to presume that, because their worldview was different from a modern one, they were merely deluded or unintelligent. But a first reading of *God* always involves taking for granted God's active and immediate involvement in creation. Consequently, the issue of human free will in the face of God's almighty power ranked as the most consistent theological problem from biblical times at least through the Reformation. Modern atheism arose as a critical refutation of a primarily naive understanding of God (as a concept *and* as a person) in order to resolve the problem in favor of individual human freedom. The irony is that determinism has never been so rife in Western consciousness as it has been since God retired from the intellectual scene! In reaction, naive believers have been very reluctant to allow critical categories to be brought to bear on the idea of *God,* because a critique of any sort is presumed to derogate from the dignity of the person of God. In stating how basic is the naive understanding of God, I am seeking, not to settle for it, but to move beyond accommodation. For despite all the staying power that the uncriticized concept *God* possesses, the person and mystery of God is not well served by clinging to a naive understanding, as if the whole truth about God is preserved in the dream images of our cultural and religious youth. More is required of the inquiring and mature adult to get beyond the confusion prevalent in Western religious culture today.

Church

In an early Christian writing, *The Shepherd of Hermas,* there appears an old, then young, female figure, *Ecclesia* (Church) who "was created the first of all things ... for her sake was the world established" (2 Vision, 4, 1).[18] Written in a somewhat apocalyptic vein, this work was judged worthy of canonical status by a number of the fathers, including Origen (d. 275 C.E.). In it, church exists before the Savior — the most dangerous naive conceptualization of any era of Christian history. But it is a good place to begin with some preliminary remarks on the interplay of primary naivete and early ideas about the church.

Central to the myth of the church, as the author of *Hermas* understood, is the feminine character of the symbol. In the apostolic era, the author of the Letter to the Ephesians compared the marriage of a husband and wife to the archetypal union of Christ and the church. Around the same time, the book of Revelation recorded two visions of figures with similar symbolic potential: the "woman clothed with the sun" (who gives birth to the messianic ruler, 12:1, 17) and "the Bride, the wife of the Lamb" (19:7–8 and 21:2, 9, 17). Thus within the New Testament itself, the two images of the mother and the bride entered the mainstream of Christian imagination and fixed a feminine symbolic value to the notion of the church or the assembly of God's people.

In the second century, Irenaeus's analogy between Eve's disobedience and Mary's obedience, making Mary the real "mother of the living" (Gen 3:20), began the interweaving of the symbols of Mary/mother and church/bride so characteristic of Catholicism. Had the bridal imagery maintained an equal footing with the maternal imagery, history might have looked somewhat different. But when the Council of Ephesus (431 C.E.), to affirm the complete unity of Christ's divinity and humanity (the problem of the *communicatio idiomatum*), declared Mary to be *Theotokos,* the God-Bearer ("mother of God" in the vernacular languages), the priority of the maternal archetype over the bridal was established.

In mythopoetic terms, this intersignification of Mary as the mother of God and mother of the faithful has had an enormous impact on the shape of the Catholic imagination. It has also served to promote celibacy and virginity, especially consecrated virginity for women, and has led to the highly ambivalent role that women have had in both religious life and in marriage. There can be no doubt about the significance of church as mother as a primal image in our inherited symbol system, but as with our common notion of God, a first reading or naive understanding of the church is only a place to begin our reflection.

Almost inevitably, symbolizing the church maternally claims a priority and an unconscious authority for the church that is in Mary's image.

But when the mother of God (the *Dei Genetrix* of myth) became the powerful Virgin (*Virgo potentissima*) of medieval spirituality, the authority of Mother Church grew apace. So anxious were medieval adherents of the cult of the Virgin to promote the priority of Mary (now associated with the church) that they applied to her the mythic image of preexistent Wisdom from Proverbs 8:22 ("the Lord begot me the first-born of his ways") just as *Hermas* had predicated preexistence of Lady Church. The habit of using Luke 11:27 as a verse in honor of Mary ("Blessed is the womb that bore you and the breasts that nursed you") without the addition of Jesus' reposte in v. 28 ("Rather, blessed are they that hear the word of God and keep it") removed Mary from the context of the gospel and took her from "among women," exalting her above all creatures. By promoting the priority of the Virgin Mary in our salvation, celibate ecclesiastical authority was happy to include itself in her glories and to give out the message that access to her all-powerful intercession was available through the ministrations of the church.

Combining the authority of the heavenly mother of God with male, patriarchal forms of authority has proved a very powerful recipe for institutional continuity over the centuries. When papal authority found itself in conflict with the Western emperors and then with kings of the nascent nation-states, it was so convinced of its all-encompassing (maternal and paternal) authority that it juridically insisted on its right to depose kings and queens. One might say that the interplay of the mythic substratum of church authority and the political philosophy that came to predominate in the Middle Ages embodied the carrot and stick principle of control more thoroughly than any other political institution has done. Again, it would be too hasty to dismiss these primarily naive understandings of the symbolism associated with the notion of church or to judge them too harshly. The resilience and renewability of Catholicism over the centuries certainly testifies to the strength of associating the church with such primal human symbols.

But the naive symbolizing of the church as a parental matrix converges with the problem of modern unbelief more than coincidentally. It makes for a fitting transition to the oppositional moment in our analogy of growth and development. Both personally and in the life of Western religion and culture, there comes a point, a moment or stage of development, when questioning, dissatisfaction, even revolt become almost inevitable. This is the crisis of criticism, when critical reason is set up over earlier, mythopoetic understanding. In the last years of this millennium, it has become a universal, if varied, phenomenon. Once we have studied the impact of this developmental movement and the crisis that it brings for naive understanding, both on the historical and the individual level, we will be in a better position to understand the full range of the forms of faith that lie to hand for Catholics today.

Bibliographical Essay

Andrew Louth, *Discerning the Mystery: An Essay on the Nature of Theology* (Oxford: Clarendon Press, 1983), has a chapter, "The Return of Allegory," that corrects the perception that allegory is by definition dishonest and recovers critically (by reference to the work of Henri de Lubac) the sense in which allegory sought to grasp the ever new aspect of the mystery of Christ. Another author who helps put allegory in historical perspective is B. Smalley, *The Study of the Bible in the Middle Ages* (Notre Dame: University of Notre Dame Press, 1964).

Peter Brown's *Augustine of Hippo* (Berkeley: University of California Press, 1969) is a magisterial work that looks deeply into Augustine's intellectual, psychological, and spiritual contribution. He compares Augustine's explanation of the need for a language of signs with that of Freud:

Both men... assume that the proliferation of images is due to some precise event, to the development of some geological fault across a hitherto undivided consciousness: for Freud, it is the creation of an unconscious by repression; for Augustine, it is the outcome of the Fall. (261)

On Augustine's own scriptural method, he writes:

There is no doubt that, as Augustine would use the Bible, it was the fuel of the blast furnace: for in interpreting it so much as an allegory, Augustine was finding in it all that he had always valued in his intellectual activity — hard labour, the excitement of discovery and the prospect of endless movement in a philosopher's quest for wisdom. (262–63)

Arno Gruen, *The Betrayal of the Self: The Fear of Autonomy in Men and Women* (New York: Grove Press, 1988), fills out some of the notions of the impact of early child-rearing on a child's "autonomy." By this word he describes the integrating factor in personality allowing one to experience freely one's own feelings, perceptions, and needs. It leads to what Erik Erikson calls a sense of self-constancy, which lies at the basis of self-esteem (*Identity and the Life Cycle* [New York: W. W. Norton, 1980], 67–73). Ernest Becker's *The Denial of Death* (New York: Free Press, 1973), with its attempt to "take psychology and deepen it with religious and metaphysical associations so that it becomes actually a religious belief system with some breadth and depth" (273), has been very helpful in my efforts to look at parallels between early development and the basis of our understanding religious truth. E. Kurtz, *Not-God: A History of Alcoholics Anonymous* (Center City, Minn.: Hazelden, 1979) recounts in the testimony of Bill W., the founder of A.A., how retaining the archaic form of unmet emotional needs into adulthood can lead to the bind out of which alcoholics seek to drink themselves (14).

Chapter 3

The Crisis of Criticism

Organic change, both in bodies and in societies, occurs at different rates in different parts. It always creates discrete tasks whose accomplishment affects the organism's health. We call the problems and opportunities that accompany such changes "vicissitudes," and the adaptive tasks required for growth "stages of development." But stages, like historical periods such as the Renaissance or the Enlightenment, always overlap as their dominant tendencies shift and readjust to new vicissitudes. This means that we can describe personal and cultural change in stages without being committed to a picture of development that presumes sudden, wholesale shifts of total paradigms.[1]

In organic development, then, we recognize purposive movement as the general framework or pattern in which a particular organism in a particular environment responds to the stable (innate) and the labile (environmental) elements involved. Stages are not automatically better or worse; they describe the extent to which persons or societies, on the basis of their innate capacities and their environmental circumstances, have adapted to particular historical vicissitudes. Developmental stages are said to be progressive and regressive in relative, not absolute, terms. In other words, the end is not predetermined except by the process by which the vicissitudes of nature and nurture interact to create the end or goal of the organism. This process is what we refer to as general laws of development. Accordingly, theological tradition, just like all living organisms, has innate (stable) as well as environmental (labile) elements. Only if there is a fruitful interaction of both will the task of faith affirmation be healthy. This rule of thumb should help us guard against absolutely identifying any already existing mode, experience, or form of faith with the not yet of the mystery of revelation.[2]

Up to now I have proposed that there are analogies between infancy and early mythopoetic religion and between latency and the development of the capacity for thought and action. Here I wish to extend the analogy to see the crisis that modern scientific culture has caused for religious belief as not just ending a naive stage of awareness but inaugurating another stage in the development of a more mature way that faith seeks understanding and affirms its object.

The Crisis of Adolescence

Latency ends when children experience a renewed irruption of instinctuality brought on by the physiological processes of puberty. The word "adolescence" catches something of the dynamic quality of this stage of life, derived as it is from the verb *adolescere,* whose past participle *adultus* indicates that the process of growing is complete. Adolescence (combined with what we commonly call young adulthood) creates a veritable divide between childhood and maturity. During these years, the tension between the stable and labile elements in the personality is so great, and the array of developmental tasks so daunting, that conflict of one sort or other is inevitable.[3] Because the physiological tasks, which are biologically programmed into the organism, occur without forewarning, adolescent life borders on chaos. The physical appearance of secondary sexual characteristics and the bodily growth this entails often create the false impression that, once physical maturity has been achieved, the adolescent has indeed grown up. Society generally recognizes this with "majority" status at ages sixteen to eighteen through various celebrations and rewards for young adults, e.g., graduations, weddings, professional salaries, athletic scholarships, etc. But all the while these physical changes have been occurring, there are primordial elements of the personality that remain stable but are masked by the pace of lability. This makes for an imbalance between evident physical change and unaccomplished emotional maturity. Because physical, social, and educational development seem to be the chief tasks of this stage, affective and spiritual development are treated with benign neglect in the hope that the adolescents can catch up with these other tasks when they settle down as adults.

But before adults emerge, adolescents must deal with their internalized ideas about who they are. Even while they are breaking free of their parents' external influence and control, the internal struggle continues to rage. While the outer conflict gets more attention, it is often the hidden struggle that accounts for outbreaks of parent-teen enmity. Overt conflicts are often acts of a drama rooted in earlier childhood. Inner-developmental tasks are a great deal harder than external adaptation but get far less press in popular culture.

Despite our ability to plot phases of this stage of development, there is a significant hidden aspect to adolescence that cannot be accomplished within the period we call adolescence/young adulthood. In childhood we introject (cast inside) emotional reactions or mental images that are acted out only in the adolescent's struggle for separation-individuation.

But the resolution of identity, the working through of the childhood introjects, only happens even later. Adolescence and early adulthood, then, is an uneven stage in which young people achieve higher orders of rational thinking while simultaneously "acting out." This has been called that special form of remembering in which an old memory is reenacted in such a way that the memory is cut off from any real resolution from within or without.[4]

This disparity between the inner and outer creates a tip-of-the-iceberg phenomenon. The raging against parents, the negative identity that so many young people revel in, their intolerance, self-involvement, even their occasional asceticism, idealism, and high-flying intellectual feats are only small indications of the developmental chaos below the surface. Despite the young person's ability to engage in second-order thinking, to bring thought and action into efficient amalgams, and to look and act independently, this stage of development really serves a longer-term working-through of the necessary disenchantment that adolescence entails. Much of the developing adolescent's inner struggle relates to the ambiguity caused by loss of an early certainty about self and world and by the newfound freedom that is dawning: it is exhilarating and frightening at the same time. This causes some of the overreactions alluded to above: ideological identification, peer group overidentification, romantic involvements, the loss of self inherent in mass movements or musical subcultures, and, tragically, the compulsion to avoid it all through suicide.[5]

While engaged in the overwhelming task of separation-individuation, the adolescent experiences mainly conflict and discontinuity with the past. As they begin to emerge from their adolescent struggles, young adults sense that their early life lies across a chasm that separates them definitively from childhood and from the world of their primary naivete. But the truth is normally longer in emerging. In later maturity, when further developmental tasks have been accomplished, the introjected memories can emerge as a source of integrating one's whole self — but never without loss or pain, and rarely without mourning. This thumbnail sketch of the vicissitudes of adolescence and early adulthood can now help us put the struggles of Western religion and culture over the last three hundred years into a longer-term developmental framework.

The Crisis of Modernity

The cultural, social, and religious changes of the Enlightenment bear close comparison with the anomalous changes of adolescence and young adulthood. On the surface, the Enlightenment's emerging secular consciousness rejected its parental matrix; but deeper down, there have been struggles with ancient memories and symbols whose outcome is still in doubt. Radically departing from what went before, much as adolescents scorn their childhood identity, Enlightenment figures saw themselves as demystifying human consciousness and disenchanting the mythopoetic imagination, leading humanity from its "self-inflicted bondage."[6] Enlightenment rationalism (and its claim to modernity) was conceived as an arrival point, an end in itself, not a staging point for further development. Its thinkers' trust in human rationality and intellectual autonomy was, from our perspective, understandable. But as a stage of cultural (and religious) development, the Enlightenment too needs to be complemented. First, however, we must engage its acting out its external struggle with mythopoetic authority before we can begin to work through to some resolution of the internal struggle between Western culture's ancient religious symbols and their critical negation by secular reason.

As a complex historical phenomenon, the Enlightenment's impact has been difficult to assess. Best spoken of as occurring in phases roughly equivalent to the seventeenth, eighteenth, and nineteen through early twentieth centuries, it affected all Western institutions, but not in the same degree. England, the Netherlands, France, Germany (and to some extent Peter the Great's Russia and Poland) were most affected; Spain, Italy, Greece, and the Slavic countries less so. But this neat division does not do justice to the entire cultural, social, and religious — not to mention political — landscape. Suffice it to say that, in the seventeenth century, a movement exalting critical reason and anthropocentric concerns (itself continuous with Renaissance humanism) and downgrading religious creeds and theocentric institutions began to influence philosophy, education, politics, economics, and, eventually, Christian belief itself. That movement still influences the West and, through it, global society, much of which was colonized in the nineteenth century by countries becoming secular at home while exporting their brand of national religion. Today, aspects of the Enlightenment's technological self-confidence are waning, but it remains, in its political, social, and scientific contributions, an indisputable foundation of modern cultural life.

The analogy between adolescence/young adulthood and the Enlightenment might appear to founder on the disparity between the former's base in raw, instinctual energy and the latter's in rationality. As I hope to show, the tasks of separation-individuation, possible only because of the high levels of instinctual energy available in adolescence and young adulthood, resemble what the Enlightenment accomplished for liberal politics and economics. Just as adolescence mixes chaotic emotions and second-order thought in a highly combustible brew, so too the Enlightenment combined iconoclastic activity with scientific rationality, with explosive results. Like the adolescent's unconscious reenactment of his or her early dramas of independence, *philosophes* like Bayle and Kant consciously delved back into the rationalism of antiquity for much of their reforming energy, unearthing even the motto *aude sapere* ("dare to know") from a classic pagan source.[7] Just as adolescence and young adulthood prepare the way (often in spite of themselves) for another configuration of a person's affective and rational life, so the Enlightenment (for all its mistakes) has prepared the way for a new paradigm of cultural, social, religious — and even political — maturity that we are still just able to glimpse, at least on our good days. Therefore, I wish to move our investigation forward by demonstrating how the critical moment in the history of Western culture and religion has been a necessary step in our dawning ability to place mythopoetic religious imagination on a footing other than primary naivete.

For all its brash newness, the Enlightenment's critical reflection had roots in classical Greek and Roman philosophical reflection, Jewish monotheizing, and the Christian habit of correlating faith and reason.[8] Even in the Middle Ages Aristotelian literalism sought to reduce exaggerated spiritual claims and ground them in what could be grasped by sensible reason. In their turn, Renaissance thinkers consciously appropriated classical antiquity — without the Christian overlay — creating a humanist outlook that undid the foundations of medieval Christian society and questioned its hallowed self-understanding. In Italy, Lorenzo Valla engaged in source criticism (c. 1440), showing that traditional documents (such as the Donation of Constantine, which gave central Italy to the papacy) were forgeries. Erasmus of Rotterdam produced a critical edition of the Greek New Testament in 1516 (based on Valla's annotations), and Thomas More, though a rigidly orthodox believer, wrote the philosophical and ethical tract *Utopia,* completely ignoring theology. Nor should it be forgotten that, in 1492, Christopher Columbus found what he wasn't looking for by sailing in what most people thought was the wrong direction. Thus as the sixteenth century dawned upon still undivided Western Christianity, *alternate sources of authorization* (classical antiquity, biblical criticism, historical investigation, philosophy detached from the schools, exploration, empirical science) had already begun to challenge the traditional pillars of the society that had survived recognizably in the West from the time of Augustine and, beyond him, the world of the New Testament. (A century after the Reformation began, when Galileo Galilei championed the heliocentric theories of Copernicus, he was punished, not for his confidence in what "the evidence of our senses have made us sure and certain of," but for threatening the authority of scripture.)[9]

In addition to these revolutionary sources for critical reflection, we must take into account the enormous disrepute into which Catholic central authority had fallen in the two hundred years previous to the

Reformation. First there was the Avignon captivity of the popes (1308–78), during which the papal court gained a reputation for worldiness and financial greed. The Western Schism immediately followed, with two and then three rival claimants to the papal throne (1378–1417). Then, under Sixtus IV (della Rovere), Innocent VIII (who married his son to a daughter of Lorenzo de' Medici), Julius II (della Rovere), Leo X (de' Medici), and Clement VII (de' Medici), the papacy was effectively but one of a number of warring Italian principalities. The disarray in which Holy Mother Church had fallen through the abuse done her by the Holy Fathers in Rome set the stage for a revolt against authority. This occurred via a change in the symbol system of Christianity.

Protestantism found the energy for separation in its discovery of the Bible as an authority sufficiently powerful to challenge the millennial authority of the papacy. Its preference for the Word over sign, for *sola scriptura, sola fides,* and *sola gratia* (scripture without tradition, faith without [scholastic] reason, grace without works) purposefully set Christianity off balance in order to rescue it from an authority too willing to compromise (as the Renaissance papacy so lustily did) with pagan art, pagan philosophy, and pagan ethics. From this perspective, the Reformation was clearly a rebellion of *logos* against *mythos,* of plain meaning against complex image, of literal truth against ambiguous symbol. In many places, the protest adopted a harsh iconoclasm that led to the wholesale destruction of "graven images," statues and stained-glass windows, in literal obedience to Exodus 20:4: "You shall not carve idols for yourselves in the shape of anything in the sky above or on the earth below or in the waters beneath the earth."

In the churches of the Reformation, the symbol of identity became the Word, spoken and proclaimed (at great length) but no longer pictorially represented. It is a historian's commonplace that the invention of the printing press was the technological premise of the Reformation's success in founding Christianity anew on the (now printed) Word, just as it was the rise of vernacular languages that provided the reformers with a revolutionary program of information sharing. To a Europe mired in an obfuscated language of symbols (and increasingly ignorant of Latin, the language of ritual and learning), Protestantism introduced the symbol of living language, of words that revealed rather than concealed, of a spiritual word that contained all the metaphysics they needed. However, when the conflict moved from pulpits to the battlefield and the ensuing religious wars produced megaviolence, sanguinary self-righteousness, and widespread devastation, a second, more drastic separation, ensued.

Although Luther never espoused the literalism that later came to characterize Protestant orthodoxy, the literalist emphasis of the Reformation helped to focus attention on *apparent* meaning. This validated the empirical inquiry that scientists like Francis Bacon (whose anti-Aristotelian *Novum Organum* was published in 1620) were pioneering. A second trajectory, which preceded the Reformation but continued to influence the period, had arisen in the nominalism of William of Ockham (d. 1347). Nominalism undercut a concern with the metaphysical essence of things, emphasizing, instead, the conditions of the subject's knowing. Nominalist thinkers proposed that we cannot know universals, only singulars. Their names or obvious qualities, not their essences, made them intelligible. These two movements, empiricism in the natural sciences and nominalism in philosophy, challenged both Aristotelian (and Ptolemaic) physics as well as Aristotelian (and Thomistic) metaphysics. The search was on for another model of how to know and more accurately describe the world. Conveniently, there were at hand skeptical and experimental intellects who wished to replace older, credulous, and metaphysical answers with newer ones. The age of intuitive reason and inductive method was aborning.

René Descartes's *Discourse on Method* (1637) provided a catalyst for this new intellectual development. Beginning by radically doubting the bases of knowing and being, of cognition and essence, Descartes sought to rid the mind of all accepted ideas, opinions, and beliefs, because he saw the mind as untrustworthy, not just in everyday affairs, but metaphysically as well. What could not possibly be doubted had the greatest claim to certitude: the "I" whose mental activity, even in the act of doubting, is an undoubted existent. This is the Cartesian *Cogito ergo sum,* "I think, therefore I exist."

With Descartes and other thinkers of the seventeenth-century Enlightenment, the logically deductive (metaphysical) basis of human knowledge was replaced by a new inductive ideal that sought knowledge through constructing a body of evidence. Knowledge became physical science, whose methods desymbolized and demetaphorized all terms of knowing. Enthralled by the self-evident data of mathematics, Descartes developed his methodological reduction of metaphysical existents to the thinking subject, though he still included God as the designer of this schema. After him, thinking subjects depended less and less on God for their "clear and distinct ideas" and more and more on experimental science to refine them. Subsequently, apparent meaning was available only in the physical sciences, not through metaphysical inquiry.[10]

Meanwhile, another major factor led to the discrediting of the traditional, primarily naive symbol system of the Bible and Christian tradition (both Catholic and Protestant). Forces other than philosophical or scientific ones were at work in the seventeenth century, making it more and more difficult for growing numbers of people, newly convinced of the logic of scientific induction, to accept the notion that truth resided in traditional religious faith.

Religious Conflict and Rationalist Reaction

Just ten years after Luther's theses were posted in Wittenberg, the forces of the Catholic Hapsburg Charles V marched on the city of Rome and sacked it. The Medici pope Clement VII, holed up in the Castel Sant'Angelo, was powerless to stop the brutality of the emperor's troops before he escaped. The ferocity of the sack and the terrible damage and loss of life both in Rome and throughout Italy were due, in no small part, to the presence of Lutherans in the army, whose righteous anger against the pope was given free play. Though Clement was to crown Charles Holy Roman Emperor three years later in Bologna, someone witnessing the events of 1527, an extreme chapter in the centuries-old papal-imperial rivalry, could be forgiven for not fully understanding that some irrational and revolutionary genies had been loosed in Europe and would not be put back in the bottle for a long time to come.

Evidence of this strange new irruption had already shown up in the social chaos caused by the Peasants' War of 1524–25 in Germany. In the wake of Luther's attacks on the papacy and the established order, peasant armies led by the radical reformer Thomas Münzer took to the field only to be crushed and annihilated by the nobility — and with Luther's blessing. Despite the Catholic emperor's attempts to accommodate Protestant princes in the Peace of Augsburg (1530), within a few years the first Protestant military alliance (the Schmalkald League) had formed. So antagonistic were the two Christian sides that the league refused to join the Catholic emperor in common military action against the Turks who were advancing on Vienna. In 1535 the Catholic king of France took advantage of the religious strife in Germany and joined with the Protestant league to make war on the Holy Roman Emperor. In France itself, a Catholic slaughter of Waldensians coincided with Henry II's burning of heretics. This practice was used in England by Henry VIII's chancellor Thomas More (1529–32) and was taken up again by Mary Tudor during her brief and unstable reign (1553–58).

In the medieval perspective, politics and religion were intertwined as two aspects of a unitive worldview. Though many in authority did not see it, that order was passing away. The Renaissance's exaltation of antiquity and humanism, plus its affirmation of vernacular languages, helped create a new sense of things, subverting older notions of a unified Christendom under papal authority. Forces of disintegration had been loosed, and the violent actions and reactions waged in the name of Christ only sealed the disintegration of an authority anchored in the naive, mythopoetic worldview that Christianity had adopted more or less whole from the Bible and from Hellenism. From the Peasants' Revolt to the Peace of Westphalia (1648), the religious history of Europe wove a brutal tapestry of vicious plots, calculated counterplots, assassinations, coups, wars, thefts, and massacres up and down the political and religious landscape.

In France, a series of reciprocal slaughters by Catholics and Protestants began in 1560 and culminated in the 1572 St. Bartholomew's Day massacre of five to ten thousand Huguenots. This mass killing was occasioned not by anything these Protestants had done but by the failure of the plot by Queen Catharine de' Medici (the niece of Pope Clement VII) to assassinate the Huguenot Admiral Gaspard de Coligny. Rather than await a possible reprisal, it seemed better to bloody the drawn sword before returning it to its scabbard. Between 1588 and 1610, first Henry of Guise, then Henry III, the last Valois king, and finally Henry IV, who thought "Paris...worth a Mass" and converted to Catholicism, were all assassinated in the societal madness caused by Catholic-Protestant strife. All in all, in the years 1560–95, a total of nine civil wars had been fought in France over the issue of religious hegemony.

Before this last Henry was despatched, he had sponsored the Protestant League of Alhausen against the Catholic League of Würzburg and the Hapsburg emperor. Though war did not follow immediately, within ten years a European donnybrook (the Thirty Years' War) had broken out. Before the exhausted parties stopped in 1648 (though France and Spain would continue till 1659), Spain had attacked Holland, Austria had defeated Bohemia, the Huguenots had revolted in France (only to be put down by Cardinal Richelieu), the Danes had invaded Germany unsuccessfully, German Protestants had allied with the Swedes under Gustavus Adolphus (financed by Richelieu), and the French had wrecked the Treaty of Prague (1635) because it left Germany dangerously united. In England an intra-Protestant civil war was being fought and, when the Calvinists were victorious under Cromwell, they celebrated by invading Catholic Ireland, driving the population "beyond the pale" into the infertile west, and massacring thousands.

All over Europe, but especially in Germany, wrote one historian, "unparalleled destruction had been wrought...by the campaigns of thirty years. Population had declined; towns had been abandoned; education had disappeared, and the lower classes were brutalized."[11] In the seventeenth century, warfare involved artillery, musketry, and standing armies — all at the disposal of rabid religious loyalties and rising nationalism. With the exception of the followers of Jan Hutter (burned at the stake in Innsbruck, 1536), Menno Simons (d. 1561), George Fox, the Quaker founder (1650), and their followers, Protestants took over the just war theology from Catholics and used it against them. Faithful to their medieval heritage, papists consistently fell back upon the two swords theory of church and state and expected the civil authority to suppress heresy, expunge error, and punish heretics, a program most thoroughly enacted in Spain and the Netherlands. In the low countries, the burning of heretics (the *auto da fé*) was so fierce that eventually both Protestants and Catholics fought together to win their independence.

After this gruesome period of strife, dynastic and nationalist politics resumed unabated, but with discrete rather than general warfare. For most of Europe, politics after 1648 took the short-sighted, nationalist form it has borne into the twentieth century. Catholics and Protestants seemed somewhat chastened, perhaps, by all the bloodshed, so with a few tragic exceptions (Ireland's Battle of the Boyne was fought in 1690), religion ceased to be the explicit cause of political and national division. But the truce was not motivated by religious conviction. Though politics took on a less religious shape, religious antagonism continued unabated in Europe, North America, and in the colonies that European countries planted throughout the world. In other words, peace broke out not from religious but from secular considerations. While exhaustion may have added to the parties' willingness to forgo sacred slaughter, the rise of secular rationalism and its impact on politics, culture, and biblical religion had more to do with putting an end to the sixteenth- and seventeenth-century religious conflicts than did Christian faith.

Perhaps it seemed that religion just was no longer worth fighting for. Disgusted with the violence around them, Enlightenment thinkers, like the children of alcoholic parents, repudiated, in the words of Voltaire, both "Geneva and Rome" and drew upon pagan antiquity's rationalism to found their own program of religious toleration. But soon they repeated what they had turned their backs on, as rationalist turned on rationalist and re-created the dysfunctionality of the parental matrix. Not unlike many young people convinced of their need to be independent, the Enlightenment turned on its parent-institutions, decided they were dotty and naive, set out to correct their errors, and promptly made most of the same mistakes, and even worse besides, in the name of rationality, science, education, philosophy, secularism, materialism, and humanism. The wars fought in and by the West since 1648, although not devoid of religious trappings, have been waged for profit and/or conquest, to secure national boundaries, achieve or maintain ethnic or colonial hegemony, or for racist/political ideology, not for God and true religion — and for this believers should be thankful. There is substantial tragedy and irony in the failure of critical scientific rationality to do much better than naive religion did in establishing social harmony and international concord. But this perspective is a postcritical one that will have to be fleshed out as we proceed. Here I wish to suggest that seeing the Enlightenment as a movement of autonomy will help us understand more sympathetically a number of the significant cultural and religious phenomena of the seventeenth through twentieth centuries. It suggests that, both culturally and personally, our contemporary situation must take into account the dynamics of separation-individuation as the

parameters for overcoming the hostility that has characterized the relationship of traditional Christianity and modernity since the seventeenth
century.[12]

Today, we look back on the attacks that the various rationalist and
secularist movements mounted against believers and religious bodies
(the Catholic Church in particular), and, while empathizing with our ancestors in the faith and admiring their steadfastness, we need not adopt
their response to movements that in the past seemed inimical to faith
but may well contribute to faith's maturing in a later era. For example,
when the emperor Joseph of Austria issued his 1781 Edict of Toleration stating that "all coercion of consciences is detrimental and...that
great profit arises to religion and to a state from truly Christian tolerance," it was denounced by Catholic authorities.[13] In the late eighteenth
century, this rationalist political perspective was abhorrent to Catholics
and to some Protestants, but today the principle has been enshrined in
Catholic teaching.[14] How far toleration goes, how much modernity faith
can come to terms with, and how we decide these questions are what
concerns us in the present work.

Because the conflict between critical reason and beleaguered, traditional faith is so broad-based, it is impossible to trace all its manifestations over three centuries. So I propose to examine how critical
reason has critiqued the mythopoetic imagination at the heart of religious symbolization and affirmation in the Bible. Specifically, I will look
at the vicissitudes or ups and downs that critical biblical investigation
has undergone. For in the history of biblical criticism we have the laboratory conditions necessary to determine the roots and the scope of the
conflict between Christianity's symbolic tradition and its treatment by
critical reason. If we can understand something of the outcome of the
development of biblical interpretation in the critical period, we should
be able to understand more clearly the parameters in which the Bible
can still contribute to our understanding of the scope of religious symbolization. This will help us decide how much critical rationality can
contribute to the shape of belief today.

As the sixteenth century closed, more and more educated persons saw
the Bible as the source of enchantment that was keeping human awareness childish. As a result, they set about to establish a new intellectual
environment in reaction to the Bible's world. Yet despite the overt clash
between criticism and revelation in the last three hundred years, we have
today begun to understand the critical period initiated by the Enlightenment, in the words of James A. Sanders, as "a gift of God in due season,
in the fullness of time, if its limitations are carefully observed."[15] If I
can make these elements clear — both the gift and the limitations of
historical-criticism — I may be able to take this inquiry beyond past im-
passes and consider the new opportunities of our postcritical situation.

If successful, this endeavor should be a little like wrapping up the tasks of adolescence and young adulthood and moving to a perspective of maturity. In turn, it may help us describe the parameters for a mature form of faith.

Criticism and the Bible

It is difficult for us to recover the excitement and confidence that critical reason and the empirical method touched off in intellectually active people in the seventeenth century. To some extent, we are still living in the aftermath of the intellectual and cultural Big Bang set off at the dawn of the scientific era. Today the promise of new knowledge still continues to summon thousands into research labs at universities and hospitals and in the corporate sector. Many of them cope with years of workaday laboratory drudgery, scraping up funds from government and private enterprise, waiting for the discovery that will justify years of effort. For them, discovery remains as persuasive a personal and professional goal as it was when Archimedes first cried *Eureka!* ("I found it!"). The modern roots of today's discovery-oriented scientific culture began in the early 1600s. Then it was no longer the rediscovery of classical antiquity, as in Florence of the early Quattrocento, or the rediscovery of the power of the Word of God, as in Luther's sixteenth-century Wittenberg that appealed to a whole new class of scholars and learned (middle-class) laity. Instead, it was the discovery of laws of nature that, in their newness and seeming inevitability, promised more than metaphysical validity.

The writings of Baruch Spinoza, who was born in the Netherlands fifteen years before the Peace of Westphalia, reflect both the age's loss of confidence in traditional, religious authority and its excitement over its discovery of the powers of impartial reason. The motive force behind his restless life is arguably the promise of transcending religious strife through an unprejudiced, methodical search for truth. Though not the first to write "in an attempt to bring warring Christians to admit that theology should be based first on reason and only secondarily on scripture and tradition,"[16] Spinoza's work became the most notorious. Excommunicated from the Jewish community in 1656, but only after absorbing the rationalist tradition of Maimonides, Spinoza published his *Tractatus Theologico-Politicus* in 1670 in order to try to help warring Christians overcome their mutual animosity and hatred by providing a method capable of avoiding murderous disputes over truth. Convinced of Descartes's philosophy and his own use of rational method, he undertook a fresh reading of the scriptures, from which he emerged believing "that the Bible leaves reason absolutely free, that it has nothing in common with philosophy, in fact, that revelation and philosophy stand on totally different footings."[17]

Spinoza was able to reach his professedly impartial conclusion because he took at face value the primary naivete of the scriptural idiom, in particular its way of attributing everything directly to God. But he accounted for this by reference to what he called the "Hebrew idiom," such as he would have learned from his kosher butcher, baker, and candlestick maker as a child. So, since the Bible dealt idiomatically (hence, inaccurately) and not literally with God's relationship to the world, he declared that the Bible corresponded to humanity's imagination, not its reason. This left philosophy free to construe the realm of the real on the basis of reason's investigation into the history of nature. The Bible was good and useful for the masses, who were not adept at abstract philosophy or deducing self-evident ideas in the manner of geometry problems. For Spinoza, positive religion, composed of doctrine and ritual with commandments and organizational structure, was tantamount to superstition.

Spinoza's intellectual daring is typical of critical reason's grandiosity, the raw psychic energy that the Enlightenment needed in order to achieve adequate separation-individuation from its authoritarian religious matrix. The entire milieu of post-Reformation Europe resembled a violence-ridden home where parental authority has been thoroughly squandered through misuse. Catholicism, the parental authority (being a paternal/maternal amalgam), even after one hundred years of bloodletting, still thought that its spiritual authority was intact! Protestantism (a younger, rebellious sibling), in its disunity and reforming counterviolence, only compounded the problem. The exception to this rule of abusive Christian behavior was the peace churches, whose unique witness provided them with *refusenik* martyrs created by both sides of the conflict. But this minority witness was not enough to sustain the case for Christianity.

By recognizing the nonliteral quality of the mythopoetic elements and the naive conceptualization of the biblical worldview, Spinoza anticipated by two hundred years the work of later biblical scholars. It should be no surprise that he couldn't manage the appropriate distance from his discovery that would enable him to see how primary naivete conditions, but does not necessarily invalidate, the religious authority of the biblical text. Though Spinoza took account of the different realms that *abstract reason* and *mythopoetic imagination* occupy, he did not integrate them. Instead, he helped to establish the habit of interpreting the Bible one-sidedly, by dissociating reason from imagination, criticism from appreciation, philosophy from theology, separating *logos* from *mythos* and putting all one's eggs in reason's basket.

From another perspective, the exaltation of Reason over Revelation was a reaction both to the irrational principles in Luther's and Calvin's systems of justification and to the supernatural excesses of Baroque

Catholicism. Add to these exaggerations the irrationality of the religious wars and it was inevitable that *autonomous critical rationality* became the reservoir of energy for a whole new set of responses to a whole new range of questions that emerged at the dawn of modernity. Today we have much to regret about the conflict between critical rationality and religious consciousness as it has shaped Western religion and culture to the present. Perhaps we must admit some level of inevitability to it. Rarely do the stable and labile elements in developing bodies cooperate optimally. But it also should be possible for believers to admit how much internecine Christian conflict contributed to the growth of rationalist religion (deism) as it was followed by naturalism, agnosticism, and atheism.

When Spinoza turned his attention specifically to the scriptures, he was again ahead of his time in proposing a method for their linguistic, theological, historical, and canonical investigation. Recognizing their pastness in a new way, he sought to determine their specifically historical meaning. While he clearly subordinated scriptural investigation to philosophical rationality, he continued to maintain that theology and philosophy each has its own proper sphere. In the years immediately following Spinoza's death (1677), but independently of him, Richard Simon published critical histories of both the Old and New Testaments. A French priest forced to leave the Congregation of the Oratory because of the controversy he created, Simon was the lone Catholic of his time attempting to investigate issues such as the Mosaic composition of the Pentateuch and historical questions about the text of the gospels and epistles. Like Spinoza, Simon thought that rational investigation would serve to undo "disorder in state and religion," but his project pleased no one. Condemned by Protestants and Catholics alike, he offended political authorities as well, and when he died in 1712, his legacy as a believing critic was highly in doubt.

By contrast, the archetype of traditional religious authority was Bishop Jacques Bossuet of Meaux, tutor of Louis XIV's son and defender of absolutism both monarchical and religious. His published history of the Catholic Church revived Eusebius of Caesarea's political theory that all history was in the hands of God and gave evidence of the providential progress of the church "ever assailed and ever triumphant, ever the same from the beginning of the world." Not surprisingly, he led the fight to suppress Simon's biblical criticism because it called a naively providential view of the Bible into question and could only be a detriment to salvation.[18]

Spinoza's and Simon's careers are themselves indicative of the "divine nerve" that William Dilthey saw at the heart of the Enlightenment's *Lebensgefühl,* or vitality, and of the vicissitudes that biblical scholarship began to suffer at its hands. The excommunicated Jewish scholar prefigured the triumph of critical rationalism in liberal Protestant scholarship from Emmanuel Kant to Adolf von Harnack, Friedrich Schleiermacher, and Paul Tillich. His methods for scripture study also pointed ahead to the development of the historical-critical method that eventually flowered in the work of Julius Wellhausen, Hermann Gunkel, Rudolf Bultmann, Ernst Käsemann, and others. By contrast, Simon's fate prefigured the period of prolonged latency in which Catholic theology stayed frozen for centuries. Forbidden by ecclesiastical authority to cut the umbilical cord and launch out on its own, Catholic biblical scholarship had to wait three centuries for Pius XII's 1943 encyclical *Divino Afflante Spiritu* to begin its own journey toward autonomy. As a result, it has had a less chaotic adolescence than its Protestant sibling, and it has profited enormously from the youthful excesses as well as the competent work — in textual, tradition, form, redaction, and literary criticism — of its separated sibling. Thus even though the critical period of biblical interpretation was shaped early on by a rationalist trajectory, it eventually yielded much fruit for twentieth-century breakthroughs, but not before it reached many dead ends as it separated itself from its mythopoetic matrix in the Bible. When Simon died in the early eighteenth century, criticism still focused on the reasonableness of truthclaims rather than on establishing their historical form or investigating the manner in which the past influences the present. These concerns of modern historiography would not emerge fully until the 1840s, and it was not until the 1860s that biblical criticism would decide that historical rather than rational questions were the most productive for it to pursue.

In the wake of Spinoza another rationalist, John Locke, attempted to unify the variety of theological schools by propagating a natural religion that would replace all supernatural forms of faith and dogmatic religions. His work *The Reasonableness of Christianity, as Described in the Scriptures* (1695) was part and parcel of both his commonsense empiricism and his desire to reconcile Christianity and reason. But not everyone was set on reconciliation. The philosopher Leibniz's theory of the monad expressed a different passion, one that sought the source of all unity and differentiation. A polymath who was also searching for a way to overcome the hostility that Catholics and Protestants continued to express for each other, he set forth his arguments that God was the source of all rationality in the world. According to his reduction of physical possibilities to logical ones, this had to be the best of all possible worlds and thus God became a guarantee of the utter rationality of the world. But once God's role was so reduced, it was a short step to dismissing the deity from the picture altogether. As the eighteenth century dawned, divinity and redundancy were becoming coefficients.[19]

Despite the vigorous effort to accommodate religious truth to rationality, David Hume dared to posit rationality as sufficient reason for itself and dismissed God as unnecessary to the equation. Following him, scholars like John Toland and Matthew Tindal rejected Locke's position on the reasonableness of Christianity and his reducing it only to what was reasonable, thereby evaporating the essence of revealed, dogmatic religion. The outcome of this move was deism, which became quite popular in England, on the continent, and in the new world. In Germany Johann Solomo Semler published his *Treatise on the Free Investigation of the Canon* (1771–75), in which he expressed some of the same concerns as Locke but insisted that dogmatic considerations had to be set aside completely so that the Bible could be freely investigated on its own merits and in reference to its own times, not with reference to the present.[20] Reacting against the sacred nature of the Bible, Semler and others saw the canon (or established body of scripture) as an arbitrary, artificial, and unjustifiable delimitation that rational, historical-criticism removed in order to carry out its impartial investigation. In Semler, the historical-critical method found one of its earliest proponents. After him, the *diachronic* study of the Bible (investigating it as a historical source) became the dominant model of biblical studies. So strong did this emphasis become that almost 150 years would pass before critical scholarship would return to take up a *synchronic* investigation of the Bible (a complementary concern with its ongoing meaning for the communities that continue to read it to encounter a revelatory message).

The same narrow, historical emphasis is found in the works of Hermann Reimarus, published after his death by G. E. Lessing as *Fragments of an Unknown Person* (1774–78). Albert Schweitzer tells us in his remarkable survey of German theology from the seventeenth to early twentieth centuries that Lessing undertook the publication because he believed "the introduction of the historical element would transform and deepen rationalism."[21] There can be no doubt that Reimarus himself was dedicated to this task, as he also wrote *The Leading Truths of Natural Religion* and titled one of his unpublished fragments *The Decrying of Reason from the Pulpit*. But Reimarus's spare reconstruction of early Christian history, which separated Jesus the Jew from the apostolic preaching, was so thoroughgoing that even Semler objected. He backed off from his own historical approach and responded to Reimarus with a literary explanation of Jesus' teaching. In it, Semler tried to show that there was both a "sensuous, pictorial" mode and a second, more "spiritual" message in Jesus' teaching; by this he avoided the gap that Reimarus had introduced between Jesus message and that of the apostles. But both Reimarus's radical critique and Semler's response furthered Lessing's own aims, for he was convinced that "accidental truths of history can never be proof of the necessary truths of reason." For him, historical criticism was important in order to destabilize the past's hold on the present. Between the present and the past there was an "ugly, wide ditch" that forced the interpreter to seek some universal, rational truth behind the historically unreliable text.[22] Before he died in 1781, Lessing's vision of a noble rationalism that would subsume all revealed religion was spreading deism to Germany. But equally important, he had recognized that with the geographical, intellectual, and cultural changes that had occurred in Western society, the past had become historical in a new way.

In some sense, all of the events we have traced from the Renaissance onward cumulatively added to this growing distance between the ancient past and dawning modernity. Today, we call it historical consciousness, the burden of having a history. Once installed, it rarely disappears unless repressed. After Lessing named what had begun to be evident from the time of the Renaissance, more thinkers understood that as moderns we have no direct, smooth, or immediate access to events, facts, perceptions, or realities of the distant past. History, as a "wide, ugly ditch," had became a threat.

As criticism of the Bible widened its impact during the nineteenth century, Lessing's recognition gradually took hold. Not all critics understood the ditch or gap between them and the Bible to be either so wide or so ugly. Pietists then, like fundamentalists now, denied it, asserting that faith made an immediate experience of intimacy with God available. But sooner or later all serious interpreters of the scriptures and of the experience of belief based on their witness came to admit that the gap between the then of biblical revelation and the now of believing is real. Lessing maintained that there were ethical truths available to reason alone that transcended change and bridged the gap between modernity and the historical past. But few since have been as confident that even the most critical reason, all by itself, spans that gap adequately. Alternately, Hume and those who followed his disenchanted empiricism decided that God was really silent and that the origin of religion had to be sought in human nature, the one constant that linked the past with the present. Kant (d. 1804) would build upon this naturalism and remove the concept of God from the foundations of human knowing. Human awareness had a parent, but in this world it had become orphaned. His various *Critiques* sought to explore the conditions under which real knowledge was possible in this world, and this led him to reduce the notion of God to the highest moral good. Though not explicitly concerned with problems of the historical meaning of the Bible, his Enlightenment epistemology called on humanity to accept the disenchantment of the world and the "loneliness of autonomy." It was a position quite like Lessing's: stranded on this side of the ugly, wide ditch, modern people are cut off from the mythopoetic past of their origins. For Kant, it was the price of being an adult, responsible human being.

There was no other noble fate for *homo sapiens* than really to "dare to know" and to grow up.

In the nineteenth century, other movements were afoot that eventually clarified how the biblical revelation as past can be understood as still present for believers. Like the maturing adolescent, critical rationality learned that it couldn't go home again on the same terms that it left. Slowly, it began to come to terms with who its parents were and what their limitations were. This discovery has opened up new possibilities for a mature relationship with the mythopoetic past. The rest of this survey will try to show how the last two hundred years have begun to provide the wherewithal for critical reason's journey homeward.

The Ugly, Wide Ditch of History

One poetically inclined interpreter stands out for his early recognition of the problem, his investigation of the critical issues, and his harmonious approaches to them. Johann Gottfried Herder (1744–1803) combined to an uncommon degree both historical-critical expertise and a "divining power of imaginative reconstruction."[23] He saw how differently the synoptics and John presented the figure of Jesus. He also saw that there existed an oral stratum in the tradition, and postulated the priority of Mark's gospel — insights that scholarship would take another hundred years to absorb and sort out. Herder's appreciation for the poetic element in the Bible and in theology explains his influence on the nineteenth-century Romantic tradition, with its high regard for the aesthetics of storytelling. But Herder was an exception among the Bible's critics. As the nineteenth century unfolded, philosophical and historical investigation influenced biblical scholars more than aesthetics. The Bible was like a locked treasure chest from the ancient past whose secrets could be divulged only if the right historical or philosophical key were found.

In any survey of intellectual or cultural history, one encounters the anomaly that thinkers wield influence for reasons other than they intended. This helps explain why scholars should be reluctant to write their own epitaphs: what one really contributes may be incidental to one's own understanding of one's life work. This paradox may help us appreciate Friedrich Schleiermacher (1768–1834) and his impact on the nineteenth century's attempt to travel across the ugly, wide ditch to the ancient world of the Bible. A phenomenally successful teacher, preacher, and apologist for Christianity against its cultured despisers, Schleiermacher is considered the founder of liberal Protestant theology. To the modern eye, he presents us with a capsulized view of liberal Protestantism's strengths and weaknesses. Positively, since he was confident that humanity's native intuition allows us to feel an absolute dependence on the divine, he affirmed the notion that all believers possess a natural ability to read the Bible with competence. For Schleiermacher, human consciousness and God-consciousness are related, hence the journey across the historical divide between the Bible and our religious experience is bridged by the intuitive bond between the believer and God. Though sin interrupts and destabilizes God-consciousness in the individual, it is remedied by Christ, who is perfect God-consciousness and who sends his Spirit to enliven the redemptive community of the church. In place of the traditional understanding that the Bible is divinely and uniquely inspired, he theorized that our latter-day divinatory intuition is the psychological reexperiencing of the original revelation. In a way, his subjectivism denied that there was much of a ditch to cross, yet his awareness of language and its role in communicating meaning allowed him to formulate exacting questions that interpretation theory has struggled with ever since. It led him to see that philology and exegesis had to be subordinated to the more general problem of how historical understanding occurs at all. Though he was a Romantic theorist, he had an important critical impact because he tried to formulate universally valid rules for hermeneutics, or what he called "the art and science of understanding."

Hence, for the first time since Spinoza, understanding the Bible was not a question of reason alone, but a combination of the art (poetic intuition) and the science (reason) of understanding the *language* in which the Bible had been written and handed down. Schleiermacher did not develop this combined model of interpretation sufficiently, but he had followers who continued where he left off and in whose debt we are today. I will return to pick up this shortly after looking at another, even more comprehensive attempt to elicit universal answers to the Enlightenment's hard questions about how we come to know God in Christ through belief in the biblical revelation.

The most all-encompassing solution to the problem of historical, religious, and philosophical truth was formulated in the early years of the nineteenth century by Georg Friedrich Hegel (1770–1831). If for no reason other than that Karl Marx was an early member of the circle of young Hegelians who sought to extend the master's influence after his death, we can say that Hegel's impact on Western religion and culture has been major. Unlike Spinoza, who distinguished between philosophical reason and religious imagination, Hegel claimed that the content of philosophy and the content of theology were identical: philosophy presented the truth in the pure form of reason; religion expressed the same truth in sensible representation. Over the course of his career at the center of Prussian society, Hegel worked out a prodigious system in which all opposites were seen to be in the process of mutual reconciliation by way of the well-known formula *thesis + antithesis = synthesis*. We come to know ourselves, life, truth, and God by the same process by which self-consciousness, living things, truth itself, and God all become self-realized: a thesis is posed, but then meets its self-contradiction, which forces a resolution at a higher level of self-awareness. This dialectic of the self-realizing Spirit (which Hegel identified with the Trinity) characterizes all life and knowing and is finally resolved in Absolute Mind. In his system, Hegel sought to account for all human consciousness and to show the way toward overcoming all human conflict.

In theory, it was beautiful, although not all of Hegel's contemporaries were equally enthralled. Among those who were, however, rank two of the most significant nineteenth-century interpreters of the Jesus of the gospels and of early Christianity: David Friedrich Strauss (1808–74) and Ferdinand Christian Baur (1792–1860). As a young preacher, Strauss sought to recover the intellectual concept that, as he saw it, lurked behind the mythic elements of scripture. But for Strauss myth "is nothing else than the clothing in historical form of religious ideas, shaped by the unconsciously inventive power of legend and embodied in historic personality."[24] In other words, the events or personalities in the Bible represent eternal ideas that, through their dissemination in the Bible, enter human consciousness. Beginning with the publication of his *Leben Jesu (Life of Jesus)* in 1835, his impact on Protestantism and on scholarship was enormous. His Hegelian reading of the scriptures, with particular reference to the person of Jesus in the gospels, not only cast aside the naive historical interpretation still common among lay people (of the gospels as real-life accounts) but dealt a blow to the minimalist interpretation that Schleiermacher and other rationalists like Heinrich Paulus had popularized. In Paulus, rationalist reduction had reached its nadir. He went further than Schleiermacher, explaining away the ascension of Jesus as a mistaken report: a cloud had interposed itself between Jesus and his followers so that when he walked off into the sunset and two men came along, they were mistaken for Moses and Elijah or two angels. In this way, Paulus rationalizes both the transfiguration and the ascension as two different mistaken reports.[25]

In contrast to this rationalist but banal interpretation of the gospels, Strauss said that the evangelists, especially John, were all consciously involved in myth-formation. In his own mind, this young Hegelian was freeing the mythic narrative to deliver up the eternal verities of Christian faith. According to one historian of the era, Strauss's *Leben Jesu* was of "epoch-making significance" because it forced scriptural interpretation to adopt specifically historical norms of investigation of the New Testament (what kind of literature it was, who wrote its books, in what circumstances they were written, how accurate a portrayal of persons and events they possess).[26]

It should be no surprise that Strauss's *Leben Jesu* was not popular in church quarters. His revolutionary portrait of Jesus the myth threatened him with such personal and professional rejection that he was forced to revise his book and then recant his whole method. Toward the end of his life he could not say that he and his followers were still Christians, but he felt that they still had a religion. Sadly, Christ-less German idealist religion, when melded with pagan mythological politics, turned in on itself and became narcissistically self-involved. Fearing its own deprivation, it became overinflated, persecutory, and brutal in its treatment of non-Germanic elements of its culture. Romanticized by artists such as Richard Wagner, the mythology became fertile ground for the seeds of Nazism's racist anti-Semitism and militarism. At the end of this chapter, I will make explicit the distinction between my concept of the mythopoetic and Strauss's. Here it should be sufficient to note that Strauss saw myth only as a costume for philosophical ideas to wear. He attributed to the writers of scripture either an unconscious expression of truth in mythic clothing or a conscious disguising of the sublime in cruder form. Since neither is properly symbolic expression (for they lack any proper sense of tension), his concept of myth resembles storytelling more than it involves truth-telling in any form.

The second and older Hegelian, F. C. Baur, turned the master's distinct methodology away from the Jesus of the gospels toward the problems of Christian origins. Baur criticized his pupil Strauss's interpretation and sought instead to reconstruct early Christian history by applying the Hegelian dialectic to the forces that he understood to be at work there. Unlike Strauss, Baur took a conservative stand toward the New Testament sources, treating them as historical documents whose contents could be mined for an actual framework of events. In this, he may have been influenced by the growth in Germany of historiography as a distinct area in the human or social sciences under the influence of Leopold von Ranke (1795–1886). Based on his studies of archival material and ancient documents, Ranke began to promote scientific or reconstructionist historiography. His model was based on the empirical method that allowed one to discover facts hidden from the ordinary observer. Ranke became convinced that with careful perusal of ancient documents and all available records of the ancient past (which were just beginning to come to light through archaeological discoveries), the historian could reconstruct an event *wie es eigentlich gewesen ist,* "as it actually happened." The confidence of Ranke and his scientific historians matched the earlier confidence of the early Enlightenment rationalists.

Consequently, Baur sought to read the documents of the New Testament as if they had only recently been dug up, revealing lost chapters of history. In them, he discovered tensions between authorities in the early church, evidence of the dialectical process at work in history: Jewish particularism (Peter) was the thesis, Pauline universalism the antithesis, second- and third-century Catholicism the synthesis. With this theory, Baur founded a school of interpretation (tendency-criticism) that came to be associated with Tübingen, where he taught. If books of the New Testament evidenced a tendency toward Jew-Gentile conflict (Galatians, Romans), they were adjudged to be early (hence more authentic historically). But if this tendency was replaced by its opposite and the issue was resolved (Acts), the writing was judged to be late and hence not as authentic.

Truly Hegelian, Baur's criticism searched out the grand sweep of events and missed finer details that have led most scholars to doubt his dating of New Testament books. Yet Baur's *Tendenzkritik,* though distorted, had an unplanned impact, for it established the principle "that the task of the historical criticism of the New Testament writings is only fulfilled when the historical place of origin of a writing within the framework of early Christian history is also established." To a great extent, the works of Strauss and Baur represent the acme of the influence of philosophical reason on the interpretation of the Bible. But in their different ways, they both forced the historical question upon New Testament interpretation. After them, biblical criticism would "not be interpreted on rationalist or anti-rationalist, but on historical lines."[27]

The initial impact, then, of critical reason on the interpretation of the Bible was disruptive in the extreme. For centuries the Bible had been the cultural and religious icon of immutability in European religion and culture. Once unleashed in the late eighteenth century by *philosophes* like Voltaire who scoffed at the disedifying material in its books, criticism of the Bible, even in the hands of believers, became iconoclastic. Like adolescents who often form a mistrustful and negative identity in reaction to parental authority, some scholars reveled in negative skepticism. Spurred on by the work of Strauss, Bruno Bauer (1809–80) sought to bury once and for all the simple faith of old-fashioned Christians. Even the skeptical Schweitzer sensed a unique *odium theologicum* in the work of this Bauer, an angry intolerance explainable in developmental terms as a defense against identity diffusion.[28] Bauer's *Life of Jesus,* one of a long line of skeptical lives, displayed the antichristological Jesus that has blossomed in such works as D. H. Lawrence's *The Man Who Died* and Hugh Schonfeld's *The Passover Plot.* The energy behind Bauer's *odium* has helped the negatively credulous to consider the very existence of Jesus of Nazareth a dubious historical fact.

Nineteenth-century Germany's virtual monopoly on theological and biblical interpretation was not absolute. Still, the one non-German who deserves a notice here owed his thunder to what he learned from them. A French ex-seminarian, Ernest Renan (1823–92), delivered to the formerly sheltered Catholic world, in one blow, the full brunt of the

Enlightenment's search for alternative religious authorization. Able to picture Galilee and Jerusalem vividly because he had traveled there, Renan published his *Vie de Jesus (Life of Jesus)* in 1863 during a particularly tense period of Catholic-secular conflict in France. French Catholics faced each other across their own divide, with liberal intellectuals like Lacordaire and Montalembert on one side promoting reconciliation between the principles of the revolution and Catholic belief and on the other the irreconcilables. This latter party (still active today as followers of the late excommunicated Archbishop Marcel Lefèbvre) associated themselves unashamedly with the ancien régime and, in the person of the influential editor of the newspaper *Univers,* Louis Veuillot, advocated the rejection of the parliamentary system as heresy. In this charged environment, Renan's *Life* went off like a bomb in a fireworks factory.

His notion was that the gospels themselves were meant to be incentives to further revelation and to inspire one's religious imagination. Hence, he developed a "fifth gospel" that his imaginative identification with Jesus and his own wandering through the hills of Galilee had inspired in him. After its publication, "whatever wore a soutane and could wield a pen charged against Renan, the bishops leading the van," wrote Schweitzer. As a first introduction to the results of almost a century of the critical investigation of the Bible, Renan's writing was a disaster. The outcome for any Catholic acceptance of criticism was predictable. Schweitzer concluded his consideration of his only non-German with this trenchant comment: "Everything in the nature of criticism, and of progress in religious thought, was associated with his name, and was thereby discredited."[29]

Despite Renan's French debacle, the 1860s in Germany saw a consolidation of the historical, as opposed to the rationalist, method of understanding the Bible. Though admiring Strauss's reconciliation of philosophy and theology, C. H. Weisse (1801–66) tried to reconstruct a historical picture of Christ in the place of Strauss's myth-oriented portrait. His investigations confirmed Herder's theory of the priority of Mark, and he further hypothesized the existence of another major source upon which Matthew and Luke were mutually dependent. In time this became known as Q, or the *logia* (sayings) source. In 1863, Heinrich Holtzmann gave his name to this two-source hypothesis, which he grounded "so carefully that the study of Jesus henceforth could not again dispense with this firm base."[30] In the same years, Albrecht Ritschl (1822–89) extracted from Baur's tendency criticism the first sociological conclusions to result from historical study of the New Testament. He recognized that early Christianity developed around various communities with different orientations ("settings in life"), not around the conflict of doctrines. Ritschl's son-in-law Johannes Weiss, applying what came to be known as the history-of-religions (or comparative religions) method, recognized that the historical message of Jesus shared an orientation to the end-of-time with other eschatological literature of the period. His *The Preaching of Jesus concerning the Kingdom of God* (1892) placed Jesus within the setting of the first century of the common era in Roman-occupied Syro-Palestine and within the setting of the religious movements shaking that part of the world. Weiss's book became an anchor for all subsequent research into the historicity of the gospels. Once this principle was accepted for study of the gospels, its implications for other biblical texts, both Hebrew and Christian, was assured. We will return to Weiss's impact shortly after picking up the thread that linked biblical criticism to the study of communication as an art and a science.

William Dilthey (1833–1911) addressed another set of concerns that will prove significant when we seek to bring closure to this chapter. As his mentor Schleiermacher's biographer, he remained a Romantic interpreter, stressing psychological participation of the later interpreter in the creation of meaning from ancient texts. But he went beyond his teacher when he schematized the distinction between the *explanation* of the natural or empirical sciences (*Naturwissenschaften*) and the *understanding* of the humanities (*Geisteswissenschaften*). The first (empirical) method involved mapping the physical causality of events; the second (imaginative or interpretative) method involved discovering how humans share meanings over time. At the same time, Dilthey worked within a strong, new tradition of historical investigation: history is knowable in its particulars, not deducible in its universals. Not naive about facts, Dilthey formulated the position that historical knowledge is a "science based on traces." Written history, or "inscribed experience," is always distanced from the actual events, so that it presents us with evidence, not of objective facts, but of expressed experiences that we can share by understanding the mode of written historical expression. Though Dilthey shared Kant's turn to the subject, his strong sense of the interconnectedness of vital, intuitive subjects as knowing what is real makes him post-Kantian. Lastly, because this knowledge is real and belongs to the individual, Dilthey's belief in the intuitive and interpretative basis of subjective knowledge put him in the anti-Hegelian camp of the late nineteenth and early twentieth centuries.[31]

With Dilthey, for whom history and hermeneutics are firmly linked, we have come to a point far from Spinoza's rigid distinction between a rational philosophy of nature and an inferior theology of imaginative discourse. We saw that, after Spinoza and Leibniz, the standard of reason developed into various forms of critical rationality: *empirical science,* which sought to explain the shape of nature; *historical investigation,* which sought to understand the shape of the past (while using explanatory or scientific tools); and *philosophical inquiry,* which, with

Kant, analyzed the conditions in which knowledge is possible. But despite Spinoza, theology as it arises in biblical interpretation has not rested content being labeled a species of the imagination. Though it does not operate in the same realm as empirical science, it does deal with expressible human experience (where epistemology and history meet). Hence, theology, or the study of God's Word, is best understood as *interpretation*. After Dilthey, we can say that theology and past human experience (history) are firmly and properly linked and that the business of theology is the interpretation of human experience as it has been expressed historically in the texts of the Bible and in Christian tradition. History itself does not conform to either Spinoza's or Lessing's optimism about the power of rational ideas to unite past and present experience and make sense of the whole. Rather it is historical human experience itself, as revealing something of God, that theology seeks to make available in the present as a paradigm for our encounter with the universal dimension of our particular experience. Theology does not interpret history in itself. The practice of theology is an *art* that seeks to profit from history, which itself is a *science* based on traces. After completing this sketch of the impact of the crisis of criticism on the Bible's mythopoetic core, we will return below to this provisional formulation of the evolving understanding of the role of theology as interpretation.

Schleiermacher's heritage came to different fruition in the long career and writing of Adolf von Harnack (1851–1930). Like his predecessor, Harnack was influential and successful in Berlin, the center of the German Empire. His *Das Wesen von Christentums (The Essence of Christianity)*, published in 1900, became the dominant expression of liberal theology. By the time that Harnack finished tracing Christianity from its roots in the Hebrew scriptures to the post-Reformation period, he had boiled down its essence to the personality and teaching of Jesus. Like Marcion, who had jettisoned the authority of the First Testament, and like Luther, who rejected the dogmatic tradition and ecclesiastical organization, Harnack reduced the message of the New Testament to "the Fatherhood of God and the brotherhood of men."[32] Like Schleiermacher's, his hermeneutic was psychological, emphasizing the personal impact of Jesus, toward whom the believer can be drawn, moved by strong sentiments of sympathy. But shrink the essence as he might, his historical scholarship, which included an edition of the writings of the fathers, was impressive, establishing the historical-critical paradigm for biblical scholarship so firmly that it eventually undid the novelistic string of liberal lives of Jesus that had been the rage since Schleiermacher's own efforts.

A second factor that helped impugn the Victorian portrait of the life of Jesus was that Weiss's work — on the original eschatological force of Jesus' preaching of the kingdom of God — had made this issue part of any responsible reconstruction. This point was pressed home in both Wilhelm Wrede's *The Messianic Secret in the Gospels* (1901) and Albert Schweitzer's *Sketch of the Historical Jesus*. These works delivered the one-two punch to any vestige of the claim of Schleiermacher's followers that they could extract from the gospels a lifelike portrait that clearly and distinctly revealed the personality of Jesus and his simple faith. Wrede did this by highlighting the eschatological material in the preaching of Jesus on the kingdom of God and by demonstrating that the hiddenness of Jesus' messianic identity (the "messianic secret") was a dogmatic convention supplied by Mark and taken over by Matthew and Luke, not part of an earlier historical stratum.

Since the time of Holtzmann (1863), Mark had been seen not only as prior to the other gospels (John having been assigned a later and decidedly theological position) but as giving the most historically accurate and theologically neutral account. When Wrede exposed the theological concern in Mark to explain Jesus historically nonmessianic career and Schweitzer accounted for the eschatological material by reference to Jesus' own expectation of the kingdom (which did not come when he expected), the entire notion of a Jesus easily accessible in the gospels vanished. For Wrede, Schweitzer, and others, this collapse had only one consequence: if *thoroughgoing eschatology* (the imminent expectation of the kingdom) was the most basic historical material in the gospel and the kingdom did not and has not come, then *thoroughgoing skepticism* is the only response moderns should give to the message of Christianity. When both of these scholars later studied Paul's writings and theology, they found neither the Paul of Augustine nor of Luther, nor a recognizable first-century messianic Jew like Jesus, but the founder of a new religion of mystical salvation, Christianity. For them and for more and more men and women living in the secular environments of the twentieth century, there has seemed only one conclusion: the stoic acceptance that we are stranded on this side of the ugly, wide ditch of history. On the far side, receding into the mists, are the mythopoetic, biblical origins of Christian faith.

From the beginnings of the Enlightenment in the seventeenth century, the conditions for rationalist skepticism about the truth of Christian origins had been growing. For a long time, both philosophical skepticism and the growth of anti-Christian polemics were contained to circles of the literati and others at educated levels of society. But as the nineteenth century ceded to the twentieth, philosophical ideas were being diffused more broadly through political and social movements for change and through the gradual increase in the numbers of educated members of society. As a result, skepticism about religious truth has grown from its initial matrix in rationalist circles to affect wider circles of educated people. Skepticism about anything deeper than a vague belief in a God-figure is a societal condition that any educated person is exposed to and that everyone absorbs through cultural, telecommunicative osmosis. Yet the wages of skepticism are not merely generalized agnosticism.

The Enlightenment's disenchantment with the primarily naive worldview of Western religion and culture up through the Reformation gave rise to both its sense of autonomous freedom for new attachments and its sense of bitter loss. This occurred in some of the same ways that adolescents/young adults continue to struggle with, and must mourn over, the loss of their primary love objects. Most of the time, they accomplish this by falling in love or acquiring new objects of affection. Rarely can such loss occur without some compensating search for new, often idealized, objects. This stage of individual autonomous development has been recapitulated in the development of Western religion and culture since the seventeenth century. The final part of this sketch will attempt to show how the twentieth century has begun a subtle shift in the direction of transcending the losses that have taken up so much of our cultural and religious energy in the previous three hundred years.

Sacred Events or Sacred Texts?

We have seen that critical history, like critical reason before it, at first produced a skepticism inimical to any notion that the Jesus of the gospels was either recoverable or believable. Like Strauss, Wrede demolished both traditional and critical attempts to paint a simple portrait of Jesus in the gospels. Like Renan, Schweitzer ended his magisterial work on a note of pure subjectivity; all of Jesus' adherents have only one source of knowledge: "they shall learn from their own experience Who He is."[33] Schweitzer's later career as a Unitarian humanist doctor who spent the last years of his long life in Africa overshadowed his earlier role in popularizing skepticism about the gospels. When Victorian-Edwardian optimism collapsed in the cataclysm of the Great War, both autonomous rationality and autonomous history (especially in its progressivist orientation) took a deserved beating. But in the wake of the war, biblical scholars rebounded energetically and began to uncover overlooked aspects of the Bible, which have subsequently shown us how we can begin to overcome the crisis of criticism and the loss of naive credibility and to shape postadolescent, mature forms of faith.

The dead end at which thoroughgoing eschatology and skepticism arrived was the occasion, if not the cause, for a shift in the critical paradigm of interpretation. Though fundamentalists today still resist the impact of criticism, responsible biblical interpreters have sought to come to terms with the losses that criticism occasioned and to shape a postcritical model of appropriating the message of the scripture. Their attempts will, in a later chapter, guide our constructing a mature framework for religious belief. But, first, this sketch must take account of the changes in biblical interpretation that have occurred in this century. The Gordian knot in which Wrede and Schweitzer tied gospel scholarship was not slashed in two, but was slipped in a fascinating display of synchronicity. At the conclusion of World War I, Karl Ludwig Schmidt (1919), Martin Dibelius (1919), and Rudolf Bultmann (1921) discovered what the real object of the concern for history was all about in the first place. For if it was true — as Gunkel had said — that "religion, including biblical religion, has its history as does everything else human," then it followed that it was not a history of amorphous ideas, nor a historical account of Israel or of Jesus that the Bible preserved.[34] Rather, some real apprehension of the Bible as revelation was available in the history of the text of the Bible, in its own *textuality*. While this insight would be a long time maturing, these three scholars developed a new type of historical-critical tool, known as *form criticism,* the study of the original, oral forms that underlay the gospels. Recognizing that these writings developed as folk literature rather than as cultured or scholarly productions allowed critical history to make its appropriate and valuable contribution to biblical scholarship. But the shift in emphasis to the text and its subtexts did not immediately break the hold of positivist historicism in biblical studies. In First, or Old, Testament scholarship, attempts to date the strata and assign authenticity to only a few old strands abounded. Historical reductionism still tended to consider the bulk of the Hebrew scriptures as postexilic, deriving from a time that was stereotyped as a period of legalism and decline ("late Judaism"). In the New Testament, the material that reflected Jesus' situation-in-life was minimalized; most scholars continued to identify most of the gospel material as reflective of the setting of the early community or of the evangelists.

But as form criticism was complemented by redaction criticism and then supplemented further by rhetorical, audience, canonical, and even structural criticism, the recognition finally became established that the bridge across the wide, ugly ditch of history is the *text of the Bible in its depth and breadth, its antiquity, ambivalence, and surplus of meaning.* Before historical consciousness had become part of the intellectual tools and cultural presuppositions of biblical interpreters, the text itself tended to be taken for granted. Part of the familiar furniture of the church and the academy, the Bible as text had been presumed to be revelatory either spiritually (as in medieval exegesis) or directly and immediately (as in the actualism of the Reformation). But historical consciousness and the historical-critical method had challenged and subverted the immediacy of the Bible. By emphasizing the distance between the interpreter and the originating experience (Lessing's "ditch"), scholars had to find the human or cultural constant with which modern readers could cross the divide. Having abandoned the authority of the church as a timeless bridge to the revelatory past (a lingering Catholic notion) and unable to sustain the role of the Spirit as immediate interpreter (one Protestant model), scholars had to posit other constants. The candidates for this role were natural Reason (Locke, Lessing), the unity of God and Nature (Herder), eternal myth (Strauss), Absolute Mind (Hegel), and human sympathy (Schleiermacher, Dilthey, Harnack). But all of these were finally revealed to be elements of historical experience, not themselves outside of history!

When it was recognized that the Bible itself contained different historical strata and sources and even competing worldviews, a new but fruitful problem arose, the problem of *distanciation*, the existence of an original gap between the revelatory event or experience itself and its written expression. This earlier distancing seemed to imply that the actual biblical literature itself was far more the product of the cultures, events, and particularities in the lives of its authors than had been recognized for centuries. Critics have evaluated this distance between the event/experience and the production of the text in different ways. Some saw the historical stratification of the text as an indication that only the earliest layers had escaped a dogmatic overlay. Others noted the intrusion of foreign elements that had to be strained through a sieve before modern readers could get to the meat of revelation. But this original distanciation is really the Bible's original grace. It is, in fact, the necessary precondition for the text to be revelatory over time.

Yet this original gap between the originating sacred event and eventual sacred text is difficult to factor into the interpretation of scripture. It seems to require that we retroject our ambiguity and ambivalence, our lack of certainty, back in time and admit that those times were also distanced from the Holy in some of the same ways our times and our experience seems to be. Our desire to believe that "there were giants on the earth in those days" — as old as Genesis 6:1–4 — appears threatened when we have to admit that the distance between creation and Abraham is not four thousand but billions of years, that the gap between Habakkuk's vision and its fulfillment still requires us to plead, "How long, O Lord?" and that the promise of the resurrection and its fulfillment in the parousia may not be very soon. Distance, quite simply, implies loss and terrifies us, culturally, in much the same way that an infant experiences the terror of abandonment when its mother leaves the room, that adolescents undergo it when they have to "leave home," and that adults endure it at all the stages of maturity until death. None of us ever readily endures loss, but life requires that we undergo it.

This dawning consciousness that the original distance from or loss of immediacy with the Holy underlies all experience of revelation is a challenging idea. If it gives us a new paradigm for understanding our contemporary situation, it also allows us to understand more deeply that it is the precondition of all human autonomy. Thus the original loss is merely the realization of original grace, not its refusal.

As this affects the way we evaluate the Bible, we understand it as the Word of God — not literally but metaphorically — because it is a word from God, moving toward us to become one with us in a way that presumes some genuine alienation as prelude to reunion. Hence, the Bible is "testimony concerning the Word...a medium and a mediation...the testimony about revelation."[35] But the Bible has in no way escaped the vicissitudes of history; rather it has been shaped by them. The Bible's expressed experience is historical, but it does not deliver up history "as it actually happened." The Bible's own inner development, then, reminds us that history is a science of traces, a humbled understanding of what historical study can deliver, but one that allows us to recover from the verbal symbols that the original writers used what they were inspired to express. We see in the surplus meaning of these traces of divine-human encounter a relative norm for our own experience, a paradigm for our own struggle. When we overcome "the Cartesian and Enlightenment dream of the control of all reality through the autonomous and self-regulating techniques of a pure and immediate consciousness" — when we overcomes modernity's grandiosity — we are led back to the text, both of the Bible and of our historical lives, as these two texts mutually interpret each other.[36] The text of the Bible, in its historicity, its ambiguity, its metaphorical richness, and its indeterminacy invites its interpreters into a dialogue. Without new readers it cannot speak; but without the Word we don't have much to say.

Within a generation of the rediscovery of the historicity of the text, the text in turn led back to a renewed theological endeavor. Rudolf Bultmann and Karl Barth debated existentialist as against dialectical interpretation; Gerhard Ebeling and Ernst Fuchs engaged in the new hermeneutic. Catholic scholars advanced the *sensus plenior* as a way of being faithful both to patristic exegesis and modern historical discoveries, and their cautious yet firm historical method had a great impact on the ecclesiology of Vatican II.[37] For the first time since the Reformation, new paradigms were in the air. Older dualistic antinomies (scripture or tradition, reason or religion, *logos* or *mythos*) had begun to be seen as inadequate to capture the excess of meaning that God's first word at creation and God's eternal Word become flesh cannot fail to contain. Scholars in biblical and related fields have recognized that, in such comprehensive and mysterious matters as life *and* death, God *and* humanity, *mythos* and *logos,* revelation *and* reason, theology *and* history, the spiritual *and* the empirical, a purely dialectic methodology, an either/or attitude, had to be overcome. In the late twentieth century, bruised, disenchanted, and chastened, but autonomous nonetheless, critical rationality has begun to move toward a reintegration that recognizes the coincidence of unity and duality, of dialectic and analogy, of stability and adaptability, of truth and indeterminacy. Perhaps we have finally reached the point of understanding that " 'both/and' is the only attitude through which human mental functions can address the nature of reality with any hope of accuracy."[38]

I am seeking to do more here than give the Devil his due in recognizing the autonomy of critical rationality and historicity, of science, historiography, and their contributions. I am, in fact, contending that normal human development necessarily risks grandiosity and self-inflation as coefficients of freedom and autonomy and as defenses against loss and despair. Transposed into another key, the critical moment involves a risk, but it is the same kind of risk that Jesus thought it was necessary for the rich to take in order to enter the kingdom of God (Mark 10:23–27). We must thread our primarily naive faith through the eye of the needle of critical and historical autonomy. Difficult, no doubt. But if the issue is faith in God for whom all things are possible, then it is something we should allow God to help us attempt. By juxtaposing my earlier expansive analogy between adolescent grandiosity and Enlightenment autonomy with a metaphor of diminishment (the eye of the needle), I am attempting to describe the essential paradox modern believers (if not modern culture) must face. We are rich in cultural and historical baggage (both religious and secular), but to enter the kingdom and achieve mature, postcritical faith and understanding we are going to have to let go of some things about belief that we currently think are necessary. For some this will mean abandoning their hypertrophied rationalism and their demand that everything make sense to them on their own terms. For others it will mean abandoning their credulity, their need to believe without reference to faith's proper object (God and only God), their clinging to a system of belief that gratifies their craving for certainty.

In passing through the eye of the needle of criticism, the believer inevitably encounters loss. The loss closely parallels both the loss of immediacy and the attendant loss of innocence that we associate with adolescence and the beginning of adult development. For a period of time (often for all of adolescence, some years of early adulthood, and even longer), the naive believer on the way to adulthood often experiences a loss of faith as those categories and beliefs (or better, naive images and concepts in which belief is first experienced and framed) fall away. This is not universally the case but, as I hope to demonstrate later, many who do not experience the loss at this stage of psychosexual development endure other experiences of loss, either comparable or compensatory ones, at later stages of life. These necessary losses that everyone endures in the course of developing into adulthood can tell us something about how faith matures. Like all experiences of burn-out or dead-ends, these vicissitudes can become the start of a new stage in a journey. The next chapter will take a further step on that journey, to the land beyond grandiosity and self-inflation into the realm of maturity, the place of faith's recovery.

Bibliographical Essay

On the precursors of modernity: See Amos Funkenstein, *Theology and the Scientific Imagination: From the Middle Ages to the Seventeenth Century* (Princeton: Princeton University Press, 1986); David C. Lindberg, *The Beginnings of Western Science* (Chicago: University of Chicago Press, 1992).

On the Enlightenment and its impact: Peter Gay's *The Enlightenment — An Interpretation: The Rise of Modern Paganism* (New York: Random House, 1966) details the roots of the seventeenth-century Enlightenment in the Renaissance; see also Michael J. Buckley, S.J., *At the Origins of Modern Atheism* (New Haven: Yale University Press, 1987). Anthony Giddens's *Modernity and Self-Identity: Self and Society in the Late Modern Age* (Stanford: Stanford University Press, 1991) catches something of the irony that this chapter traces when he affirms: "In respect both of social and natural scientific knowledge, the reflexivity of modernity turns out to confound the expectations of Enlightenment thought — although it is the very product of that thought" (21). Ernest Gellner (*Postmodernism, Reason and Religion* [London and New York: Routledge, 1992], 23) rails against the fashionable relativism of "postmodernism" and its suspicion of objective reality, defending the Enlightenment's "fundamentalist rationalism," against which he sees all religious belief as an opposing fundamentalism. Many other authors do not accept Gellner's naive view of religious belief.

On Galileo and his controversy with Rome: See J. Brodrick, S.J., *Galileo: The Man, His Work, His Misfortunes* (London: Geoffrey Chapman, 1964), and, more recently, Richard J. Blackwell, *Galileo, Bellarmine, and the Bible* (Notre Dame: University of Notre Dame Press, 1991). The classic Catholic perspective on the Renaissance papacy is found in Ludwig von Pastor, *The History of the Popes from the Close of the Middle Ages,* vol. 7 (St. Louis: B. Herder, 1908). For the previous period, see Guy Mollat, *The Popes at Avignon: The "Babylonian Captivity" and the Medieval Church* (New York: Harper & Row, 1965). An important portrait of French ultramontanism is found in Dom Cuthbert Butler, *The Vatican Council 1869–1870* (London: Collins and Harvill Press, 1930), 44–62.

On the history of biblical interpretation: See Werner G. Kümmel, *The New Testament: The History of the Investigation of Its Problems*

(Nashville: Abingdon Press, 1970); Albert Schweitzer, *The Quest of the Historical Jesus* (New York: Macmillan, 1960); Robert M. Grant with David Tracy, *A Short History of the Interpretation of the Bible*, 2d ed. (Philadelphia: Fortress Press, 1984); D. K. McKim, ed., *A Guide to Contemporary Hermeneutics: Major Trends in Biblical Interpretation* (Grand Rapids: Wm. B. Eerdmanns, 1986); Werner Jeanrond, *Theological Hermeneutics: Development and Significance* (New York: Crossroad, 1991); as well as the works of Paul Ricoeur listed at the end of chapter 2. Alec R. Vidler's *The Church in the Age of Revolution: 1789 to the Present Day*, Penguin History of the Church 5 (1971), provides a general picture of the clash between reason and faith in European Christianity.

Chapter 4

The Onset of Maturity

The Loss of Immediacy

For all the gains that the individual makes in adolescence and early adulthood, there are also losses. The two most basic are the loss of immediacy and the loss of innocence. Adolescents, having lost childhood intimacy and innocence, find themselves in a disenchanted world, devoid of familiar comforts and assurances. Just so, Western religious culture today has endured a loss of revelational immediacy and historical innocence, living in a cosmos where the magic has died. Worldwide religious fundamentalism has reacted against these losses with massive denial. Mainstream churches have stretched the accommodation of the Bible's mythopoetry and reason to the limit. Few have argued that faith affirmation has suffered necessary and beneficial losses that can allow for something more mature to develop.

The familiar expressions "cutting the umbilical cord" and "untying the apron strings" are popular ways of expressing the challenge involved in taking the first steps of what psychologists call the separation-individuation process. Both popular wisdom and developmental theory agree that there will be trouble if, at the appropriate time, young people cannot take the steps necessary to become independent. As unpleasant as it is, the only real route beyond the pain of loss to the gains beyond goes through loss. Ducking or denying it makes for trouble. Similarly, if believers today resist the journey through the critical eye of the needle, they will achieve little except to store up energy for a future depression or explosion.

The basic developmental struggle in adolescence is the consolidation of personal identity vs. the diffusion of that identity. The task of solidifying a sense of identity confronts adolescents with confusion, often accompanied by fear, loathing, and self-disgust that, though disguised, is acted out by adolescents both individually and jointly as members of the youth culture. When adolescents become novice adults, if they have not sufficiently figured out "What am I going to make of myself?" or "What do I have to work with in life?" they will not be able to make the kind of life plans that are the basic developmental tasks of young

86

adulthood. But before that further stage is reached, adolescents have to endure the irruption of the biological factors that propel them to find a new matrix for their growth outside the family. These almost always involve narcissistic self-involvement that expresses itself in new attachments (a peer crowd, gangs, spring-break sprees, rock groupies) or in new affective relationships.

When adolescents move out of the nest, they are often estranged from their families because the earlier system of family relationships cannot easily readjust. This move recapitulates the original drama of the separation-individuation stage that we associate with the "terrible twos and threes" — the anal period of development. Children who successfully negotiate this primal stage of independence will, as adolescents, have a much easier time of taking on the greater pressures for independence that assail them. On the other hand, children whose testing of their own motor skills and the trustworthiness of their environment met nothing but resistance will most likely engage in a full-blown adolescent revolt. If parents were successful at attending to their young child's newfound instinctual demands, they will have an easier time when their adolescent seeks to achieve emotional and social autonomy.

The loss of immediacy between parents and children, both as prefigured in early childhood and lived out in adolescence, has its biblical counterparts. Various biblical figures assume the responsibility of standing on their own two feet and, in doing so, achieve a spiritual autonomy, even at the price of rebelling against God. Adam and Eve's so-called sin and the rebellion of the builders of Babel are mythological events that account for the normal framework of life in ancient Hebrew society.[1] In other words, these narratives of the way life works presume that the human condition developed from an earlier, undifferentiated unity with the creator. Genesis is patient of such independent stands as Abraham makes when he confronts God "on his way to court" to judge the people of Sodom (Gen 18:16–33). The theme of testing and rebellion asserts itself during Israel's most adolescent period: the wandering in the wilderness. So prominent is the issue of struggle in the human-divine relationship that it reappears as the inaugural event of the ministry of Jesus in the synoptic gospels. In Mark, God's Spirit "expelled" Jesus into the wilderness to be "tested" by Satan. As in the book of Job, Satan is merely doing his job — making sure that obedience is authentic. In the biblical taxonomy of struggle, Satan's tempting and God's wrestling with Jacob function in much the same way. Consequently, the apostle Paul saw Israel's disobedience and rejection of the gospel message both as provoking or testing God and, at the same time, provoking the Gentiles to accept salvation (Rom 11:11–12). Israel's jealous God would, in turn, counterprovoke them. For, when God called or named Jacob the wrestler "Israel" (Gen 32:29), God gave him a call that, Paul says, is irrevocable (Rom 11:29). Like the most extraordinary human parents (cf. the prodigal's father in Luke 15:20–32), God's merciful love encompasses God's children's rebellious distancing, their making a journey toward autonomy. God sends the sun and rain on both the just and the unjust (Matt 5:42) and consigns both Jews and Gentiles to disobedience so that God might have mercy on them all (Rom 11:32).

Thus, the one Gerard Manley Hopkins called "Thou mastering me God" was no stranger to the prophet Jeremiah or to the authors of those psalms that accuse God of abandoning his own chosen or anointed one (Ps 69:20 and 89:52). The anguished cry *Eli, Eli lama sabachtani?* ("My God, my God, why have you abandoned me?" in Ps 21:1) records this normative crisis most powerfully. In the New Testament, such texts of revilement and abandonment are the backbone of the synoptic passion narratives as well as the basis of the atonement theology in the Letter to the Hebrews. In Mark 15:34, the one and only saying of Jesus from the cross recorded in Mark repeats the psalmist's cry of seeming abandonment. So crucial is this experience of human distancing from God that it seems everyone, including Jesus (if we read the hymn of Phil 2:6–11 as another example of biblical separation-individuation dynamics), can attain to full sonship or identification with God only as a result of an abandonment or the risk of total identity diffusion. The Bible, in its own mythopoetic way, adumbrates humanity's loss of immediacy (the condition for every mature form of religious belief) in much the same way that adolescents move toward autonomy.

Analogously, the Enlightenment enacted a similar struggle over human identity, one crucial to both mature personal and cultural development. When the mythopoetic view of humanity as created immediately by God began to be challenged, a crisis of identity ensued. Just as adolescents face the threat of identity diffusion behind a barrage of defense mechanisms, so enlightened thinking responded to the crisis of human identity with some predictable narcissistic defenses such as inflating second-order thought through conceptual self-involvement. The inflation (technically known as *hypertrophy*) of the power to think — from Descartes's *Cogito, ergo sum* through Kant's epistemological turn to the subject — represented Western culture's egocentric regression in order to achieve a new objectivity about itself and the world. Subsequently, the growth in critical, objective consciousness about the world has involved modern men and women in fundamentally new emotional attachments that have accompanied modernity's intellectual grandiosity and its outbursts of both creative and destructive energy.

Since the Enlightenment, Western society has lurched back and forth between these poles of creation and destruction because of the inherent difficulty that all developing human beings have with balancing powerful intellectual and affective acquisitions. Scientism and Romanticism have remained split off from each other (except in science fiction) instead of integrating, thus producing the twentieth century's profusion of wars, the Soviet gulag, the Holocaust, the nuclear arms race, the Cambodian genocide, and purely eugenic abortion. The imbalances that occur when abstract concepts (national defense, racial purity, economic parity, personal rights) become the object of affective attachment regularly give rise to ideologies that lead to disaster. The skewed notion of autonomy results, in the words of one psychotherapist, in people being capable of a "thoroughly dispassionate contemplation of atrocity."[2]

Modernity's turn to the subject and its individualistic enactment have pushed the narcissistic self-involvement of philosophical reason to new heights. Kant's transcendent subject tends to view things from outside history, devoid of much sense of belonging, making it difficult for scientific rationality to coexist with affective intuition.[3] The inflation of scientific reason has also resulted in the empiricism that sought to overcome any lingering feel for knowledge. In the logical atomism of Bertrand Russell, reality, broken down into its smallest (atomic) parts, could then be examined in the same clear and distinct way that atomic particles could be classified and objectified. Philosophical empiricism, though seemingly hard-headed and scientific, is just another form of the narcissistic aggrandizement that has characterized thinking since Descartes. Like adolescents whose sense of omniscience masks their real vulnerability, philosophical atomists (or logical positivists, as they came to be known) perceive their own perceptions as more real than the web of relationships though which they participate in life. Their desire to control reality becomes the substance of the real.

One of the more curious results of the supremacy of rationalism has been the attempt on the part of theologians to occupy the same ground as their rationalist critics. Seeking to give objective weight to theological formulations, some theologians have sought the same kind of validation for theological concepts that empirical scientists seek when they describe the way physical and chemical phenomena work. This leads theologians to abandon analogical modes of expression and to use literal definitions that virtually reify aspects of religious mystery. As we shall see at a later point, when theology stresses the reasonableness of mystery, it is yielding to the same egocentric epistemology popular since Descartes. Not unlike the practitioners of inflated reason, these theologians are in flight from the threat of immersion in bodiliness and in history and all the indeterminacy and ambiguity in which both the body and history involve human beings.

A certain kind of fideism has reacted to rationalism by reducing all theological meanings to affective movements of the heart. These alone avail for salvation; the mind grasps images of objective truth only if they are apprehended by affective loyalty, not by intellect, which cannot grasp religious truth adequately. The rationalist-fideist dispute, which raged in the nineteenth century, represents another example of the tendency during periods of intense lability to overidentify with one set of new acquisitions of the developing organism at the expense of the other. When either part is identified with the whole or when the part substitutes for the whole, the way is open for ideology to take the place of a tensive view of reality that balances the claims of both intellect and emotions.

The inflation of either critical rationality or affective loyalty can easily lead to pseudoscience that dresses up irrationality in scientific garb (theories of racial superiority) or to pseudoreligion that makes irrational superstition the object of faith affirmation. But as tragic as these simplistic solutions are, neither individuals nor culture nor religious faith can reach maturity without weathering developmental vicissitudes that risk veering off toward one extreme or the other. In the history of Western religious culture, tipping the balance in favor of scientific reason led to the rejection and attempted extirpation of religious faith. This hostility to religion fits within the developmental dynamics of identity consolidation vs. diffusion as those dynamics illuminate the merging organism's reaction to authoritative, if not authoritarian, institutions. Angry rationalists like Bruno Bauer represented the curious combination of rational conviction, fueled not by its own cool and calculated analysis but by the white heat of its own affective rejection of religious authority. Like adolescents struggling for their own voice, some rationalist critics of religion use their anger to give them the energy to take on forces that they perceive as oppressive.

Anger is also a predictable response to the loss of immediacy, because the latter demands that a new and separate identity be shaped. The anger that distorts or resists religious faith in such periods of development is often a defensive reaction (an abreaction) against an earlier credulity. Adolescents typically express their ongoing need for something to believe in by adopting the opposite of familiar forms of belief. Adolescent faith often becomes reversed and so expresses itself "in loud and cynical mistrust."[4] Angry protests against religious authority and its real or perceived arrogance have shaped the religion and culture of the West from Luther to the gay protest group Act Up and have produced important, even necessary, developments in critical negation (see chapter 9).

Beyond these reactive positions, real autonomy or individuation comes only through a process of reintegration of the intellectual and affective acquisitions of adolescent/early adult development. But in the thick of change, few can step back and observe their overinvestments in either rational capacity or affective ability. What is true of all developing human beings is true also of religion and culture as they have endured change in the last three centuries. While there is a stage at which narcissistic inflation is an appropriate coping mechanism, moving beyond it involves surrendering the defenses that seemed so necessary to consolidate identity. Adolescents do not easily accomplish it, because the grandiosity that accompanies narcisssistic attachment to one's intellectual or affective acquisitions seems so effective. Only when grandiosity is spent (when adolescence ends in truth rather than chronologically), when defensiveness is spent and identity diffusion no longer threatens, can young adults enter a stage of mature reflection and so integrate the range of their acquisitions.

But changes as deep and as significant as this do not occur all of a sudden or once for all. Genuine change occurs through the interaction of social, economic, personal, and intrapsychic forces in people's lives, through their own personal action on one another, and through the interrelationship of people and of people with ideas. These are the aspects of what is natural to human beings that grace "elevates and perfects" — not in smooth or magical continuity, but often in critical interventions by which nature's own entropy is overwhelmed by its inner tendency to grow. Organic models of growth rather than mechanical ones make more sense because change does not operate in a clearly linear, progressive direction but by the subtle interaction of the stable and labile elements involved. In fact, change is often initiated, paradoxically, by regressive movements so that the organism can achieve the energy needed to undertake growth. Regression then can be the first step to integrative movement forward.

Movements of change, in organisms as well as in societies, rarely occur smoothly — at the same intensity in all the different parts of the body. Therefore, if modernity is going to be able to move beyond its current polarization between its intellectual and affective acquisitions, it will have to face the chasm of distrust, opened centuries ago, between the critical rationality of the Enlightenment and the naive, mythopoetic, religious imagination from which it has distanced itself. Only if we deal with the chasm between *logos* and *mythos,* between objective, empirical reason and subjective, inner meaning, between (scientific) explanation and (intuitive) understanding, will we be able to begin to reintegrate the parts of our divided cultural psyche and achieve a mature religious perspective. Only if we admit to the breadth and depth of the chasm can we discover the wherewithal to cross it, to reclaim both sides of it as parts of a whole.

For some believers, the very thought that there is a gap we must cross to reappropriate the source of religious belief only threatens the presumed immediacy by which they are present to themselves and God is present to them. For some Catholics, such a form of belief takes it for granted that the gift of the Spirit poured out on the church and entrusted to the hierarchical magisterium acts as a divine guarantor of the immediacy and authenticity of divine communication and normative religious experience. They expect ecclesiastical offices to deliver spiritual benefits and carry spiritual weight automatically. For them, Catholicism is the stuff of divine guarantees that operate without fail, *ex opere operato*. But neither a mature theology nor a reflective reading of history allows us to be so naively confident about the governing, sanctifying, and teaching offices of the church and what they claim to guarantee. Historical consciousness, or taking the ugly, wide ditch of history and its ugly truths seriously, involves us in a loss of immediacy that modern culture and faith have irreparably endured. We turn now to describe another element of the ugly, wide ditch that is our modern condition, the loss of innocence and the challenge it has created for a mature form of believing.

The Loss of Innocence

When mythopoetic self-awareness begins the process of separation-individuation, there inevitably occurs a crisis of authority or authorization. Both adolescence/young adulthood and the Enlightenment are critical precisely in the sense that they demand a *krisis,* a judgment of whose authority is the source of identity — one's own or one's parents'. For when adolescents truly admit that they no longer immediately inhabit the world of their parents and that life is bearing down on them individually, they experience, in some form or other, the wound that renders them both victims and victimizers. I call this wound the loss of innocence that accompanies the loss of immediacy. It is every bit as daunting as the first loss, and the two together set up a series of hurdles that are the natural obstacles to adult maturity.

At the same time, because no developmental change takes place instantly, there is always an overlap in which earlier parental authority uneasily coexists with the adolescent's budding self-authorization. Mini-crises of authority occur in this overlapping space, particularly when earlier parental authority has begun to wane or has been discredited and then seeks to assert itself in the face of emerging independence. This conflict between traditional authority and newfound self-authorization takes its toll on both parties. But without some clash of authority, growth to real adulthood is deferred. All adolescents and young adults have to learn to negotiate the demands of authority, but only those who internalize the best of what authority offers will successfully authorize their own separation-individuation and begin to acquire a mature sense of identity.

On the one hand, the adolescent given free rein by authority will achieve freedom, but one that risks becoming delinquency. Underneath the obvious lack of constraint lurks a sense of abandonment that sends him or her in search of a surrogate authority. Inhibited adolescents, on the other hand, have a hard time standing on their own feet, and often remain symbiotically attached to a parent or parents well into adulthood. Having never separated from parental authority (in the literal sense that they were authored by their parents), they always lack self-authorization and find adulthood a threatening and lonely fate.

In general, the character of the authority under which we find ourselves before and during adolescence has a great deal to do with the way we learn to authorize ourselves and undertake our own journey to maturity. When a young person's parents are honest and straightforward, have always been clear about permissions and prohibitions, do not lie, and candidly share in appropriate ways the decisions and crises that each family faces, then a boy or girl can build upon fundamental trust and come to respect parental authority, advice, and guidance — even when a crisis of authority occurs. In this situation, parents have earned their children's cooperation and generally get it. Parents, from their perspective, can expect to be given the truth in return, and they find it easier, when their children leave the nest, to let go and surrender control of their lives and fates — all the while continuing to maintain open and frank communication and an ability to disagree and even be disappointed. In such a situation, one's family history (both as it is consciously recalled and unconsciously traced in the psyche) lays down a firm foundation for a properly autonomous and self-authorized completion of the young adult's maturational tasks. Here, the loss of innocence that attends growth and development is not severe, because the young adult has gradually been introduced to the painful tasks of accepting responsibility for his or her own choices. In such optimal (and rare) settings, adolescence and young adulthood are less overwhelming as stages of growth.

But most personal lives haven't been shaped so cooperatively and, accordingly, loss of innocence brings with it a higher crisis index. Only recently have we have begun to understand some of the short- and long-term consequences of a child's too-early loss of innocence. An adolescent who has been abused as a child either sexually or emotionally and has either repressed the trauma or had the truth hidden will find personal self-authorization very difficult. Similarly, if adolescents have been lied to about family problems or have had to deal with drugs, drink, or violence as the background of family life, their inner sense of deprivation, of innocence withheld, will make their sense of self a shaky business. Ironically, adolescents forced to take responsibility for themselves and their siblings because of absent or irresponsible parents find real, personal autonomy very difficult to achieve, no matter how independently they act. Later in life, they often repeat the kind of abuse that they suffered from themselves, so deeply embedded in them is the wound of lost innocence. In these situations, the adolescent lost a sense that the world was *not harmful* (the literal meaning of "innocence") long before they could understand what had happened. So often early childhood abuse, parental loss, the deprivations of poverty, or the violence done in home settings are repressed as children try to go about the essential tasks of surviving. But in such dysfunctional settings, the loss of innocence is more severe because it preceded adolescent separation-individuation. The victims of such abuse — betrayed at their most vulnerable period of awareness — can rarely learn to trust either others or themselves. Their ability to stand on their own feet as emotionally autonomous adults is severely hampered. When they try to come to terms with their history, whether it be the part they have consciously retained or its unconscious traces, they face a daunting challenge, one that keeps even many adults in the dark about their early loss of innocence.[5]

Adolescent development is daunting enough; but when complicated by the introjected contempt resulting from childhood abuse, growing up becomes traumatic. The unconscious acting out contained in adolescent rebellion, contrariness, or the whole range of what we call negative identity often occurs in response to the sense that parental authority is hypocritical, that the world is not what it seemed when they were kids — to a sense of betrayed innocence. Again, the underlying issue in loss of innocence is the passing of the authority of one's mythopoetic, naive matrix with its sense of oneness and wholeness. In its place one has to find the source of one's own authorization. The many forms that adolescent belonging takes are attempts to moderate these demands for self-esteem, to provide a group identity where no individual identity has yet formed. But all such group identity as a substitute for authentic self-identity is a ruse that sooner or later collapses.[6]

Few adolescents or young adults overcome loss of innocence early in this phase of their development. Resolving the crisis normally awaits some further growth when the pain stemming from trauma or introjected contempt become conscious and can be worked through in a process best described as mourning. Yet before this can occur, the fears accompanying the retrieval of the traces that history has seared into one's deep self have to be faced. Adults can remain attached to certain mythic representations of their childhood and of their idealized parents rather than face the loss of the security they receive from their memories — even when they are really hiding deeper and more unpleasant truths.

When fear of unearthing the source of pain causes people to keep trauma and its memory repressed, they generally engage in repetitive, compulsive, or obsessional behavior, as the mind-body unity presents its bill and torments the victim to face the truth. But healing cannot occur unless we recognize the source of our self-contempt in its introjection at its origin.[7] This often involves a loss of confidence in once-trusted persons or parents. Along with the experience of shame, burned deeply into one's psyche, these are the wounds that accompany loss of innocence. Though commonly associated with adolescence, they find their roots in early childhood losses. When these early losses are later compounded in adolescence, then history itself can become a trap. For when childhood idealization passes and we begin to understand ourselves historically, the first response may well be panic. Adolescence and its addiction to now, cannot yet cope with having a history, and so resolution has to await a later stage of consolidation. But mature adulthood means dealing with the vicissitudes that make our story our own peculiar history. It is a maturity that eludes child-adults who have not mourned their loss of innocence, who have not faced up to the failures of those set in authority over them, who have not learned to authorize or take responsibility for their own further personal and spiritual development.

These considerations are relevant for individuals, for social organisms like the church (called the Body of Christ), and for our religious culture at large. The temptations that exist to idealize the past and smooth over the abuses of parental authority are multiplied when it comes to our judgments of Holy Mother Church and the access she promises to God the Father. Today, if we would be adult believers, we have to face the loss of mythopoetic innocence that we have too long sought to repress. Our spiritual parentage cannot live up to our ideals for it, and our history has been replete with forms of abuse that we have only just begun to face. To make matters more difficult still, we have to face the additional loss of the adolescent self-confidence of the Enlightenment and its presumption of autonomy and clear-sightedness as well as its own self-idealization. Today Western culture is experiencing an adolescent liberation from its mythopoetic matrix and has become as ambiguous and guilty as its "parents" ever were. Expelled from the garden of pre-ambivalent harmony, Adam and Eve's son killed his brother. And so the drama repeats itself.[8]

Therefore, to overcome Western religion and culture's loss of innocence and to profit from the loss in order to gain a more mature sense of how and what we believe, we must face the ambiguity of our history and the abuse that both religious and secular parties have doled out in abundance. We must face the disheartening truth that there is no source of authority that has lived up to its own myth or its own ideal representation of itself. Without facing the ambiguous condition of authority in Western culture and religion and without taking some responsibility for the harm that both religious and secular authorities have caused, we cannot mourn the wounds that our authorizing institutions have inflicted. If we do not mourn them and face up to the introjected contempt that believers and unbelievers carry around within them, we cannot as a religion or a culture be healed. If believers do not seek healing and the self-authorization that comes with internalizing their spiritual journey, they cannot reach the stage of mature faith.

Facing up to our collective loss of innocence is the only way that we can deal adequately with the question of religious authority. But before I can spell out what a fully mature faith involves for individual believers, it will be necessary to correlate the question of the authority of the church with the issue of the authority of the Bible. Though the first seems a particularly Catholic issue and the second a thoroughgoing Protestant one, I will try to show that the problems of one illuminate the other. If I can show what a mature model of interpreting the Bible is like today, then I can turn to describing a mature model of ecclesiastical authority, one that helps believers both to stand on their own two feet and to lean at the same time upon God.

I argued earlier that the Enlightenment's championing of critical rationality has resulted in a net gain for the contemporary appropriation of the biblical revelation. Through it we have achieved a renewed understanding of the Bible as text spanning the divide that historical consciousness has made endemic of modernity. Despite the scriptures' lack of strict historical exactness, their confused transmission history, their embarrassing particularism, their failed prophecies, their patriarchal bias, and even their theological tendentiousness, the Bible remains for believers the primary witness to the events and persons whose encounter with the living God represents the church's basic myth. Despite the problems that arise when the Bible's ambiguity is frankly admitted, the mainline Christian churches have accepted the critical disenchantment of the Bible that conditions its authority, whether or not individual bishops, curial congregations, scholars, or believers admit it.

In similar fashion, a critical perspective on history yields an ambiguous and disenchanting recital of how religious authorities have cooperated in wartime atrocities, social discrimination, intellectual dishonesty, racial injustice, the suppression of dissent, the persecution of heretics and nonbelievers, blatant anti-Semitism, colonialism, misogynism, imperialism, and the like. This recital demands that we face up to the shame of Western Christianity's historical text and seek to extract from it, as we do from the Bible, the truth beyond the failures, the word of grace in the midst of sin. Instead of engaging in the age-old habit of apologetics, throwing the best light possible on dubious persons and tragic events, we need to face the text of our history as a condition for a mature encounter with the truth beyond our naive adherence to, or our angry rejection of, our history. Only when we overcome our loss of immediacy by healing the split between critical reason and religious imagination, only when we overcome our loss of innocence by mourning the damage inflicted in the name of faith, only then have we earned the right to reconstruct a truly mature way of believing in the closing years of the twentieth century.

It would be a serious mistake to think that a postcritical, mature interpretation of the Catholic tradition of faith in the contemporary situation will allow us to put the uncertainties of the postconciliar period behind us and seek to restore a traditional, precritical version of what is proposed for belief. Our religious culture has endured too deep a loss of naivete to allow this simplistic solution. But rather than lament the loss of our immediate connection to the biblical world or regret the loss of our naive innocence, I wish to move warily into the future to discover new possibilities for a religious response to the changed conditions of humanity's relationship with God at this labile stage of our religious and cultural development. Disregarding any nineteenth-century progressivist optimism about our own best efforts really being God at work in us, I invite both restorationists and progressives to squeeze through the eye of the needle that criticism and history insists that we have to thread in order to discover postcritical maturity. Because we are bereft of both immediacy and innocence, it is difficult to know where the energy, the skill, or the wisdom will come from to help us formulate what postcritical faith might look like.

Ironically, some of the energy, wisdom, and skill necessary for this step forward toward religious and cultural maturity may have been provided by a professed opponent of religious belief. Without knowing it or meaning it, our unwitting benefactor discovered that the healing of our losses could begin only with Western culture and religion's regression to a primal level of self-awareness and with the dethroning of critical rationality's autonomy. When these primal truths are spelled out fully, we shall be able to stand on our own feet, finally aware of our wounded yet healed condition, and proceed to a more mature expression of religious belief. I wish now to trace the beginnings of this regression in favor of development and see how, despite its starkly critical, antireligious position, it has contributed to a more mature form of Catholic faith.

The End of the Enlightenment

By the late nineteenth century, Christianity found itself beleaguered. The advancing claims of positivist science, critical rationality's latest rage, along with the rise of modern industrialism, had convinced many of the bourgeoisie, as well as scholars and laborers, that the traditional world of the Bible and the church was no longer their world. Hegel attempted to rehabilitate the Christian religion by presenting it as the sensible, imaginative expression of the same truth that philosophy expressed in the purer form of reason, but it didn't stick. Instead, Kierkegaard denounced Hegelianism's objectification and depersonalization of Christian faith, and Marx put the lie to Hegel's purely hypothetical and intellectualist system, reducing his dialectic of self-realizing Spirit to a materialist program for communist revolution. His a priori atheism seemed not only logical, but necessary, as a way of exposing the alienation of the majority of society from the fruits of their own labor.

Simultaneously, the impact of Darwin's *On the Origin of Species* had led to a general discrediting of the historical reliability of the Hebrew Bible just when scholars had also begun to dissect the New Testament portrait of Jesus. Few believers have had the vision or the ability of John Henry Newman (1801–90) to balance deep faith with acute critical abilities. A strong opponent of rationalism and of liberalism (which he understood as opposing dogmatic religion), Newman balanced the old and the new during his career in the Catholic Church (1845–90) as few have been able to do before or since. He protested against the antagonism between theologians and scientists and expressed no shock at Darwin's theory, which was rocking the religious establishment of the time. Astute enough as a theologian to give the "profound submission" due as an act of obedience to Pius IX's 1864 *Syllabus of Errors,* he nevertheless denied that it had dogmatic force requiring an act of faith. With the same astuteness, he defended the new historical methods for investigating the Bible in an essay on "History, Criticism, and the Roman Catholic Church," published when he was eighty-three years old! But Newman was an exception to the rule of virulent antipathy between critical, scientific investigation and religious faith.

Onto this stage of conflict between Enlightenment culture and traditional Christianity arrived a man who developed a theory he thought powerful enough to deliver the coup de grâce to the "utterly pernicious illusion" of religion in general and Christianity in particular. The heir of rationalist philosophers like Ludwig Feuerbach, whose *The Essence of Christianity* (1841) had popularized atheism, Sigmund Freud (1856–1939), as a student at the University of Vienna in 1874, declared himself "a godless medical student and an empiricist." He dedicated his life's work to mapping out "the dream of the Enlightenment: to expose artificial moral constraints on the expansive self-feeling of the life-force," a task that would lead to the fading away of traditional religion "with the fatal inevitability of a process of growth."[9] More than fifty years after his death, Freud still raises the hair on the necks of religious believers who seek to dismiss him as a footnote to the twentieth century's immoral thought. While Freud and the psychoanalytic movement no longer generate hysterical reactions from religious authority, to date there has been little Catholic recognition of his contribution to our awareness of the human psyche's complexity and of the role sexuality plays in human development. Yet any attempt to interpret our contemporary situation without Freud and psychoanalysis is flaccid from the start. Because psychoanalysis, in the words of Paul Ricoeur, "conflicts with every other interpretation of the [human] phenomenon," the effort to appropriate it for a mature form of faith can tax our best efforts. Yet the attempt must be made, because Freud's interpretation, as refined by psychoanalytic authors, has contributed to the postcritical situation in ways we have only begun to fathom.

At the same time, I am not principally concerned with vindicating or critiquing Freud. (I cannot claim the competence to do so.) But I have sought to learn from him, his followers, and his interpreters and to factor what I have learned into this rethinking of the forms that faith takes. My own psychoanalytic journey from misunderstanding to recognition is the background to my reading of how Freud's adversarial, antireligious interpretation of human existence can help flesh out a more mature religious response.

Freud saw himself as an Enlightenment thinker, fully convinced that "there is no appeal to a court above that of reason." Defending this position, not as a philosopher but as a scientist, he argued that scientific investigation was sufficient for finding out whatever about the nature of the world had any practical interest. Beyond that, there was no way of knowing what is real. Religion, then, was nothing but an illusion, the illusion of thinking that "what science cannot give us we can get elsewhere."[10] Though once tempted toward theism by a professor (Franz Brentano, a former priest), Freud remained consistent in holding that religion and empirical science made mutually exclusive claims. He was equally concerned to set off psychoanalysis from philosophy and, to that end, defended his speculative theory as based on strict empirical method in the same way that physics is. His scientific positivism suggested to him that his work was analogous to that of the archaeological excavator of Troy, making him a veritable Heinrich Schliemann of the mind.[11] Unlike more poetic and philosophical writers such as Goethe, Schiller, and Nietzsche, who inferred the existence of twilight realms of consciousness, Freud sought to discover "manifest proofs of the existence of the unconscious."[12] So intent was he on his scientifically oriented search that he could write in a 1931 letter, "I have rejected the study of Nietzsche although — no, because — it was plain that I would find insights in him very similar to psychoanalytic ones."[13]

His commitment to positivist science and his background in medicine and neurology prejudiced him in the direction of a strictly physical, or bodily, explanation for psychical, or mental, phenomena. This, in turn, led to the frequent charge that Freud's method is reductionist, that he ignored or even suppressed evidence that did not fit into his single-minded theories, and that he built the enormous edifice of psychoanalytic theory on the too-narrow base of instinctuality. Yet the "simplicity" pole of this theory (his propensity toward neat generalization) has to be balanced by a corresponding complexity pole (his thinking also ranged broadly and deeply as he sought to investigate all of human emotional and cultural life). His theoretical thinking oscillated fruitfully between these two poles — an evaluation that is more balanced than dismissive accusations of Freud's reductionism or psychologism. I will argue, in fact, that his empiricist, critical reason, divorced from any wisdom matrices in philosophy or theology, was virtually necessary to allow him to pierce through Western religious culture's defensive armor in matters of the body and sexuality. Without someone as brash, cocky, and overbearing as Freud could be — and despite the problems he caused for himself and for the reception of psychoanalytic theory by his flawed character structure — it is doubtful that the contribution of the psychoanalytic movement to deepening our understanding of interiority would have made headway against the mind/body dualism favored by Western religion and culture.

It is helpful to remind ourselves that Freud's stark empiricism endowed him with unsentimental clarity. Comparing his reluctant public to a tyrant out of touch with both his people and himself, he urged them, "Turn your eyes inward, look into your own depths, learn first how to know yourself! Then you will understand why you were bound to fall ill; and, perhaps, you will avoid falling ill in the future."[14] Passages such as these have contributed to the commonplace comparison between Freud and Augustine. Both men understood human consciousness to have undergone a specific dislocation that has caused language and communication to become indirect and symbolic when it deals with interiority. Both took starkly naturalistic views of human beings, whose pride had to be confronted over and over with the uncomfortable truth that "we are born between urine and feces."[15]

Like Augustine, Freud saw a historical dimension to humanity's need for humility over against its collective self-importance. As part of his plea for looking inward, the founder of psychoanalysis took Western culture's self-inflation to task (he termed it narcissism) for its three-time opposition to modernity's critical eye of the needle. Our wounded narcissism opposed

the discoveries of Copernicus for they stripped us of the illusion of being at the center of the universe; it opposed Darwin's evolutionist theories, which plunge us into the vast flux of life; finally, it resists psychoanalysis because this latter shakes the primacy and sovereignty of consciousness.[16]

The merit of Freud's thinking lay in its essentially modern recognition of the self-alienation of human consciousness. From a decidedly irreligious perspective, Freud pressed home that we cannot understand ourselves directly by simply expanding our immediate cognitive capacities. Humankind is afflicted by "some geological fault across a hitherto undivided consciousness," an ugly, wide ditch, as it were, in our self-understanding.[17] To cross that divide, Freud took a detour through scientific explanation to enable us to recover understanding, not via the deductions of philosophy and philosophical theology but by the empirical route of the natural sciences.

Despite his reductive analysis and even his exclusion of contrary evidence, Freud has contributed to our dawning ability to overcome the split between scientific explanation and intuitive understanding and to recognize that they are not opposing, but asymmetrically paired, styles of fathoming human nature. Like history, a science that interprets traces of events in the available evidence of the past, and like biblical criticism, a science that interprets traces of the human-divine encounter in the canonical text, psychoanalysis interprets traces of repressed and distorted consciousness in the text of human life to help heal the wounds of self-misunderstanding that are at the root of alienation.[18] Psychoanalytic interpretation offers a way of making a whole story out of disconnected and fragmented memories and of reuniting one's conscious, rational understanding with one's unconscious, affectively oriented other half. As a work of interpretation, psychoanalysis involves as much art as science, as much intuition as ratiocination, because it takes us on a journey that we can negotiate only via "the detour of signs" (Ricoeur).

In the mid-1890s, Freud began a friendship and developed a theory that would mutually interact to plot the initial course of the psychoanalytic movement. In correspondence with Wilhelm Fliess (with whom he remained an intimate for ten years before their friendship broke up bitterly), Freud poured out his early theories and doubts and expounded on his own self-analysis. This correspondence is now regarded as the foundation of psychoanalysis. During the same years, Freud wrote but did not publish a paper outlining how he wished to develop a scientific psychology (his "Project"), built upon his earlier neurological research, that would explain mental functioning in terms of "quantitative considerations." He was seeking nothing less than "a sort of economics of nerve force."[19] His theories of both normal psychology and psychopathology were an offshoot of his early laboratory experience. He wanted to discover the physical causes and effects of mental energy as an actual physical force. At this stage, Freud sought to describe, quantitatively and empirically, the forces or stimuli that arise either as perceptions from the outside world that impinge on the mind or as instincts (internal excitations) that disturb the homeostasis or constant mental energy of the brain/mind. As a research scientist, he presumed that these psychical events were caused by the movement of material particles or neurons in the brain.[20]

Comparing his psychological speculations to the work of physicists, he tried to map the mind according to the laws of thermodynamics. His materialist mindset clearly embraced the principle "Nothing existed but particles and forces — all else was illusion."[21] He defined feelings or affects, as well as ideas, as encoded messages translated by the mind from the stuff of instinctual charges sent up from its inner core. Thus instincts are never known in themselves, but only by the way they are represented as ideas or affects in the complex organism that is the brain. Central to the thermodynamic principles of energy with which Freud was working is the notion of constancy — the quantity of energy remains constant. When there are serious disturbances in the force, as it were, the organism itself seeks to restore constancy (Freud's definition of pleasure) by reducing the tension loosed by the charge of neurons (which he associates with unpleasure).

But for all his speculation on the materially organic mode of mental functioning, he did not publish his 1895 paper and soon moved to a speculation for which he was convinced he had evidence, the sexual etiology of neuroses. When Freud left behind his "Project" and published instead "The Aetiology of Hysteria" (1896), he left the laboratory for the clinic and, ultimately, the analyst's couch. Freud would never abandon his conviction that his work on the human psyche was strictly scientific (and deterministic as well). But where he once used the word "cathexis" to mean, literally, a storing up of energy flow (indicating a different level of psychical attachment to a person or idea), he eventually settled for a distinctly psychological meaning to the term. Today "cathexis" is understood on analogy with a physiological investment of a unit of the brain with specific memory content.[22]

The startling discovery that Freud presented in that paper on hysteria at a meeting of the Vienna Society for Psychiatry and Neurology was based on eighteen patients he had been treating. He claimed that the origin of their neurotic behavior (called hysteria at the time) could be traced to their sexual abuse as children. Despite Freud's conviction that this discovery would finally launch his career and bring him the fame and fortune that had so far eluded him, he got an "icy reception from the donkeys" and a rebuke from the presiding psychologist. In the words of a biographer, "It was an evening Freud chose never to forget; the traumatic residue it left became a ground for low expectations, a justification of his pessimism."[23]

But the significance of this rejection is more than biographical. He subsequently abandoned his seduction theory (now known as the trauma theory) as the cause of neurosis and substituted a drive (or instinct) theory. According to this substitute theory, infant sexual fantasies and emotional conflicts were responsible for what his patients later reported as actual memories of sexually abusive incidents. To this day, Freud's shift in his thinking, which led to much of the superstructure of orthodox psychoanalysis (infantile sexuality and its stages, the Oedipus complex, penis-envy in women, the division of the psyche into id, ego, and superego) remains controverted. Though some see Freud's freeing himself from "the unfortunate seduction theory" as allowing him to develop the mature insights of his self-analysis, not everyone is so convinced that this move was fortunate. Others have seen Freud caving in to adult defense mechanisms (including his own), which were powerfully present in "Victorian" Vienna. For when he shifted the burden of his theory from actual events of abuse to the sexual desires of infants, he made children and their instinctual endowment the problem and let parents and abusive adults off the hook.

Alice Miller's corrective reading of one of Freud's most famous cases ("The Wolf Man") is particularly strong evidence for this latter interpretation. With material made available after Freud's death, Miller has shown convincingly that the founder of psychoanalysis overlooked the severe sexual abuse suffered by the Wolf Man. She has speculated that Freud, perhaps unconsciously, overlooked it because of its similarity to incidents in his own childhood and then read problems of his own past into the case history of his patient. Miller's own early work in the field of child abuse, its prevalence and its long-lasting impact, has been startlingly vindicated of late. Still, she has not repudiated Freud's groundbreaking contribution. Rather she credits him with developing heuristic tools that have pointed the way toward handling complex problems previously uncomprehended in any organized or therapeutic way. His contribution is best honored, she insists, if it is not made into an immutable system of psychoanalytic dogma.[24]

In similar fashion, Otto Rank, Carl Jung, Karen Horney, Harry Stack Sullivan, D. W. Winnicott, John Bowlby, Erik Erikson, and Ernest Becker have all parted ways with Freud without repudiating his breakthrough discoveries. Religious writers, like Paul Ricoeur, Gerald May, W. W. Meissner, and James W. Fowler, all regard Freud's work as a major contribution to religious self-understanding, despite Freud's irreligious stance. For while the Enlightenment's scientific rationality sought to perfect the project that Max Weber referred to as *die Entzauberung der Welt* (the disenchantment, or demystifying, of the world), Freud, an Enlightenment knight-errant, discovered that in its depths human consciousness refuses Descartes's reduction to clear and distinct ideas. Paradoxically, though Freud proposed to eliminate any but rational considerations of the human condition, he instead rediscovered and regrounded the irreducible enchantment of human self-knowledge. Critical rationality's tools for grasping the object world of the senses, for verifying the real, and for excluding the fantastic have all sought to liberate human knowing from the mythopoetic world of primary naivete. But Freud uncovered the discomfiting truth that moderns had not only lost immediacy and innocence vis-à-vis the object world, but could no longer know themselves immediately and innocently by a direct appropriation of data, facts, measurements, or intuitive insights into their subjective state. At the end of his life, he could only adopt a stance of stoic resignation, because he had become convinced that human beings were always poised precariously between the death instinct (*thanatos*) and the basic life instinct (*eros*). Fight it though he did, Freud brought the Enlightenment full circle by subverting pure reason.

After Freud, we understand that knowledge of the physical world and self-knowledge function in analogous but not identical ways. Self-knowledge proceeds via interiority (as in Augustine) and indirectly, via the detour of symbols in which analytic reflection is complemented by synthetic interpretation. The interpretive work of critical psychoanalysis first disenchants primary naivete to bring to light the contents of the unconscious, always symbolically conceived, as a way toward setting self-knowledge on its own feet. It then helps the autonomous individual to overcome the loss that this enlightenment involves in order to reintegrate what he or she knows into a secondary, postcritical naivete. This knowing is both factual and mythopoetic, analytic and synthetic; it recovers what has been lost, but from a mature perspective of forgiveness and responsibility. In cultural terms, the contributions of psychoanalysis have been limited by our continuing beguilement with individualist presumptions that autonomy equals happiness and that the purpose of psychoanalytic work is to liberate an individual from his or her past rather than to reintegrate the liberated person into the ongoing stream of life of a community where human meaning must be found.

Religiously, most of Western culture still clings either to primary naivete (philosophical myths) or to critical, skeptical forms of un/belief bordering on irreligion (this century's version of deist humanism). The conflict between these two forms of faith affirmation has hampered efforts to reintegrate the gains of critical rationality with the precritical, mythopoetic world of symbol. In the following chapter, I will explore whether the terms of Freudian psychoanalysis can help us pioneer a model for postcritical, or mature, religious belief.

Chapter 5

Freud and the Crisis of Modernity

Repression and the Unconscious

Cardinal Newman, it is said, noted that some people's mistakes are more important than other people's truths. Freud's explicitly irreligious understanding of the instinct-laden human being seems to be a prime example of such a mistake. For in its narrowness, it pierced the veil of spiritual idealization that has prevented faith affirmation from recovering from history's traumatic impact upon it. In this chapter I wish to trace the implications of Freud's thinking on the defensive grandiosity of both naive belief and critical reason in order to fashion tools for overcoming our double loss of immediacy and innocence.

Freud based psychoanalysis on his observations that adults act hysterically, or develop neurotic symptoms (pervasive guilt, obsessions, compulsions, phobias, eating disorders, alcoholism), because they unconsciously have repressed unmastered childhood conflicts. As a physical determinist, Freud described repression as a psychic event that happened *to* the individual's consciousness. Today we understand repression more positively as part of the adaptive mechanisms of the developing body/mind amalgam. Repression naturally allows people to bite off only what they can chew of life. Hence, neurosis occurs along a normal spectrum. Only at one end of it do we find clinical neurotics, who bite off *more* than they can chew. These neurotics are overwhelmed by the excessive responsibility that comes with ingesting more reality than they can handle. It follows that neurosis is "another word for the total problem of the human condition," a condition that has become neuralgic in modern Western culture precisely because of the explicit loss of experience with the transcendent.[1] Neurosis always tempts human beings, but not because they have had to repress childhood fantasies about sexuality, as Freud thought. Rather, they either cannot completely forget tragedies that they actually experienced (e.g., loss of a parent, sexual abuse, etc.) or are protecting themselves from being overwhelmed by the innate tragedy of their natural limitations, most dreadfully death it-

105

self. Repression and neurosis, then, name the pervasive restlessness that modernity has exacerbated; they both contain not just individual, but historical, import.

Having discovered repression, Freud sought to explore it as a condition of latency in which ideas and memories lie in a storeroom of the mind beneath a barrier of censorship. This realm, the unconscious, represents a condition of mental reality that deductive principles of knowledge have ignored because they stress the conscious mind as the agent of knowing. Conditioned by the unconscious, then, both knowing and the known are not necessarily what they appear to be. But this does not lead to philosophical skepticism. For dreams are the royal road to the unconscious. Once alerted to unconscious reality, we understand it as the storehouse of the anxiety that bubbles to the surface of our waking awareness as well.[2] Irrational anger that we either disguise by saying that we're having a bad day or resist through addictive habits is the clearest sign that deep down things are not right. Anxiety tells people who disguise their woundedness that their lives are not what they want them to be. In brief, anxiety substitutes for many repressed feelings that hide from conscious awareness.

For Freud, mental functioning was determined by psychical laws as mechanistic as physical laws. This made the unconscious like "a maximum-security prison holding antisocial inmates...harshly treated and heavily guarded, but barely kept under control and forever attempting to escape."[3] Today the special characteristics of the unconscious system make it seem less like a prison than a country club for subversives. In the unconscious, instincts or wish-impulses are timeless and unregulated by censorship (unless they try to rise to consciousness), bothered neither by principles of contradiction nor by problems of doubt. Side by side in the unconscious dwell traces of a person's nature and nurture, discarded remembrances and restless feelings awaiting furloughs that are readily granted by dreams and neurotic acting out. Described by Jung as "the whole living past in the lower stories of the skyscraper of rational consciousness," the memory banks of the unconscious hold the stuff of our personal and community myths, of artistic creativity, and of imaginative play. They are home to the restlessness that writers from Augustine to Hegel have seen as the motive force behind our desire for union with the All.[4]

Though Freud saw it more narrowly focused, the idea of the unconscious has changed the way we look at the workings of the mind, at the emotions, at personal motivation, at the consequences of childhood trauma, and at the role of images and language in the formation of consciousness. Because the unconscious conditions the way things attain meaning, it follows that no ideas are so clear and distinct as Descartes imagined. Today, the thinking that humans do must reflect on itself, taking into account how unconscious processes act like a hidden rudder guiding even the most clear-minded reasoning.[5]

Narcissism

The word "narcissist" normally describes people whose lives are distorted by their self-involvement or absorbed with their own self-image. Technically, such persons are afflicted with secondary narcissism, a personality disorder in which defensive grandiosity seeks to keep a failed sense of self afloat. As we saw in chapter 1, primary narcissism is not a pathology. It is the fundament of psychosexual development that names how the human organism's vital energy is self-absorbed for the sake of survival. Most of us revert to this primary stage of self-love when we are sick or sleeping. Because Freud described narcissism as an instinct or drive, he misrepresented it as a latent tendency to predatoriness.[6] In actuality, the primary narcissism of newborns is a protective shell against vulnerability. Arising as both energy and need, it connects human beings at a level of relationship deeper than subjects and objects. From day one, according to Ernest Becker, the human being's "sense of self-worth is constituted symbolically," not just biologically. We naturally desire ourselves to be objects of primary value, not just one of a crowd. An infant's primal energy-for-living instinctually senses that it is worth being cared for. When this energy is checked or frustrated (as it almost must be to some degree), the infant suffers wounds to its narcissism. As a result when they become children, they constantly compare themselves with one another, checking for advantages or special favors a sister or brother might receive, in order to insure they are not being shorted of what is necessary to affirm themselves. Even later, when, for example, an executive who has made it to the top gathers status symbols around him, he is enacting the same need for affirmation. This is the survival of wounded narcissism: the "tragic destiny" that decrees we must somehow stand out and know that we matter.[7]

More positively, differentiation through self-worth is spoken of as emotional autonomy, which is not a derivative of pathological narcissism. Children achieve a capacity for life-affirming emotions, for the ability to express both joy and sadness, by being allowed access to their own feelings and needs through the actions of those around them. For an infant's natural vitality to develop well enough, it must be mirrored back and affirmed, not frustrated and denied. How a child sees itself in the care-giver's eyes will influence how the child views both itself and its world.

This means that knowing one's self and one's world is always intersubjective. An infant's capacity for relationships (from its earliest object relations) is either established or impaired by the developmental vicissitudes of upbringing. In those early stages of establishing basic trust and emotional autonomy, the foundations of one's later life and belief system are laid. Even in good enough care-giving settings, however, children necessarily suffer from narcissistic wounds because life in relationship can never match the omnipotent expectations of the human organism's vitality. The inevitability of these wounds requires that all human beings engage in some kind of repair work as part of their individual development. When individuals do not take the journey (the stage of individuation), they inevitably suffer from unconscious idealizations in which authority figures or fantasized relationships function as replacements for the inner vitality that they never developed.

When such ideas or figures dominate one's religious worldview, the believer's need to live communion with God immediately and innocently domesticates the spiritual realm. This makes revelation (objective faith) and religious belief (subjective faith) into manageable mystery, with no depths to penetrate, no unsolved paradoxes to be struggled with, no losses to overcome, no history to live down or atone for. Instead, there is only clarity, certainty, and consequent obligation.

But because things aren't what they seem, they cannot be this simple. Though we should need no reminder that seeing and believing (knowing "deep down things") cannot be immediately correlated (John 20:28; 2 Cor 5:7), Freud's antilogic of the unconscious has provided us with a fresh confirmation of an ancient truth from a critical perspective. What is different is that seeing and believing need not refer to two different realms of reality, one material and the other spiritual. Freud laid the basis for reintegrating religious faith beyond our historical and personal loss of immediacy and innocence by a highly reductionist view of human sexuality. To that ambiguous gift, which somehow tells us about God's image within humanity (Gen 1:26–27), we now turn.

Personality and Sexuality

Freud's theory of human personality was first schematized in *The Ego and the Id,* published in 1923 when he was sixty-seven years old. However, the theory that saw personality emerging from a conflict between an id, an ego, and a superego was formulated during and immediately after the Great War. Freud had first identified a censorious aspect of the ego (which he would later call the superego) in the essay "Mourning and Melancholia." As heavily as the war had weighed on his thinking, the death from influenza of his daughter Sophie, pregnant with her third child, dealt him a heavier blow still. Stoically he wrote to Sándor Ferenczi, "Since I am the deepest of unbelievers, I have no one to accuse and know that there is no place where one can lodge an accusation."[8] Freud felt that sorrow and anger or joyful ecstasy welling up in the id could easily run away with the ego, a hapless rider barely able to contain the steed it rode. The ego for its part had to hold on and do as best it could, so he endured and worked on stoically.

The theory, especially as it came to link the superego with the unconscious, was a pessimistic response to the pretensions of Christian Europe and its highly developed civilization. In reducing the accomplishments of culture to an extension of the superego's ideals that disguise our destructive aggression, he sought to burst the bubble of Germanic (Christian) culture, to which he always remained an outsider. What was more, his thoroughgoing pessimism led him to lump together all forms of culture into the police state that, for him, all civilization more or less aped.[9] As a "godless Jew," yet a proud one who had felt the sting of anti-Semitism, his antitheology was a strong antidote both to the reactionary and racist Catholic politics of the Hapsburg Empire and to the religious liberalism whose strongest proponent had been the Prussian court theologian Adolf von Harnack. Despite Harnack's preaching that the essence of Christianity taught the infinite worth of the human soul, neither Enlightenment theology nor Rome's antimodernist piety had done anything to prevent the senseless slaughter of millions of young soldiers and civilians during the war.[10]

Thus, Freud thought his pessimism was realism. His reductionist analysis both of the ego's control and of civilized society's norms sought to administer a needed dose of cold reality to Europe's narcissistic self-inflation. His clinical approach to moral duty had none of the panache of Kant's a priori moral imperative. It revealed that, unlike Becket in *Murder in the Cathedral,* most people rarely do the right thing for the right reason. Their actions reveal the inauthenticity of the ordinary conscience, much as Kierkegaard claimed in his description of "automatic cultural" people who play the fictional games society prescribes for them.

Yet the conflicts that make up the structure of personality result in the paradox that normal people are not only much more immoral than they believe themselves to be, but also far more moral than they know.[11] On the one hand, society offers high cultural and religious standards of morality, but few people live up to these ideals. To promote them, morality allies with the superego, but often in a way that is neither healthy nor genuinely virtuous. On the other hand, average people under siege by the passions of the id and the censure of the superego manage to cope and do as well as they do with only their precarious sense of themselves (their ego) to guide them.

Freud's deterministic scenario of morality sought to counter both philosophical and naively religious conceptions of the way people function. But as a reaction, it pessimistically attributed to the normal ego the self-alienation and weakness of a neurotic ego, one whose center of gravity has shifted to the outside world.[12] In the last half century, psychology has redressed this pessimism and has stressed the extent to which the human personality is a system open to adaptation, rather than a closed one comprised of competing inner forces. An individual develops emotional autonomy by adaptively dealing with inevitable conflicts. One's sense of self grows as it interacts with others, especially those key persons in the family network who are one's earliest object-relations. Hence, personality and individual character are not necessarily or solely the result of a struggle of conflicting inner forces, but of the web of human relationships they share.

The ego, id, and superego do not denote things in the mind but, more flexibly, point to the way that the text of one's life develops from the interaction of endowments and experiences. They stand for the stable and labile elements of individual personality, which grows by negotiating between the instinctual body (id) and social duty (superego). The ego is not the self, but a symbol of the irreducible something that negotiates the dualistic of flesh and spirit, body and soul, matter and mind but which cannot be completely identified with either.

Another matrix of conflict out of which Freud saw the superego developing arises from a child's being in love with one and hating the other member of the parental pair. The idea of the so-called Oedipal complex emerged from Freud's self-analysis of his dreams and early memories carried out within a year of his father's death in October 1896. Perhaps these familiar circumstances account for both its familiar ring and its strained application to all individual development. In normal circumstances, Freud theorized, the Oedipal complex arises from the conflict caused by a boy's straightforward sexual-object attraction (*cathexis*) for his mother and from his identification with his father, which makes the father first his model and later his rival.[13]

While the Oedipus complex has been criticized as simplistic, male-oriented, and all-encompassing, it seems that Freud put his finger on something — but on what? Infantile sexuality? The possibility of non-sexual bonding we call identification? The love-hate ambivalence in all human relationships? Freud's own peculiar triangulation with his parents? A lot depends on how the familiar ring of the Oedipal complex is interpreted. Rather than retain Freud's instinctual reading of it, we can recognize that he consistently ignored the ways in which the infant's legitimate narcissism is often wounded and how that trauma lays the groundwork for neurotic symptoms that reappear later in life. Hence the Oedipal complex as he formulated it blames the child-victim, a habit as old as the Oedipal myth itself. The newborn infant Oedipus had his ankles pierced and bound by his parents, who abandoned him on a mountain to die. From such violent beginnings little good comes, but few have paid attention to how the tragedy of Oedipus is rooted, not in his killing his father and loving his mother, but in wounds inflicted on him in early life.[14]

Looking more closely at the myth, then, allows us to shift our understanding from the child's sex drive for mother and anger with father to the relational complex common to all children, who occupy an anomalous family position because of their biological closeness to the mother. Feelings of rivalry toward the father, jealousy, powerlessness, and even sexual stimulation occur in the Oedipal triangle of mother, father, and child. The issue then is not child libido or sexual desire, but the relational conditions in children's lives. If infants or older children are sexually stimulated by their parents, other children, or adults, neurotic attachments will most likely be created in the space between the deed and its defensive repression. Though infants can act upon their environment, their capacities are limited and easily frustrated. Hence the Oedipal complex is not chiefly about sex. It has more to do with power — the struggle that children (wedged between the parental pair as they are) must engage in to be allowed their own feelings. Without access to their own emotions, they cannot develop empathy for others.[15]

Freud sensed correctly that something goes on within the father-mother-child complex, but he described it from too narrow, personal circumstances. As part of a larger trauma of powerlessness, Freud's complex can be better understood as a project that all children undergo as they seek to take the measure of the world and struggle to get on top of it. Spinoza had a term for it: the *causa sui* project, our (understandable but pathetic) attempt to become our own cause, parent, or creator. As a child grows and achieves motor skills and learns language in order to deal with its world, it seeks to shape that world to its own expansiveness. This is why children at a certain stage give their parents orders, proclaim *no* to just about anything said to them, and test their parents incessantly. A child deprived of any sense of power will have a difficult time attaching emotionally to or identifying with parents and other adults.

Also, as children experience bodiliness (curiosity about sex organs, for example), their experience recapitulates the Fall — but here it is, as Becker noted, a "fall out of illusion into sobering reality."[16] They cannot help but become aware of the arbitrariness of their bodies and that their bodies are not all they are. At the same time, children experience an inner self that is capable of imaginative symbolizing of reality. They go nowhere without their first not-me possession, want stories read and reread, ritually play with the same toys, develop relationships with both real and fictional characters who inhabit their world. By contrast, bodily reality represents determinism and boundedness (and ultimately, dying). No matter how the body is played with, manipulated, firmed, shaped, or exalted, it cannot of itself transcend its biological limits.

This defeat leads children to submit to social reality and to the formation of a mature (socialized) character. As a defeat, it explains why
Freud saw the individual superego and the oppressive structure of society as the Oedipal complex writ large.[17] Less narrowly, it symbolizes the
many triangular situations into which biology and the vicissitudes of social and political life thrust every person. Reinterpreted as a life-project,
the Oedipal complex is a rehearsal for life's greatest and most continuing
challenge: dealing with body determinism and social limitations through
symbolic freedom. The inner and the outer power struggles that inevitably result tempt human beings, in the course of their development,
to veer off in one of two directions: toward the grandiose escape of too
much possibility or toward the depressive path of too much necessity.

Children who suffer narcissistic trauma and then repress their
wounds as part of their brave attempts to get on top of their world and
master it have a more difficult project to enact. They symbolize their
place in the world very differently from those who learn a healthy level
of self-repression. But all human beings must undertake this spiritual
project, which Freud identified but reduced to sexual politics. It involves
nothing less than understanding the full impact of bodiliness (including
sexuality) on humanity and on each individual's symbolic constitution.

During Freud's Paris sojourn (1885–86), he was impressed by
Dr. Charcot's observation about a young woman's nervous disorders. In such cases, said Charcot, *"c'est toujours la chose genitale,
toujours...toujours...toujours"* ("it is always the genital thing, always"). Ten years later, he expanded this notion by claiming that genital
sexual abuse was the root-cause of hysteria in eighteen patients whom
he was treating.[18] But his thesis was rejected as scandalous, and he
suffered some professional isolation as a result. This disaster was followed in two weeks by the ambitious doctor's fortieth birthday, which
coincided with the fatal illness of his father, who died in October of
the same year.

During the same period, he entered into his self-analysis. Four years
later in 1899 Freud, in *The Interpretation of Dreams,* began to spell out
his theory of the Oedipus complex and the way dreams distort, disguise,
condense, and displace their subjects while symbolically expressing un-
thinkable thoughts, including aggression and sexual material. Still it was
not until 1905, with the publication of *Three Essays on the Theory of
Sexuality,* that his libido or drive theory, with its frank supposition of
infantile sexuality, was proposed. A brief look at these three essays will
help us understand their impact on twentieth-century society.

In the first essay, "The Sexual Aberrations," Freud arranged not only
the most disgusting perversions, but also normal sexual activity and neurotic symptomology, along a continuous spectrum. He theorized that
neurosis itself comes from unmastered instinctual (sexual) conflicts in

childhood, for which neurotic activity was a kind of screen or compensation. In the second essay, "Infantile Sexuality," he claimed that the noticeable "precocious sexual activity" of small children, normally up to the age of five or so, was evidence of the existence of a sexual drive in childhood. Although he would not add until later his notion of the oral, anal, and genital stages of sexual development and gratification, the suggestions in these essays were "as tightly packed as a hand grenade and as explosive."[19] Freud not only defined "libido" (pleasure or desire) as a component of the instinct of self-preservation in the smallest child (narcissism), he also labelled infants polymorphously perverse. Full genital expression of sexual pleasure came only later in life, of course. But the period of latency itself was caused by children's repression of early Oedipal desires out of fear of retaliation (castration for boys, loss of love for girls). This repression cut a swath of amnesia into childhood, masking earlier memories of erotogenic activity that, he claimed, was primal, natural, and not the least bit depraved.

His third essay, "The Transformations of Puberty," described how the development of the genital organization (which is ordered to end pleasure) did not cancel out the earlier erotogenic organizations (oral and anal), which remained available for the production of forepleasure. But once the genital organization emerged, there came the challenge of consolidating sexual identity in the face of the revival of unremembered Oedipal attachments.

The book contained only three modest-sized essays, but the shrapnel is still falling around us. By speculating that the nature of sexuality was primal, polymorphous, and possessed of a natural tendency to the perverse, Freud dealt a blow to all task-specific, role-specific, and period-specific views of sexuality that would deny its pervasive and general nature. Linking it with the Oedipal attraction of children for their parents probably made the structure of his sexual theory too big for the base on which it was built. Nevertheless, the gauntlet that Freud threw down is still lying at our feet, a major challenge to all previous definitions of sexuality. At the core of his theory, he stated that normal sexual development does not naturally occur. Though arising in the human sexual instinct, mature sexuality is achieved only through experiences of psychical inhibition. Lacking these, a person with all the conscious willpower in the world will still not be able consciously to control sexual ideation and activity. Oppositely, he linked forms of nonsexual activity innocently indulged in to sexual drives that had been repressed. Linking adult sexual instinct with unremembered childhood experiences, pre-latency sexual attractions, neurotic activity, and sexual perversity, Freud tied together varied phenomena always held to be distinct. If they had been linked at all, it was under the label of sinful concupiscence. Discovering a unity underlying activities that had been widely separated threatened a very old, dualistic worldview where sexuality, being only of earth, was naturally corrupted.

Most significantly, when Freud despecified genital organization, defining it as different only in degree, not kind, from other sexual activity, he uncoupled heterosexuality and reproduction. He also argued that heterosexual pleasure was a goal that not everyone reached. Genital union always was "a victory over the libido's original dispersion towards zones, aims, and objects regarded as deviations from the mainstream of genital heterosexuality" — a victory that some individuals would not or could not attain.[20] Chief among these were homosexuals who, according to Freud, acted aberrantly, but only because they were still dealing with unmastered childhood conflicts. Again we can see Freud's economic understanding of available sexual energy at work in his concepts of dispersion, inhibition, and redirection of sexual energy. The psyche's energy, not just the body's organs, were the key to the outcome of sexual maturation. But the psyche was more complex and more instinctually determined from childhood to maturity than anyone had guessed.

Almost ninety years later, his theory of sexuality is faulted for making sexuality the all-important factor in the formation of human character and for reducing all physical satisfaction to sexual satisfaction. By compressing a host of expressions in infants and children (curiosity, jealousy, autoeroticism, and physical sensations) into infantile sexuality, he derogated from the centrality of the issues of power and autonomy at work in early development. Even forms of adult sexual acting out are today understood (as in cases of explicit pedophilia) to be about the adult's own sense of powerlessness (his or her narcissistic deprivation) rather than the satisfaction of explicit sexual desire.

Yet beyond the narrow confines of his instinctualism, Freud raised correctly the problem of how human beings interrelate force (instinct) and meaning in their lives. Libido is not a quantity of sexual energy but the energic source of a grammar of desire rooted deeply in human affectivity. Meaning, though it attains consciousness through language, is rooted in preverbal experience that has its own unique language rooted in our unconscious depths. While Freud reduced meaning to the interaction of physical forces in the body, others have seen a deeper paradox at work in the way bodily function and transcendent meaning are intrinsically related.[21] According to Becker, what psychoanalysis has revealed is that the body and sexuality are inseparable from our existential paradox, the duality of human nature. "The person is both a self and a body, and from the beginning there is confusion about where 'he' really 'is' — in the symbolic inner self or in the physical body." In other words, the demands of bodiliness, which first involve awareness of the physicality of the feeding mother, the awe (rather than sheer envy) of the father's penis, the parents' sexual involvement, and which also induce narcissistic play — all are components of the "confusion over the meaning of [human] life," a meaning that can only emerge adequately through some reconciliation between the dual realms of symbolic freedom and bodily fate.[22]

Becker's post–sexual revolution perspective allows us to sort out the wider significance of fetishism and sexual perversion. Because anxiety over the body continues from childhood to adulthood, people take refuge in substitute objects or fetishes. Some are used as aids in sexual functioning magically warding off a person's sense of vulnerability. They help people deal with the totality of the human condition by allowing them to partialize or symbolically to invest purely individual meaning in an activity in which they seem to enjoy little freedom (sexual desire).

Fetish charms also exist in polite society, but they are usually disguised. According to Becker, the secret ritual, the secret club, the secret formula "create a new reality . . . a way of transcending and transforming the everyday world of nature, giving it dimensions it would not otherwise possess and controlling it in arcane ways."[23] In more cases than we credit, this leads to the sado-masochistic activity of the overintense high school athlete, the anorexic cheer leader, the do-it-all mother, the ninety-hour-a-week lawyer, the all-suffering minister. All engage in masochistic activity that is different in degree, not kind, from the seeking of bodily pain as a condition for sexual arousal. Such activities seek to transform suffering and pain (symbols of our limitations and our being-unto-death) into sources of pleasure.[24]

Likewise, sadism and the kicks that people get from inflicting pain exist along a continual spectrum that includes a child's pulling the wings off a butterfly, an adolescent's bullying of a young child, a father's spanking a child in punishment, and a rapist's threats and forceful penetration of his victim. These are all actions that help (momentarily) to achieve mastery over our weakness and provide us with perverse satisfaction, if not real pleasure — whether sexual or not. In general, then, sado-masochism reveals that both philosophical and interpersonal issues are rooted in physicality — which is why much sado-masochistic activity involves a sexual component.

As we know, not everyone is immediately capable of the psychic inhibitions that Freud specified as the road to normal sexual organization. Though Freud tended to underestimate the power of the integrative ego to encompass the demands of instinctuality, he nevertheless opened up new vistas that have helped those after him to see how, though creatures of earth, we transact more than materiality in our creative illusions. Our greatest limitation (our body unto death) is at the same time the springboard of our capacity to transcend species limitation and attain self-transcendence as well.

The greatest test of this perspective arises from the problematic of sexual differentiation. If today we have moved beyond Freud's repetition of the ancient equation of the male as normative human, humanity's spiritual member, we should be able to achieve a more mature understanding of male and female sexuality by attending to the symbolic significance of their varied genital structures. For more than other body parts, the sexual organs seem mysterious, even autonomous, and often not under conscious control. Hence, they have a tendency to be split off in our unconscious and to remain unintegrated in our overall identity. It might seem paradoxical in the extreme to speak of the symbolic sense of things as tangible as sexual organs. But the very fact that no one treats the primary or secondary erotogenic organs as if they were elbows or kneecaps means that they have a special meaning. And in the structure of our knowing, nothing achieves meaning without their being symbolized.

Long ago, Paul sought to convince his formerly pagan congregation in Corinth about the importance of communal harmony by appealing to the natural symbolism of the body. Paul argued that "God has so constructed the body to give greater honor to the inferior part [the genitals] so that...all the parts may have the same concern for one another" (1 Cor 12:24–25). He was establishing for his Gentile congregation a symbolic value for the human genitalia, which they traditionally had in Judaism, but not in the Roman Hellenistic world. He was resymbolizing the sexual organs as a way of promoting more than sexual chastity (which is why the hymn to love follows in chapter 13). Today, the whole range of vulgar Anglo-Saxon words that name penis, vagina, intercourse — which polite society avoids — are used also in a symbolic way to demystify or render accessible exactly what polite society doesn't like to have up front, in its consciousness. Teenagers, males in the locker room (real or figurative), liberated women, and anyone wishing to titillate do the same. All such vulgar symbolism seeks to neutralize the sexual organs by feigned contempt for them, but of course it means quite the opposite.

Because the sexual organs themselves express a tension between physical, erotic capacities and reproductive, social significance, they are not easily incorporated into a person's self-image. This leads to the tendency to leave them "out there" and hence see them as manipulable for casual, detached pleasure. Contrary to traditional moral theory, pleasure is not the problem; rather, it is the failure to integrate the self and its body parts that makes moral and spiritual wholeness difficult to attain. When women report the experience of rape and claim that they did not really feel present, or when people remain emotionally uninvolved with their own sexual feelings, it is a clear sign that they are disengaged from themselves, engaging instead in a defensive maneuver to protect their inner selves from being hurt by the activity of their momentarily split off sexual organs. While our sense of the natural symbolism of the sexual organs cannot be the same as Paul's, there is wisdom in admitting the more than literal meaning of the sex organs as a way of internalizing their connection to our whole self. Otherwise we end up allowing them to take their place as one of the factors "out there" that define our sexual personhood in literal, naturalistic terms. Although there are other ways that human beings dissociate or split off parts of themselves, it commonly occurs in sexuality.

In an atmosphere of alienation from the body, where body-guilt or body-denial prevails, or in a culture where only the finest and fittest bodies will do, internalizing sexuality makes enormous demands on an individual's maturity. But it will be more possible if we take seriously the natural symbolism inherent in the genital organs rather than hide our own discomfort behind prudery or pretended virtue. Because the penis and the vagina, the testes and the womb, mean more than their physical properties and signify more than is anatomically evident, they symbolize both life and death in a way that their prurient exploitation and prudish avoidance belie. Their symbolic significance, something Freud's peculiar narrowness helped recover from our mythic past, also helped to open up in a new way the perspective that male and female symbolize the duality of the fully human. In biblical terms, male and female taken together are the only full signification of our human identity, the only complete manifestation of the "image and likeness of God" (Gen 1:27).[25] Today, that text speaks to believers differently than it once did. Freud's attacks on hypocritical Victorian morality, with his brash theories about anatomy and personal destiny, made it necessary for twentieth-century society to reconfigure the full personal, social, religious, and political significance of sexual differentiation.

Beyond Neurosis

Not content to map the micro-structure of the human mind, Freud was convinced that he had discovered the macro-structure of history and culture. His overweening confidence led him to make some of his most creative, comprehensive, and absurd suggestions. From his earliest treatment of art, culture, and religion, Freud saw into the heart of things, but he often saw only a narrow swatch. In a 1908 essay, "Creative Writers and Daydreaming," he identified unconscious ideation, wishes, and the survival of unconscious memories as sources from which all writers draw. Poets, writers, and children at play were genetically linked. Artists, too, are like daydreaming adults, transposing the stuff of the world into a new, more pleasing order. This meant that neither play nor artistic creativity were real: "The opposite of play is not seriousness —

but reality."[26] Childhood play became adult fantasy (since pleasure is never surrendered once it has been enjoyed), and both activities, said Freud, reflected states of dissatisfaction: "the happy person never fantasizes; only the unsatisfied one does." Freud explained all symbolic activity via his famous example of a child at play, making a toy disappear and reappear. The child is teaching itself to master brutal reality — to cope with the loss of instinctual pleasure. Mother leaves and baby doesn't know if she is coming back, so it pretends through the use of symbolic objects that life is not so bad after all.

Freud named this assuaging of the loss of pleasure "sublimation," partly a social constraint and partly a binding and transformation of energy, which society requires everyone to try but at which only some really succeed. The artist, however, has the best chance of escaping the either/or framework that society imposes — either repress your libido (via neurotic inhibition) or become sexually obsessed, either be dominated by the culture or be dominated by your libido. Artists are a third type, whose creative work is a form of adult play that seeks to make reality more palatable.[27]

Because Freud saw art not as analogous to dreams and play but as identical to them, he theorized that works of art were stenosigns or masks for something archaic. His narrow conception ignored the way symbols properly speaking have a more complex structure, not one that can be reduced to simple, one-way references. Works of art cannot be interpreted as merely expressions of a person's private (conscious or unconscious) world. Works like Michelangelo's *Moses,* Sophocles' *Oedipus Rex,* and Shakespeare's *Hamlet* are artistic creations not because they are projections of the artist's neurotic conflicts but because they sketch their solution. They disclose or manifest something of the present or the future of human striving for dignity and meaning. They are not merely regressive symptoms of an artist's unresolved conflicts but progressive interpretations that escape the individual limitations of the artist's own story.[28]

The missing link, then, in Freud's theory of artistic creativity is the absence of any positive evaluation of the role of suffering in the life of the artist — or in human life. In similar fashion, he reduced enjoying works of art to inducing a mild narcosis, but one not potent enough to allow human beings to forget their real misery. Thus, according to Freud, art is a narcotic and a shaky refuge from suffering, nothing more. Hence, sublimation of all kinds merely masks pain, for artistic creativity and enjoyment are merely substitutes for neurosis.

Although Freud's 1908 essay connected fantasies, dreams, the unconscious, and imaginative writing, he later located the wellsprings of artistic creativity (and scientific investigation) in the avoidance of reality rather than in an ability to engage it no matter the risks. Had he explored the unconscious as a source of artistic expression, he might have realized how much neurosis is a secondary symptom of the artist's situation, never the cause of the artist's creativity but that which gives shape to the artist's life. This means that there is a link between personal suffering and its record in creative work because the source of creativity lies in the creative person's capacity for suffering his or her own history as part of a more general narrative of pain and pleasure. Hence, the difference between the artist and the neurotic is a talent. The neurotic is an artist manqué who lacks the artist's ability to transform suffering through symbolism.[29]

Neurotics repress their suffering, continuing to deny it and thus giving it no expressive (artistic) outlet. Lacking access to their own inner voice, they experience a loss of self that results in underlying rage and destructive desires. What is more, there are those who begin as artists, but whose arts fails them and who end up engaging in antisocial pathology. Native talent, then, is no guarantee that suffering will produce art, because there has to be the wherewithal, the emotional autonomy, to transform inner suffering into an external act of redemption.[30]

Equally, performance artists, from comedians to opera and rock stars, turn their personal joy or pain into art, the symbolic stuff of their performances. The obvious meaning of the narrative they are performing stands in tension with a further, perhaps unconscious, meaning that cannot be explained in footnotes, exhibition catalogues, or critics' columns. Its being *performed* stands in the place of any final resolution of life's anomalies. Thus, the symbolic content of art cannot be seen as a substitute for reality, as if it only covered over an underlying problem. Art makes available elements of the seen and unseen aspects of life that cannot be perfectly resolved, but that remain tensively related to each other. Therefore, the symbolic is not less than real; rather it is *hyperreal*. Any genuine act of artistic symbolization involves an exploration of reality in its depths, not merely on its surface. Artistic activity does not hide the ugly reality that we cannot be perfectly happy; it braves transforming human suffering by making its individual chapters symbols of humanity's narrative of wounds and its healing.

The significant overlap of art, culture, and religion is a major theme in both *The Future of an Illusion* (1927) and *Civilization and Its Discontents* (1930). In them, Freud developed a perspective first set out in *Group Psychology and the Analysis of the Ego* (1921). For Freud, civilization (and culture, which is indistinguishable from it) is a ruse, because it pretends to be what it isn't and to accomplish what it can't.[31] For similar reasons, religion is an illusion. Civilization, so-called, "is largely responsible for our misery," he wrote, because it prevents the individual's achievement of happiness, the only kind of happiness he thought possible. This radical individualism arose not only out of

Freud's evolutionary instinctualism but from rationalism's dissection of political society into individual units of aggression and of economic action. The "neighbor" is, for Freud, "not only a potential helper or sexual object," but also someone on whom one is tempted to satisfy aggressiveness. Any more-than-individual, other-than-instinctual happiness is doomed to failure because civilization is at war with itself. The life and death instincts that lie at its foundation alternately war against each other and collude with each other to incite and forbid individual happiness.[32]

This bleak picture emerged because Freud's description of civilization limits itself to the most pathological aspects of civilization and culture. Some developments in civilized society stem from a high degree of mixing libidinal and aggressive aspects of human nature (scientific advances resulting from war-fighting technology, patriotic bonding around warfare). But these phenomena are not inevitable and may one day be judged to be outside the bounds of what civilized society allows. Freud was aware that his theoretical (even mythological) system tempted him to judge "the normal entirely by the standards of the pathological" (he called that a Charybdis which he tried to avoid). But he seemed more anxious to avoid the "Scylla of underestimating the importance of repressed consciousness," so he kept substituting what he learned from extreme cases and constructing a universal symptomology upon them. It is no wonder, then, that he claimed to be able to offer his fellow human beings "no consolation."[33]

Again, it seems only fair to note that Freud's mature years (he was fifty-eight in 1914) coincided with the suicidal debacle of World War I, the rise of the culture of "Dollaria" (his name for the United States), Fascism, the Great Depression, and the eventual triumph of the Nazis. With the passing of the Enlightenment's passion for clear and distinct ideas, he was forced back upon the narrow base of his instinct theory, which he elaborated more and more convolutedly.[34] Still, Freud's insistence that civilization is a ruse deserves to be heard, even if we do not accept his narrow premises. Oskar Pfister, a Lutheran pastor who was a student and friend of Freud, was only the first to point out that culture and civilization are not the same thing. We might even paraphrase Freud's earlier work *The Ego and the Id* and affirm that normal *civilization* is not only much more immoral than people believe, but human *culture* is far more moral than people know. For culture ("what is good and worthy of protection") did not have to be opposed to human nature but could be seen as a natural development and extension of what is good in that nature.[35]

Separate from his pessimism, Freud's clinical insights have contributed to a healthy suspicion about even the best intentions of society's political and cultural leaders. Unconscious motivation has much to do with the way power disguises itself and pretends to be something other than it is. This is perhaps even truer, and trickier, in a society fifty years more advanced in extending personal freedoms to individuals and lowering its requirements for instinctual renunciation. Unlike bourgeois European societies (and later Marxist ones), in which the individual was more clearly at the mercy of the power of the community (what Freud called "the decisive step of civilization"), late twentieth-century democracies have lessened the burden of instinctual sacrifices imposed on their members and today bribe their constituents with personal freedom by providing access to a plethora of instinctual enactments. Mass delusion has a whole new meaning after the micro-communications revolution.

The ruse that Freud took culture to be, then, looks much different from a late twentieth-century perspective. Individuals have been freed from many of society's repressive demands, which no longer can be charged with causing the neuroses that afflict members of advanced capitalist society. The challenge of culture is to help individuals ground their lives in healthy repressions so that they can invest themselves in more-than-individualist schemes for meaning and transcendence. This option, from the perspective of religious faith and post-Freudian realism, will play an important role in a mature understanding of faith.[36]

As noted earlier, Freud's cast of mind had a way of converting a good analogy into a firm identity. In a 1907 paper, "Obsessive Actions and Religious Practices," he offered the straightforward identification that set the tone of his later work: "neurosis as an individual religion, religion as a universal obsessional neurosis."[37] Here again was an opportunity to carry through what eighteenth-century rationalists like Voltaire had started and what Feuerbach and Marx had devoted much of their intellectual energy to accomplish: the debunking of religion. Freud warmed to the task but did not stop with a general indictment of religious faith. In 1939, in the months before his death, he published his final blast. In *Moses and Monotheism* he reiterated his dubious anthropological views from *Totem and Taboo* (1913) on the origins of religion. More significantly, he tendentiously identified Moses as an Egyptian (an outsider, not a Jew) and speculated that he was murdered by his own people (founder and victim). As he had done before in analyzing the *Moses* of Michelangleo, Freud was identifying with Moses, writing about himself and his own ambivalent identity. Sadly, the book's legitimate suggestion that anti-Semitism persisted because of Christian jealousy and envy might have had some impact had it not appeared in a work whose outrageous claims guaranteed easy dismissal.

The Future of an Illusion, his earlier and more polite attempt to debunk religious belief, had sought to provide for average believers some critical distance from their unreflective participation in society. Though Freud had little confidence in the masses (whom he considered lazy, unintelligent, having "no love for instinctual renunciation") he hoped to coax them beyond their identification with their rulers and beyond the "substitute satisfactions" offered by culture, so that they could recognize civilization's religious ideas for illusions. Avoiding the charge that religious ideas were errors or falsifications, he contended that they correspond rather to the wishes of a small baby. A child's menaced self-regard calls for consolation and, in its helplessness, it needs a father-protector. In the same way, humanity had created a "store of ideas ... built up from the memories of the helplessness of ... childhood" as the material for religious teaching, which, he insisted, had no evidential force. It was not true, but its influence had to be explained. This he did by deepening humanity's store of memories to include historical recollections of an event that was a product of Freud's own imagination: the killing of the primal father.[38] The combination of these childhood and historical memories overwhelm the majority of people, who become religious instead of being neurotic. Freud's coup de grâce deserves to be quoted:

Religion would thus be the universal obsessional neurosis of humanity; like the obsessional neurosis of children, it arose out of the Oedipus complex, out of the relation to the father. If this view is right, it is to be supposed that a turning-away from religion is bound to occur with the fatal inevitability of a process of growth, and that we find ourselves at this very juncture in the middle of that phase of development.[39]

This returns us to his initial analogy become identity: "the universal neurosis spares [believers] the task of constructing a personal one." To replace illusionary religion, which was withering away, Freud offered the soft "voice of the intellect," which will finally succeed in installing "our God, Logos," the personification of "science [which] is no illusion."[40]

Oskar Pfister's friendly and respectful response to Freud, fittingly called "The Illusion of a Future," was published in *Imago,* the periodical founded in 1912 by Otto Rank and Hanns Sachs. Pfister was acquainted with Freud's Enlightenment agenda, his desire to supplant religion with his own substitute in the guise of reason; so his response went to the heart of the matter. He took up the central insight of Freud's own argument (and life work), that the "intellect is powerless in comparison with [our] instinctual life," an issue that, for all of his trumpeting of reason, Freud had never adequately dealt with. This is the illusion that Pfister pointed out to Freud: that reason can provide, by itself, what religion has contributed to culture over the years. But Pfister went deeper and brought home the issue that the Enlightenment had obscured and that Freud, the originating genius of psychoanalysis, had himself missed:

We human beings are not only thinking apparatuses, we are living, feeling, desiring beings. We need values, we have to have something that satisfies our hearts and souls, that vivifies our desires. ... In analysis, do we not often have to deal with clear-thinking people who drive themselves almost to starvation and despair with their thinking?...Religion, with its partly sublime, partly attractive symbols, with its poetic splendor and its shattering interpretations of reality, with its overpowering personalities who by their heart-warming deeds and sufferings charm people, and by their faults and weaknesses warn yet inspire the fallen person with courage to aspire to his ideal with new strength — religion is an educator that science with its theories cannot replace.[41]

Perhaps to prepare for such a response, Freud had predicted in his essay that "defenders of religion will...make use of psychoanalysis in order to give full value to the affective significance of religious doctrines." It was probably Pfister that he had in mind. It was a significant concession, one the pastor was quite capable of taking up. Not least among his penetrating insights was one that Freud was in no position to know first-hand but that Pfister as a pastor knew full-well. The claim that religion was a prophylactic against neurosis ignored the pastoral truth that "neurotic manifestations are, in fact, generously distributed among pious believers." Again, it's not a case of either/or; there are many cases of people who are both religious and neurotic, a peculiar observational and evidentiary fact that Freud, a self-described wicked pagan/godless Jew, had no opportunity to witness! Certainly, Pfister's points are telling, but I would like to build upon them by developing Becker's perspective on illusion and its significance in the light of his claim that "the best existential analysis of the human condition leads directly into the problems of God and faith."[42]

Unlike Freud, who saw life and death instincts pitted against each other, mutually subverting the individual, Becker noted that *life itself* awakens us to our being-unto-death. "Creatureliness is the terror," because we are "self-conscious animals." Our symbolic selves are capable of creative expansiveness, imaginative depths, and spiritual heights here and now, and yet our bodies sicken, age, cripple, and die. It is this painful paradox that is repressed from infancy as a result of our organismic primary narcissism, our attempts to cause ourselves, and the boon of repression by which we lower our sights and accept a safe identity from society. Civilization encourages (or coerces?) us to play by the rules and to conform to achieve happiness (the practiced self-deceit of so-called mature character), as if this solved our dilemma.[43]

Becker based his merger of religion and psychoanalysis on the similarity between Kierkegaard's school of anxiety and the analytic experience in which analysands experience the demolition of all their unconscious power linkages or supports. Severed from infant narcissism, disabused of adolescent rebellion, unimpressed by one's early adult accomplishments, stripped of convenient excuses, weaned of perfectionism, exposed to one's unconscious dream-world, and naked in one's grief, the analysand discovers something of the deep hole known in religious thought as the dark night of the soul. There, the acceptance of cosmic vulnerability, of powerlessness to change the past, of woundedness, and of emptiness allows persons — if they but *suffer* them — to let go and surrender themselves to grace, to healing, to the creator who loves specks of dust and expanses of nothingness.

Conceived as a series of steps, this perspective revalues suffering not as a punishment but as an opportunity.[44] It is founded on the explicitly religious (if nondogmatic) admission of the transformative role of conversion, the turning toward grace that changes certain dying to risky living, the move from loss to recovery. In the void, suffering is finally borne — albeit "with loud cries and tears" — rather than played off as pleasure (masochism), imposed on those weaker than ourselves (sadism), or philosophically resented but accepted (stoicism). The light goes out externally only so it can glimmer internally. But the catalytic moments and illuminating events are more than balanced by hours, weeks, and sometimes years of struggle before the needed act of self-surrender can be conceived, entertained, and enacted. This is not magic but the discovery of a transformative dimension to suffering not unlike that of artistic creativity. The psychodynamics of therapeutic healing seeks to make it available to all of life's artists.

At this point, we are far from Freud's understanding of religion as a recrudescence of an infant's sense of its helplessness. Adults are not helpless from day to day, unless they are clinically neurotic or have succumbed to psychosis. In fact, like Kierkegaard's "automatic cultural" people, society's average adults work very hard to obliterate any anxiety stemming from cosmic helplessness, to block out any gut-wrenching encounter with life or with death's claim upon them. They forget, so as to avoid conscious awareness; they stay drugged or overinvested, though play, work, money, or sex, to ignore the persistent scratchings on the lid over their unconscious. Likewise, the fear that they might wake up to painful memories of being wounded or of wounding others, to recollections of childhood abuse or failures of care and love, can be paralyzing far into later life. The helplessness of the adult is the retained, unconscious memory that something is dreadfully wrong with me, the world, my life. Its repression in the storehouse of the unconscious cannot protect us. Rather, it becomes pathogenic of the normal neurotic interactions we learn to live with — society's lie of character that rewards maladjusted individuals for their dominance of others — or of sociopathic acting out that occurs in a dizzying variety of ways.[45]

To turn farther away from that helplessness or to ignore our complicity by muting our own pain, we turn to human relationships, to sexual love, romance, marriage, family, and children. There we are trapped again, but this time there are other victims involved. Not that these choices are unworthy or wrong. But Becker wants us to face our culture's overevaluation of "the romantic love 'cosmology of two'" and how, as overvalued, it is bound to fail: "When you confuse personal love and cosmic heroism you are bound to fail at both." Without discouraging loving relationships, Becker seeks to move beyond any level of accepting the average person's security "that the cultural game is the truth, the unshakeable, durable truth." Neurotics know that this is true, but as failed artists, they cannot create or enact a way out of the game they see more clearly than others.[46]

What we are being told, then, is that creatureliness denied, though rewarded by the cultural game, risks grandiosity and self-inflation (too much possibility) and that creatureliness repressed or internalized (too much necessity) leads to depressiveness. So how can we live and express our created-unto-dying life? Becker relies on Rank's paradoxical answer: "To be able to live one needs illusions, not only outer illusions such as art, religion, philosophy, science and love afford, but inner illusions which first condition the outer." His suggestion takes other provocative forms. He calls for human beings to discover "life-enhancing illusions" or to practice "legitimate foolishness," so as to be capable of the paradox of simultaneously affirming themselves and yielding, to "lean on God and give over everything to Him and still stand on [their] own two feet." But this paradox cannot be enacted in either simple or individual terms. The category I would propose as a way of summarizing these insights is that of *spiritual artist*. It requires nothing less than heroism, but a day-to-day heroism that orients human beings "beyond their bodies...and toward...myths of heroic transcendence." This heroism can be termed spiritual artistry because it demands engaging in healthy repressions that help us deal with the fact that we "cannot experience everything."[47]

But how do we get to be spiritual artists, and how do we know that our creations are not mere fabrications? Clearly, spiritual artists are made, not born. We saw earlier that the distance artists achieve from the source of their own pain, while creating works of art, can also prolong their suffering. Is suffering itself the source of the spiritual artist's life-enhancing illusions? Or is it not knowing how to *suffer* suffering, how to sing a song of the Lord in a foreign land, that unseals the fount of creative life? Spiritual artists must become adept at imaging their own, as well as the world's, predicament from a new or unique angle. Their symbols and illusions must engage and modify the ideas, images, hopes, and fears of their community in order to help them as well as others cope with life's ineluctable contradictions.

The mature religious awareness I term "spiritual artistry" is based on a human capacity illustrated by rereading Freud's case of the child and its self-administered game of peek-a-boo. In contrast to Freud, whose model child would cathect the toy as a substitute satisfaction and then decathect it when its mother comes back into the room, this alternate perspective presumes that real growth or development takes place when the infant relates to the world outside. Children who early in life experience traumatic abandonment or successive deprivations and whose environment may not even provide for toys or dolls lying to hand for consolation may well develop an object-constancy disorder, because their experiments with transitional objects would only have been failures. As a result, they are not so much instinctually deprived as lacking any sense of their presence to the world. As we saw in chapter 1, transitional objects allow a child to practice contributing something from its private, subjective world (the positive meaning of projection) and thus to interact meaningfully with reality around it. Rather than merely mastering an absence by such play and substituting a toy in the place of reality, the child is accepting a new *presence* composed of the object and his projection of a symbolic identity upon it.[48]

We have, then, in transitional phenomena or positive illusory experiences a realm that is proper both to objective reality (without either exalting or debasing it) and to subjective reality, a realism that is not delusional or a total derivative of subjectivity. The child's healthy narcissism is here beginning to expand by way of prospective illusion or symbolization to include itself in the real world of objects. If this is not a prime example of legitimate foolishness, I do not think we will find one. We actually include ourselves in the real world of experience through our projection of our symbolic expansiveness. Our ability to create illusions or symbolize the meaning of things, objects, or people also bespeaks a "capacity to transform reality into something permeated with inner significance," because in this revised perspective, human beings cannot do without illusion, for it gives meaning and sustenance to human experience of the self.

Transitional *phenomena,* then, refer to real objects in their capacity to stand for and make known relational reality. Because transitional phenomena are defined as intermediate areas of experience that allow for an illusion in time and space where both union and separateness exist, they are prime examples of how objectivity and subjectivity cohere in human depth experience. Transitional phenomena undergird the adult's capacity for artistic creativity, as well as for cultural and religious expression. Though illusion rated the lowest place on Freud's reality denominator, it has been rehabilitated in order to express the paradox at the heart of the human expression of meaning.[49]

As an indicator of the vital role that symbols of all kinds play in our negotiation of what is real beyond the merely obvious, transitional phenomena are significant in helping us examine other situations in which we experience a space or a gap created by distance and potential loss, especially as this involves religious experience. Not all illusions will be appropriate for developing spiritual artistry, so we must learn to be critical of the likely substitutions by which believers, in periods of personal or historical transition, are wont to deal with the withdrawal of either the object of faith or the loss of their own subjective belief. Freud's characterizing religion as illusion, then, was far more paradoxically truthful than he could ever have imagined. It completely changes the terms of the supposed impasse between religion and reason and affects the way that we describe spiritual artistry and mature faith.

A religious community poses its image or doctrine of God and begins to teach it to young people through what we have called mythopoetic imagery, stories, and prephilosophical ideas. As this was in the beginning, so it continues to be, and it is perfectly appropriate. As children become more capable of abstraction and their formal education advances, they become more capable of receiving nuanced presentations of both the stories in the Bible and the doctrines of their tradition. But then comes the crisis of criticism, a highly significant transition both for culture and for adolescents. At this time, experiences of withdrawal, distance, or loss occur frequently. It is rare that there is not some turmoil in the religious life of the adolescent/young adult. When the separation begins to take place, as with the infants they once were, their response is going to depend upon their illusions or their dominant symbols. The separation is threatening for young people, but they will be the last to let any adult know that. In the face of their subliminal panic, they can act like most victims of fear: they obsess. But their obsessions vary. For some young people, the idea of displeasing God is intolerable because it is too threatening. These generally give themselves to more fervent forms of prayer, rituals of obedience, vows of chastity, and rigid notions of doctrine, and entertain fixed notions of reward and punishment.

For their opposite numbers, the idea of displeasing God, if they think about it at all, couldn't be more pleasing. If you're going to revolt, why not against the Big Guy? But this does not mean that the panic of separation is not acted out. These adolescents too, obsess, but more through immersion in a subculture, through adulation of rock stars, through a hypercathexis of clothes, cars, and speed, or through actual addictive behavior with drugs, smoking, or alcohol. It is not hard to see this as the regression to primary narcissism, the narcotic that Freud saw operative in art and religion. It is the behavior of adolescents threatened with too much necessity — the necessity to leave the matrix of childhood and make it on your own, which is the only way adolescents imagine anyone ever makes it.

These alternatives sketch out the way young people deal with their separation from early personal and religious understandings. Most adolescents will combine the reactions in their desperate attempts to enact their *causa sui* project. But no matter how they enter this crisis — a long one, to be sure — they will emerge from it dependent on the character of their illusions and the durability of their dominant symbols. The concept of transitional phenomena makes us attend to both the objective and subjective elements of faith and, beyond them, to the mode of their combination, the shape of young believers' illusions, the quality of all the symbols that have nourished them in the early mythopoetic period of the formation of their basic religious images.

The shared illusions or symbols by which a community of faith hands on its continuing life are its life-blood, the food with which it nourishes its members in this cosmic transitional space that Paul called "living here in the body while we are away from the Lord, walking by faith and not by sight" (2 Cor 5:6–7). In this space we can at best achieve a mediated immediacy because subject and object, self and other, affirmation and denial are not absolutely distinct but actually coinhere. Meaning is both given and achieved; we are simultaneously both "in the body" and beyond it. To describe this paradoxical mode of living, Becker resurrected Kierkegaard's symbol of the knight of faith as an example of the energy and dedication necessary to live transcendent myth in this blood-soaked world. My suggestion is that believers today, in a period of banality rather than of trial, have great need for spiritual artistry to weave new life-illusions out of the storehouse of our mythopoetic, unconscious memories of communion with God, to explore more deeply the depths of our symbolic consciousness of our God-struggle, to teach us how to be legitimately playful and wisely foolish in our worship of God, to restore the "joy of our youth" when we go to the altar of God. Have there been such artists who have captured but transcended the panic we experience as we endure transition, distancing, and loss and who have invited us to see the meaning of these gaps or spaces for ourselves and for God? Perhaps not too many. But one of them, the second Isaian prophet, created this poetic illusion for Israel to discover in the space between them and their Lord. It is as good an example as we have of why some poems, songs, and symbolic expressions become canonical.

> But Zion said, "The Lord has abandoned me; my Lord has forgotten me."
> Can a mother forget her infant, be without tenderness for the child of her womb?
> Even if she should forget, I will never forget you.
> See, on the palms of my hands I have written your name;
> Your city walls are ever in my sight.
> Those who will rebuild you are hastening to you,
> while your destroyers and spoilers are fleeing.
>
> (Is 49:14–16)

Since we cannot live properly human lives without images of hope, symbols of restoration, and experiences of legitimate playfulness, religious faith needs, not to entertain illusions, but to create, refine, rework, deconstruct, and create them anew. That will demonstrate how true and how adequate are our illusions for negotiating the loss of immediacy and innocence that maturity requires.

The Healing of Memories

As a major contribution of Freudian theory to society, psychoanalytic therapy (and analytically based counseling) remains controverted. In the rest of this chapter, I will argue that the work of critically appropriating the illusions adequate for personal maturity happens in the therapeutic setting mainly because of transference and that therapy and transference combined provide further heuristic tools to overcome the impasse between naive religion and critical culture.

In his 1933 *New Introductory Lectures*, Freud set out the aim of therapy as the strengthening of the ego to make it more independent of the superego, to enlarge its perception so it could appropriate more of the unconscious id. He summed up therapy in the famous phrase "Where id was, there ego shall be": therapy raises unconscious conflicts, introjections, and repressed memories to consciousness so that the patient can manage life better through expanded ego-adaptation. Yet by 1937 Freud began to stress the pervasive strength of the inborn drives and the death drive's resistance, expressed most virulently in character deformations resistant to analysis. Again, Freud's unsentimental clarity was never far removed from pessimism.

In some ways, Freud could justify this lowering of expectations for individual patients as he became firm in his conviction that he had cured humanity's historical narcissism, contributed to the eventual disappearance of religion, and helped people "prepare for life" by allowing them, more realistically, to "prepare for death."[50] Trapped in the paradox that people cannot live without civilization but cannot live happily within it, individuals could hardly seek to escape "Necessity" while "Eros" and "Thanatos" raged within. Speaking of cure, then, sounded naive or grandiose; so Freud did not give much hope, claiming to have sought to cure neurotic misery in order to introduce the patient to the "common misery of life."[51]

Though a counterbalancing optimism has been proposed — it sees therapy as enabling "an individual to solve his problems himself...to regain his spontaneity...to give him the courage to be himself"[52] — I would argue that historical neurosis or the more-than-individual effects of history's wounds place us between pessimism and optimism when we deal with therapeutic practice. Any adequate understanding of therapy must help us deal with the persistent taunt recorded by the prophets Jeremiah and Ezekiel, "The fathers have eaten sour grapes, and their children's teeth are set on edge" (Jer 31:29; Ezek 18:2). This dirge highlights not only the reactive nature of the neurotic personality but also the generational conditions under which a great deal of neurotic symptoms are formed. Because during much of childhood we have no outlet but our feelings, repressed emotions stemming from not being loved as one truly is, or from being ignored, beaten, misunderstood, or seduced are programmed into our memories and cannot easily be worked through. They will likely be acted out in personal, societal, political, or religious agendas that substitute for facing the narcissistic abuse that even good-enough parents and childhood settings commonly involve. Later in life it is easier to blame society's institutions rather than to deidealize our parents.

Given the depth of the unconscious content of our neurotic symptoms, the task of working them through in therapy cannot be easy. Therapeutic work does not aim to correct a person's fate. It helps by uncovering the pain that results from scarring incidents, relationships, and introjections; by overcoming resistances to knowing how one's parents failed or became idealized in one's psychic imagination, and by initiating a process of therapeutic mourning of those failures, which leads to forgiveness for historical wounds that were introjected. In place of the internalized wounded self, more empathic self-objects or a resymbolized personal story must be constructed. When people resist calling such memories to the surface or when they block or deny wounds, both psychosomatic and neurotic illnesses follow.[53]

Freud saw unconsciously based resistance as one of the most significant factors in therapeutic work.[54] Find the stumbling block in the patient's memories, detect what has been forgotten, determine the significance of silences or of intellectual avoidances, and the analyst can begin to ferret out what is being unconsciously blocked. Both personal and societal amnesia, the unconscious repression of historical or background material, seems to protect the organism from the pain of memory and the pain of awareness. Since our conscious awareness of the cause of our plight is blocked, the only thing we have to go on is the unconscious information that links us to the sour grapes. So we taste them to see whether the fruit really is a bad as we remembered! Hence those who are ignorant of (or forget) history are condemned to repeat the same mistakes, over and over again.

How can the cycle be broken? How can members of a new generation escape the pattern and loosen the hold of the "fathers" upon their fate. Only by leaving the "paradise of preambivalent harmony," the place of our childish nostalgia for the days of immediacy and innocence.[55] Since mourning cannot take place in a vacuum, it must have an object and must respond to real situations. These are discovered in analytic therapy through a reexperiencing of the pain and grief that was, often long ago, stored away, repressed, shoved into the lowest, most secret level of our Pandora's box of the unconscious.

In therapy, through free association and the unique communion between analyst and analysand censored questions can be faced: "I always meant to ask them about that." "Why did she say that to me and smile the way she did?" "Why have I never had the courage to discover that about him?" What rises to consciousness in these questions is not just information (some of which is attainable, some not) but a new level of personal responsibility, often suppressed along with childhood memories or prohibitions. But none of this ever comes to the surface without causing distress. The mourner must begin to let go of the unconscious object and face life without the unconscious ball and chain affixed so long ago. Individuality emerges as the work of mourning brings freedom from introjected contempt for the weakness, impotence, and uncertainty in one's self and others.[56] Coming to terms with the past, which nothing and no one can change, means coming to terms not only with the traces of history lodged in the unconscious but also with our historical condition (our lives are conditioned by choices others have made). Avoiding ambiguity (the good and bad in parents, uncles, aunts, siblings, babysitters) so as to preserve an ideal past prevents us from being free of the past.

Therapy creates a real setting in which those wounds can be reopened vicariously. It is technically called work because of the attention to and the suspension of normal reference required to weep over the pain inflicted and begin to dress the wound with our newfound authority and strength. Psychic or spiritual healing is the result of therapeutic mourning; paradoxically the only portal through which healing comes is marked "woundedness." The ability to accept our vulnerability, imperfection, and introjected self-contempt and to accept, simultaneously, the bruised child within as loved in spite of its ugliness is the key that unlocks the door. Pain is never good in itself but only as transformed in the suffering of it, in our allowing ourselves access to our inner selves, bruised and pathetic though they be. It is a singular pathology of our competitive and self-contemptuous culture that pain today has become not the portal to truth but to victory. Athletes poison themselves to achieve the muscular edge, not in order to discover their unique potential or perform to their utmost, but to win. Strength has become an end in itself, not a means to health, happiness, or wholeness. Without the awareness of this paradox, the joy of winning is reduced to being merely "the mirror image of the fear of being a failure!"[57]

Our impoverished and enfeebled cultural ideal of strength has a hard time holding on to the paradox recorded in following mythopoetic dialogue.

Therefore, that I might not become too elated, a thorn in the flesh was given to me, an angel of Satan, to beat me, to keep me from being too elated. Three times I begged the Lord about this, that it might leave me, but he said to me, "My grace is sufficient for you, for power is made perfect in weakness." I will rather boast most gladly of my weaknesses, in order that the power of Christ may dwell with me. Therefore, I am content with weaknesses, with insults, hardships, persecutions, and constraints, for the sake of Christ; for when I am weak, then I am strong. (2 Cor 12:7b–10)

This startling corroboration of an ancient religious text by the practice of psychoanalysis says something about spiritual artistry and its time-lessness. The analytic cure as a work of mourning contradicts any philo-sophical or scientifically positivist remedy for our self-misunderstanding. Again, the truth of psychoanalysis, as it impacts on real people, "is closer to that of Greek tragedy than to that of modern physics" because it presumes that we "learn by suffering."[58]

But for this learning to be therapeutic or healing, we must look at the catalytic role played in both theory and practice by transference. Freud formulated the notion of transference on the basis of his 1880s work with hypnosis and his study of hysterical patients, who were helped by uncensored talking. Though he had abandoned hypnosis by the early 1890s, it revealed that the patient's attachment to the hypnotist created an energy field, as it were, that seemed to motivate reluctant patients. In papers written in 1912 and 1914, Freud spelled out the virtues and liabilities of the attachment, emphasizing that the analyst's role was to ally himself to the "normal" aspect of the patient's psyche and become a "dependable partner — the listener shocked by no revelation, bored at no repetition, censorious of no wickedness." Aware of the innuendo and suspicion that would surround such an intimate arrangement and of the possible misunderstanding of his statement that "it is essentially a cure through love," Freud undertook to warn analysts of the pit-falls and urge them to carry out psychoanalytic care and healing "in abstinence.... One must permit neediness and yearning to remain as forces favoring work and change, and one must beware of appeasing [patients] with surrogates."[59]

The therapist not only serves as interpreter of the text of the patient's symptoms, dreams, and reminiscences but, more important, bonds in an ambivalent way — the bond itself becomes a productive problem in the course of therapy. This occurs when the analyst's imagined re-lationship to the analysand (or vice versa) adds to resistance so that unconscious factors remaining hidden can be discovered and raised to consciousness. The popular caricature of analysis as paying for a friend, plus well-publicized complaints by the victims of bad analysis and actual malpractice, have contributed to skepticism about analysis. It requires both emotional ascesis and uncommon interpretative skills — not an easy or natural combination and one that is perhaps beyond many of its practitioners.

When the therapist properly becomes the patient's auxiliary ego, the work of mourning so crucial to freeing up unconscious memories and introjects can make real progress. Here the therapist's empathic receptivity to the patient's introjected contempt is key. It allows the patient's deeply rooted unconscious to emerge and be reexperienced as both present and past so that its content can be grieved over and its unseen power dissipated. Wounds relationally inflicted can be healed only in an equivalently relational context. Therapists needs to remain outside the relational traps that neurotics, given their repetitive behavior, set. But simultaneously they must remain in relationship and be savvy about what is occurring, able to interpret their own feelings as a "lost key to still invisible doors" (Freud's notion of unconscious reconstruction). If they can, and if the analysand cooperates, the cycle of contempt can be broken and mourning can lead to healing.[60]

The energy field of the analytical setting can alternately be seen as a transitional space where autonomy and dependency coexist, creating the subjective objectivity and objective subjectivity that serves as my model for all revelatory situations. In some of the same ways, group therapy, when it involves an intense experience of communion, creates a similar space where members enact surrogate relationships that are themselves heuristic fictions. Though artificial, these relationships enable participants to experience conflicts and connections that free them to deal with the real relationships in their lives. Transference occurs, then, across a spectrum from the more to less intense.

To my knowledge, Freud did not understand transference as reversing the effects of the superego's severity with the ego. But if the superego represents the introjection of parental-societal norms that censure the ego's expansiveness, then the therapist has a good chance, in the transferential relationship with the patient, to relieve much of the introjected harshness of the patient's superego figures. The pervasive disapproval, from failure to be adequately mirrored as a baby to unreasonable demands for achievement or parental inability to show approval — all basic narcissistic wounds — leave a person with an underdeveloped and bruised ego onto which neurotic symptoms attach like leeches. When a patient reexperiences vulnerability in the analytical situation and receives encouragement rather than censure, developing an empathic inner-object is more possible. To paraphrase Freud, we can say that therapy seeks to bring a patient to the point that "where the superego was, there ego shall be." People still acting out of an internalized need for the approval of their parental-societal introjects cannot assume responsibility for their own sense of themselves and for their own actions.

The analytical setting provides another benefit in its transferential significance and therapeutic value that is, frankly, spiritual in its full breadth. I suggest that it puts the patient in an actual transitional space that potentially creates the kinds of illusions we examined earlier. If the analyst practices ascesis in the relationship, the analysand can occupy a vulnerable space such as we occupied whenever we did not know where we stood with our parents, with loved ones, or with life itself. In those alienating spaces we don't change or grow; we get emotionally stuck in our own inner space. But in the analytic encounter, one regains the chance to inhabit the empty space of one's own self, to stage the nothingness that is feared the most, to face the nobody we're terrified we are, and to discover someone we have never known before. In trusting dependence on this nonparent, nonlover, we play at a relationship that, if artificial, is very intimate and real. In this illusory but actual experience one masters an absence (lets go of introjected self-contempt) and accepts a presence (that self-child growing at last to full stature, not out of duty but out of love).

But this rarely happens without tears, which are truly the gift the spiritual masters have said they are. The surrender and letting go involved in being self-forgetful enough to mourn one's pain does not represent defeat but triumph — an inner victory never before experienced. If the therapeutic setting provides this illusory space where the spiritual artistry of both the analyst and analysand meet, the grace of transference bestows an emotional maturity that allows one access to life as God wants to grant it. Now grace can get at nature and make some progress. Now religious faith can get really interesting.

Transference is not based merely on a personal or idiosyncratic experience open to a few who can afford therapy; rather, it is grounded more deeply in the structure of our creatureliness and is basic to the human condition. History witnesses to subtle as well as blatant examples of fascination with a person who holds or symbolizes power, along a spectrum from Francis of Assisi to Adolf Hitler. This uncanny phenomenon is more than a factor used in healing neurotics; it is a universal predisposition to merge with figures more powerful than ourselves. It reveals, says Becker, how false is the "lie of self-sufficiency, of free self-determinism, of independent judgment or choice." In daily life, it describes the transferring of our emotional attachments from parents to teachers, superiors, impressive personalities, idealized heroes, or rulers — or to dictators, revivalists, or sadists.[61] Transference explains the conduct of naturally shy people who become bold in crowds, the frenzied attempt to win against impossible odds, and even the "terrifying sadism of group activity." It uncovers why "participation in the group redistills everyday reality and gives it the aura of the sacred — just as, in childhood, play created a heightened reality."[62] If this sounds exaggerated, a little reflection on the dynamics between leaders and members of football teams, police assault teams, and combat units, or on the bonding of fraternity brothers, religious fanatics, or gang members, or still yet on the enthusiasm of opera fans, rock star groupies, or Catholics at a papal audience — all give evidence of the power of "the *magical heroic transformation* of the world and of oneself" at the heart of so much "transferential" activity in daily life. Yet transference does not explain genuine heroics at all; too often it involves cheap heroics, gained by merging one's real self and hiding one's own fears in the group that is "following the leader."[63]

So transference is an inherently ambivalent potential expressing a cowardly reflex at the same time as it also reveals a "reflex of the urge to heroism and self-unfolding" that testifies to our attraction to the good, the true, and the beautiful and our desire to merge with the All. Yet it is also responsible for our apartness, our uniqueness, our fear of absorption. Transference reveals that to be human means to balance singularity and union and that this ambivalence is the source of our natural guilt and inner dissatisfaction. Accordingly, it is both a universal neurosis and a marvelous talent, or what Martin Buber called our "imagining the real" and accepting from others the nourishment that our self-transcendence requires. As a universal passion, transference reveals that we need to project ourselves outward in what Becker called "creative projection" or "life-enhancing illusion," which only a religious understanding of the world allows.[64]

Rereading Freud — In Spite of Himself

Freud's pessimistic antitheology sought to humble the West's cultural and religious self-inflation and introduce it to unromantic realism. It coincided with Wittgenstein's critique of the attitude that saw the "self-communing self, radically independent of relationships" as the starting point for philosophical reflection.[65] Both men insisted that modern self-consciousness had no access to self-presence, self-knowledge, and the immediate presence to Being. Like some philosophers, naive believers were tempted to adopt forms of narcissistic wish-fulfillment when they did not subject their ideas and ideals to critical processes. Their critiques of immediate self-consciousness affect the way we look at objects as well. No more than the *self, things* are not so simple as they once seemed. In psychoanalytic terms, objects in the world are first of all objects of desire. We know the objective world first as an extension of ourselves, then as projections of something of the self that flavors our experience of the world and builds into our most "objective" view of the world an element of indeterminacy that can never be wholly eliminated. From the beginning of life, subject and object are involved in an interactive dynamic that clearly conditions the way that we come to know what we know of ourselves and the world. This psychodynamic nuance in our idea of how we know does not necessarily lead to skepticism but it does insist on the role of the subject in the object's being known. We know the world by means of heuristic tools that allow us to approximate the impact of the objective world on the knowing subject. We have no access to an impersonal, objective representation of the world totally separate from the conditions of how we know it.

This chastened view of the way we know reality draws our attention again to a second loss of immediacy beyond humanity's loss of immediacy to God (which the mythopoetic worldview expressed), namely, our subsequent loss of immediate self-awareness. The Enlightenment's turn to the subject had outcomes different from what most of its heroes, Freud included, would have expected.[66] For in the face of our pretensions that our conscious selves, efforts, desires, intentions, interactions, and thoughts have clear and obvious meanings, the discovery of unconscious elements of awareness proclaims that things are not so obvious. Immediately, we know less than we think we do about ourselves and about the world.

Though Freud sought to establish psychoanalysis as a hard science, it is better categorized as a hermeneutical or interpretive science (more like history than physics) because it involves itself in the "deciphering of a hidden meaning in an apparent meaning."[67] Language, when it is called upon to express our hidden, unconscious depths cannot denote precisely what we are thinking or feeling. It connotes, in metaphorical and symbolic ways, a deeper and more complex reality that cannot be objectified. Early in his career, Freud called his therapeutic efforts a "talking cure" because freely associated words, representing ideas or affects, were the first entrance he found into unconscious reality (dreams came second). The only access to repressed material is our expression (verbally and otherwise) of symptoms, introjects, revived repressions, and the images that well up from our unconscious in dreams. This means that psychoanalysis is a work of interpretation; it seeks to heal through a recovery of split-off symbols that make up the distorted text of a person's life. In the presence of the analyst, who helps interpret the meaning of these traces of the past and whose empathy allows them to be worked through in the place of their unconscious acting out, the analysand can resymbolize the meaning of events or memories in a new, though humbled, text of his or her life. The past and its traces cannot be changed; but they can cease to control the present if they are raised to consciousness, mourned fully, and reunderstood as part of a chastened self-consciousness, devoid of the crippling neurosis or partialization that had seemed so necessary to stay alive.

As a mode of interpreting the text of a human life, psychoanalysis moved away from Freud's early goal of scientifically mapping the brain, a task in which neurology has made great strides since the great doctor left the lab. Accordingly, we have seen that neurosis, the unconscious, narcissism, the id, ego, and superego, the Oedipal complex, and repression are all capable of denoting certain clinical states or operations — but as clinical definitions they do not name discrete *things*. They symbolize elements of the human condition, complexities in human relations, and conditions of the body-mind-soul that cannot be examined under a microscope, but are real in their impact and effects. Practitioners of the science (*logos*) of psychoanalysis must be versed in theory, but their successful practice demands that they develop unmeasurable skills like empathy, intuition, and trustfulness; they must be spiritual artists capable of interpreting *mythos*. Despite advances in the diagnosis and treatment of neurological and chemical disorders (no longer lumped together with emotional disorders as mental illness) psychoanalysis is not likely to be replaced by physicians prescribing pills. It treats not disease, but humanity's wounded desire.

By revealing how thoroughly psychosomatic are our knowledge, our will, our love, and our human predicament, psychoanalysis has given both its practitioners and our broader culture a valuable set of tools. While not complete in themselves, they have proven remarkably adaptable, allowing us to map more accurately than naive conceptualizations ever made possible moral intentionality, the normal spectrum of human sexual activity, the paradox of bodiliness, the unconscious impact of parenting, the ambiguity of cultural (and some religious) truths, the source of our symbolic potential, and the capacity for the healthy repressions by which, *pace* Freud, even simple tailors, and not just inhibited saints, may find some happiness in life.

But for most of us this occurs only after a journey in which our resymbolized or reintegrated self-consciousness has to overcome our loss of innocence, a loss now revealed as liberating, a condition for growth. But our guilt in the face of lost innocence does not stem from Freud's strange mythology of the murder of the primal father and its repetition in the murder of Moses or in the homicide-crucifixion of Jesus. To account for why human beings feel guilty about themselves it makes no sense to replace the enduring mythopoetic narrative of Genesis 2– 3 with Freud's alternative and unsatisfying mythology. But it helps to recognize that when Freud replaced old mythopoetic symbols with new "scientific" ones, he showed that the Enlightenment's project to derive certainty from the self-manifestation of clear and distinct ideas was essentially an adolescent reach for an unambivalent certitude.[68] Once we can humbly admit that, we can surrender both precritical innocence and critical willfulness and advance, humbled and chastened, toward genuine maturity.

Bibliographical Essay

In addition to Ernest Becker's *Denial of Death* (New York: Free Press, 1973), noted above, I have used in my rereading of Freud for our post-critical settings W. W. Meissner, S.J., M.D., *Psychoanalysis and Religious Experience* (New Haven: Yale University Press, 1984). A training and supervisory analyst at the Boston Psychoanalytic Institute and University Professor of Psychoanalysis at Boston College, Meissner is the author, most recently, of *Ignatius of Loyola: The Psychology of a Saint* (New Haven: Yale University Press, 1992). I have also relied on G. G. May's *Will and Spirit: A Contemplative Psychology* (San Francisco: Harper & Row, 1982) and *Addiction and Grace* (San Francisco: Harper & Row, 1988). I have benefited from the full-length studies of Paul Ricoeur, *Freud and Philosophy: An Essay on Interpretation* (New Haven: Yale University Press, 1970) and of Peter Gay, *Freud: A Life for Our Time* (New York: W. W. Norton, 1988). Gay writes that "Ricoeur's Freud is not my Freud" (745) but provides no details about his objections. Another recent rereading of the impact of Freud's Jewishness comes from Yosef Hayim Yerushalmi (*Freud's Moses: Judaism Terminable and Interminable* [New Haven: Yale University Press, 1991], 90), who claims that Freud fruitfully applied psychoanalytic concepts to the relationship between Judaism and Christianity. Historical Christian anti-Semitism rests upon a repressed and denied fratricidal guilt of "having usurped the birthright of which Christianity is never completely secure so long as the Jews, obstinately refusing to acknowledge the usurpation, remain a witness and a reproach" (93–94).

Helpful in reappropriating Freud beyond his own instinctualism have been Alice Miller's *The Drama of the Gifted Child: The Search for the True Self* (New York: Basic Books, 1981) and *Thou Shalt Not Be Aware: Society's Betrayal of the Child* (New York: New American Library, 1986); Karen Horney's *New Ways in Psychoanalysis* (New York: W. W. Norton, 1939); Arno Gruen's *The Betrayal of the Self: The Fear of Autonomy in Men and Women* (New York: Grove Press, 1986); and works by Erik Erikson, including *Identity, Youth and Crisis* (New York: W. W. Norton, 1968) and *Identity and the Life Cycle* (New York: W. W. Norton, 1980).

Chapter 6

Reweaving *Mythos* and *Logos*

Characteristics of Maturity

Autonomy and Individuation

Maturity lies beyond chronological adulthood. It is a state of spiritual self- and other-awareness reached "only by a fortunate few."[1] Similarly, religious adulthood follows earlier stages of faith awareness only with a struggle. In the late twentieth century, the average religious person resembles a hapless adolescent in the throes of losing immediacy and innocence, unsure how and where to move next. Contemporary religious culture, even when it is interested in balancing its mythopoetic heritage and modern critical rationality, works out uneasy compromises between them or keeps them segregated. Some religious groups (ultra-orthodox Jews, Mormons, some fundamentalist Christians) seem to live a bifurcated existence: primary naivete is reserved to private experience and critical rationality flourishes publicly. But such resolutions of the wrenching tension between two internal worlds can only endure within subcultures. Within the broader culture, the mythopoetic is banished to the realms of entertainment (science fiction, horror films, fantasy epics) and scientific thinking goes unquestioned.

Whereas a few hybrids like Scientology merge scientific rationality with religion, more and more the heirs of the Enlightenment and the up-holders of traditional religious faith square off and battle each other in fruitless culture wars. Modern though we are, we have come up short of maturity, lacking adequate models to resolve this crisis in our cultural and religious development. Postcritical religious maturity will be possible only when we come to terms with the stark fate of modernity and move beyond our losses by incorporating them into our religious worldview.[2]

Having begun a journey away from the parental/mythopoetic matrix, every individual and every interpreter encounters the risks of emancipation, the twin vicissitudes of too much possibility or too much necessity. The first threatens to inflate the emerging ego with grandiose schemes for enhancing its own significance. It bends desire back around on the self, making all and sundry pay homage to its need for nourishment. Respecting no boundaries in its quest for significance, it consumes everything within its reach. Alternately, too much necessity blocks progress because fate, the system, one's past, a confederacy of dunces, or any number of oppositional forces are experienced as overwhelming. Faced with real or imagined opposition, the schizophrenic (at the end of this spectrum) revolts against official reality and takes the exit of severe dysfunction or, tragically, sees necessity as death and chooses suicide.

So natural are these extremes that adolescents most often overcompensate for conscious or unconscious weaknesses by investing in a one-sided *persona.* Stressing their best suit — either intellect or affectivity — they rarely develop different sides of their personalities simultaneously. Within bounds, these one-sided developments are correctable later when real individuation begins. Paradoxically, adolescent emotional autonomy, though involving separation and threatening the emerging individual with isolation, establishes the foundations for genuine individuation. In turn, the individuated person is most capable of achieving interpersonal communion and participating in a community. Individuation has little in common with the crippling individualism that has made mutuality so difficult in modern Western societies. As the task and the goal of personal maturity, individuation occurs when adults are born again and become like little children — ancient images, not of childish dependence but of spiritual maturation. With this second birth comes a "detached concern with life itself, in the face of death itself," which yields the wisdom about things that is most characteristic of real maturity and quite different from Freud's resigned stoicism.[3]

Individuation is different from individualism, or the self in its separateness. Positivist psychology often seeks to put the self or the ego at the helm, improving on the natural expansiveness of the relatively healthy person's ego and stressing the human potential that makes life and its problems manageable. Psychology as a technique guaranteeing mastery caters to the subjectivism that is responsible for Western culture's crisis of communal identity. In fact, no encounter is more central to our self-understanding than the encounter between an older understanding of the *psyche* as soul and its modern sense as self. If the two understandings are mutually exclusive, then autonomy can only represent a revolt against the creator and individuation must become willful solipsism. In other words, despite our best efforts we would be trapped, as Freud himself ironically concluded, with compulsively repeating the original sin for which we were once expelled from paradise, our only redemption being further rebellion.

But the historic encounter between soul and self does not require their opposition. For when the developing ego (the conscious part of maturing awareness) risks the isolation of the desert (the place of testing) for the sake of maturity, it necessarily risks being its own, autonomous self, responsible for knowing its own inner states. But that is not where development ends. The ego must also risk the deeper solitude of the return journey home — the fuller significance of the stage of self-realization that I have introduced under the figure of individuation or spiritual maturity. Achieving autonomy (emotional independence, or the journey "out") allows the psyche to gain a capacity for the specifically human goals of communion and community. Achieving individuation (affective communion, the journey "in") allows the person to undertake the rarer goal of full integration and communion with God. In this framework, the psyche as soul (*anima*) corresponds to the earlier, indeed primitive, mythopoetic (theological) image of the self coming forth from its nondifferentiated matrix ("in the image and likeness of God"); the psychological self (*animus*) corresponds to a critical and anthropological view of the self as human creature (differentiating itself even from the rest of creation). Both are stages of a journey, each with its own validity. Their reintegration into a mature whole will allow us to overcome their perceived opposition and discover something deeper about the full spiritual capacity of the *psyche*.[4]

Without autonomy and full individuation, any notion of mature faith is illusory. Without a sense of separation and autonomy, a person cannot escape the temptation to reachieve a childish symbiosis or primal union with God that respects neither the complete otherness of God or one's own unique identity as not-God.[5] The grace of midlife spiritual crisis (a crucial time for autonomy to become thoroughly individuating) is that it causes the breakdown of one's well-planned spiritual project and sends one back to the drawing board. While naive believers dread the "prospect of a nonbenevolent and nonprotective God," anyone desiring a real relationship with God must endure some experience of genuine separateness. Identification without secure separation is dangerous and disrespectful both of creator and creature.[6]

Persons who lack autonomy cannot properly engage in transferences as these occur at stages in the deepening of friendships, mentor relationships, and mutual love. If their lack of autonomy stems from an incomplete separation from a parent (with whom they are still emotionally merged), they will never be able to invest anything but diffuse emotional energy in relationships that threaten the primal matrix. They may be able for a time to borrow some feelings as if against a prior investment, but these are usually called back with interest and the new venture collapses. Persons in the grip of an unresolved relationship with a deceased parent or spouse can suffer the same fate, if they have never emotionally separated. They cannot invest themselves in any relationships in political society or care for anyone who does not provide care for them.

In terms of object-relations theory, such individuals remain confused about the essential subject-object differences at the heart of stable relationships and sometimes even about society's distinction between mine and thine. Children or adults with compulsive acquisitive tendencies — either kleptomaniacs like compulsive shoplifters or emotional sponges who soak up loose feelings when they walk into a room — suffer from an inadequate sense of their own separateness. They have never developed an ability to invest in transitional objects, to project themselves meaningfully into the world around them, or to project meaning upon the in-between or illusory aspects of experience where subjects and objects overlap. Having trouble with healthy illusion, with imagining themselves securely as part of the world, they also lack a capacity for symbols. They rarely use or appreciate metaphor and are suspicious of any except literal meanings, often suspecting that jokes told in their presence might be about them because anything not sufficiently "out there" and obviously distant from them just might be "in here" and about them!

To the extent that separation of the self from one's primary-care matrix involves loss, it is the absolute presupposition and foundation for reintegration. Without developing personal autonomy and working at individuation, the individual cannot expect to develop any self that is worth valuing or loving. With no valuable self, the whole world of culture and religion will have no worth or meaning or will be acquired or consumed for its own sake, a substitute for interiority. Alienation from one's self leads to the search for replacement figures, generally one-dimensional and slick, like the hollow creations of Hollywood and TV-land, whose predictable emotional crises, sexual adventures, and superhuman feats give people a sense of participating in life on the edge when in reality they're couch potatoes. Alternately people today merge with sports heroes, our culture's best incarnations of the *puer aeternus,* professional Peter Pans who will never grow up. In all too many cases, these stars of stage, screen, and stadium are themselves victims of their own and others' hypertrophied needs and suffer tremendous personal emptiness. Since no amount of money or stardom can fill an internal void, many turn to drugs, promiscuity, or mystical endeavors. Having only these hollow transference figures to relate with, individuals incapable of separation or autonomy have little chance of knowing themselves, their fellows, or God except as wish-fulfillment.

Attachment and Detachment

Attachment names a basic component of desire that allows humans, from infancy, to include themselves in a network of relations that makes up their world properly speaking. Referring to what Freud called cathexis minus his biological determinism, attachment is the way we make our desire count, the effective glue of our social relationships. However, desire (as *cupiditas*) tends to double back on itself and become almost attachment to attachment — an addiction to neediness. Attachment then becomes full-blown lust, a determining factor in social injustice as well as in private psychological suffering and in the production of violence. Just as young children rage when their desire is frustrated, so adults who are attached to a particular self-image or an insecure national self-definition violently react when challenged. Similarly, racial prejudice plays on ideologies of attachment to "our own kind" of people. The kind of anger that cuts off one's own nose to spite one's face can also be said to come, not from the frustration of actual needs, but from our immature attachment to a particular solution or outcome of a conflict. On a more intellectually sophisticated but no less immature level, ideologues of all stripes become so attached to their own certainty of analysis that they will countenance great suffering (on the part of others) rather than yield their point or doubt the world-image to which they are neurotically attached.

Extreme attachments to persons, ideas, or objects represent neurotic partializations and so constitute the basis of fetishes. All of us employ fetishes of one kind or other, but it might be helpful to understand them in the light of early attachment behavior that has not been outgrown. In particular, immature attachment behavior is present in the way religious doctrines as well as devotional objects and practices can devolve into fetishes from the fear of losing the source of good one feels is necessary for security. When an ideological mentality is wedded to fetishization, the combination makes for fanatical behavior that, again, will impose any amount of suffering rather than accept other perspectives or allow what is perceived as deviant behavior. Theologians in particular are particularly prone to cathecting words and formulas or becoming attached to them inordinately. Theology is principally kataphatic or expressive about its object. Yet as mature theologians have comprehended, the apophatic corrective of mystical religious experience exposes theological systems as inadequate to express the truth of the unseen God adequately.[7]

Liberation from neurotic attachment occurs through detachment, though in Christian piety detachment has often been dualistically conceived, approximating Stoic *apatheia* (lack of emotional movement) if not Manichean disdain for the flesh — freedom *from* rather than freedom *for*. However, because the characteristics of maturity relate as asymmetrical pairs, not dualistic opposites, detachment as a personal goal and a hermeneutical model of faith affirmation is not the reverse of attachment but its accomplishment on another plane, a capacity for loving self-forgetfulness. But to be maturely self-forgetful rather than neurotically self-effacing, a person must seek to allow desire to pass over into God, our source and end. This spiritual truth can be lived by mature human beings capable of genuinely letting go of the need to be right, to be approved or vindicated by others.

Self-forgetfulness allows us, even if we only taste it now and then, to take ourselves less seriously and God more so. It gives the mature individual an ability to play with grace and confidence, to develop a capacity for healthy illusion, to risk mythopoetic formulations that invite participation in the mystery rather than compel begrudging obedience to imposed demands. It allows mature individuals to see the insecurities at work in others as similar chapters of the same ego-oriented drama once acted out on one's own stage. This allows one to understand the part one is being asked to play in relational dramas and to switch roles so as to avoid confrontation, defuse a crisis, or give the last act a different ending. Surely Jesus meant as much when he propounded nonviolent solutions to crises caused by personal attack, coercive litigation, and enemy occupation (Matt 5:38–48). Turning the other cheek, giving your shirt as well, walking the extra mile are prescriptions almost bordering on buffoonery that can be carried out only by a person self-forgetful enough to play the fool. They are also serious, subversive acts capable of transforming violent situations. Only one who stays cool and detached under pressure can respond as Jesus taught; they are not prescriptions for provoking adversaries to greater violence. Instead, as the legitimate foolishness of nonviolent self-forgetfulness, such strategies seek to redeem not only the drama but all the players in it.

Without self-forgetfulness, a genuine capacity for illusion is not possible. To the ideologue, truth is either completely objective or totally subjective, not the creative interplay of both. The world is either the companion of the flesh and the devil, or it is all-there-is, never the playground of God's first friend, Lady Wisdom. Literalistic, philosophically dualistic, and moralistic religious awareness is always either/or about us and them, flesh and spirit, God and humanity, male and female, child and adult; it rarely sees the Incarnation as a revelation about both elements in these asymmetrical pairs. We don't always have to choose one or the other. Hence maturity does not involve abandoning everything childhood was about but rather rediscovering and reintegrating the childlike qualities of playfulness (the original workshop of personal and spiritual integration) with the best of our critical capacities in a postambivalent garden where mature children of God can disport themselves.

Overcoming Narcissism

The significance of primary narcissism in early life and the prevalence of its secondary derivatives in neurotic disorders make it clear that maturity must deal with the problems narcissism poses for the human condition. Because narcissistic vulnerabilities are a universal human condition, so easily introjected to become resident insecurities, the issue of self-esteem lies close to the heart of maturity, especially as this involves our interaction with authority at all stages of life. People for whom grandiosity or self-inflation remains a response to the threats life poses will act out their recrudescent narcissistic needs in sexual excess, addiction, or more civilized forms of self-aggrandizement (cornering the junk-bond market on Wall Street) to guarantee attention and a powerful sense of self.

After childhood, narcissistic emotional involvement with others arises from need rather than desire; this makes the narcissist's love not a giving but a taking. Receiving love does not lead to gratitude but to fueling the narcissist's appetite for more. Narcissists find it hard to care for children because they become rivals for the available attention. In general they will react to authority ambivalently, either cathecting the institutions of religion and culture as a way to bolster their own damaged self-esteem or regarding them as oppressive and neglectful intrusions on their individual welfare.[8] Not even the attention of everyone in the room will fill the abyss of need in the narcissistically wounded person, and the failure of life, society, or loved ones to fulfill that need leads to monumental depression, from which the narcissist hides in increasingly grandiose scenarios. History is full of the evidence of the tragic lengths to which narcissistic leaders and their blinded followers will go and the pain they will inflict in the name of patriotism, group loyalty, or religious truth.

How can a mature person overcome the narcissistic wounds that life has dealt and overcome the addiction to neediness that lies behind so much personal and political ambition? Healing of narcissistic trauma and recovery from it comes through mourning. Only by facing the wounds of childhood and the residue of vulnerability they leave behind can a person be freed from the introjected contempt that fuel the narcissist's defenses. With mourning comes a renewed sense of wholeness despite woundedness as the mature person receives life again as a gift. The acceptance of one's damaged but now restored self has enormous potential for helping a person overcome expressions of secondary narcissism. On the one hand, it accepts no human parent as the agent of the rebirth, but God the Giver. On the other, it helps us reparent ourselves in a way more appropriate to actual, ongoing human needs. Then the love others have for us can sink in and take the place of the introjects that make so many people needy their whole lives long.

The reborn or, in William James's terminology, the "twice-born" achieve new levels of understanding and a patience for ambiguity (a capacity for illusion). Once-born narcissistic personalities wedded to inflexible value systems have problems with a pluralistic approach to religion or culture. They feel constrained to punish anyone whose convictions violate their need for their own group, ideology, or church to be certainly correct. St. Alphonsus Liguori was expelled from the religious order he founded because his continuing (mature) development as a religious teacher no longer fit the far less flexible standards of his younger followers. Their grasp of truth had become so absolute that even their founder no longer fit their need to be secure in their identity as religious. The test of the mature is the way they respond to the charges and accusations of their humorless and self-righteous persecutors, who normally affirm that they are actually "offering worship to God" (John 16:2). Because maturity allows one to detach from the need to belong and to be right, authority can never adequately reside in once-born institutional or political affiliations. Mature believers find authorization in their journey through woundedness to the source of all healing and all authority.[9]

Reintegration

Individuation is not a product of our willful effort to create a more functional and socially acceptable self, but a rerooting of the autonomous *ego* in the givenness of life. One approaches it not directly, but as if circumambulating the center — a God-given self — slowly gathering in what was formerly scattered.[10] Just as the apocalyptic writers saw the final shape of things (*Endzeit*) as the reappearance of the prealienated shape of the world (*Urzeit*), so every person seeking full maturity comes back around to an encounter with a chastened but fuller self. This means that we are in a long process involving both *dis*-covery and *re*-covery. Much as we change over the course of a life, we are who we always were, if in an unrealized fashion. Our end is also our beginning, both because we are dust and unto dust we return and because our source is also our destination, as Augustine wrote: "You have made us to be *toward* Yourself, O Lord, and our hearts are restless until they rest in You."[11]

Full maturity for the human person, then, involves a reintegration of what earlier seem to be oppositional realities. As this affects Western religion, we saw that Enlightenment autonomy was achieved at the price of further splitting apart objective and subjective, intellectual and imaginative, rational and irrational, realism and idealism, scientific and mythopoetic, public and private, capital and labor — and seeing them oppositionally. To these contrarieties can be added activity and passivity, masculine and feminine, strength and weakness. It is not unfair to say that in modern Western culture (secular or religious), we have honored objectivity, intellectuality, rationality, realism, science, masculinity, activity, and strength to the detriment of subjectivity (except as individuality), imagination, irrationality, idealism, the mythopoetic, the feminine, passivity, and weakness.[12] Because these pairs are seen as oppositional, it seems more profitable to exploit their differences and promote adversarial understandings of them. As a result, a maturity based on reintegrating oppositional tendencies, personally or culturally, will not be easy to achieve. It will require more than merely juxtaposing them or trading off their different capacities. Reintegration, like being born again, involves real change, a shifting synthesis of asymmetrical elements that has no predetermined or final shape.

Basic to this stage of maturity, then, is the conviction that opposites not only attract but should eventually coinhere. Spiritual theology refers to this as the *coincidentia oppositorum*, the union of opposites by which, at a high level of integration, truth is revealed in paradox and contrarieties, rather than collapsed unities. Maturity lies beyond our ordinary perception in the same way that God is revealed beyond both affirmation and negation (through the coinherence of the kataphatic and apophatic, the *via positiva* and the *via negativa,* the way of knowing and of not-knowing).[13] Positive language about belief in God must be reintegrated, all along life's way, with the experience of emptying silence; only thus can belief be doxology rather than ideology.

Analogously, for reintegration to occur, the conscious and unconscious elements of the self must meet and remeet so as to be rewoven into a whole fabric. All through life, we encounter and profit from "others" or opposites, spouse, friends, mentors, or the like. These engagements help us overcome the hypertrophied autonomy we developed in order to break from the parental matrix. But beyond these personal relations, we reintegrate ourselves by coming to terms with our "shadow" side.[14] If the dark side of the self has been hiding repressed (introjected) trauma or abuse, reintegration will be accompanied first by anger and then by mourning, though this is often resisted mightily. With the right kind of therapeutic support, the defensive, bitter, and conscious self will be able to recognize its partner in the damaged and ashamed unconscious. In reweaving them together, people discover an empathic capacity that had always eluded them, despite all their willful efforts at personal improvement.

These theological and personal analogies can now be brought to bear on the major problematic of this work: that Enlightenment rationalism has been unable to bring about a mature religious or cultural product because it has been unable to come to terms with its shadow side. In disdaining the imaginative, mythopoetic, idealist, feminine, and unconscious elements of religion and culture and preferring only the rational, scientific, realist, masculine, and conscious, Western society remains stuck at an impasse of its own willful making. Our religious culture has been handicapped by equivalent imbalances in which either the rational or the affective elements of faith affirmation have been prized, not an integrated model that subsumes them both. We have only begun, in this century, to comprehend how the textuality of scripture provides us with a bridge across the "ugly, wide ditch" of history that divides our modern selves from our mythic history. In the canonical books the normative images and symbols at the basis of premodern Judaism and Christianity (as well as much of Islam) enshrine the mythopoetic and unconscious roots of faith affirmation. If we can learn to reintegrate these images and symbols with our rational, scientific, and historical consciousness, we may find a way to a mature religious culture beyond the impasse.

Postcritical Maturity

The Bible as Canon

As we saw at the end of chapter 3, twentieth-century scholars have recognized that older antinomies (scripture or tradition, reason or revelation, *logos* or *mythos*) were no longer adequate for appropriating the full textuality of the Bible. This truth came home to the Roman Catholic Church as the outcome of a skirmish that was a watershed in the history of the Second Vatican Council. The preparatory commission had prepared a schema called "On the Two Fonts of Revelation" in order to set off Catholic doctrine from the Protestant position of scripture alone (*sola scriptura*). The old battle was to be rejoined.[15] But the council rejected the commission's antagonistic statement. Three years later it promulgated *Dei Verbum,* the Dogmatic Constitution on Divine Revelation. Refusing post-Tridentine polemics, *Dei Verbum* sought to integrate the Catholic understanding of tradition and of scripture by grounding *both* in the earliest apostolic preaching (8). The constitution did not solve all the problems exercising nascent Catholic biblical scholarship, but it created a new opening for Catholics interested in recovering their scriptural heritage and ending the defensiveness of the previous era.

The most startling position in Vatican II's teaching on divine revelation, especially given its Latin title, was its avoidance of the simple identification of the Bible and the Word of God. According to *Dei Verbum,* the gift of revelation is prior to the written word; it is the event of God's self-communication "realized by deeds and words" (2), chief among which is the event of Christ, "the eternal Word" (4). The "transmission of divine revelation" is said to occur through the apostolic preaching, through the committing of the message of salvation to writing, and through sacred tradition, which is imaged as the apostles "handing over their own teaching role" to their successor bishops (7, quoting Irenaeus). Yet tradition is not a separate body of teaching. Rather, it is defined as an activity that

develops in the Church with the help of the Holy Spirit...through the contemplation and study made by believers...through the intimate understanding of the spiritual things that they experience, and through the preaching of those who have received through episcopal succession the sure gift of truth. (8)

Tradition and scripture, then, "form one deposit of the word of God," whose interpretation is carried on by the "living teaching office of the Church" (10).

In later chapters, I will take up the question of the magisterium, or teaching office. Here I wish to present the implications of Vatican II's teaching for the question at the heart of this inquiry: "how [we] bridge the gap between biblical meanings and contemporary cultural categories of thought."[16] The council's teaching on the role of the Bible in Catholic faith, which broke through the historical Catholic/Protestant impasse traced above, can overcome the mythopoetic/critical impasse as well. For if tradition is a varied activity that combines contemplation, study, experience of spiritual things, and biblical preaching, it requires methods by which both critical-technical and intuitive-imaginative aspects of traditioning can be woven together. For neither criticism nor charismatic inspiration (of individuals or of hierarchies) can by itself be adequate to what is required.

My sketching out of a method for reintegrating criticism and imagination (*logos* and *mythos*) is based on *canonical hermeneutics* as developed by James A. Sanders, author of the seminal work *Torah and Canon*.[17]

According to the Catholic scholar Fr. Dominique Barthélemy, Sanders best reconciles criticism with canon (the Bible as the church's book) because he details the ways in which tradition ("the holy Scriptures... actualized in the Church," 8) is critically accomplished.[18] Sanders defines canonical hermeneutics as the quest for

a midpoint between the hermeneutical task of the historical-critical method, which seeks original biblical meanings, and the hermeneutical task of spanning the gap between those recovered meanings and modern cultural systems of meaning.[19]

Sanders attempts to rehabilitate the authority of the scriptures (as revelatory) from *within*, to demonstrate that the Bible is canonical not merely as an "authoritative collection of books" but, more basically, as the actual record of a long "process that started way back with the first case of repetition long before Scripture was fully penned [and] continues today in the believing communities that find their identity in it, as well as indications for their life styles."[20]

Sanders originally came to this recognition by tracking a number of critical investigations demonstrating that canon (as a dynamic lying behind the Bible) had its own history. First he investigated the inner dynamics of the way the Torah was shaped as "ancient contributors and communities bridged gaps between earlier authoritative traditions, and wisdom, and their own time and contexts." What later became the Bible had canonical content, not because its earlier oral and written collections provided timeless doctrine, but because its traditions functioned authoritatively over time, providing "ever new generations with faith (identity) and direction for life (obedience)."[21] The stable elements of the story were sufficiently adaptable (or labile) in new circumstances to allow for growth to take place while continuity was also preserved. Only after the writings had existed over time and been reshaped by the vicissitudes of Israel's history, providing answers to the various challenges to the people's historical identity, did they begin to take on an invariable shape that is the common sense of "canon." Hence, the Bible as canon is both an end of one process (scripture) and the beginning of another (its ongoing interpretation, or tradition).

Sanders next investigated the transmission of the text of the Hebrew scriptures (including their translation into Greek in the Septuagint). He found that as the texts themselves became fixed and authoritative, they began to be understood as "oracles, signs, riddles, as well as story." As a result, because the text (not just the story) was now the stable element, it became adaptable by being interpreted in different settings, either by the application of rabbinic rules or through patristic allegorization.

Both historical and textual investigation, then, indicated that over the centuries "the very ontology of scripture had changed from sacred story to sacred text as [had] the fundamental understanding of its inspiration or authority."[22] In other words, the very notion of canon has evolved. Beginning with oral traditions that became written versions, through triumph and disasters and a process of trial and error, the Bible reached a final stage in which certain texts were canonized because they had been existentially verified in the long history of Israel and in the catalyst of the early Christian struggle over the identity of Christ.[23]

At the beginning of the critical period, Sanders claims, the history of the canon was ignored, and the concept of canon was narrowed; as a result scholars lost "sight of why those communities had canonized the text in the first place."[24] Today we recognize that the Bible represents a canonized dialogue between memory (stable tradition) and ongoing faith life (its adaptable uses). The Bible as canon is more than a collection of literary works; as a complex intertext, it is itself a metaphor productive of great artistic and religious indeterminacy. As both *logos* (written traces of the past) and *mythos* (symbolic of more than itself) it has meaning. The Bible, then, must be read in a way that fosters the mutual relationship of stable canon and labile community.

Some hermeneutical implications of canon

1. By accepting the canon of scripture as a starting point, we involve ourselves in a continuing historical process that is different only in degree, not kind, from the traditioning activity at the roots of the Bible-as-canon. By conducting a dialogue or conversation with the canon of scripture (a less-one sided image than "interpretation" as if the whole

were inert matter and we could have at it with a scalpel), we keep the Bible out of the museum and it keeps us, as a community of faith, out of the dustbin of history. The past of the tradition and the present of believing coinhere through the dynamics of canon.[25]

2. This means that scripture and tradition are and always have been asymmetrical pairs that cannot be collapsed into a single principle of revelation. The Bible, even though understood at one time to be composed of ahistorical, oracular utterances, actually constitutes a relatively pluralistic and ambiguous body of literature. Its contents stem from such different contexts that it even confidently contradicts itself. The biblical canon, then, bestows upon the church of every age stable, but also fluid, paradigms "for God's work from creation through re-creation out of which we may construct paradigms for our own works."[26] The canon and its ongoing interpretation ("tradition") also mutually coinhere and need to be reintegrated as a matter not merely of style but of adequate truth.

3. The Bible-as-canon because of its intertextual make-up consistently presents a "theocentric, monotheizing hermeneutic, that is, the focus is on what the One God of All has done in given human situations and then what God would yet do in another."[27] By this Sanders means that despite the various crises that challenged their religious identity, the Bible's formers continued to resist polytheism in all its popular forms. The same God who called Abraham from Ur of the Chaldees led Israel into Egypt, brought them up "with a mighty hand and an outstretched arm," and sent them into captivity, but then redeemed Zion as well. God the Redeemer could also be known by his works, and even when this was "firstborn" Lady Wisdom, the Lord was still "Lord alone." In New Testament terms, the same God and Father "who did not spare his own beloved Son" from the cross also "did not let [his] holy one undergo corruption" and so "exalted him high above every sovereignty, authority and power." *Ehad hu*, God is One (Deut 6:4), the message embedded in the canonical literature, was as relevant in the struggle against ancient polytheism as it has been against later dualistic and fragmentizing portraits so inherent in Western modes of thinking. The temptation to idolatry and polytheism, which apportions and divides God from God, is the same temptation that I have called partialization. Because the totality of reality can be so overwhelming, we are tempted to bite off only as much as we can digest and create fetishes to make it less overwhelming.[28] The Bible, however, continues to insist that divine justice is one, though composed of tensive operations. For just as it is not unjust for God to proclaim, "I will have mercy on whom I have mercy, and I will have compassion on whom I have compassion" (Exod 33:19 in Rom 9:14–15), so God's justice reaches its purpose when we recognize that "there is no distinction between Jew

and Greek; the same Lord is Lord of all and is generous to all who call on him" (Rom. 10:12).

4. This principle of the coinherence of justice and mercy is most explicitly celebrated in the Bible by what Sanders calls the Bible's "most common theologoumenon" — that God's grace works in and through human sinfulness (*errore hominum providentia divina*). He affirms that God's prevenient grace (which anticipates us at every step and encompasses our missteps) can be said to underlie some three-quarters of biblical literature. It is because this scandal is so central that the canon could preserve the paradox that salvation occurs as much through unexpected rescues as through destructive historical events. This means that God's grace and God's judgment also mutually coinhere. God is never *our* God (the redeemer) to the exclusion of God's being the creator of all flesh. Canonical hermeneutics demands that communities that take their identity from the Bible must discern that identity afresh: Is God our savior or our judge in the present? Does God remain *our* God even in the face of disaster? How is it that God will raise up a people after this storm passes? Providence, from a canonical perspective, does not presume that everything that happens happens by God's "will and pleasure." Rather, it implicates God in the role of cosufferer with his people, even as God is the horizon of their hope.

5. Though the traditions of creation and salvation appear in tension, the general rule Sanders upholds is that "one must read the Bible theologically before reading it morally." What stands at the center of the revelation is what God is doing to create and save, but our fetish is often like that of the (neurotic?) rich man of Mark 10:17–22, who was concerned principally with what *he* had to do to be saved. His question to Jesus ("What shall I do to inherit everlasting life?") centered not on God but on himself. When Jesus invited him to join the company of the disciples — minus the encumbrance of his wealth — and be part of *God's* dawning kingdom, the man could only walk away sad because he was unable to let go. The full, canonical meaning of the Bible will often be lost if we yield to the tendency to moralize before we theologize, before we seek the Integrity of Reality, the oneness of God, in the face of ancient or contemporary polytheizing.[29]

Reading the Bible as a pluralistic whole (as canon) helps us discover how preponderant the theocentric, monotheizing hermeneutic is, even though the wisdom tradition tends toward anthropocentrism and some of the New Testament emphasizes Christ's unique role in salvation. Taking the Bible as an intertextual whole contrasts with most modern hermeneutics, which develop a "canon within a canon" so as to emphasize one aspect of the revelation as opposed to another (law vs. gospel, grace vs. free will). Not surprisingly, this leads to a partializing of the whole and produces interpretations of the Bible that veer off in one of two directions. Either they smack of too much possibility and ignore the persistence of sin, evil, hardness of heart, emphasizing human perfectability at the expense of our creatureliness; or they express too much necessity, emphasizing judgment as punishment and God's arbitrary divine will, at the expense of the good news of unmerited grace and the unstrained quality of divine mercy.[30]

6. The last of these initial implications of the full canonicity of the Bible takes into account what most people mean when they speak of the "canon." Some books are part of it, some are not. At one time, the process of adding books and of reediting the ones that were considered canonical came to a halt. Not uniformly and simultaneously, but over some centuries, there was a change in what Sanders calls the "ontology of canon." What had been an unfolding sacred story, incrementally handed on first orally and then in fluidly shaped documents for centuries, became a stabilized, fixed, and sacred text. While the historical circumstances are too complex to take up here, some further hermeneutical implications of this implicit change in the idea of inspiration and authority behind the change in the canon's ontology, which Sanders has worked out, must be detailed.

Stabilizing a formerly fluid text led to its relative dehistoricization. No longer did a scribe have the liberty to clarify or update the reference of a text or to render it with the same freedom as did Paul of Tarsus or Matthew the scribe once the text, rather than its message, became the "Word of God." Stabilization preserved relatively ancients texts, but it also increased the temptation for inverting the message. For once the original context was lost sight of, it became unmoored and free-floating in a way that allowed the original point to be lost. As Sanders argues, "A frozen text written for one set of problems can create new ones when read in a totally different situation." The metaphorical indeterminacy of the canonical text, then, demands critical controls that keep its paradigmatic interpretation honest.[31]

Hard and fast textual stability also led to the sacralization of the text. But paradoxically, the freezing of the sacred text permitted "a pluralistic text that has remarkably resisted assimilations and homogenizations of readings" to survive. Had this not occurred, the interpretive battles fought by Jews, Christians, and heretical groups might well have given rise to wholly altered and increasingly sectarian Bibles. Though textual stability gave impetus to atomizing the Bible and carving it up to support party platforms, it also preserved the original witness. Again, a static text can lead the unimaginative to presume that a once-for-all, unchanging meaning exists (this perverts rather than preserves the historical sense of scripture) but such interpreters cannot snuff out the dynamic tensions fixed in the text itself.[32]

A final observation that flows from the Bible as canon concerns what

we might call the sociology of inspiration, and of interpretation as well.
The deeper mystery attending the Bible as canon is that the Spirit of God
not only hovered over the whole canonizing process but still attends us
that we might hear God's Word. Yet this rarely occurs in the privacy
of any author or preacher's study. Our scholarly or academic prejudice
in favor of individual authors at their desks needs correction. The communities and congregations for whom, with whom, and by whom the
scriptures were produced still remain the context for their ongoing interpretation: "The community shaped the text as it moved toward canon
and the text or tradition shaped the communities as it found its way
along its pilgrimage to canon." This renewed emphasis on the community's encounter with God's Word draws our attention to the primary,
experiential, and partly unconscious theological process at the heart of
the scriptures. Only after we have taken this primary process into account can we consider the canon as resulting from a secondary process
available to us through critical or analytic categories of interpretation.
Self-conscious authors have had, at best, an auxiliary role in creating
the texts of the canonical tradition. Scribes served the community, not
the academy, when engaged in their various tasks over the centuries.[33]

The point is worth stressing because, in contrast to the early
twentieth-century view that the text was the bridge across the ugly, wide
ditch that separated moderns from ancients, canonical criticism has expanded on this awareness to name the intertextual traditioning process
to which the canon witnesses as the bridge, "precisely because the same
thing is going on now in the believing communities as went on back
then." Most of the creative and attentive people who are responsible for
the shape of the Bible are anonymous. Even in the case of Luke-Acts, the
most self-conscious author in the New, or Second, Testament, Sanders
sees evidence to support the position that "what Luke wrote and passed
on to us in his literary work undoubtedly reflects what went on in the
educational and liturgical programs of the congregation."[34]

This intertextual traditioning process at the heart of canon means
that the authority of the Bible as canon does not stem primarily from
ecclesiastical decision-making. The rabbis and church councils made
decisions about the extent of their respective canons, but a more informal *consensus ecclesiae* had already laid the parameters for those
later decisions. The canon is not the product of a divine or ecclesiastical voluntarism but results from an experiential (and inspired) impulse
to hold fast to the word of truth (the stability pole of canon) while going forth to encounter the new thing God has done (the adaptability
pole). The canon of scripture witnesses to the various ways in which
the biblical communities negotiated holding fast and going forth. Consequently, it provides texts of various extension — liturgical recitals,
psalms, prophetic oracles, laws, parables — that illustrate how contin-

uing biblical communities can hold fast and go forth even today. What is more, the canon provides examples of how old texts can be asked to address new situations. The *how* is called hermeneutics, the "bridge between responsible exegesis and homiletics," shorthand for the craft of theology as ongoing interpretation.[35] The Bible itself, then, in its textual traces, has recorded something about how we can travel across this bridge when we attend to some of the rules for reading available in its pages. From the Bible's own maps, Sanders has extrapolated some rules for our interpretive journeys.

Some "Unrecorded Hermeneutical Rules"

The triangle of interpretation. Close scrutiny of some of the explicit conflict situations in the Bible can help us understand how we can learn to bridge the gap between old texts and new situations. In their original setting, both Jeremiah and Jesus applied the scriptural traditions of their people in a way that contradicted an established understanding of the divine promises. Neither Jeremiah, nor Jesus, nor their various opponents disbelieved in God's covenant fidelity. But as prophets who respectively predicted the destruction of the First and Second Temples, they both understood God to be exercising that fidelity, not by protecting the Temple from Israel's enemies, but rather by allowing it to be destroyed. The message of covenant fidelity could not just remain static; it needed to be adapted to changing circumstances.

From this biblical pattern, Sanders has developed a model for interpretation that puts traditions (texts), their sociopolitical contexts, and their application (hermeneutics proper) into a triangular relationship. When we seek to apply a text by taking it out of a past setting and inserting it into a contemporary situation, we must do so with a view to the kind of application we are making. Only the text itself is relatively "frozen" or stabilized; the context must remain labile, lest we misappropriate the text by placing it in a context alien to it. Hence the way we apply it must remain adaptable to the circumstances (or context) of our community. Understanding the historical situation to which it referred or in which it was written down (and these are often not the same) is important, but once that it is done, the third angle (the mode of adaptation) still remains to be understood.[36]

Interpretations that comfort or challenge. A text or tradition is adapted *constitutively,* to support a program of obedience or a policy of the community, or *prophetically,* to critique the community and call it to reform. Neither mode is always and everywhere right. Canonical hermeneutics understands that there are times for comforting the discomfited and for discomfiting the comfortable. No hard and fast rule determines when either hermeneutical angle is the right vantage point in the ambiguous situations of history. Affirming the basic ambiguity that has always attended hearing and prophesying the Word of God is good preparation for dealing responsibly with contemporary ambiguity. Again, the Bible's metaphorical indeterminacy is both a challenge and an opportunity, ruling out literalist interpretation.

Biblical paradigms. The Bible-as-canon, then, provides us with a paradigm, in the sense of a pattern, exemplar, or model, in which one or other mode of application created the conditions for faith. In some settings, a supportive reading can give the faithful courage to endure; in others, the same interpretation might cause people to commit grave injustice. But the Bible-as-canon also gives examples of subtler combinations of supportive consolation and prophetic challenge. For instance, in Jesus' basic message — "The time is at hand and the Kingdom of God is drawing close. Be converted and believe this good news" (Mark 1:15) — the two notes are sounded together. First, the message that God's kingdom was drawing near was pure comfort for Jews living under Roman occupation, hence constitutive. But embedded within the gospel was a demand straight out of the judgment preaching of Jeremiah: You're straying away and you need to turn back and attend to what God wants for you and from you. Because the message is sublimely symbolic, the proximity of the kingdom demands a complex response to both its constitutive and prophetic elements. In other words, the gospel message of salvation transgresses the distinction between comedy and tragedy. The supreme moment of this divine drama occurs in Jesus' victorious cry as he dies on the cross in John 19:30 (*Tetelestai:* "It is accomplished!"). Like the announcement of the kingdom and the cry from the cross, the sermon in the Nazareth synagogue (Luke 4) is a paradigm of the complex combination of text, setting, and mode of application that alerts us to how challenging it is to bring the biblical paradigms into new situations.[37]

Dynamic analogy. The creative fidelity necessary to give these complex paradigms new life creates Sanders's rule of dynamic analogy. In order to place a text in the right context, the interpreter has to identify elements in the contemporary situation that are dynamically equivalent to those in the situation in which the canonical material arose. Dynamic analogy enables one to avoid the trap so many have fallen into (which Sanders calls "polytheistic good guy/bad guy thinking in reading the Bible") by insisting that we transcend the convenient and self-serving dualisms we too readily bring to our understanding of the text and to "breathe the ambiguity of reality into the ancient situation or context."[38] In other words, we should not too quickly identify ourselves with any one figure in the biblical narrative, because yesterday's hero (Moses, David, Peter) can be tomorrow's goat, and vice versa. What is heretical in Jerusalem will seem very orthodox for the remnant in Babylon. Likewise, Jesus' critique of religious obedience and Paul's critique of circumcision for Gentiles made one kind of sense when "the shape of the world was passing away" but wrenched from their end-time contexts and appropriated undynamically, those truths laid the foundation for the falsehood of anti-Semitism.

Dynamic analogy is far more helpful as a rule of interpretation than typology. This was a feature of the Antiochean school of patristic biblical interpretation (which the biblical theology movement sought to rehabilitate), which located historical *types* in the scriptures and identified them as the essential components of the inner coherence and validity of the Bible, also making them patterns for Christian experience. Dynamic analogy seeks, by contrast, to account for what is different when comparing two analogous biblical passages or applying either or both of them to the present. Without sufficient attention to the internal ambiguity of the textual material and to the ambiguities that attend our contemporary situation as well, an interpreter will end up engaging in static analogy or applying texts in a manner that assimilates them to the dominant culture of the time. Sanders notes that this is the particular fault of fundamentalism, which expresses, not biblical faith, but bibliolatry or the worship of the Bible in the place of God.[39]

Resignification or intertextuality. Another of the unrecorded hermeneutics unearthed by canonical criticism rests on the liturgical practice of canonizing texts and then reusing them in various settings. Over time, they inevitably take on various meanings. Historically, "repetition or *relecture* with concomitant resignification" allowed the Bible to survive as an intertext with a plurality of meanings. By definition, canonical material is multivalent and pluralistic because communities and congregations once chose to listen to it, despite their distance from the material's origins and the different context in which they lived. The notion that the author's original intention determines the present-day meaning of the scriptures fails to deal with this phenomenon of resignification.[40] Canonical criticism, by articulating the ever-shifting paradigm of text, context, and mode of application, opens the way for our interpretation to become more honest. Insisting on the normativity of plural readings of scripture in the context of the believing community, it helps us to affirm the relative rather than the absolute value of critical methods. It also presses us to learn how to reintegrate the critical perspective with the mythopoetic elements that constitute the founding vision of Christian faith and, hence, sets the stage for mature interpretation of faith identity today.

The Canon as Paradigm

This review of the principals and procedures of canonical hermeneutics confirms Barthélemy's claim that Sanders shows us the how and the wherefore of *Dei Verbum*'s notion of revelation as an ongoing appropriation in the community of believers (whether this is portrayed with a heavy emphasis on hierarchical teachers or not). Sanders has helped us to reintegrate, in a critical perspective, the *logos* into which the Bible was frozen with our ongoing sacred story (or *mythos* contained in the Bible). For the Bible-as-canon contains and means both *mythos* and *logos* simultaneously and interactively. Canonical hermeneutics demonstrates how these seemingly opposite aspects of the revelation mutually coinhere. They help release the potential of the biblical *mythos* to be appropriated as our story, while retaining the biblical *logos,* so as to respect the historical and particular nature of both the story and the text. We can't have one without the other. Canonical hermeneutics brings the two together asymmetrically, respecting their differences. They allow us access not just to the word but what the word is about in this day and age by freeing the Bible to reveal paradigms of challenge and comfort, of judgment and grace, of gospel (the ongoing story) and law (its ethical demands). The active coinherence of these asymmetrical pairs in canonical hermeneutics renders it a mature theory of interpretation of the Bible.

Canonical hermeneutics, by reintergrating the Bible's story-event character and its textuality, changes, if not the "ontology" of scripture, then certainly our access to it. By moving beyond both *sola scriptura* and a static notion of scripture and tradition, canonical hermeneutics situates the historical-critical quest for explaining the text in the interpreting community that labors to understand it paradigmatically for the present. It teaches us that the Bible-as-canon, from a postcritical, mature perspective, belongs to the community first and to the scholar/interpreter second. It vigorously promotes critical efforts to exegete ancient texts, but refuses to canonize only the most ancient meaning.[41] It insists that as we interpret the texts, so the texts must be given a chance to interpret us as well. It also asks the community to make the story its own by reappropriating the words so that the Spirit may breathe life into them. Thus the text of the Bible and the text of a community's life are rewoven in new acts of intertextuality.[42]

This approach makes the Bible not so much an inspired text as the inspired catalyst of our ongoing, inspired search of the scriptures, that in them we may find life. By repositioning the authority of the Bible-as-canon within its function in the community of faith, as that faith is shaped and reshaped, canonical hermeneutics makes an important contribution to a mature understanding of the divine initiative to which faith responds.[43]

Dynamic Analogy and the Symbolic Imagination

As we saw above, insufficient attention to the ambiguity behind and in the textual material, and to contemporary ambiguities as well, will lead an interpreter to engage in static analogy, to misapply texts and distort a biblical message. Static analogy occurs most frequently in cases of literalism, the style and conviction of biblical interpretation that avoids the metaphorical indeterminacy of the Bible. Fear that the world might be stood on its head and that God might not be our God quite as we require often motivates such avoidance. The difference between static and dynamic analogy is similar to the difference articulated earlier between a stenosymbol (or mere denominator) and a symbol properly speaking. Stenosymbols express one-to-one correlations between the signifier and the signified. If the name tag says "usher," the safest bet is that the person wearing it will lead you to your seat. But static, one-to-one correlations are not adequate when we seek to interpret the Bible. Dynamic analogy, requiring that we "breathe the ambiguity of reality into the ancient situation or context," elevates the text to symbolic significance.

This means that scripture-as-canon possesses an excess of meaning characteristic of all symbols properly speaking. The texts of scripture have a canonical thickness to them because they have meant different things at different times during the process of canonization and during their history in the community of believers. Their thickness or polyvalence is not the result of their doctrinal of moral content, their predictive quality, or their multiple senses. Rather, it arises from their symbolic polyvalence. As the product of intertextual resignification, the scriptures require that we continue to read them as more-than-literally true — or else they would hardly be revelatory! Above I defined a symbol as a word, image, phrase, or thing whose thickness or excess of meaning resulted from the tension between its apparent (or literal) sense and its less than obvious signification. In somewhat similar terms, Sanders describes the canon, with its duality of stable text and adaptable meaning, as "a history of efforts to get those texts to say what they do not apparently say." In other words, in canonical texts (as both stabilized and sacred), there is always a tension between apparent meaning and their interpreted or signified meaning. As the shape of a text (its extent, its pairing with other texts) is adjusted in the various settings-in-life of the church (liturgical, dogmatic, moral, spiritual, or political), it will take on various constellations that defy its being locked into a single referential meaning.

As this raises the relationship between the literal truth and the historicity or veracity of texts, it is important to point out that historical factuality represents only one factor in our coming to understand the ongoing meaning of biblical narratives. For example, even if we grant that Pontius Pilate's wife actually did try to intervene in Jesus' trial (Matt 27:19), its facticity would still not determine our assessment of how to interpret Matthew's passion narrative today. Brute facts contribute to, but do not control, the meaning of biblical texts.

Similarly, because we lack historical evidence for Luke's census requiring that "all the world" be taxed (Luke 2:1), we determine that it
is not literally factual but is a fictional approximation of events such
as might have been the cause for Jesus "of Nazareth" to be born in
Bethlehem. But the discrediting of the census as fact has not led to our
denying significance to the infancy account. Instead, today we have a
better awareness of its symbolic riches that were overlooked precisely
when it was taken as a historical or literal account of events. Most
people's knowledge of the Christmas story ignores the fact that it is a
modern (midrashic) amalgam of elements of Matthew and Luke's accounts with a dose of Psalm 72 (the "kings" who bring the gifts come
from this text). Its lack of historicity is only one factor in our assessment
of its meaning and significance, not a decision that it has none.[44]

It follows then, that even the literal sense of biblical passages cannot
be correlated on a one-for-one basis with individual facts of history. The
literal sense is simply what the Bible says. To determine it, we must use
all the tools that historical and literary criticism make available. But that
is just the beginning. The temptation to presume that, once the Bible was
finally committed to writing, its meaning and not just its textual form
was frozen is present even in *Dei Verbum*. Paragraph 12 seems to index
the meaning of the text to the author's intention as the best indication
of "what God wanted to manifest." But even this bit of positivism is
conditioned by the constitution's admission that tradition "develops" (8)
and that the church moves toward a "deeper understanding" (23) of the
contents of the Bible.[45]

Today, it is perhaps more possible for us to see that determining this
deeper understanding must take into account the ambiguity of reality,
both as our ancestors in the faith once encountered it and as we experience it as a contemporary community of faith. While at first this
ambiguity may seem nothing less than an enemy of truth, canonical hermeneutics allows us to see it as an ally of our freedom and dignity to
choose a relationship, in faith, with the living God, rather than with self-
derived substitutes. The believing community always faces the challenge
of not merely knowing what God said in the past but of responding
to the present invitation of God's Word. Understanding dynamic analogy helps us to render faithfully in a modern context the dramatic
sweep of the monotheizing of the biblical narrative. Canonical criticism,
by summoning the faithful to seek what Sanders calls the Integrity of
Reality beyond our tempting partializations, has presented the Bible's
interpreters with a fitting challenge toward maturity.

But the Bible contains Christocentric and anthropocentric hermeneutics as well, and these elements of revelation are less immediately
applicable by means of the historical orientation of dynamic analogy. As
we saw, dynamic analogy centers on the community's faith-identity in

the story (*mythos*) of scripture. But there is an additional task to biblical interpretation: uncovering what Sanders calls indications for community lifestyles (*ethos*) in the Bible. This second concern, much less worked out in Sanders's essays on canonical hermeneutics but clearly present in his own preaching, may reflect a traditional Catholic concern for lifestyle or sanctification issues as a complement to a history-of-salvation justification emphasis.[46] Not for a minute would I dispute Sanders's preference for theologizing before we get around to moralizing, but living out of the Bible's witness, especially from a renewed Catholic interest in its authority, leads me to articulate a more sacramental or symbolic approach for appropriating the full range of latter-day biblical meanings.

Because scripture abounds in excess meaning, whether we are dealing with major narratives (such as the Joseph account), theophanies, prophetic oracles, parables, sayings, or even the wisdom material, it cannot be reduced to a doctrinal or moral text, a casebook for ethical concerns, or a convenient source for catechizing the ignorant. Its pluralism will not allow us to shrink it to a Sunday school primer. Rather, the primacy of the symbolic in the biblical writings brings us up face-to-face with the need to apprehend its truth by engaging in a controlled but imaginative "suspension of the literal."

Before proceeding to spell out how this works, we might look at some analogies in human life that also require such a suspension. At the beginning of the Romantic period (itself a reaction to the rationalism of the early Enlightenment), Coleridge liberated drama from the tyranny of the neoclassical unities of time, place, and action by arguing that a willing suspension of disbelief constitutes poetic faith. Truth cannot be limited to any linear, literal engagement with its component parts when truth's supposed limits are in fact one's own temporal, spatial, and local limitations.[47] It follows that appreciating a work of art requires that we accept provisional rules, not for deluding ourselves but for opening ourselves up. When we do, something manifests itself that cannot be subjected to laboratory analysis or to any one-to-one correlation of artistic detail to "real" truth hiding inside or behind the work of art. These provisional rules, which operate in the kinds of transitional spaces that link a child's play and a maestro's art, are responsible for our capacity to "infer 'otherness' — the transcendent" through intuitions deeper than language. In these open-ended spaces beset with ambiguity, George Steiner says, "Grammatical normality 'fails' where meaning is set free." Therefore, nothing that has any potential for manifesting deep truths "escapes the risk of interpretation." Despite all our attempts at defining or exhausting these privileged contexts for meaning, Steiner affirms that in them "our experienced reconstructions of the past are grammatical and textual 'truth-fictions.' They are carpentered out of the availabilities of the past tense. No finally external verification attaches to them."[48]

The suspension of the literal reaches its acme in music. Music is more basic even than metaphor in language; it actually represents

an evolutionary modulation or translation into more semantic, representational codes of the arc of melody.... The energy that is music puts us in touch with the energy that is life; it puts us in a relation of experienced immediacy with the abstractly and verbally inexpressible but wholly palpable, primary act of being.... Thus do we seem to harbour at the threshold of the unconscious, at depths precisely uncapturable by speech and the logic of speech, intimations, incisions in the synapses of sensibility, of a close kinship between the meanings of music and those of humanly-enacted meaning itself.

More than any other aesthetic experience, music creates the spaces that communicate to us something of the first encounters with the self, at the "nativity of consciousness." "The time which music 'takes,' and which it gives us as we perform or experience it, is the only free time granted us prior to death."[49] Steiner's insights cannot help but explain the heightened significance of music in both high and popular forms of culture. However obsessional or shadowy they may seem as "inferences of otherness," rock, pop, or rap music (especially as they combine with erotic passion) stand for something else, a desire for breakthrough, for manifestation beyond the confines of the self or of the now.

We also engage in the suspension of the literal in games and sporting events. Basic to every game we ever play is a set of rules that creates an artificial environment for those involved (and for the spectators) for as long as the game lasts. Literal, daily reality becomes suspended during the game. We are recreating, (re-creating) our ability to participate in reality's stringent demands by relaxing the constraints of the workaday world and by attempting to master "fate." At play, or by running, swimming, cycling, working out, we restructure reality (and perhaps our bodies as well) so as to achieve a sense of control that life, in its literalness, linearity, or its chaotic irrationality, denies us. Competitive sport intensifies this suspension of the literal and requires of athletes far more physical intuition than intellectual control to perform maximally and achieve mastery. Those who cannot be self-forgetful enough to let the game *play* them, to allow the rhythms of the team's movement or the physical demands of the game to take over — to suspend rational control and allow psychic and physical intuition to call the shots — will not enjoy themselves. (They probably won't win either.) Just as sports and games are living metaphors of life, so the pages of scripture are redolent with the parables, mythopoetry, and metaphor that, like Lady Wisdom, delight in playing on the literal surface of reality as a means of revealing truth.

The paradox that we must suspend the literal to get at meaning reminds us that the very structure of symbols in human knowing and in self-expression derives from the experience that we have more ideas than we have words. As I have argued, before there was language, and behind language's most secret thoughts, we imbibed images and symbols, what Kant called those representations in which imagination binds up or concentrates so many ideas that they "arouse more thought than can be expressed in a concept determined by words." This means that when we are touched by those aspects of life that go below the surface, threaten our control, or bespeak the ultimate, when we are undone by the wobble in human experience that is both weakness and grace, the normal shape of things must bend so that we do not become overwhelmed by either too much possibility or too much necessity.[50] Religious language, which only developed as a language of concepts secondarily, is thickly planted with metaphors that bend our categories out of shape in order to push our understanding toward otherness.

Symbols, parables, and myths are necessary as modes of religious discourse because revelation is necessarily encountered at the limits (or in the depths) of human experience. Concepts schematize and draw out what revelation presents as otherwise unknowable facts. But the indirect, symbolic, and metaphorical forms of languages, such as the parables, primally and profoundly confront our imaginations with what Paul Ricoeur calls "the indirect presentation of the Unconditioned." We achieve genuine self-and-other knowledge (as distinguished from information) not directly and immediately, but indirectly and often paradoxically, through the detour of symbols. The dispossession of the conscious ego as the house of meaning gives us a humbled knowledge of God and of ourselves, but it is a real, not just notional, knowledge, allowing us a properly religious, middle, or transitional space where the sacred and the profane mutually coinhere as sacramental. But in being so dispossessed we can rediscover the potential of symbol and metaphor to involve our participative imagination really and sacramentally, in the sphere of the Unconditioned.

I am suggesting that the narratives and symbols of the canonical tradition, because they do not originate in individual self-consciousness but in a historical community of tradition, possess a transitional potential through which the past and the future invade the present through the wobble or wound of our historically conditioned lives. Directly, these symbolic narratives of creation and re-creation (and the way they are sacramentally reenacted) cannot demonstrate with probative force that we are assured of a victory of life over death. Such a victory is not the apparent reality we live with from day to day, nor can we claim to know it merely rationally.[51]

As occupying a place on the boundary line, the symbolic narratives and their sacramental enactment function for believers in the manner of transitional phenomena to invite us to suspend the merely literal. They are meant to function as the stuff of creative illusion, by which we enact, not all at once but little by little, our integration into a transcendent community of meaning and living. As we read and reread these narratives of faith, we are invited to trust in a story of gracious judgment that enables us to hold on and to let go simultaneously. We all live unto death in a world that we cannot control. But in the free and playful spaces of word and sacramental encounter (see chapter 10), our imaginative knowing learns graciousness and gratitude in the face of our predicament. Our engagement of these mythopoetic narratives helps us achieve a sense of particular identity within the wholeness or Integrity of Reality.[52]

As in the early stages of life, when we must overcome the loss of the security of our parental matrix, we stand to overcome the culture's loss of religious immediacy via the transitional phenomenon of the Bible-as-canon in order to enact a religious and cultural maturity. Dynamic analogy (as a reading strategy) and symbolic imagination (as a lifestyle strategy) represent a mature mode of engaging the central elements of Christianity's religious symbol system. They create the possibility of our journeying to the boundary line between objective realities that we have no way of controlling and subjective realities that tend to solipsism by playing creatively with the traces of memory and hope that abound in the narratives and symbols of our religious tradition.

Earlier we saw that creative illusions allow us to grow personally, to engage the world on both objective and subjective terms and to bite off just enough of the world to chew at various stages of life. The biblical tradition makes available symbolic narratives that act as transitional phenomena in the illusory space where reality makes itself known in and through the subject's risking meaning beyond itself. Though the analogy is risky, I am suggesting that the play by which we engage the traces of the divine-human wrestling match (cf. Gen 32:28) is an essential element of developing faith as well as of growing in hope and love. Receiving the symbols that the tradition makes available and making them their own accomplishes for mature believers something of the same goals and discoveries of the infant discovering the world and self through the transitional phenomena that take it from its cradle to at least its early schooling.[53] Let me press the analogy.

The fact that our society prizes science more than poetry may help us understand why it may be hard for children to suspend disbelief (except for grossly literal dramas in soap operas and movies) as a means of believing in themselves as agents of their own personal and spiritual maturity. Children who are encouraged to engage their religion and culture imaginatively gain a far more accurate sense of who they are and what they are capable of than those trained merely to control information and engage in quantitative operations. It is precisely the uselessness of the humanities, their gratuitous and unprofitable catering to the expansiveness of the child's developing imagination, that is their real value. This is so precisely because literature, art, music, and the interpretative (or social) sciences such as history should seek not merely to impart information but to develop the creative powers by which students can imagine a future.[54]

In other words, the person who significantly involves the self in the larger world of meaning is necessarily less self-involved. If the conviction grows from infancy that one's needs are real and worthy of oneself and that the world is an inviting place that provides one with opportunities not only for physical sustenance but for affective gratification and welcomes one's involvement in it — if it allows a child to play and welcomes its illusionary creativity — then that child will become an adult whose aims, goals, and affectivity will not be mere derivatives of narcissism. It will not be cut off from its unconscious because the wounds stored there are too hurtful; rather it will be able to have access to its dreams, personal myths, and proper illusions and know how to participate in relationships, to live in society, and to seek the unseen God.

By contrast, a literalism that is incapable of metaphor, irony, symbol, and the suspension of the literal arises in individuals or from cultures that are narcissistically self-involved. Literalism's demands for certainty and its inability to handle either historical, textual, or cultural ambiguity in the past or the present reflect an individual or collective self that feels vital only when it cathects the objective world for its own needs. In response to the threat that it might be set adrift and be on its own (the fate of either too much possibility or the rebound phenomenon of too much necessity), the neurotic self (or society) reacts by partializing reality, by fetishing objects. Sanders charges that biblical fundamentalists (for whom the Bible *is* the Word of God, no symbols allowed!) are guilty of bibliolatry — they have fetishized the Bible as their headlock on reality, as their guarantee of grace. Faith, in this neurotic arrangement, becomes willful assertion, hope devolves into waiting for the rapture, and love expresses not desire but supernatural Need.

In contrast to fundamentalist literalism, dynamic analogy activated through the symbolic imagination seeks to complete the journey to maturity by reintegrating the rational, conscious religious quest with the unconscious, imaginative material available in the mythopoetic symbols of the Bible-as-canon. I argued above that maturity, beyond adulthood, is aided by the reintegration of what, in earlier stages of development, is seen as opposite features of the human person. Similarly, personal and hermeneutical maturity should follow from the reintegration of the primarily naive, mythopoetic stage of awareness (complemented by early rational and linguistic activity) and of autonomous critical rationality. After criticism has run its course, gotten over its grandiosity, and felt its own weakness, it can become the developmental partner of its former adversary. Because infancy and childhood are succeeded by adolescence and young adulthood, nothing seems so dialectically opposed to growing up than being childlike on any level. As we have seen, reacting to the parental matrix with a certain amount of rebellion is quite natural in adolescence, and even healthy for the development of individual autonomy. Failure to separate oneself from the symbiotic union brings illness later in life — often psychosomatic illness — precisely because of the unnaturalness of sustained dependency. This is why for a good long time historical-critical investigation of the biblical material has remained in a state of autonomous separation from its matrix in the mythopoetic world of God the Father and Mother Church. Graced as this paradoxical process has been, the time has come for reintegrating the primarily naive, mythopoetic, symbolically charged biblical material with the critical perspective of modernity so that postcritical religious maturity is at least in our purview.

The rule of dynamic analogy, arising from the intertextuality of the Bible-as-canon, and its application by means of a symbolic imagination, arising out of the psychoanalytic perspective, will enable us to accomplish this reintegration by combining serious text-traditional study with playful homiletics and symbolic theology. In the chapters to follow I wish to describe more fully this postcritical hermeneutic with which I will seek to fill out a morphology of contemporary faith.

Bibliographical Essay

On individuation and reintegration: Jolande Jacobi (*The Way of Individuation,* trans. R. F. C. Hull [New York: Harcourt, Brace & World, 1967], 10) contrasts Freud's "genetic-analytical" depth psychology with Jung's "teleological-synthetic" viewpoint and credits Jung with developing a psychology for "life's afternoon" in contrast with Freud and Adler's "psychology of life's morning" (41).

On biblical hermeneutics: Cf. R. E. Brown, S.S., and Sandra M. Schneiders, I.H.M., "Hermeneutics," *New Jerome Biblical Commentary* (Englewood Cliffs, N.J.: Prentice-Hall, 1990), 1146–65. Barthélemy's comparison of J. A. Sanders's approach to canonical criticism with Brevard Child's canonical approach is seconded by W. Meiers, "The Hermeneutical Dilemma of the African American Biblical Scholar," *Stony the Road We Trod: African American Biblical Interpretation.* ed. Cain H. Felder (Minneapolis: Fortress Press, 1991), 40–56. Cf. also Frank Kermode, "The Argument about Canons," *An Appetite for Poetry* (Cambridge: Harvard University Press, 1990), 189; Kermode suggests Sanders's approach might mediate between more extreme positions.

Sandra Schneiders (*The Revelatory Text: Interpreting the New Testament as Sacred Scripture* [San Francisco: HarperSanFrancisco, 1991],

102) chooses the term "paschal imagination" to describe a comprehensive New Testament hermeneutics. Her combining a dogmatic treatment of the New Testament as a medium of revelation with a hermeneutical treatment of how we get at what a text means today has much in common with Sanders, because she seeks to show how the paschal experience behind the texts can be newly appropriated. She is also dependent on the hermeneutics of Paul Ricoeur, whose works are almost too numerous to cite. In "Metaphor and the Central Problem of Hermeneutics" (*Paul Ricoeur: Hermeneutics and the Human Sciences,* ed. J. B. Thompson [Cambridge: Cambridge University Press, 1981], 177) Ricoeur draws the explicit analogy between the way metaphors and texts function. To interpret a text means to apprehend "the proposed worlds which are opened up by the non-ostensive references of the text."

Richard B. Hays (*Echoes of Scripture in the Letters of Paul* [New Haven: Yale University Press, 1989]) provides one of the most stimulating studies of Pauline hermeneutics, in which he seeks to learn from the Apostle "the art of dialectical imitation" (183). Learning how to read the Bible from Paul will help us *"appreciate the metaphorical relation between the text and our reading of it"* [ital. original] allowing us to grant "a broad space...for figurative intertextual configurations...for metalepsis. The troping of the text would be the natural consequence of locating our lives within its story" (186). Hays's conclusions help substantiate the role of dynamic analogy in biblical interpretation articulated by James A. Sanders and of the symbolical imagination that I have tried to spell out.

Terrence Merrigan (*Clear Heads and Holy Hearts: The Religious and Theological Ideal of John Henry Newman,* Louvain Theological and Pastoral Monographs 7 [Louvain: Peeters Press, 1991], 186) cites John Henry Newman's theory of the polar interaction of reason and intuition as evidenced in this excerpt from his *Grammar of Assent:*

Real assent...is in itself an intellectual act, of which the object is presented to it by the imagination.... The imagination has the means, which the pure intellect has not, of stimulating those powers of the mind from which action proceeds. Real assent then or belief, as it may be called...does not lead to action; but the images, in which it lives, representing as they do the concrete, have the power of the concrete upon the affections and passions and by means of these indirectly become operative.

The intuitive and rational processes are integrated in the illative sense, which itself expresses the ceaseless interplay by which Newman claimed that the act of faith possessed a properly cognitional character.

Chapter 7

Mourning Lost Innocence

The Bible-as-canon has given us a perspective in which the *mythos* and *logos* of the Bible, so often set against one another, mutually coinhere in a way that helps us overcome our loss of revelational immediacy. But mature believing also must face the question: What is it that authorizes belief expressed in doctrines that themselves have a history? For any honest look at the ambiguities in the history of faith affirmation reveals that believing today has also lost its innocence. To overcome this loss, we must undertake an equivalent act of reintegrating the mythopoetic shape of doctrine with historical criticism. As we seek to do so, we will find that, like the Bible, our ambiguous doctrinal history is also canonical: it contains the traces of sin and repentance, of oppression and liberation, of death and resurrection that, when critically appropriated, can help us retrieve adequate paradigms for mature Catholic identity.

From Newman to Vatican II

John Henry Newman (1801–90) was virtually unique in his ability to cross the no man's land that separated primary naivete and nineteenth-century rational criticism. As a young Protestant, Newman saw how the words and images of scripture create and sustain an affective vision whose intuitions theology developed into a more abstract, notional system. In passing back and forth between images and abstractions, Newman saw an "implicit, more or less unconscious, reasoning" that made faith affirmation explicit. These were his first intimations of the dynamic notion of development, which would eventually move him from the alleged primitivism of Anglicanism to Roman Catholicism. But the fruits of Newman's life and works would take most of a century to mature. They would not be harvested in Rome, however, but in Belgium and France, where theologians grasped that development had to characterize any dynamic presentation of truth. It was an idea whose time had come.[1]

Inspired both by Newman and by the praxis-oriented philosopher Maurice Blondel, theologians of the *Resourcement* retrieved the patristic writings in order to cure theology of the scholastic rationalism that had dominated it into the twentieth century. As an abreaction to the Enlightenment rationalism, Catholic theology had unintentionally accepted many of its adversary's premises in favor of rational autonomy, theorizing about a state of pure nature (separate from grace) as the ground on which to contest secular rationalism. It was a two-story theology in which natural knowledge of God, a natural religion, and a natural morality inhabited the ground floor; the mystery of our communion with God lived upstairs over the realm of nature. Rarely did the natural and supernatural mingle.

Among the shortcomings of this theological perspective was its hyperobjectivism. Rationalist theologians presumed that their expressions of religious truth were actually equivalent to the religious realities of which they spoke. This resulted from an exaggerated use of Aquinas's principle that human knowledge resulted from the equivalence between the thing itself and what the mind knows (*adequatio rei et intellectus*). Thomas had adopted Aristotle's notion of equivocation, in which concepts analogically mediated, but never completely captured, the objects of the knowable world. This allowed Aquinas to treat symbolism correlative to Augustine's neo-Platonic view. According to both, "our concepts of God are, so to say, pictures of pictures, representations of representations. Our self-knowledge is, therefore, the image of God closest to us, because it is the least mediated."[2] After Aquinas, however, natural knowledge and its newfound possibilities flourished without any sense of the tension between ideas, and images and how concepts represented them. Instead, the nominalist passion for univocation, the knowing of things in their individual, not their universal, essences predominated. Like their deist opponents, scholastic theologians presumed that there was a real correspondence between their knowing subjectivity and the unchanging objects of the metaphysical superstructure of being. God had decreed that the order of nature and the order of grace (supernature) should mirror one another in such a way that rational argument was our surest passage to the natural heaven that all rational beings could desire. Happily, communion with God would top their unitarian expectations. In this way, Descartes's clear and distinct ideas eventually gave rise not only to an effective scientific intellect but also to a hypothetical and idealized theological schema with less positive consequences.[3]

In contrast, then, to scholasticism's rationalism, the *Resourcement* discovered in the patristic divine economy the sense that revelation took place via the historicity of the human condition. Yves Congar and others pointed out that scholastic theology's notion of the invariance of truth-affirmations, as well as its conceptual-deductive methods, was inadequate for dealing with the whole of revelation. A renewal of Christian affirmation demanded the study of historical periods where stable aspects of the tradition fruitfully interacted with its labile or adaptable elements. In the early twentieth century, then, theologians turned their attention to the patristic engagement of tradition and culture, for it had produced writings whose hermeneutical character made them the counsel of history that ailing scholastic theology needed in order to be cured of its objectivism. As commentators on the scriptures, the sacraments, and the life of faith, patristic writers into the Middle Ages had preferred symbols and images over rational argument, the concrete over the abstract, and the intuitive over the conceptual. Because these works were interpretive of humanity's historical engagement with revelation, twentieth-century scholarship learned from them that no single theological language could be totally adequate to the mystery, as all language emerges from contingent situations. Theology would never come to the end of its search for new ways of presenting the message and, hence, all theological efforts remain hermeneutical; they seek to understand God's activity through the various languages of faith that arise in the course of history.

Though the proponents of the *Resourcement* were criticized by Pius XII and silenced by the Roman Curia, they had proven themselves both more traditional than their detractors and more creative as well. Most of them were eventually called to Rome to help write the documents of Vatican II.[4] Thus are history's suppressions and startling liberations primary data for what we call the ambiguity of reality and its impact on the shape of theology. It does not ride above the tide of human affairs but always emerges in the ebb and flow of historical life, bearing history's wounds no less than did the crucified. Doctrinal teaching, as faith's self-affirmation, develops in order to live. Because it develops, its various forms can be traced in the record of the symbols, words, metaphors, and concepts that have made up its written expression. And because it develops, it undergoes change, growth, and decay. In other words, by looking at the historical vicissitudes of faith affirmation, its own woundedness, we can determine something of the shape of our lost innocence. Because the resurrection of Christ is the supreme event of revelation (*Dei Verbum* 4), it stands as the epigenesis of Christian faith. By undertaking a genealogical inquiry into the way belief in the resurrection has been expressed, we can determine how healthy theology is today, to see if faith affirmation can overcome its loss of immediacy and loss of innocence and attain some maturity.[5]

A Genealogy of Faith's Woundedness

Like any growing self-conscious organism, Christianity has maintained its identity and developed its lifestyle responses by managing the interaction of its stable and labile elements. Even before the closing of the

New Testament canon, Christian identity was up for grabs in that its fundamental self-understanding was being impugned, not by outside opponents, but by history: The world had not passed away. Jesus had not returned, and some believers were beginning to doubt if he would.

The second letter of Peter, written as late as 150 C.E., gives evidence that the delay of the Parousia had become neuralgic, for the issue dominates the whole letter. To reassure his congregation that "the coming of our Lord Jesus Christ" was not based on "cleverly concocted myths" (1:16), the pseudonymous author wrote "his" reminiscence of the Transfiguration. Against the "false teachers" (2:1) who scoff at the "promise of his coming," saying that "ever since the fathers fell asleep, all things have continued as they were from the creation of the world" (3:4, itself an echo of Ecclesiastes 1:9), Pseudo-Peter claimed that human ways of counting days were inaccurate: "For with the Lord one day is as a thousand years, and a thousand years as a day" (cf. Ps 90:4). Restating the "tradition" that what "we await are new heavens and a new earth where justice will reside" (cf. Isa 65:7; 66:12 in 3:13), he sought to shore up his congregation's "stability," praying that they "grow in the grace and knowledge of our Lord and Savior Jesus Christ" (3:17–18).

This letter is prima facie evidence that Christianity, once it began to suffer history, began to undergo crises of development in order to preserve its essential identity over time. As we have seen, in times of crisis the danger of identity diffusion always looms large: the stable and labile elements can become so unbalanced that the inner sameness and continuity of the community are threatened. In the course of growing and changing, then, efforts to adapt the stable core of Christian faith have been tempted by the twin developmental dangers that every life form subject to the human condition must endure: too much necessity and too much possibility. For a healthy adaptation despite history's wounds and to escape long-term illness (ideological fixity), a balance must be struck between these two tendencies, especially as they also represent the *incarnational* pole at one end of the spectrum of Christian theology (as the flesh clearly bespeaks necessity) and the *eschatological* pole at the other end (as the end-time is ultimate possibility).

When theology seeks to fill the gap between the already of biblical revelation and the not yet of the Parousia, it has to risk the temptations that come with filling the void created by the hiddenness of God. This means that the natural expansiveness of the theological endeavor mirrors the normal neurosis of the human condition. It takes the dangers of reaching out beyond the mere normalcy of life to another level of risk. While most believers probably opt for a faith response short of the intensely self-conscious God-wrestling of theologians, average believers still have to undergo their own trials and tribulations. Life's wounds are real enough even without the effort to make God-sense of them. Doing so inevitably tempts theological reason to adapt pathologically in the direction of either too much narrowness or of too much openness.

The sketch that I will offer here will look at significant periods in which Western Christian theology has suffered history. If it is true that "some people's mistakes are more significant than other people's truths," then it also true that some of Christianity's failures are more important than some of the church's triumphs. When contemporary Christians present their history mainly as a series of victories (in alternative Catholic and Protestant versions), they deny their woundedness. Such history represents either a naive attachment to mythopoetic introjects or a critical deidealization that risks becoming its own negative identity. Both reactions hamper the faith community's maturing beyond our historical loss of innocence.

Augustine: *Doctor Gratiae*

Few Christians have lived their faith more controvertedly than Aurelius Augustinus, bishop of Hippo (354–425 C.E.). Born a century after Rome had celebrated the thousandth year of its founding, he died as Roman Africa was being dismantled and destroyed by Vandals, themselves Arian Christians who were expelling or torturing to death their Catholic counterparts. His life, endeavors, and extensive writings have done much to shape Western religious culture down to the present.

Although a Catholic Christian for only thirty-seven of his seventy-one years, Augustine wrote voluminously, citing the Bible, by actual count, 42,816 times. From these extensive writings, we can trace how he appropriated the Bible's symbolic world, merging it with that of pagan antiquity.[6] When Augustine was converted, first to wisdom when he was nineteen and then to Christianity fourteen years later, he would take his adopted neo-Platonic worldview on an inward journey to the depths of the human heart.[7] Combining it with the affective language of the Bible (principally the Psalms), he sought God in his personal depths, for he had come to believe that God dwelt "deeper than my inmost being" (*intimius intimo meo*). Before his full conversion, he had steeped himself in sensuality, being "in love with love," as he later wrote in his *Confessions* (III, 1. i). Later he embraced the dualism and rationalism of the Manichees, whose drastic worldview sought a necessary connection between the created world and an evil principle that had invaded the kingdom of Light. Splitting off the Hebrew scriptures and the creator God from their Bible and separating any responsibility for evil from God and from themselves, the Manichees held Augustine's loyalty for ten years. Their creed allowed him to be austere, spiritual, but not yet continent — he really did pray, "Lord, give me chastity and continence, but not now" (*Conf.* VIII, 7, xvii). He was protecting himself, for as long as he could, from being overwhelmed by his own ambivalence through adopting a rigidly partialized system of belief whose adherents considered themselves superior to all other Christians. Referring to Catholics as semi-Christians, the Manichees joined moral optimism with a strange divine passivity — a combination that Augustine rejected after reading Cicero and after he met a man much like that ancient Roman, Bishop Ambrose of Milan.[8]

Augustine was swayed by a combination of Ambrose's eloquence and spirituality, Plotinus's doctrine of the good, and a maturing ability to confront his own unhappiness. When he eventually "put on the Lord Jesus Christ," he left behind the narrowness of the Manichees that had so attracted him as a young man. As a neophyte, he wrote philosophy, migrating decidedly toward the seemingly unlimited possibilities of the spiritual life. His mind, he wrote, had "in an instant of awe...attained to the sight of who God is" (*Conf.* VII, 17, 23). Returning to Africa, he sought to continue his life of contemplation; but shortly after moving to Hippo, he was acclaimed by the crowd in the cathedral and ordained by Bishop Valerius. Within two years, Augustine, though only a presbyter, was preaching and expounding the scriptures, though this was contrary to church law in northern Africa. He engaged a former Manichean opponent in public debate, beating him so badly the man had to leave town. Then he took on the Donatists, even publishing a popular song against them when they refused to debate him. Augustine's energy for engaging in controversy matched his capacity for internal conflicts.

During the ten years before he wrote his *Confessions* (in 397, when he was forty-three), Augustine was still beguiled by the spiritual potential of the soul to ascend straightaway from the "old man" of the senses to the "new man" of the spirit. Commenting on the Sermon on the Mount, he exhorted bishops to love their wives as they did their "enemy," as Christ had taught. But soon his neo-Platonism began to fray around the edges. Newly impressed by the inability of the will to act with the complete freedom that spiritual possibility should have allowed, he rethought the problem of evil from an interior perspective. Memory and the impress of past actions upon it created internal states that a strangely weakened reason had trouble dispelling. In this frame of mind, he returned to the writings of Paul and read him, not through neo-Platonic lenses, but through the prism of flesh vs. spirit. Progress in the spiritual life no longer appeared as a vertical ascent of the mind/soul to ethereal realms; it depended solely on the unfathomable will of God. With this chastened spiritual awareness, catalyzed by his own life-review that produced the introspective *Confessions*, Augustine would later affirm that

Whoever thinks that in this mortal life a man may so disperse the mists of bodily and carnal imaginings as to possess the unclouded light of changeless truth, and to cleave to it with the unswerving constancy of a spirit wholly estranged from the common ways of life — he understands neither What he seeks, nor who he is who seeks it.[9]

This turn from spiritual accomplishment to yearning, from the upward flight of the soul into the depths of the wounded heart, represented another conversion, from grandiose to limited freedom, for Augustine had confronted necessity and come down to earth. As a bishop, he waged controversies against the Donatists and the Pelagians with long-lasting results. The first considered themselves spiritually pure, a chosen people who lived apart from an impure world, a continuation of the church of the martyrs. The second probably have a worse reputation than they deserve because they lost out in the controversy over grace (not unlike the later Jansenists). Their spiritual program came right out of Hellenic stoicism — self-control was enough to protect the free choice between good and evil — more than it flowed from the gospel of the crucified and risen Christ.

Since Augustine had become convinced that the conscious mind was so surrounded by dark shadows that the mind "cannot trust its own report" (*Conf.* X, 32, 48), he considered Pelagianism spiritually false. For him, perfection no longer lay within the span of human life, which he increasingly saw as a journey or pilgrimage, extending beyond death. Rather, the mind achieved truth by indirection, through the material signs of spiritual realities, interpreting the ambiguities in the Bible (and in life) by "the fertility of human reason" so that truth could "grow and multiply" (*Conf.* sc xiii, 24, 36–37). The angels might be able to see everything clearly and agree unanimously, but human beings needed to learn from one another and be bound together by *caritas* in their task of learning.[10] Though himself no sluggard when it came to ascetical discipline (which he also demanded from his clergy, whom he gathered in celibate, semimonastic communities), Augustine's realism about the human condition and the necessarily mixed condition of the church as a human society disallowed his reading out of the church the average person not eager for perfection. Freedom from doing evil could not be chosen by an act of the will; it had to be achieved by a slow process in which grace and free will became bound together in a healing process as the soul was drawn slowly by the source of all desire toward communion.[11]

Yet Augustine's realism had its downside. The necessity pole did not allow him merely to debate and engage in controversies with his theological opponents. What was at stake was the future of Roman society as well, threatened as it was by destruction from without. In 410 C.E., *the* city, Rome itself, mistress of the known world, was sacked and burned by Alaric's Goths. In response both to pagan accusations that the abandonment of the worship of Rome's ancestral gods had caused this disaster and to an upsurge in Donatist activity, he wrote a series of pamphlets that would take him thirteen years and twenty-two books to complete: *The City of God.* In it he postulated that "two cities, the one of God, and the other of the world," were intertwined in perpetual struggle, inextricably mixed in historical time. Gone were any of Origen's ideas of successive worlds of increasing perfection and Eusebius's lionizing of Constantine and the Roman Empire as God-sent. Like the soul on its journey, the citizens of God's city (the ideal church) were on a pilgrimage from Babylon to Jerusalem, from captivity to that final judgment when Christ would separate humanity into two groups of citizens, depending on where their loyalties had resided. For Augustine, apocalyptic judgment was woven into the structure of history itself. Just as the body was no longer merely the tomb of the soul but its contentious partner, so history had become the place of unique events that had inexorable consequences. In this necessary scheme of things, even heresies had a role, as providential challenges that helped the church to discern how best it could live out its citizenship in God's city though living as otherworldly wanderers on earth.

His thoroughgoing realism led him both to hymn creation as God's gift as well as to comment how even little babies were envious of one another (and hence fallen from grace). It also involved his acceptance of civil authority, flawed as it was, as an instrument of corrective punishment of heretics. As anyone familiar with the growth of the just war tradition knows, he was no pacifist. God's ways of dealing with erring humanity seemed to him to be made of sterner stuff in this grim life (especially after the sack of Rome). He promoted the legal suppression of the Donatists by the same logic that allowed God, who once chose the Jews, to reject them (the unfathomable will of God, the doctrine of predestination). But even this splitting off of some in the human race for glory and others for hellfire did not solve all of Augustine's dilemmas when he sought to live in the dissolving world of the empire. Salvation, it seemed, was reserved for the few; most of humanity was a "damned lump" (*massa damnata*), unleavened and unleavenable — except for the gift of God's grace.

Just when we are ready to dismiss Augustine as a paranoid schizophrenic, projecting onto the world his own unresolved conflicts, overwhelmed by his own limitations and by the finitude of the human condition, he surprises us. He is not the first or the last analyst to pronounce the human condition sick. Still, his final years were spent waging the case for grace and healing as God's first and last word of revelation.

His last controversy was with a second generation of Pelagians, led by Bishop Julian of Eclanum, Italy. It revolved around an issue that recapitulated Augustine's own career first as a Manichee and then as an enthusiastic neo-Platonist. One might even say that the controversy pitted his early loves, with their realist and idealist pretensions, against one another and then threw them back at the aging bishop. Like the Manichees, the Pelagians were rationalists, but they reasoned very differently about the human condition. Humanity had not fallen in the garden; it had just taken a wrong turn and could, with the right amount of coaching and determination, turn again and choose the virtuous life. Having once followed the example of disobedient Adam, people could now choose to be good and follow the example of Christ. Like the neo-Platonists, the Pelagians presumed that progress in the life of the Spirit followed as the night the day, if only one followed God's law and arranged one's life in such a way as to preserve virtue. In many ways the conflict between Julian and Augustine adumbrated the heat of the nature/nurture argument in social psychology centuries later. The Pelagian theologian insisted that a good environment would make a person better, while Augustine countered that human nature, because of its sexual and emotional conflicts, was more complex. For the Pelagians, moral freedom came as a human endowment. For Augustine, it was achieved only through an inner struggle: "The understanding flies on ahead, and there follows on, so slowly, if at all, our weakened capacity for feeling."[12]

Portraits of Augustine as obsessed by the issue of sexual desire and the weakness of human capacities based on concupiscence are, nevertheless, unfair. He was more astute, recognizing that human behavior is very convoluted. The Pelagians stressed Christianity's abilities to change deep-seated habits through moral reform. Augustine understood that removing one source of temptation (as puritanical societies have consistently tried to do by legislation) only repressed a desire that, if a person did not heal, would only spring up elsewhere.[13] Choice, in and of itself, could not unite knowledge and will, understanding and emotion. That unity would be found only beyond human self-determination, in our dependence on God, in the love God bestows, in the help we receive to be healed of the wound of our mortality, in Grace. Thus, finally, the mystery of grace, God's life bestowed in Christ's outpoured Spirit, mitigated Augustine's terrifying flirtation with a depressive picture of human fate: we are born between the urine and the feces and we die no matter what we do.

If Augustine was tempted by too much necessity, he was saved from it, and from himself, by grace. It did not prevent him from splitting off the damned from the saved nor seeing sexual desire as anything but a "dark mirror-image" of a fierce longing for God, a "leaden echo of true delight."[14] Nor did it prevent his accepting a tyrannical view of authority or endowing the church with a capacity for a violence that it has only today begun to repudiate. Instead it led him to pit his darkened humanism against the neat compartmentalizations of more Hellenized thinkers like Bishop Julian and John Cassian, for whom sexuality was merely what free choice made it. For Augustine, concupiscence was a tragic flaw precisely because the soul was meant to love the body but the body's genitality was sadly discordant with the will, a flaw that, he argued against Julian, was God's punishment for Adam's willful act of disobedience.[15] The aristocratic Bishop Julian's philosophical idealizations created a system useful only to a few highly educated people like himself. Augustine did not invent shame for the body in its relation to either lust or death, but the vicissitudes of his own sexual life and his hypersensitivity to them led to his fetishizing the indeterminacy of the body's sexuality as the reason for human unhappiness. Unlike more enthusiastic ascetics like Jerome and the stoical Ambrose, who asserted that the married remained under the law, while pious virgins were under grace, Augustine sought to keep some balance between the body and the person, between sexuality and the believers' spiritual possibility. Still, when his diagnosis of the human condition was repeated by others outside the broader context of the pilgrimage to healing (the controlling metaphor of his life and writings) his fuller thinking was lost and his teaching came out unbalanced.[16]

On the positive side, Augustine did bequeath to Catholic theology in the West, in concert with other writers of both East and West, an appreciation of the multileveled sense of the Bible, a belief that not everything had been said, a conviction that the church was not a coven of the spiritually perfect but a society of redeemed, if struggling, sinners. This amounts to a paradigm of moderate possibility: the redeemed life is a gift, and to lead it "the Spirit, too, helps us in our weakness" (Rom 8:26). His blindnesses are as much part of his legacy as his clear vision and his introspection. After him, Western religious culture is decidedly guilty, because it possesses a shadow-side comprised of a dark current of sexual shame. With him, Catholicism has flirted with too much possibility only for its professional classes (the clergy and religious), not for the laity or for society as a whole. Though he recognized that Christianity had relevance for all humanity, he seemed unable to open his mind or heart wide enough to admit the many to salvation. Still, after him, the Catholic Church would never be a church for the few. It sought to lessen life's harshness with sacramental mysteries and their promise of a life better than this vale of tears. Because Augustine's balance was imperfect, his legacy for the church's journey through history between the Scylla of too much possibility and the Charybdis of too much necessity is an ambiguous one. Without facing that ambiguity, especially in matters of human sexuality, no postcritical appropriation of belief will be possible.

Managing God's Monarchy

Augustine's victory over the Pelagians is said to have begun the transition from the classical to the medieval world. After the brief resurgence of the Byzantine imperial authority in Italy (527–65), the papacy, strengthened under Leo I (440–61), emerged as a monarchy under Gregory I (590–604), filling the vacuum in the West created by the collapse of the imperial power. In North Africa, the contentious Christian churches disappeared under the onslaught of militant Islam, whose advance west and north was only halted at Tours in France in 711. Throughout the seventh and eighth centuries, Celtic monks from Ireland and Iona off the coast of Scotland replanted Christian churches as far south as Bobbio in Italy. The feudal order emerged as cities shrunk, leaving castles and monasteries to anchor what passed for organized society, religion, and learning.

Though Charlemagne's crowning by the pope on Christmas of 800 is often presented as reestablishing the political and ecclesiastical order, his kingdom fragmented on his death. Only after another hundred years did a social and political order eventually emerge that became the seedbed of medieval and modern Europe. Thousands upon thousands of anonymous peasants, soldiers, monks, and nuns lived and died (often violently) exercising little freedom, having few options about their circumstances, hoping for a better world beyond the nasty, brutish, and short life they knew. Diminished possibility and ineluctable fate defined daily life. People thought themselves fortunate to escape the fierce judgments of God in this world and prayed that they would do so in the next as well. In place of the classical worldview of human possibility within providential bounds, the medieval West labored under the threat of rape and pillage, looking only back to the "empire" of Charlemagne as a time of peace, prosperity and unity.[17]

The Eastern empire, though itself shrunken by the expansion of Islam, endured the iconoclast controversy and imperial intrigues, as Byzantine Christianity took on a different flavor from its Western counterpart. As representatives of New Rome, its missionaries turned north and, in the tenth century, while Poland was being evangelized by Western missionaries, brought Duke Vladimir of Kievan Rus and his people into the Eastern (Orthodox) fold. The East/West fault line, which the formal split between Rome and Constantinople in 1054 C.E. solidified, was becoming not only a cultural but a theological chasm. Christianity was becoming either Latin and Western, or Greek and Eastern. As Latin Christianity shifted decidedly toward the necessity pole, it closed itself off to many elements of spiritual possibility that characterized Orthodoxy. This meant that, in the West, the possibility pole would continue to be associated with classical humanism.

In the tenth century, the Roman papacy sank to its pre-Renaissance nadir as the office of bishop of Rome was held by a succession of local rogues.[18] When society no longer comprised an urban network under centralized authorities but dissolved into fractious duchies, the shape of church ministry also changed. Though bishops and their cathedral chapters continued to be the norm in cities, a clear episcopal-presbyteral-diaconal structure ceased to function both in monasteries and in the towns that clustered near the fortified seats of counts, dukes, and prince-kings. A bevy of proprietal churches arose whose upkeep depended on the secular authority. Bishops were rarely in the position to provide and maintain clergy for outlying areas, let alone educate them. Hence church order was mainly presbyteral, dependent on lay potentates for maintenance and on monasteries for liturgical and theological leadership. Church life survived for the average Catholic without the leadership of an Ambrose or an Augustine. When a reorganization began in the eleventh century, the impetus came, not from bishops or from the minimally educated lower clergy, but from the monasteries.

Already in the tenth century, reforms had revived monasticism. From this newly confident milieu Emperor Henry III appointed Gregory VI pope in 1049. Gregory brought with him to Rome other monks itching to bring the fruits of reform to the church at large. Still, in the harsh conditions of the time, he and three more popes came and went by 1061. By then, the East/West schism had occurred when one of Leo's reforming monks, Abbot (later Cardinal) Umberto, excommunicated the patriarch in Constantinople. Another reforming monk, Hildebrand, was elected pope in 1073 and took the name Gregory VII. With him, monastic zeal invented and installed a new model of defining and sustaining the identity of the church.

From its fourth-century emergence as a prominent element in Roman imperial society, Christianity's standards (or canons) of belief and practice had been the Bible, the writings of the fathers, the records of the local councils and their decrees, and the sacramentaries, or standard books of worship. This would soon change as the reforming monastic papacy undertook to reorganize church life. Gregory's first efforts involved sending legates to revive the practice of local regulative synods. Few had much effect, given the centuries-long habit of purely local control that had led to the combining of ecclesiastical and social authority. Counts or dukes who were also bishops or abbots were reluctant to surrender their longstanding authority to synods.

Under Gregory VII, the reform movement shifted the base for its efforts and chose as its cry *Libertas ecclesiae!* ("freedom for the church"), by which they meant to deprive lay "secular" authorities of their time-honored rights to appoint ecclesiastical ("religious") officials. This novel distinction allowed the reformers to subvert local laws and customs

and overturn longstanding traditions. In their zeal, the monastic reformers formulated a theology that erected a rigid distinction between two
earthly societies: the civil and the ecclesiastical. Augustine's scenario of
two cities in the world was split further and applied to the church,
which was no longer one society, but two, one clerical and one lay.
Armed with this spiritual distinction read into law, the monastic papacy
forbade laymen from exercising any *potestas* or authority over priests,
because priesthood was a unique spiritual office. When it came to *potestas sacerdotalis,* no earthly, secular authority could interfere, because (as
Aquinas would later state) "the power of the priest does not depend on
any higher power except divine power."[19]

Church historians have commonly lionized Gregory VII as an un-
alloyed hero whose bravery in the face of the emperor Henry IV's
"cynical traffic in bishoprics and abbeys" preserved the identity of the
church after the depredations of the "dark ages."[20] Reviving the notion
of fullness of power (*plenitudo potestatis*) from Leo I — for whom it
might well have a moral rather than a legal sense — Gregory sought to
make canonical legislation emanating from Rome the supreme authority
in regulating church life. The *Dictatus Papae,* which was entered in the
papal register in 1075, listed the principles on whose basis the Roman
Pontiff laid claim to a revolutionary status for his office, one of near
absolute authority. Among its twenty-seven titles or provisions claiming that all bishops, clerics, and lay persons, including emperors, were
subject to the pope, were these:

7. That for him alone it is lawful to enact laws according to the needs of
   the time, to assemble together new congregations, to make an abbey of
   a canonry and, on the other hand, to divide a rich bishopric and unite a
   poor one.

8. That he alone may use the imperial insignia.

10. That his name alone is to be recited in the churches.

12. That he may depose emperors.

26. That he should not be considered a Catholic who is not in conformity
    with the Roman Church.[21]

This self-conscious inflation of the spiritual and temporal power of
the pope would appropriate many more titles and prerogatives before it
reached its zenith. The pope became Vicar of Christ and Vicar of God,
whose sway extended over all human beings. This became explicit in
Unam Sanctam, a dogmatic bull of Boniface VIII (1294–1303): "We declare, state, and define that it is absolutely necessary for the salvation
of all that they submit to the Roman Pontiff."[22] Perhaps the pressure

of conflict with civil authorities, and in particular with the renascent French monarchy, pushed Boniface to the logical extreme of the reformers' position. When Philip the Fair retaliated by issuing a call for a general council, the pope drew up a bull of excommunication and deposition. To prevent its promulgation, the French imprisoned him in his home fortress, where he died within the month at age eight-five. In consequence, from 1305 to 1378 the popes were "guests" of the French monarchy at Avignon — one result of the monastic papacy's decision to fight worldly power with worldly power disguised as "spiritual."

What contributed to the popes' claim to such a grandiose authority that could never be exercised in fact? Part of an answer lies in the mindset that had been developing since Hildebrand's days. The instrument for the developing theories of universal primacy and cosmic sovereignty was the rediscovery of a unique form of "possibility" — code law, a set of rational principles for societal conduct that was ancient Rome's contribution to the Hellenistic world.

Beginning in the eleventh century, both clerical and lay scholars had begun to study the rediscovered *Corpus Juris Civilis* of Justinian and to frame laws for a society driven by violence for half a millennium. These scholars had a dream that law, harmonized with the moral and spiritual force of the church, could create a renewed civil society. In 1140, the monk Gratian produced an enormous volume (known as the *Decretum)* whose full title expressed its outsized purpose: called the *Concordia Disconcordantium Canonum*, this collection harmonized all discordant church laws and sought to eliminate any doubt "about the pope's omnipotence or about the precedence of church law over secular law." As the founder of ecclesiastical canon law, Gratian sought to provide a uniform jurisdictional and sacramental code for the church. The effort also promoted order in society as well, by subordinating everyone to the supreme legislative authority of the pope.[23]

This ideal, however, was impossible to realize outside an imperially coercive system. For code law (as opposed to statutory law) legislates universally, providing for exceptions through a system of dispensations by the legislator. Necessarily comprehensive, it presumes the omnipotence and omniscience of the legislator. It is also totalistic, fitting only in a highly unified society whose variations can be contained and whose social nuances can be subordinated to its dominant worldview. Because canon law was modeled on a code of legal decrees (in which the pope took the place of emperor), the entire superstructure was based on the will of the legislator. The whole canonical mentality, convinced of its unlimited capacity for regulating human affairs, courted too much possibility. Even on one of his most grandiose days, Augustine would have scoffed at the effort.[24]

Because the model for canon law was not the Bible but a philosophy of civil law, its practitioners tended to reduce law to its purely regulative and coercive function.[25] Though law can be viewed analogically, all biblical, ecclesiastical, or civil laws were identified as variant species of the same God-given genus. Though Albert the Great cautioned that the variability of the real should make legislators hesitate to locate all human actions under one and the same universal rule, and Aquinas called for applying laws according to the principle of *epicheia* or equity, canonists legislated (and judged) cases in a literal vein. Issues of morality were subsumed as a subset of juridical matters, and code law, though it had been revived as an exercise in the instrumentality of reason, became more an exercise of spiritual willfulness.[26]

In the canonical perspective, the laity were negative creatures, defined by what they were not (not clerics). The church became formally identified with those in authority, who held "ordinary power" and could dispense to a passive faithful the helps necessary for salvation. Under Alexander III (1159–81), who sat with his cardinals in consistory *every day* to hear and decide lawsuits, the Third Lateran Council (1179) formally removed any lay role in the election of bishops and invested it exclusively in the cathedral chapters. Equivalently, sacramental mediation no longer proclaimed the graced *possibility* that a life of worshipful praise offered here below; rather, it was understood through the minimal conditions legally *necessary* for their potent validity.

As the high Middle Ages ensued, the lawyers' desire to legislate all areas of life and morality not formerly subject to public law was combined with the new academic method of dialectic and its ever greater distinctions between what had formerly been seen as parts of the whole. Legalistic rationality reached its early peak at the Fourth Lateran Council in 1215. Its canons literally separated out the holy from the profane, legislating that Jews wear distinctive clothing, that married priests be forcibly separated from their wives, and that homosexuals be segregated from the society around them.[27] Behind the monastic papacy's attempt to regulate purity of life and segregate the sacred from the secular lies a complex temptation toward both too much possibility and too much necessity. The compounding of the two led to a fixity that turned otherworldly symbols into this-worldly privileges. Rather than seek a balance or compromise between infinity and finitude, the hierarchical mechanism of law was subverted by the dread necessity of its own spiritual power.

There were dissenting voices, but they could not derail the papacy's attempt to legislate an ideal Christian society into existence. Even a giant like Bernard of Clairvaux, who still operated out of the nondialectical world of the fathers and saw the dangers of the new literalism in the concept of papal authority, yielded to the combination of papal power, military might, and grandiose conviction about doing God's will by preaching a holy war.[28] Such had the necessity of violence and counter-violence become that even an otherwise saintly and wise man could send Christian soldiers (who would not stop fighting one another) on a crusade, a war for the cross of Christ. As we saw, when identity is un-balanced, one response is a negative identity, a decision to be bad rather than to be nobody, or even to be dead rather than not quite somebody.[29] The Crusades, a politico-religio-military adventure of great import and great evil, sent thousands of "bad boys" off to redeem themselves, not by changing their violence but by declaring it good and making the enemy evil. Here is one more instance of Christianity's spiritual possibility buying into necessary evil, splitting off all its own violence and projecting all its ambivalence about itself outward onto others — priests' wives, Jews, homosexuals, Muslims — and seeking to segregate or drive them out.

One great dissenter to the age's Faustian pacts between spiritual possibility and military necessity was Francis of Assisi — not that he lacked his own form of spiritual grandiosity. Accepting poverty, chastity, and obedience without the protection of a monastic enclosure and a brother cellarer, kissing lepers, taming the wolf of Gubbio, dousing what food he did eat with ashes lest he enjoy it too much, walking barefoot in the snow, and going alone on crusade not to fight but to convert the Sultan by preaching the gospel of love to him in person — these are not the actions of a simple lay brother. Rather, Francis accepted the great possibility of the call to be like Christ because he had seen through all the neuroses of health that had first attracted him as a young man itching to be a chivalrous knight on horseback.

In seeking to become like Christ his *Signor*, he sought true self-transcendence, a goal he may have reached shortly before he died. Despite the adulation he received in his lifetime, he constantly called himself a sinner and pushed himself further. He was uniquely able to complement his spiritual grandiosity by opting, not for cultural or religious heroism, but for the possibilities of a cosmic spirituality. He accomplished this to the extent he did, not by mystically trying to leave the flesh and the world behind, but by never being more than two inches away from his finitude, his creatureliness, his mortality. Francis learned to a stunning degree that Christ's death and its outcome in resurrection had tamed necessity to such an extent that the mystery had come around fully and revealed death to be, not the opposite of spiritual possibility, but its entranceway. Refusing any of the false asceticism that denied creatureliness, Francis bonded with irrational creatures (even speaking with them, we are told) and created a wholly new devotion to the humanity of Christ. He stayed close to the earth. A few years before his death, he had experienced the limits of spiritual possibility in this life with the vision of the crucified Christ in glory (the paradox of life in death) and from it came away wounded with the marks of Christ's love for all humanity (the stigmata).

A rare spiritual artist whose life testifies to the possibility of self-transcendence, he reintegrated and wove together former antinomies, seeing in them the coincidence of opposites to which his biographer St. Bonaventure testified at the conclusion of his own masterpiece, *The Soul's Journey into God*.[30] His dying words commended his own radical poverty to his brothers and sisters, a legacy whose spiritual possibility would tempt some perhaps too greatly. His legacy, while bequeathing to Catholicism large numbers of loyal male and female religious, also pitted Franciscan spiritual possibility against papal power, presaging the Reformation and the separation of political power from spiritual authority in the modern West.

Paradoxically, Innocent III won approval for the Franciscans, against the determined opposition of the Cistercians, at the same council (Lateran IV) that was opting to exclude impure elements from Christian society. Papal support for the burgeoning company of poor brothers and sisters was forthcoming because the Franciscans and their fellow mendicants, the Dominicans, gave the papacy leverage in a struggle that had been simmering for some time. Throughout the 1100s, groups like the Poor Men of Lyons, the Beguines, the Beghards, the Albigensians, and the Waldensians had waged various spiritual and social protests against a politicized church heavy with trappings of power and wealth. They charged that the hierarchy, the clergy, and the monasteries were guilty of betraying the apostolic simplicity of the early church. To take the wind from their sails, the popes, beginning with Innocent, who personally met with Francis, encouraged apostolically poor but loyal orders like the Franciscans and Dominicans, and they flourished.

In response to the growth of universities, the mendicant orders founded houses in the new urban centers of learning. But a portion of the Franciscans sought to remain faithful to the radical vision of their father, *il Poverello*. In the heat of their conviction, the Spirituals (those who refused to live in convents, as against the Conventuals) turned and bit the hand that had fed them. Maintaining the fiction that they owned nothing (by deeding their property to the papacy), they took up the teachings of the visionary Cistercian monk Joachim of Fiore (d. 1202). Convinced of the corruption of the church and breathing an older monastic antipathy for the novel dialectical spirit of the universities, Joachim had taught that a third age of the Spirit was about to dawn, in which the decadent church would disappear. Seizing upon this rupture between the kingdom to come and a too-worldly church, the Spiritual (or Black) Franciscans predicted the collapse of the church (in 1260) and the dawn of the millennium, the ultimate possibility that constantly tempts the church-in-time.

As the Spirituals were becoming more strident, the papacy was becoming more assertive of its power over kings, princes, bishops, and church life *in toto*. By the time the Spirituals had been crushed by the Inquisition, the papacy had become compromised even further by its captivity at Avignon (whose chancery became known for its financial avidity) and by the Western schism that produced three rival claimants to the papal title. The reform of the church "in head and members" that Innocent III had sought in the decrees of Lateran IV had failed. His strategy of using the mendicants against the entrenched bishops and clergy had weakened the latter's loyalty to the papacy so that many, for instance, sided with Philip the Fair in his struggle with Boniface VIII (as they later would side with Henry VIII against Clement VII over the issue of Henry's divorce). Subsequently, general councils that included laity (Constance in 1414 and Basel/Ferrara/Florence from 1431 to 1449) sought to employ church law to correct papal rivalries and clerical abuses. Though the centralized papacy eventually prevailed over the conciliarist movement, it never adequately refuted the Spirituals' contention that it was decadent and had severed itself from the wellsprings of spiritual power. Political necessity consistently got the better of the spiritual possibility of gospel poverty. By burning critics as heretics, the Catholic Church maintained itself as a worldly power, polluting its own life-giving waters. The results followed as the night the day.

The medieval papacy, seeing its own hierarchical mediation of grace as the only link to God's eternal kingdom, overinvested in its own mythic amalgam of spiritual and earthly power. The Renaissance princes who occupied the Chair of Peter into the sixteenth century failed to stem an even more explicit challenge to the papacy's self-mesmerizing totalism. That challenge ended papal hegemony over Western Christianity and prepared the way for modernity's own crisis of spiritual meaning. While it eventually ended the papacy's pretensions to political power, it set off a reaction that led to a further hypertrophying of the papacy's will to control faith affirmation.

Divine Necessity Triumphant

Though his name is inextricably linked to the Reformation, Luther's intellectual and affective tools show him to be an heir of the Renaissance. Philosophically, he shared the nominalists' skepticism about knowing God by way of analogy, an anchor of Thomistic scholasticism. Mixed with the Renaissance's concern for mapping the material forces that shaped the world, nominalism believed that God held all things together by the force of will. God's willful activity (voluntarism) fit well with the Renaissance's projection onto God of its gamble that the human being was the measure of all things. Both the Reformation and the Counter-Reformation sowed the seeds of modern theology's dilemma. Tracing the struggle over how God's will is manifested has great importance in our search for a postcritical maturity.

A professor of scripture, Luther was a monk for whom the schools had become too full of exaggerated rationalist possibility about God to the detriment of divine freedom. Yet God's willful freedom also confronted Luther with his own doubts about how he could be saved. He had become a monk to resolve an identity crisis, stemming from his conflict with his father, a member of the rising bourgeoisie who wanted his son to be a lawyer. When being a strict and genuinely ascetic monk did not allow him to "feel his way to God," his negative identity portrayed God as a "dreadful and untrustworthy father."[31] His dilemma pitted a wrecked rational possibility from the human side against a demanding God whose unfathomable will, much as in Augustine, had to be trusted absolutely. The only anchor in this storm was the individual believer's solitary encounter with Christ, the God-man. Luther himself credited his Augustinian mentor Johann von Staupitz with the idea that faith comes first and that we can face God's son and look at him as a human. With this insight, Brother Martin took on and reshaped Christianity, aiming his charges primarily against the clergy's monopoly on the means of the individual's salvation. He did not seek to reform the church institutionally — too many had failed at that. He gave sinners a new way to trust in their salvation.

Emphasizing the individual conscience, Luther enacted a drama that modernity, in both its secular and religious forms, has been confronting ever since. Almost immediately, others drew revolutionary implications from his challenge to empire and church, launching the Peasants' Revolt. Though Luther backtracked and repudiated the lawless mob he had done so much to inspire, revolutionary Puritanism (inspired by John Calvin) continued to agitate against absolutism in seventeenth- and eighteenth-century France and England, and in America as well. Because Luther understood the human being as *simul justus et peccator*, justified by grace but still in the thrall of sinfulness, he could be no social reformer. Having freed individuals from the heavy-handed authority of Rome, he could not free them from other social and political determinations while life in this world endured. His theology of salvation had great appeal in a society still recovering from the trauma of the Black Plague and the negative identity it had inspired. If people were codetermined by both sin and grace, they had to deal not only with their own personal ambivalences but also with the mixture of good and evil in society. Against the hypertrophied rationalism of the schools, the monopoly of priestly mediation by the clerical system of sacraments, and a bloated papal monarchy (all evidence of Rome's yielding to too much possibility), he saw humankind hemmed in by both religious and secular necessity.

Religiously, all possibility was God's, except for that which God had done for humanity in Christ. Human freedom was necessarily bound up with sin to such a degree that only grace, faith, and the Word of God could break through to humanity's imprisoned will and free them to love God and their neighbors as themselves. For Luther, just as for Augustine, grace, faith, and the word of God represent the only real spiritual possibilities for the Christian believer, but in different proportions.[32] Unlike Calvin and other more radical reformers who would follow him, Luther did not so thoroughly split off the saved from the damned as the necessary correlation of God's arbitrary and unfathomable will. For him, the essential split was an internal one. The battleground for the struggle was the individual's soul (becoming a conscience) and its affective judgment about where it stood in God's sight. Perhaps it is fair to say that Luther posed the problem of reduced human possibility more effectively than he solved it. Like his patristic mentor, Luther left behind a paradigm of moderate possibility, but one that impacted in a new way on believers as *individuals*. To be saved, each and every one had to master narrowness and finitude by attachment to Christ's suffering on their behalf. That portrayal of the believer's dilemma was convincing enough to survive the Counter-Reformation assault on it. It also impacted on modern society, despite growing secularity, and through its influence there, revisited Catholicism at a later date.[33]

The Counter-Reformation began with the close of the Council of Trent in 1563 and lasted until 1963, when Vatican II's first fruits began to be felt. During those four centuries Catholicism responded to the challenge of the Protestant "revolt" by getting its own ecclesiastical life in order. But it never adequately rethought the underlying issues that allowed the Reformation the success it had enjoyed. Not willing to admit its own errors of fact or judgment or to concede any of the Reformers' positions, Tridentine Catholicism froze itself into an ahistorical mold, pretending that everything essentially Catholic had been there from the beginning.[34]

Despite being institutionally stiff-necked in the face of Protestant criticism, Catholicism's system of sacramental mediation, its main line of defense since Augustine against the overwhelming threat of damnation, was not unaffected by Luther's assault. Trent solemnly defined, for the first time, the existence of seven sacraments, a number arrived at in the Middle Ages (from a possible forty). By them the church (now identified as the hierarchy) administered to the faithful from the womb to the tomb and, beyond, from purgatory to paradise. Though aimed at saving the soul of the individual from hellfire, Catholicism's weight fell not on any individual struggle but on the validity of its sacramental mediation. In any conflict there could be no doubt which came first. Protestantism stood for private, individual interpretation within the framework of righteousness by faith; Catholicism for ecclesiastical rectitude as the surest mediator of grace. Hence the Catholic believer was bound by dreadful necessity: the church alone could assure salvation. But the church (as a clerical caste of sacred mediators) balanced this sense of doom by its sacramental potency, its grace-filled actions that, when validly administered, functioned *ex opere operato* (automatically) to render the soul capable of withstanding judgment. Protestant possibility relied on God's active sympathy for Christ, with whom the righteous bonded through an act of personal acceptance and belief, but they could make no claims on God. Catholic possibility was more robust and gave the obedient believer some claim on salvation, but the power was strictly in the consecrated hands of the clergy and hierarchy.

In the seventeenth century a resurgent Catholicism went on the offensive, fueled by the Counter-Reformation zeal of Spanish Carmelites, Franciscan missionaries, and their new rivals, the Jesuits. In 1622, the papacy established the congregation *Pro Propaganda Fidei* as a centralized missionary arm to free missionaries from dependence on Catholic monarchs. Gianlorenzo Bernini finished what Maderno and Michelangelo had begun in Rome, expressing in splendid artistic construction the continuity of the church (that is, the papacy and the hierarchy). To this day the tombs of the popes and the memorials to Catholic sovereigns in St. Peter's testify to the presumption of permanence and solidity by which the eternal church would continue to prevail against the gates of hell and the plots of schismatics and heretics. Built as a mausoleum to the apostle Peter — and despite the fact that its very construction had been a cause of the Reformation! — St. Peter's advertised the Roman Church's spiritual possibility and divinely constituted authority. The skeletons on its Baroque tombs admitted the necessity of physical death and decay, but *the* church lived for all time. This was Baroque Rome's lesson in stone, glass, and gilt, expressing its increasingly exaggerated ability to guide the course of human affairs as God willed. One hundred and thirty-one years after Luther posted his theses, the papacy was still unreconciled to Protestantism's very existence, and Innocent X condemned the Peace of Westphalia for recognizing Protestant churches as legitimate. What had begun at Trent as a program to refute error and reform weaknesses had become a hard and fast ideology that denied standing to any ecclesial rival. The claim that the Roman authorities and the pope in particular were responsible for pronouncing on all matters of faith and morals, that they constituted a singular teaching authority over the whole church, is the final chapter in this genealogy. It fills out the picture of how the Reformation's challenge to Rome's spiritual power was the midwife to the modern shape of Roman claims.

The Church's Necessary Power

In response to the Reformers' iconoclasm, the Council of Trent defended "those traditions relating to both faith and *mores* as either verbally from Christ or dictated by the Holy Spirit, and preserved in continuous succession in the Catholic Church." In the context of Trent's defense, the clear meaning of *mores* is "practices," the traditional customs of worship and devotion (including indulgences) that had been longstanding in the worship-life of the Catholic people. Similarly, the Roman Catechism of 1566 repeated the phrase "faith and *mores*" when defending the inerrancy of the church as guided by the Spirit. Neither declaration made any reference to a special competence to teach about the moral life.[35] Trent's modesty on the issue of faith and morals was nothing new. At the Council of Constance in 1415, a similar defense against the followers of the proto-Reformers Wycliff and Hus had been used. Before that, Aquinas had argued to the inerrancy of the pope's teachings in matters of faith (*2a 2ae*, q. 1, a. 10) with no mention of *mores*. Trent's argument was not in favor of papal authority (an issue it avoided) but with the more general point of the trustworthiness of the church's worship life.[36]

But within a half-century, as part of the Counter-Reformation Catholic offensive, Robert Bellarmine (d. 1621), Professor of Controversial Theology at the Collegio Romano from 1576 to 1588, propounded the spiritual power of the Roman pontiff with none of the modesty Trent had shown. He introduced into mainstream Roman theology an opinion inflating the role of the pope that reached back to the first claims for papal infallibility in the thirteenth century. Specifically, Bellarmine argued that the pope could be mistaken in matters of fact and even as a private teacher of faith and morals, but that, in concert with a general council, he could not err in laying down decrees of faith or "general precepts of morals...which are prescribed for the whole Church and have to do with matters necessary for salvation or with matters which are good or bad in themselves." Even in "doubtful matters," Bellarmine averred (here following his Jesuit founder Ignatius's rules of "thinking with the church"),

the Church is obliged to agree with the judgments of the Supreme Pontiff and to do what he commands and not to do what he prohibits; and lest it should act against conscience, it is obliged to believe that good which he orders, and that bad which he prohibits.[37]

What seems to be at work here is the totally military model of obeying orders and commands that had become popular in the Society of Jesus, whose members took an extra vow of obedience to the pope.

But there was another influence at work, one Luther himself was comfortable with theologically if not ecclesiologically. This was the notion that the supreme arbiter of the world is the Will of God (by whose absolute power the world exists) and that the laws of both nature and morality proceed immediately from the divine will. From the late Middle Ages to the present, this voluntaristic notion of law (as based on the will of the law-giver) has been a major modality by which religious culture has sought to cope with the felt limitations of its own possibility. Confronted with finitude and with a reduced sense of what we can know about universals, nominalist philosophers and their legal partners, voluntarist theologians and canonists, adopted a narrowed view of the role of law.

The same revolution that sought to abolish final causes from the study of natural phenomena and created the "ultimate prospect of science . . . a *mathesis universalis* — an unequivocal, universal, coherent, yet artificial language to capture our 'clear and distinct ideas' and their unique combinations," also created a theology that projected onto the entire relationship of God to the world a sense of necessary correlation between what is and what must be.[38] The same passion for univocal terms and the same impatience with equivocation and analogy that motivated Descartes in mathematics and Leibniz in philosophy had already led Francisco Suarez (d. 1617) to abandon Thomas's analogical predication of divine activities and to accept a completely nominalist perspective on law. For Suarez, "our justice consists in our will, which is weak and not right in itself, being conformed to the rule of the divine will, which is essentially right." Hence, the supreme norm of rightness of action is the law, and law becomes the norm of morals, since all laws derive directly from God if they are authentic. Whereas for Aquinas, law "is nothing other than a certain ordering of reason for the common good promulgated by one having the care of a community" (*1a 2ae*, q. 90, a. 4), for Suarez it became "the act of a just and right will (*voluntas*) by which a superior wills (*vult*) to oblige an inferior to do this or that."[39] From a world of rational possibility that presumed we could understand something of God by our analogical application of human terms of experience, voluntarism lurched in the opposite direction toward rational necessity. No longer convinced that it could understand via analogous reason the finality or purpose of God's law, Tridentine Catholicism closed a defensive perimeter around dogmatic theology, moral teaching, and canon law and committed itself to submit to God's Will.

For Luther, the rejection of mediatory symbols, by which God indirectly affected change in nature and in persons (hence, instrumentally), had prompted him to relate to God by faith alone. For Catholicism, it led to knowing God by reason alone and reducing the differences between the ways humans and divinity accomplish their will. Sidestepping Aquinas's caution that the differences were greater than the similarities that we predicate by analogy, Counter-Reformation theology necessarily identified the ways of God with the ways that we know them. Protests against this mania for univocation and its abandonment of metaphorical and symbolic language were exceptional and gained for writers like Pascal inclusion on the *Index of Forbidden Books*.[40] Despite the humanism inherent in the rational perspective of this theology, it reduced the mysteries of creation and redemption at the heart of Christianity to a necessary system of rewards and penalties, quantifiable divine demands and equally quantifiable human obedience.

In such a reductionist theological environment, faith was narrowed to a necessary intellectual assent to those relatively few propositions that escaped reason's exaggerated capacities, and *mores* were equally reduced to morals. No longer the whole network of doxological response (the *lex orandi*) by which believing (the *lex credendi*) was established, *mores* became literally "moral law." With this final step beyond the medieval fixation of spiritual power in the hierarchy, the nineteenth and twentieth centuries have seen Rome's pretensions to universal political authority shift into a claim to possess *magisterial* authority to bind the faithful within certain prescribed laws of human behavior.

This claim peaked at Vatican I, which, in a triumph for Bellarmine's ideology, defined papal infallibility in matters of faith and morals. At the same time, while the fathers of Vatican I obliged Pius IX by giving him a definition *that* the Roman Pontiff is infallible when speaking "*ex cathedra*...defining a teaching about faith or morals to be held by the universal Church," they were much more chary about *what* faith and morals entails (see chapter 9). There is no doubt that *mores* in this context meant requisite human moral behavior, nor that the definition spoke of a special competence encompassing the definition of certain moral responses. But to the frustration of bishops who pleaded for some explanation "of what was to be understood by that word *mores*" and of those who complained that the definition had not gone far enough, the only explanation offered — before the council abruptly ended — directed the bishops to consult a competent theologian on the subject of the extraordinary papal magisterium in morals.[41]

In the post–Vatican I period, the same theological party that had wanted a stronger statement of Roman authority continued its efforts further to inflate the areas of competence that the pope (and his Curia) were qualified to define on behalf of the whole church. Despite the efforts of Newman and others to point out the moderate and limited character of the definition, popes after Vatican I have presumed that their major role was to be the ordinary teacher of Catholic doctrine and faith response. Pius IX defined the role of the theologian as demonstrating how the doctrines defined by the church were contained in the sources of revelation. Leo XIII spawned a conservative Thomistic revival and limited the scope of biblical scholarship with his encyclical letter

Providentissimus Deus of 1893. Pius X considered Leo's theological advisors too accommodating to the spirit of modernity and suppressed the efforts of theologians and biblical scholars to benefit from advances in the historical and social sciences. Benedict XV defined the area of theological discussion as comprising *only* those upon which the Roman See had not delivered its own judgment (DS 3625); Pius XI took it for granted that this magisterium was "exercised every day by the Roman Pontiff and the Bishops in communion with him," and Pius XII repeated that the function of the theologian was to indicate how what the "living magisterium" teaches is found in scripture or tradition. Beyond that, he claimed for this centralized living magisterium (looking more and more like a caste of persons) the God-given purpose "of illuminating and unfolding what are only obscurely and implicitly in the deposit of faith."[42] Under John Paul II, the expansion of magisterial pronouncements, known as "creeping infallibilism," has speeded up to a gallop. Its effect is to treat papal pronouncements as oracles from God's vicar, something that the Living Apostle and Prophet of the Church of Jesus Christ of the Latter-day Saints claims for himself but that has no support in the defined Catholic dogma regarding the bishop of Rome.

What I am arguing is that the modern inflation of papal and hierarchical teaching authority corresponds to a mindset tempted, as were the medieval papacy's politics, by too much spiritual possibility bound up with voluntarist necessity. Like the Pelagians, whose rationalist premises declared that since holiness was possible it was obligatory, papalist theologians since Bellarmine have presumed that since it was *possible* for the church to teach on matters of faith and how to enact that faith, it was *necessary* to do this univocally and unequivocally, with as little room for indeterminateness and freedom as can be managed. This constricted understanding of how God acts in our midst — binding us not principally through an innate moral sense that allows us communion with divine reason or the Logos of God but through laws that equally bind nature and conscience — lies at the heart of the abstracted myths of Roman legal theology. In its understanding, laws necessarily derogate from human freedom, because, in the voluntarist system, freedom is boundless and undetermined except when constrained to accept the will of a superior. Over against the human possibility of rational freedom, then, the voluntarist theologian (a humanist *manqué*) understands dreadful divine necessity as promulgating inexorable decrees via divine positive law, natural law, and church law. All of them bind in conscience because they are the equivalent, for Catholics, of what Luther saw as our bound wills. Both attitudes represent relatively pathological responses to the challenge of too much possibility and too much necessity. As the spectrum along which Christian faith affirmation is normally enacted, both responses leave us with some serious healing to do.

Both the Reformed doctrine of God's freedom and the Catholic reduction of the means of salvation to a juridical system of demands and rewards have produced a further interiorized negative identity for modern believers. When critical rationality sought to shed Christianity's guilt and claim a clear and enlightened consciousness, it undergirded modern political nationalism and its communist alternative, bequeathing humanity the megadeaths of the twentieth century. This is what I have called the double loss of innocence that has left modernity wounded and abandoned on this side the "ugly, wide ditch" of historical ambiguity. We live across a chasm from the symbolic realm where the roots of both religious belief and rational humanism were planted. History mocks us with the specter of unlived chapters of religious understanding, social integration, sexual health, and unmade choices that represent our cultural and religious shadow. The wounds go deep. If any healing is to be had, those wounds need to be consciously endured so that what lives only in our mythopoetic imagination can be reintegrated, giving us some capacity for a more mature, healthier form of believing and acting. History, in its own way, recapitulates the myth of the Fall, but in the mythopoetry of the Bible the Fall is a *felix culpa,* an opportunity for life hidden in the curse of mortality.

The Work of Mourning

Alongside the triumphant rebounds, institutional robustness, and affirmations of historical continuity, Catholic history and theology really represent a "strange mixture of great good and frightening evil."[43] Hiding from this by constructing an idealized history of the church's faith affirmation and by denying this ambiguity is to hide in a "paradise of pre-ambivalent harmony" such as grievously ill adults hide in to deny their abusive or violent upbringing. There are times when forgetting the past, failing to remember or repressing trauma, helps people survive. But when the crisis is past, the past remains critical to the present and the future. Without confronting the damage done, the hurt received, or the pain doled out, health and wholeness cannot be achieved. I recognized this for the first time when, as a teenager, I watched Rod Steiger's performance in *The Pawnbroker,* a film about a Holocaust survivor who, because he had repressed the traumatic loss of his wife and children, was immune to the pain of the people of Harlem where his shop was located. Only after discovering and facing his introjected pain and mourning his great loss could he feel anything for himself or for others. Mourning cannot remake the past or make the future safe from darkness, doubts, or fears. But the only path to achieving real empathy with the whole canon of one's life, its tragedies and triumphs, the only portal to healing, is recognizing and facing the wounds that have been inflicted — and actively mourning the lost possibilities, the brute facts that have scarred our personal and communal histories.

In theological terms, we have a correlate of therapeutic mourning in repentance and forgiveness, a duality or paired reality proclaiming that without repentance forgiveness does no good, without forgiveness repentance is only anguished regret. While Catholicism has transacted this healing dynamic in various forms for centuries, it has remained focused on individual souls, not on its own guilty historical condition. But what would it mean for Catholic doctrinal teaching to mourn?

The introjected wounds festering in contemporary Catholic consciousness result from earlier chapters in the life of the church and its theological reflection, as sketched in this genealogy. But it is important that I stress my lack of ambivalence about this ambivalent history. History might have been better than it was and if we had not done this or that we might not be suffering the way we are. But life-in-time does not admit of being unwounded. While it is necessary for scholars today to engage in both revisionist history and the retrieval of lost elements of our tradition, I am not seeking to indict Augustine, Aquinas, Luther, or Suarez for not acting like critical twentieth-century theologians. Rather, I am seeking to come to terms with what our history has been so that we can work through the phobias, the violence, the splitting, the anger, and the frustration that arise from unmourned introjects. If this is not done, then the body of the church must be resigned to reenact conflicts that have gone unresolved for centuries. Maturity will remain a goal beyond our reach until we can overcome ideological conflict and reintegrate the shadows of our unlived lives, taking responsibility for the evil we have done by recognizing its threads in the skein of our contemporary identity.[44]

The traces of the past are evident not so much in the conscious shape of day-to-day Catholic experience as the unconscious realm of symbolic enactment and in the underlying dysfunctional relations between members of the church. A few examples will suffice to illustrate how unmourned introjects prevent us from overcoming our loss of innocence. Catholic teaching never formally adopted Calvinism's belief in the utter depravity of the human condition but stressed reason's ability to know naturally everything necessary to salvation. Nevertheless, our theological rationalism and legalism have left the average believer in the grip of an affectively guilty conscience. Evidence for it can be found in that singular Catholic locale (which fewer Catholics today resort to), the confessional.

Catholic people, dutiful their whole lives long and successfully repressing all their desires to be otherwise, often confess things *done to them* instead of what they have done to others. Their guilt seems to be rooted in their having feelings at all! This alone can account for the repetition of compulsive actions they have been confessing for years. The habit developed early because of the legal norm (perduring to this day) that required first confessions for seven-year-olds, the legal age of reason. Requiring confession before a child receives Communion shows how an imbalance in favor of reason has caused the introjected self-contempt of the average Catholic to flourish. The argument goes that, because children can reason about right and wrong, they can incur guilt, which can be absolved only sacramentally. What is ignored is that, when taking responsibility is the issue, it is precisely the feelings or affective understanding of the individual — not his or her rationality — that is operative. Whether seven-year-olds have developed emotionally enough to know their feelings is irrelevant. As a result, the unconscious wound of being guilty for being human (rather than being angelic) perpetuates itself in a confessional discipline that apes a juridical process. Despite the healing potential of the sacrament of reconciliation, its present form remains too narrowly based in a system of sin committed, penalty assessed, repentance enacted, absolution declared. Granted that it is neat and efficient, even when carried out with pastoral sensitivity, it rarely leads to change. Feeling this inability to change despite receiving the grace of the sacrament, people feel more guilt, until they walk away in disgust.

In particular, Catholics have developed a bad conscience in matters of the body. This occurred not only from splitting off the soul from the body and prizing only the spiritual part of the self, but also by separating church into the "many called" (the baptized) and the "few chosen" (those in vows or ordained) and further subdividing the chosen into empowered men and unempowered women. With the withering away, in the two centuries after Augustine, of almost all of the classical humanist regard for the things of this world, monastic asceticism became more and more the norm of what not just clergy but society in general was supposed to emulate. While the good sense of the faithful, the poetry of courtly love, the Renaissance's recovery of a healthy sense of the body, the Jesuit's "laxist" positions, Alphonsus Liguori's moderate moral theology, and even Pope John Paul II's philosophical reflections on married sexuality have all sought to rebalance our religious understanding of what we have split off, the realm of the secular where most of the church (the laity) live still remains unredeemed. Only the sacred can produce grace, and only those possessed of spiritual power are its instruments.

The same hypertrophied notion of spiritual power that led to totalistic interpretations of the pope's political power over kings and princes, over disposing all legal cases and dispensing all bishoprics, also centralized all ecclesiastical authority in the hands of an absolute monarch, the pope. This led, in turn, to the suppression of synodality, the ancient principle of collective decision-making by bishops in council; to the end of the election of bishops and the exclusion of the laity (and most of the clergy) from the process; and to the expansion of the authority of the bishop of Rome into an ideology of universal primacy.

Both at Vatican I and at Vatican II (and, one might argue, at Trent as well) moderate positions were formally adopted that sought to sustain some balance between the way the pope and the rest of the church, particularly the bishops, interact in teaching, ruling, and sanctifying the church. But as soon as the bishops left those councils, the work of administration once again fell into the hands of a self-interested party that has consistently sought to promote the absolute hegemony of centralized authority. After Vatican I, despite the clarification that the definition of infallibility did not mean the pope was an absolute monarch, papal centralism grew apace. We saw earlier that it slowly but certainly has sought to absorb the teaching office into a Supreme Magisterium, emphasizing always what was specifically Roman at the expense of the Catholicity of the church. Similarly, after Vatican II specifically defined the collegiality of the episcopacy both in theory and in practice, the curialists went back to work as usual.[45]

It seems that the consistent yielding to the temptation of too much possibility — here, in an ideology of too much spiritual power — cannot be accounted for in purely ecclesiological, historical, or rational terms. Absolutism of any kind, an attitude of all or nothing, arises from the threat of identity diffusion that the wound of history engenders. The need for an all-good, all-powerful figure to give oneself over to, which Freud saw as the genesis of all religion, does function in religion, but as a pathology, not as the norm.

Earlier I examined this human tendency under the rubric of transference. As a universal passion or natural desire, transference suffers from the same potential for imbalance that all *cupiditas,* or desire, suffers from: a tendency to go overboard. Hence transference can easily become an unhealthy symbiosis rather than a creative projection that mediates meaning and helps our individual lives draw upon a power that tames the terror of our creatureliness. Because Catholicism is rife with transference figures and transferential possibilities, it has shown itself resilient and strong, because, as Becker said, it took a hold of "creature consciousness — the thing [human beings] most wanted to deny — and made it the very confidence for [our] cosmic heroism."[46] But this same talent for symbolically transacting our role as a historical community in the universal shape of things has also led to a propensity to blur the distinction between the divine and the human, creating a dangerously neurotic fusion between too much possibility and too much necessity in absolute, rather than relative, transferences. Absolute transferences derive from unreal idealizations and are the modern equivalent to idolatry (see chapters 9–10). At base, the necessary tension in the shape of symbolic relationships is dissolved as holiness is literally attributed to a patriarchal figure and a hierarchical establishment.

When we seek to measure the impact of these transferences on the role of authority in Catholicism, what seems to tip the balance toward the hierarchy's assertion of absolute spiritual control of church life is the introjected sense that all authority arises in the will of the legislator. This heritage of voluntarism has been inculcated in the male clergy and though them in generations of Catholic faithful. It is responsible for the failure of Vatican II, despite its best efforts, to deploy a more horizontal or relational model of church authority in place of the patriarchal pyramid that places the pope at the tippy-top and the laity on the broad bottom. Because hierarchy has for so long symbolized inequality and subordination (particularly of females to males), not a diversity of gifts, and stressed a top-down model of authentic participation in what comes from God (the original trickle-down theory of being and grace), the postconciliar papalists have refused to surrender it or reunderstand it. Consequently, they have reshaped the actual hierarchy in some plainly tyrannical ways, sought to suppress theological dissent, and insisted on uniformity in thinking and action throughout the whole church.

By and large, the clergy and the hierarchy do not protest, even when they recognize how unjustified are the papal depredations of local autonomy and the Curia's assaults on individual members of the hierarchy or theologians. They have been trained to be good sons of the Holy Father, who sits at the top of a system of preferment that resists all input from below. The robust dialectic of the medieval scholastics and even the fraternal fracases of the religious orders are things of the past. Today we know that papal power developed through the accidents of history and patriarchal narrowness, not by some divine scheme of inevitability. Rome's assertion of an absolute veto power over ecclesial developments that threaten its hegemony in faith and morals is relatively modern. But it is a dysfunctionality that has older antecedents. They are the undigested sour grapes that have set our teeth on edge, setting off a compulsive reenactment of conflicts that are the result of earlier introjected contempt for things human that has been building since the second century.

Today, those resisting the Vatican's attempts to enclose theological discourse and the ongoing interpretation of the Christian tradition in too tight a circle can also be tempted toward their own form of too much theological possibility. Responding to the inherently dialectical dynamics of theology and the need not to be overwhelmed by the narrowness of the Roman school's approach to the mystery of Christianity, some have felt free to cut loose from the tradition in ways that mimic liberal Protestantism's nineteenth-century reduction of the gospel to "the brotherhood of man and the Fatherhood of God" (but in a more gender-inclusive formula). Not understanding the symbolic formulation of liturgy and doctrine, proponents of their own affective religious possibility abandon traditional Trinitarian formulas in favor of a purely functional notion of the Godhead: "In the name of the Creator, Redeemer, and Sustainer." On the surface, it seems to be a move to enfranchise women by desexualizing or depatriarchalizing God, but underneath its inclusive intent there lurks a narcissistic inflation of the human sense that God's existence mainly has relevance as it meets our individual needs. Alternately, certain movements of contemplative practice or mysticism also court the danger of too much possibility as they become "fused with a sense of magical omnipotence" which itself, said Becker "is actually a manic defense and a denial of creatureliness."[47]

If Catholicism in the twentieth-first century is to avoid the more pathological effects of the ongoing struggle over the loss of immediacy and the loss of innocence, it must engage in a process of repentance and forgiveness. But I wish to avoid the theological terms and call it the work of mourning. For any genuine interpretation of the validity of Catholic faith affirmation beyond the impasse between our mythopoetic tradition and its critical analysis must begin with grief. We must mourn our totalism so as to recover, not our primary innocence, but a mature, postambivalent, and empathic sense of our sinfulness and our justification. Without accomplishing what A.A.'s Twelve Steps calls an inventory of all those we have hurt and a conscious effort to make amends, the future could well see the church involved in a schism that would clearly represent a repetition compulsion. Clinically, repetition compulsion means placing oneself in a distressing situation that repeats an old experience while denying that there is a prototype; on the contrary one has "the strong impression that the situation is fully determined by the circumstances of the moment."[48] In some degree, the genealogy I have presented is a first effort at such an inventory. At the time the events occurred, they seemed to their participants to be the best or only course of action. With hindsight, we can sympathize with their choices or be critical of them, but we must allow ourselves to feel the wounds in the Body of Christ that resulted, whether inadvertently or not.

Therefore, the task of mourning our introjects will reveal, in a way we have not seen up to now, that like the Bible, our theological history (our tradition) is canonical. By attending to periods of intense formation and reformation of that tradition, I have sought to examine both the losses and gains so as to stress that there is no return to the paradise of preambivalent harmony for us. We have been cast out of Eden once for all and our loss has become our only opportunity for grace, for life, and for growth. For this *culpa* (fault) to yield any *felicitas* (blessedness), we must engage today in yet another creative reincarnation of the Christian message.[49] Just as the overarching theological perspective of the Bible can be described by the paradoxical phrase *errore hominum providentia divina* ("God's grace works through human sinfulness"), so our history today presents us with the traces of the same paradox that alone accounts for the good news that the church proclaims. Hence the only way we can escape repetition compulsion is to look again at the shape of modern Catholic belief and engage in what we have called dynamic analogy, dialectical imitation, the *metalepsis* of the symbolical imagination in order to appropriate postcritically what Catholics believe. As we shall see in chapters 9–10, postcritical maturity means that, in its most developed form, faith believes in spite of unbelief. By mature faith, we know not directly but through symbols; we see, as Paul intuited, only "through a glass darkly," sacramentally, not with absolute clarity. In faith, the symbolic imagination allows us to lose a primitive vision, endure the loss of all that seemed true, and recover, not ideological certainty, but faith.

Bibliographical Essay

On the impact of John Henry Newman: See Stephen Prickett (*Words and the Word: Language, Poetics, and Biblical Interpretation* [Cambridge: Cambridge University Press, 1986], 68), who attests of Newman's *Poetry, with Reference to Aristotle's Poetics* (1829): "There is no doubt that Newman's was the most subtle, the most satisfying, and the most comprehensive solution to the problem of the relationship of the religious to the poetic that the nineteenth century was to see. In it the 'intensive' [emotive] and 'extensive' [cognitive] views of poetry were to find some measure of reconciliation." The same author ("Romantics and Victorians: From Typology to Symbolism," in *Reading the Text: Biblical Criticism and Literary Theory,* ed. Stephen Prickett [Oxford: Blackwell, 1991], 182–224) argues that despite Newman's understanding that faith belongs primarily to the community (213), he "was as resolute as Coleridge in his insistence that to accept [the teachings of the Catholic Church] in the first place inescapably involved a prior act of the individual conscience — a point that was not so much anathema as incomprehensible to those...in Rome, who continued to feel that there was something suspiciously liberal about even Newman's critique of liberalism" (211).

On the nature/grace controversy: See J. Mahoney (*The Making of Moral Theology: A Study of the Roman Catholic Tradition* [Oxford: Clarendon Press, 1987], 72–81), who traces the increasing naturalization of natural law from Thomas to the nineteenth century and the triumph of the nature-supernature stratification. When accepted, this two-storied approach to Christian anthropology resulted in an anthropology in which grace meant that "the Christian sat upstairs on the

Clapham omnibus." H.-E. Mertens ("Nature and Grace in Twentieth-Century Catholic Theology," *Louvain Studies* 16 [1991]: 248) argues that the separation of the two orders of nature and grace in the seventeenth-century condemnation of Baius and the Jansenists, following the premises of Scotus's nominalism, "paved the way for deism." He also details Bellarmine's opposition to Baius and the Jansenists as opening the way for the rationalism of Grotius's notions of the ethical life (and international law) *etsi Deus non daretur* ("as if God did not exist," 44). According to him, the condemnation of Baius and the Jansenists is "yet another instance of a blunder by Roman teaching authority" (47). Joseph Komonchak ("Theology and Culture at Mid-Century: The Example of Henri de Lubac," *Theological Studies* 51 [1990]: 586) shows that Thomas knew of no "purely natural destiny for man" and, hence, that the later stress on rational powers and what humans could accomplish by them is a perversion of Thomism. Theological rationalism can be seen as a reaction formation to the Enlightenment and had some dysfunctional effects. See also Yves M.-J. Congar, O.P., *A History of Theology,* trans. and ed. Hunter Guthrie, S.J. (Garden City, N.Y.: Doubleday, 1968).

   On the interaction of philosophy with theology: See Amos Funkenstein (*Theology and the Scientific Imagination,* 53), who details how, after the time of Aquinas, the thingness or objectivity of reality shifted (in Scotus and Ockham) from an analogical way of speaking about nature and things. For Aquinas, the thingness (*quidditas*) of reality was mediated by universal concepts. Hence, the mind knew a thing because it was capable of the mental (and spiritual) act of abstracting from it what it had in common with the universal. By contrast, the later scholastics abandoned abstraction and taught that only the *individuality* (*haecceitas*) of particular objects was directly knowable. This epistemological shift had positive implications for the development of natural philosophy into natural science. But its consequences for theology were baneful. Funkenstein accounts for the ambiguous place of Thomas in later writers by showing how his "doctrine of analogy did as much to restrict the medieval sense of God's symbolical presence as it did to promote it" (55). He also details Scotus's rejection of Thomistic analogy on how God is present in the world and stressed that "Christ's body is in the Host in a locative, dimensional sense because God can place the same body at different locations simultaneously, in heaven and in many places on earth." Luther rejected such philosophical arguments on locative presence, holding that "like God's power and essence, Christ's body is everywhere (*ubique*) at all times. The communion is only the occasion at which Christians are instructed by the word of God where to concentrate on finding Christ's presence." Protestantism had much less to fear from pantheistic inclinations than Catholicism. On the other hand,

Protestant theology also encouraged, at least on the level of exegesis, unequivocation: it called for a return to *sola scriptura* (59).

On the impact of the Gregorian Reform: See John W. O'Malley, S.J. (*Tradition and Transition: Historical Perspectives on Vatican II*, Theology and Life Series 26 [Wilmington, Del.: Michael Glazier, 1989], 89), who parallels the two "great reformations" in the history of the church, the Gregorian Reform and the Protestant Reformation, before Vatican II. Geoffrey Barraclough (*Medieval Papacy* [New York: W. W. Norton, 1968], 75) notes a shift when the spirit of reform traveled south from the monasteries to Rome: "the first consideration was not moral rejuvenation, but the reinforcement of papal authority." Brian E. Daley, S.J. ("Structures of Charity: Bishops' Gatherings and the See of Rome in the Early Church," in *Episcopal Conferences: Historical, Canonical and Theological Studies,* ed. Thomas J. Reese, S.J. [Washington, D.C.: Georgetown University Press, 1989], 28) cites Mansi's monumental collection of conciliar documents as evidence "for over four hundred synods and meetings of bishops, Eastern and Western...between the mid-second century and the pontificate of Gregory the Great." John Boswell (*Christianity, Social Tolerance, and Homosexuality: Gay People in Western Europe from the Beginning of the Christian Era to the Fourteenth Century* [Chicago: University of Chicago Press, 1980], 277) details how Lateran III (1179) issued the first sanctions against homosexuals, which it combined with others against moneylenders, Jews, Muslims, and mercenaries. Lateran IV (1215) "forbade Jews to hold any public office, restricted their financial arrangements...and ordered them to wear clothing which distinguished them from Christians." David Knowles (*Christian Monasticism* [London: World University Library, 1969], 87) speaks of the extraordinary growth of the Cistercian monastic reform: "Within thirty years fifty-one white monk abbeys existed in England and Wales." But shortly they "were, like others before them had been, ruined by their own success," because their efficient lay brothers entered the wool business and made their abbeys wealthy (89).

On the papal sponsorship of the Franciscans: See G. Barraclough (*Medieval Papacy,* 128), who asserts that "the real cause of the heretical movements was not doctrinal difference, but protest against a secularized church." He says that

the great mystical tradition, with its implied and open criticism of the legalistic church and its hierarchy, [stemming] from Joachim of Fiore and St Francis...was a fundamental fact in the history of the fourteenth, fifteenth and sixteenth centuries, because the claim to an active religious life for all the faithful, a direct mystical communion with God...was essentially irreconcilable...with the church's claim that the only road to salvation was through the sacraments administered by a duly authorized clergy.

Hence the Reformation flowed directly from the unresolved issues in Innocent III's acceptance of the Franciscans.

On Martin Luther's position spanning the Renaissance and the beginnings of modernity: See Erik Erikson (*Young Man Luther*, 195), who says that Luther's tools were the tools of the Renaissance: a fervent return to the original texts, anthropocentrism (in Christocentric form), and the affirmation of one's own voice (the vernacular). He also makes the provocative suggestion concerning Luther's strictly masculine soteriology: "It was probably his father's challenging injunction against the little boy's bond with his mother which made it impossible for Martin to accept the intercession of the holy Mary" (123). For a portrait of European society in the fifteenth century, see the conclusion of Barbara W. Tuchman's *A Distant Mirror: The Calamitous Fourteenth Century* (New York: Alfred A. Knopf, 1978), 580:

It was time of default. Rules crumbled, institutions failed in their functions. Knighthood did not protect; the Church, more worldly than spiritual, did not guide the way to God; the towns, once agents of progress and the commonweal, were absorbed in mutual hostilities and divided by class war; the population, depleted by the Black Death, did not recover.

On the post-Tridentine treatment of the "church" as the hierarchy: See Yves Congar (*Lay People in the Church,* rev. ed., trans. Donald Attwater [Westminster, Md.: Christian Classics, 1985], 45), who describes the situation in this way:

Thus whilst Protestants were reducing the Church to an inward Christianity, to salvation, and by doing so were dissolving ecclesiology, Catholic apologists were looking at [the Church] above all as the machinery of the means of grace, as the hierarchical mediation of the means to salvation...in a word, a "hierarchology."

On the early attempts to balance the teaching on infallibility: See John Henry Newman ("A Letter to His Grace the Duke of Norfolk on Occasion of Mr. Gladstone's Recent Expostulation," *Difficulties of Anglicans II* [Westminster, Md.: Christian Classics, 1969], 328), who cited the Roman theologian Perrone that papal infallibility was not "an infused gift" but a guarantee that "there should be no error in the final step, in the resulting definition or dogma." Newman called for

caution to be observed, on the part of private and unauthorized persons, in imposing upon the consciences of others any interpretation of dogmatic enunciations which is beyond the legitimate sense of the words, inconsistent with the principle that all general rules have exceptions, and unrecognized by the Theological Schola. (337–38)

He pointed out that the conditions in the definition of Vatican I "contract the range of his infallibility most materially" (325).

On the relation between theologians, bishops, and the Roman magisterium: See Joseph Ratzinger ("Primacy, Episcopate, and Apostolic Succession" in Karl Rahner and Joseph Ratzinger, *The Episcopate and the Primacy* [New York: Herder and Herder, 1963], 38–41), who comments on the lack of balance between the centralizing Curia and the world's bishops that John XXIII's council would have to raise. Francis A. Sullivan (*Magisterium,* 77) cites and agrees with Ratzinger's 1969 statement that the loss of the distinction between the bishop of Rome's patriarchal and his strictly papal authority contributed to an unwarranted centralism. Robert Blair Kaiser (*The Encyclical That Never Was: The Story of the Pontifical Commission on Population, Family and Birth, 1964–66* [London: Sheed & Ward, 1987, published as *The Politics of Sex and Religion* in the United States in 1985]) knew many of the principals personally and describes Fr. John C. Ford, S.J. (who along with Cardinal Ottaviani produced the bogus "minority report" of the commission) as giving "the game away when he said *Humanae Vitae* reaffirmed 'the power of the magisterium to bind consciences.' For Ford, the point was not truth. It was power. The point was not to teach, but to rule." A balanced and factual account of one of the most notorious cases of the conflict between a theologian and ecclesiastical authority is found in Larry Witham, *Curran vs. Catholic University: A Study of Authority and Freedom in Conflict* (Riverdale, Md.: Edington-Rand, 1991). A recent personal, yet insightful, account of the state of the problem appears in Michael Crosby's *The Dysfunctional Church: Addiction and Codependency in the Family of Catholicism* (Notre Dame, Ind.: Ave Maria Press, 1991).

According to Thomas Michael Loome (*Liberal Catholicism, Reform Catholicism, Modernism: A Contribution to a New Orientation in Modernist Research,* Tübinger Theologische Studien [Mainz: Matthias Grünewald Verlag, 1979], 194), "Modernism" can stand for a "self-enclosed philosophical-theological *system* of thought presented and condemned in the papal encyclical *Pascendi dominici gregis.* . . . But the system itself, as a system, is an historical irrelevancy: a fiction created by Rome in order to justify its attempt to crush the real 'Modernism' " which the author defines as an intellectual tradition within Roman Catholicism. Loome uses Freidrich von Hügel's description of it: "the perennial attempt to reinterpret traditional Christian belief in the light of 'the philosophy and the scholarship and science of the later and latest times' is probably as good a definition as possible." Gabriel Daly, O.S.A. (*Transcendence and Immanence: A Study in Catholic Modernism and Integralism* [Oxford: Clarendon Press, 1980], 218–19) concludes that modernism is less important than the officially sponsored reaction it provoked.... Anti-modernism became a species of ecclesiastical patriotism enforced by an oath and initiated by a campaign which bore striking resemblances to the anti-communist activities of Senator Joseph McCarthy in the United States of America in the late 1940s and early 1950s.... The term "modernist" remained as a convenient label for any theological initiatives in the Roman Catholic Church which appeared to deviate from the neo-scholastic norm, especially in matters of dogma, biblical criticism, and Church polity.... Much of the drama and excitement engendered by the first session of the [Second Vatican] Council stemmed from the relative suddenness of the realization that integralism was no more than a schola in Roman Catholic theology, whereas the basic tenets and methodology of that schola had been widely taken to belong more or less to the substance of Catholic faith.

Chapter 8

Primal Faith and Its Misshaping

The Symbolic Shape of Faith and Morals

Catholic identity at the end of the twentieth century has been damaged by theology's objectifying, legalistic habits and its voluntaristic understanding that, because it is possible to speak about God and the ways of God, it is necessary to define and delimit the truth of everything "on earth as in heaven." Mistaking the fullness, the inclusivity, the reasonableness, and the traditional nature of Catholic faith for an absolutist system of truth, magisterial theology has succumbed to a pathology that "tries to make itself master of the past and the future and tends to become totalitarian."[1] As we have seen, literalism and legalism have gone hand in hand, converting a naturally adaptive Catholicism into a stoical ideology characterized by a desymbolized authoritarian literalism.

Though the theologians who laid the basis for Vatican II had worked to undermine the rationalist and voluntarist pillars of the post-Tridentine system, the council's balancing act (the result of political compromise) did not identify rationalism's theological pathologies. Though it did mourn for some past misdeeds (as in its repudiation of theological anti-Semitism) and accept the fact of growth (by adopting the principal of doctrinal development), the council did not have the wherewithal or historical perspective to seek healing for Catholicism's unmourned introjects. At the 1987 Extraordinary Synod that commemorated the opening of Vatican II, the hierarchy's major motivation seemed to be maintaining peace in the house rather than wrestling with the underlying tensions tearing at the body of the faithful.[2] As a result, the papacy and the hierarchy today remain confirmed in their own delusions about their ability to control the whole church's expression and enactment of its belief.

Is there no balm in Gilead? Can Catholic faithful, theologians, preachers, and teachers think about, formulate, and proclaim the truth of the tradition without being unhistorical or authoritarian? Can we negotiate our journey without succumbing to spiritual grandiosity or depressing reductionism, to precritical naivete or critical rejection of the tradition?

205

We can indeed, if we attend to the way symbols mediate and interpret faith both before and beneath abstract language. By taking into account the way theological language originally functioned mythopoetically, we can progress beyond the developmental traps that litter our historical record by regressing to an earlier stage of Christian faith experience and reappropriating the way we practice faith before it becomes the stuff of abstract argument. The shift I am advocating is from conceptualism to symbolic theology, from analysis to analogy, from demonstration to persuasion, from the logical to the rhetorical. Official theology has long ignored the extent to which all language, but certainly theological language, "is activity before it is cognition, intersubjective before it is objective, and rhetorical before it is logical." Its conceptualism has treated concepts as if they were Plato's *ideas* and then understood them via Aristotle's preference for unambiguous and univocal language. It continues to presume that if terms are narrowly defined and given conceptual fixity, they actually participate in extramental reality. Like the pathological mixtures of possibility and necessity that we saw in the last chapter, conceptualism combines an inflated sense of the human intellect's capacity for abstraction with a narrow notion of how God binds our intellect or wills.[3]

This move, then, represents a break with scholasticism's method of proving the conceptual facticity of theological statements by rational deduction to a demonstration of how theological ideas, symbolically expressed, have practical effect in the life and experience of believers. By attending to the precritical, rhetorical ("persuasive") form of theological expression, we can achieve a genuinely postcritical position that does not abandon the search for truth nor settle for a subjectivist, existential criterion of what feels real or truthful. If we can avoid the extremes of objectivism and subjectivism and discover how theological symbols disclose what biblical revelation means in the present, we can show how faith affirmation functions in the stream of life where the symbols of worship and belief give rise to thought and to action.

The symbolic aspects of revelation and faith have claimed more importance since the Romantic reaction to rationalism began. Like the poets Coleridge and Blake, such critics as Herder and such theologians as Johann Adam Möhler and Matthias Joseph Scheeben sought to open theological discourse to the perspective that there is an indeterminate element to the reality of Christian truth that cannot be rationally systematized. Like them, John Henry Newman (while still an Anglican) understood that "Religious Truth is neither light nor darkness, but both together. . . . Revelation, in this way of considering it, is not a revealed system, but consists of detached and incomplete truths belonging to a vast system unrevealed, of doctrines and injunctions mysteriously connected together."[4]

A more recent effort to recover the symbolic was Jesuit Karl Rahner's bringing together the work of Aquinas with that of modern thinkers like Schleiermacher and Heidegger. Noting that most modern explanations of how the sacraments cause grace ignore the sign-value of the sacraments, Rahner rehabilitated a properly symbolic understanding of the sacramental mediation of grace. He did this by bringing together Aquinas's notion that sacraments cause grace *significando* (by the way they signify or symbolize) with Heidegger's philosophy of language as a manifestation of being. This allowed Rahner to ground the sacraments as expressions of the church, which is itself a sign or sacrament of what Christ, the primordial sacrament, manifests. In other words, the church manifests in space and time the "eschatologically triumphant grace of God," yet it never exhausts the mystery of God's redemptive love that it symbolizes in the here and now. The sacraments give visible form to God's gift of grace; they "effect grace" by symbolizing God's gift in the here and now. This understanding of symbol retains a connection to the world of Thomistic ontology, of unseen essences somehow manifested in the physical accidents of nature. Because there is a transcendent realm not comprehensible to limited human awareness, there remains a gap that can be crossed only through indirect expressions by which one reality can be present in another.[5]

Taking over this perspective, Avery Dulles has defined symbol as "an externally perceived sign which works mysteriously on the human consciousness so as to suggest more than it can clearly describe or define," or as an entity that "communicates by inviting people to participate in its own meaning, to inhabit a world which it opens up, and thereby to discover new horizons, with new values and new goals." Unlike some early twentieth-century "modernists" who might have seen the visible symbolic communication of faith as mere instruments of deeper realities (hence, dispensable), Dulles and others have discovered that faith relates best to reason by having its symbols critically interpreted rather than reduced to concepts of complete determination. This means that the living tradition of belief continues to be vital primarily through the enacted symbols of the whole church in its life, teaching, and worship. Only secondarily do those actions (ecclesial *praxis*) become the subject of theological reflection, formal clarification, or magisterial definition.[6]

Dulles thinks that this approach to understanding revelation is superior to models of understanding that have been operative in the past. He defends symbolic theology (vis-à-vis the countercritical position of theologians who attribute objective meaning to dogmatic propositions) on the grounds that the symbolic approach does more than make cognitive claims: "Its distinctive mark is not the absence of meaning but the surplus of meaning." Symbols invite our participation in the reality of God, deficiently revealed as reality must be in the symbols of revelation.

Over against a paracritical stance that assigns different realms of meaning to science and faith, the symbolic approach insists on the necessary mediation in time and place of revelation, even in mystical experience. It refuses to isolate faith affirmation from the social and historical circumstances in which it must occur. Over against purely critical approaches (both historical ones seeking the *bruta facta* of revelation and dialectical ones stressing the biblical word's uniqueness), Dulles upholds the symbolic approach because it accounts more adequately for history's ambiguities. By refusing to equate the Bible's words with God's past speech-act, it resists locating revelation in the past. In sum, a symbolic understanding of *what* God communicates in revelation and *how* that communication occurs in the Bible and in the Christian tradition takes a middle position between overly intellectualistic (critical or countercritical) and overly experiential-expressive approaches. It safeguards the intelligibility and historicity of revelation while refusing to reduce it either to the sum of human experience or to the puzzling wisdom of a hidden God. As symbolic, revelation and faith are, as Newman said, neither "light nor darkness, but both together."[7]

As we saw in chapter 1, human awareness is, at base, relational and arises from the capacity of developing humans to bridge the gap between self and other through symbolizing. All genuine experiences of otherness are rooted in symbolic consciousness, a distinctly human capacity that represents our openness to transcendence. Grounding this spiritual capacity in the gifts unique to human beings can help us avoid explaining symbolism in terms of nonmaterial idealism or mysterious (baffling) functions of the intellect. The heavily philosophical analyses of language and being that Rahner and others have developed are a hedge against the deconstructionist project to "break the covenant between word and world" (Steiner), to see language merely as a grammatological "game of differences" and to reduce symbols to less-than-literal stabs at human self-expression. But when writers identify a symbol as "the mode of presence of something that cannot be encountered in any other way" or something that "participates directly in the presence and power of that which it symbolizes," they threaten to make all symbols in language, anthropology, or sociology appear to be apologetic variations on a religious insistence that "there's Someone out there sending us messages." This notion of symbol stems from a philosophical reflection on specifically linguistic symbols and loses touch with the unspoken and ineffable aspects of symbolical praxis.[8] Because symbols manifest reality in other than cause-and-effect (realist) categories, they tend to be lumped in with unseen powers or essences whose presence cannot be accounted for except by reference to other symbols or metaphors.[9]

What Dulles and others, then, account for mysteriously, Ricoeur more forthrightly identifies as the element of unresolved tension present in the structure of metaphor and symbol. Though symbols violate the logic of the law of the excluded middle by which something cannot be true and not true at the same time, they are not any more a mystery than the principle of indeterminacy, which violates the laws of classical physics. The surplus of meaning in all symbols — the whispered "is not" that a live metaphor always carries in its affirmation — results, not from some unseen divine power, absolute or ordained, but from a tension caused by the instinctual deprivation under which humans must resort to symbolic communication.[10]

For if conscious beings, in the act of communicating, necessarily communicated their inner life, there would be no such thing as human freedom. Human consciousness, because it is symbolic, can never fully realize or be present to itself. We only know ourselves with difficulty, by becoming adept at both conscious communication and at interpreting our unconscious states of awareness. Hence there is an analogy between God's self-communication (both in the Godhead and in the economy of our salvation) and the structure of our knowing ourselves and others. Any immediacy we have with God (and with our adult selves) has to be a mediated immediacy, one that goes (as Ricoeur says) "by the great detour of signs." Equally, any pretensions we might have to know God are possible only because any revelatory light mutually coinheres with a residual darkness. What we know is partly determined, not negated, by what we don't know. Hence all our speaking about God (theology) is ultimately silenced by "words that cannot be spoken" (2 Cor 12:4, the phrase that founds the apophatic tradition). Symbols speak the truth of the Christian tradition because they encompass silence, refusing to say more than they know. As symbolically revealed, therefore, God is not a mysterious unknown, or merely the depth dimension of human awareness, but a presence in absence. The Godhead cannot finally be conceptually defined nor can the facts of God's self-revelation be so verbally enshrined in dogmatic definitions as official Catholicism has presumed. Rather, the reality of God is disclosed least inadequately in paradox: through light and darkness, male and female, unworded Word or any other symbols that express a *coincidentia oppositorum,* like the nonconsuming fire in the burning bush which has been called "the only true speech. Human saying lies."[11]

The complex structure of symbols, the light-and-dark character that makes them so appropriate to the structure of revelation, makes the task of handing on the tradition's faith and morals an equally complex one. As Newman knew, the tradition does not ordinarily develop, as Dulles would have it, "through a harmonious interaction between the ecclesiastical magisterium and the sense of the faith inherent in the Church as a whole." Such a view idealizes a history that has been far more conflicted. When Dulles affirms that "postcritical theology, as I use the term, begins with a presupposition or prejudice in favor of faith, i.e., that its fundamental attitude is a hermeneutics of trust, not of suspicion," he can be accused of seeking to return to the garden of preambivalent harmony. Trust must be gained, not asserted in denial of the difficult lessons that come in the wake of our loss of immediacy and loss of innocence. Dulles's own method of seeing various models at work in theology has the merit of avoiding the oversystematization of past theology. But by insisting that a plurality of "root metaphors" can function side by side and, in their coexistence, "overcome the conflicts" of the past, he is too irenic. For him, there is sin, but only the "sin of the world," not any systematic distortions that the tradition itself has fostered consciously or unconsciously.[12]

Instead of denying the ambivalence of our ecclesial structures and the pathologies in our theological genealogy, and in order to face the question about the relation of symbolic theology to what is true, I wish now to describe the properly rhetorical function of symbolic theology.

Praxis-oriented

Theologians seeking to overcome the rationalistic mode of propositional theology have highlighted the extent to which participation in the worship life of the church gives access to its inner life and to the moral behavior that follows from what the church believes. Because it is said that worship gives rise to thought, then giving praise and thanks to God is what generates teaching and conduct. Doxology attains the object of faith in a way that doctrinal definition cannot do. This represents a recovery of an ancient perspective. Worship, as an act of faith, is a way of knowing, but it does not acquire knowledge mentally. Symbolic theology reflects upon worship to articulate it as an aesthetic presentation of a real but graced experience of communion with God. It also articulates moral actions in the web of human relationships that flow from our thanksgiving to God in Christ. Hence, symbolic theology operates out of a sense that "orthodoxy" means right worship (before it means holding the right beliefs) and seeks to become orthopraxis in a reasoned way. It also seeks to energize people to change and to deepen their adherence to the mystery of Christ's transformative presence in the church and in the world.[13]

Persuasive

Aristotle's analysis of the art of rhetoric showed that a key to its effectiveness was the reliability of the speaker and of the speaker's modes of persuasion. A theology that operates rhetorically takes for granted that its interpretations — their artistry, cogency, and the way they elucidate the deep structures of experience — are inseparable from its presentation of truth. Practitioners of a symbolic theology forego appealing to

coercive authority to enforce their own view of the matter they are interpreting. While rhetorical forms do not shrink from using dialectical
thinking and rational argument, they remain noncoercive in their refusal
to create a totalistic system of religious belief valid for all times and
all places. This form of doing theology bases its authority on winning
the assent of its listeners by resonating with their own deep instincts of
faith, not on claiming a priori to bind its audience in conscience.[14] We
saw earlier that the authority of the biblical canon emerged from a process of traditioning more than from its official promulgation. Likewise,
the authority of symbolic theology rests on its dynamic equivalence in
reproducing the challenges or comforts of the canonical tradition. It
does not merely repeat the past in order to be authoritative and faithful.
Rather, it engages in dialectical imitation, which does not presume that,
because certain symbols once mediated God's grace or judgment, they
are adequate at a later stage of understanding. Doing theology always
demands re-presenting fundamental mysteries in new adaptations.

Constructive

Symbolic theology by definition seeks to interpret experiences of God's
self-manifestation, but it does not end there. It seeks also to mediate con-
structively between the tradition of faith and human society and culture,
explaining each to the other and challenging both to discover deep harmonies between natural realities (the created order) and their destiny in
God (the order of grace). This requires that theology balance doxology
and analogy, respecting the integrity of the church's act of worship while
also seeking to demonstrate how the human capacity for autonomy is
not violated but liberated in faith's encounter with the living God.[15]

Nonconceptualist

Many theologians since Descartes have understood thinking as a manifestation of the mind's own internal states. In this view, meaning
happens when one establishes objective (quantifiable) descriptions of
what is being thought about or mentally conceived. Instead, meaning
can be better understood as occurring in encounter situations, in which
our reaching out is also a being met, not just by information, but by
a world that is real. It is knowable to the extent that we are part of it
and it becomes part of the knower. In the Cartesian model, meaning is
replaced by concepts, and certain terms that supposedly enjoy a privileged lock on how reality really is were removed from the stream of life.
This reduced truth to a system of propositions that left nothing unsaid.
It also allowed for theoretical knowledge that alienates its subjects from
the objects of their knowledge, creating a purely technical reason that allows those who possess it to dominate others. This way of knowing has
created the pathologies of scientific rationality that have caused so much

damage via the manipulation of physical reality. The conceptualist view of theological propositions, also, has caused damage, because it cannot account for historical change, intellectual and affective development, or tradition as a dynamic process.

Theological formulations, our attempts to put into words the reality of revelatory encounter, should correspond to what Newman called our "piecemeal" reflection upon an idea too overwhelming for consciousness. They cannot be resolved into some of the aspects or relations of that encounter and then substituted for the whole. The "idea" of revelation "is not enlarged if propositions are added, nor impaired if they are withdrawn," said Newman.[16] But seeking to ascend to the idea and encapsulate the whole in terms and concepts, to present it packaged and whole, runs the certain risk of creating an ideology. The narrowness of ideological thinking flows from the threat of being overwhelmed with the totality of reality. One of the ways to fend off being overwhelmed is to bite off only as much as one can chew. But when what the theologian has bitten off is identified with the whole, and when concepts supply for the idea of revelation, the theologian becomes an earnest, obedient, often prolific writer, but ultimately a tragic and driven figure.

Therapeutic

Because all good therapy begins with diagnosis, the uncovering of hidden, unconscious introjects and of pathological attitudes that inhibit living and growing, symbolic theology must be able to take advantage of the diagnostic tools made available by the hermeneutics of suspicion. With them, we can recognize the residual narcissism that encourages us to cling to our preambivalent idealizations of ourselves and our community of faith. Rather than seeking to refute the masters of suspicion (Nietzsche, Freud, and Marx), a postcritical theological endeavor will seek to incorporate their insights and recognize that both we ourselves and our language are devoid of innocence. We can afford to trust as long as we recognize that we are never so objectively disinterested regarding truth as we have pretended in the past.

All systems of knowledge and the arguments that support them are part of a web of personal and societal relationships. Their maintenance depends on arrangements of power and authority. Therefore, symbolic theology seeks to get beyond name-calling, anathematization, and rejection of the claims of the other that characterized so much of theology in the past. This does not mean that all truth is immediately relativized. The picking and choosing of mere aspects of the idea of Christian revelation (the original meaning of "heresy") has to be guarded against. But when theologians defend their own insights, they must be aware of their own tendency to distort and of their own impure motives, so often stemming from their need to be right, to be obedient, or to be better than they feel they really are. Theological interpretation cannot be confined merely to revealing cultural or historical blind spots but must become sensitive to its own as well.[17]

Because symbolic theology is self-consciously rhetorical, it can enact this therapeutic aspect of formulating faith and morals, first, by recognizing that symbols are essentially open and patient of many interpretations, possessing a surplus, or excess, of meaning. Their implicit hiddenness affirms that "there is, thank God, always more to be expressed; there is always much more that is left unexpressed."[18] Second, symbolic theology is therapeutic because it is inherently self-correcting and, hence, enacts the transformative role of symbolic formulations. Theologians sensitive to the tentative and heuristic rather than fixed and final, shape of their formulations understand that their own work must be patient of correction if they are out to change the community or to seek to deepen its faith.

Hence a symbolic, transformative way of doing theology does not presume that it is part of a self-enclosed world of meaning. Faith (and the way that theology formulates and reflects on it) not only develops through successive structurings through time but also, at any one time, is made up of coexistent structurings that mutually inform one another. The structures that doctrines take on do not transform or change believers because they can actually re-create the immediate encounter with God that they are about. Nor are they best understood as the grammar of religion by which believers learn the rules that allow them to practice their faith. They may engage their adherents in a demanding conversation with tradition, but more important, they are meant to engage their adherents in change, in transforming praxis. This conversion or transformation does not occur in one fell swoop, changing our worldview instantly, as if a person or a community existed in one symbolic frame of reference one day and, then, when the "penny dropped," their symbolic universe (and they along with it) could change overnight.[19]

All of these proposals say something about the way faith affirmation and teaching seek to make the originating encounter with the divine available to the historical community. But the various forms that faith takes (and the various ways that theology thematizes those forms) often overlap. The necessarily piecemeal character of our experiences of God involves us in interpreting the traces of God's presence that have become the canonical stuff of the tradition. But the same piecemeal character of our conversion implies that we do not traverse the stages of faith only once. Not unlike the tradition as a whole, individual believers find themselves falling back into earlier forms of their belief in order to recover there energic sources of growth so that they can consolidate their personal gains. This habit of regression in the service of progress can be understood as a law of change and development that affects all organic reality. Because living organisms, living persons, and living traditions are all composed of stable and labile elements, there is no determined way in which those elements of constancy and adaptability will interact in any given historical circumstance. Growth in faith will suffer the likely vicissitudes of all personal as well as societal phenomena.

Within these conditions, the truths of Christian faith as they are symbolically expressed possess reserves of symbolic capital to help the journey of faith forward, for humbling it to the dust, for shoring it up when it retreats, and for energizing its imaginative leaps beyond any cognitive straitjackets. Symbolic formulations of what we believe and how we should live not only require a measure of artistry to be formulated and appreciated; they also require a playfulness and self-forgetfulness, a capacity for seeming contradiction and for wise foolishness. How this is so will be described as I seek to identify how elements of the Catholic faith tradition, grounded in primarily naive belief (but philosophically inflated) can endure their critical negation (chapter 9) and emerge in a postcritical, secondarily naive shape (chapter 10). The journey that faith affirmation makes is rarely smooth, but it is filled with potential for recapitulating the primary rule of the canonical process: *errore hominum providentia divina*.

Primarily Naive Belief

Primarily naive belief is the place where faith is rooted, whether we know it or not. It is akin to the experience of basic trust that Erikson discovered at the intellectual and affective roots of human knowing and loving. Lacking a good enough experience of basic trust, human beings will be permanently handicapped in their attempts to know what kind of world they are living in and who they are in that world. On the basis of the maxim "Whatever is received is received according to the mode of the receiver" (*Quidquid recipitur, recipitur secundum modum recipientis*), it may be well nigh impossible for some human beings to conceive of or experience (in all but a completely unthematized way) either God's goodness or their own capacity to respond in faith. As I have stressed, I am in no way seeking to denigrate or disparage naive belief. It is absolutely fundamental to all and any belief, even the most sophisticated philosophical musings, intellectual proofs, or hermeneutical leaps.

An episode in the history of twentieth-century Christian apologetics can illustrate this point. After becoming a believer in God in 1929 ("the most dejected and reluctant convert in all England"), C. S. Lewis proceeded to become, first, a Christian and, then, a brilliant controversialist for the case of Christianity. On radio and in print, he pursued his robust brand of intellectual apology for Christian faith, vigorously defending its truth-claims and vindicating its particular story of salvation. Most of his works from this period are still in print, even though, at a point of crisis, Lewis ceased to write in this vein. His biographer traces his abandonment of philosophical apologetics to a debate with a follower of Wittgenstein. Elizabeth Anscombe, no unbeliever herself, demolished his philosophical argument for the existence of God and left him shattered. After that evening in 1948 at Cambridge's Socratic Society, Lewis never again engaged in intellectual refutation of the arguments of unbelievers. Instead he fell back to a more basic form of imaginative writing and to a more basic way of affirming that "the hardness of God is kinder than the softness of men."[20] He became a writer of theological fiction, a teller of tales whose main characters were children. A. N. Wilson sees the import of the change in the following terms:

The Lion, the Witch and the Wardrobe grew out of Lewis' experience of being stung back into childhood by his defeat at the hands of Elizabeth Anscombe at the Socratic Club.... This story is delightful, a wholly absorbing narrative in its own right. It is as though Lewis, in all his tiredness and despondency in the late 1940s, has managed to get through the wardrobe himself; to leave behind the world of squabbles and grown-ups and to reenter the world which with the deepest part of him he never left, that of childhood reading.[21]

Lewis's stories affirmed a conviction that grew out of conversations with Owen Barfield and J. R. R. Tolkien in the early years after his conversion. Thus Lewis was able to write to his fellow-poet Kathleen Raine, "What flows into you from myth is not truth but reality (truth is always about something but reality is about which truth is) and therefore every myth becomes the father of innumerable truths on the abstract level."[22] Basic to all later expressions of belief are some fundamentally naive, uncomplicated, first-order, mythopoetic construals of the world and all that is, and these can never be completely surpassed or grown beyond. These truths are not all that there is to say, but they correspond to the simple facts that children need to hear and that cannot be ultimately impugned, no matter how critically sophisticated a person becomes. If a person suffers so much damage during life that all vestiges of these primarily naive truths are repressed, they nevertheless cannot be wiped out. The kind of truth I am talking about was illustrated in Peter Berger's *A Rumor of Angels*. Speaking of a mother who, in the middle of a crashing thunder-and-lightning storm, rushes into her infant's room, cradles the child, and assures it, "Everything's all right," Berger insists that the mother is speaking a truth that is, at some level, fundamental — or else there is nothing true in our experience.[23]

The evolutionary conditions of human development uniquely explain not only our propensity but also our capacity for such fundamental truths. In chapter 1, I referred to the long period of extrauterine gestation in infancy and childhood, during which human young remain totally dependent on their care-givers. Known as neoteny, this condition produces the singular human capacities that I identified earlier with symbolization, language and artistic skills, playfulness, and transferential relationships. These natural capacities do not necessarily translate into religious affirmations, and when they are never thematized or educated, they underlie counterfeit religious responses and superstition. But they found our capacity to be religious, to be trusting of even an unknown God, and to affirm, as well as critique, the mythopoetic images at the very base of biblical religion.

Primarily naive belief, then, takes the symbolic realm as a primary datum of life in the same way that children, if they develop normally and healthily, have an innate capacity to suspend disbelief, to delight in the heuristic fictions that make up their earliest worlds (the network of their relationships, as well as their primitive cultural and educational environments). In the preceding chapters, I have traced the ongoing attempt to discredit all forms of naive believing that resulted from the onset of critical rationality. But I have also sought to show how, beginning with the Romantic movement, the normalcy, healthfulness, and truth involved in the ability to suspend disbelief arose as a reaction to rationalism's too narrow perspective. In this century, when many, not least of all Freud, expected the triumph of scientific reductionism, the irony is that society has begun to witness, not a wholesale disconfirmation of the Enlightenment's critical tools, but a renewed patience for those necessarily naive apperceptions that lie at the root of human relationships, affective sensibility, artistic accomplishment, spiritual capacity, and, ultimately, growth in faith, hope, and love.

Equivalently, we need to recognize how the rudiments of Christian faith lie in the naive, mythopoetic symbols of the Bible — without succumbing to the impatient perspective of fundamentalism, which as a reaction to human autonomy is a caricature of genuine naive belief. Faced with the threat of losing the cultural and religious security that immediacy and innocence give, naive believers balk. Personal freedom and autonomy (being a law unto oneself) are frightening possibilities. Into the vacuum that these believers refuse to fill rush emotional attachments transferred from their primal security figures to idealized, often omnipotent and magical, replacements. In healthy development, transference becomes the means by which people recoup the energy that the loss of immediacy and innocence drain from them, allowing them to project themselves into new relationships. But fundamentalist believers tend to become attached to substitutes, to religious cult leaders or to imagined relationships with Christ or God. Transference becomes pathogenic when people can't handle the emotional unhousedness that teaches us from infancy that happiness lies just beyond our firm grasp. For to be someone I must belong to someone, and thus our passion's arousal for the other who will let this happen is both the basis for our hope and a snare as well.

Religious fundamentalists attach themselves to the symbols of the Bible as if these constituted the actual events of history because they would be otherwise overwhelmed by the range of possibilities in modernity's sense of separateness from its primal beginnings. They cannot admit that the mythopoetic language of primal participation is any different from the language of molecular physics because that would mean they no longer inhabit the world of preambivalent belief. Purchasing this security at the price of intellectual honesty, they are comfortable with the wrathful God of the Bible because their own experience of emotional immediacy is the only medium of religious awareness they have. But it is a pseudoimmediacy (and intimacy), in which God is contacted in prayer by closing the eyes ever so tightly and by adopting the sincerest tones possible. Jesus, in this emotive context, becomes the adult's version of a child's imaginary friend, and God is a mixture of naive cosmological imagery and an equally naive affective projection of need.

There is another form of naivete, not such an obvious travesty of genuine naive belief, known as the pistic model. It looks more sophisticated than fundamentalism because it is undergirded by philosophical conceptualism and voluntarism in matters of morality and law. Though it usually drapes itself in ecclesiastical garb, it is still an underdeveloped form of faith. Children and underdeveloped adults appropriately retain naive belief. It can express elements of the truth that others who have not successfully negotiated their struggles with maturing can only envy. But the naive forms of faith that fundamentalist and conceptualist believers profess are often destructive of personal dignity, of moral independence, and of any religious sentiment higher than group or party loyalty.[24]

Roman Catholic officialdom since the dawn of the Middle Ages and the Gregorian Reform has increasingly become a world of conceptualized symbols and legalized moral norms. Rather than allow the symbols of the Catholic tradition full play in their potential reference, Catholicism has defined its worship, teaching (doctrine), and praxis (or ethos) in a narrow range of reference. Despite reasoned theological pleas for carrying out a hermeneutics of doctrine, despite historically informed reminders that no one in the church can claim control over the living Tradition but that "only the Church community as a whole is the integral subject of the Tradition,"[25] the magisterialists are not daunted. Ruling out dissent from their way of framing Catholic faith and morals and from their standards of Catholic worship, the pope and the Curia have cowed hierarchies into accepting the prevailing policies, translated bishops from see to see, and trampled ecclesial tradition in the name of loyalty and obedience. Ironically, this repressive behavior guarantees that faith affirmation will never rest content with wrapping naive belief in an institutional straitjacket. As we will see, critical un/belief is organically related to naive belief, especially when the natural expansiveness of primary naivete has been repressed or too tightly controlled. There is something endemic to healthy growth that insists that some will rebel and say no when credo is demanded. Martin Luther's "Here I stand, I can do no other" and Galileo's *"Eppur' si muove"* were the voices of autonomous believers seeking to stand on their own two feet. Those voices loosed a maelstrom that, if not inevitable, became so when Rome's rigidity sought to prevent natural growth. This dialectic between naive faith and critical un/belief, I will argue, is an essential element in the totality of forms that Catholic faith takes. Before taking it up, I wish to describe the shape of naive belief as an appropriate response to the data of revelation and then to detail what becomes of that response when faith affirmation is understood as defining the facts of revelation in other than analogous and symbolic ways.

The most ancient *symbols* of the Catholic faith are the creeds of the early councils, which underlie all subsequent doctrinal definitions but differ from them. The fundamental creeds are first-order declarations of belief, while dogmas represent second-order definitions of the meaning of the creedal declarations. The creeds also relate to orthodoxy in an equivalently first-order relationship because they are anchored in the doxological act of worship. When the creeds migrated from their setting in worship to the dialectical world of the university, they were seen as normative second-order treatises to be defended. From there, in the Reformation, they became confessional only in the sense of setting this group over against another, of confessing a body of particularly interpreted beliefs rather than of confessing *God* (rendering praise and thanks).[26]

The basic structure of the creeds is tripartite, as is evident in the baptismal ritual. Here the creed follows an interrogatory form that, when reversed to the declarative, has the shape of the Apostles' Creed:

Do you believe in God the Father Almighty, creator of heaven and earth?

Do you believe in Jesus Christ, His only Son our Lord, who was born of the Virgin Mary, was crucified, died, and was buried, rose from the dead and is now seated at the right hand of the Father?

Do you believe in the Holy Spirit, the holy Catholic Church, the communion of saints, the forgiveness of sins, the resurrection of the body and the life of the world to come?

In its most basic form, then, the creed makes affirmations drawn from the mythopoetic narrative of the Bible. These affirm (1) that God is the maker or creator of the whole world; (2) that Jesus is the Christ, born in an other-than-natural manner, that he escaped from the consequences of physical death, and that he shares God's ruling relationship to the created world; and (3) that God's own Spirit is related to the existence of the church as a universal community characterized by holiness and made up of a fellowship of holy ones both living and dead, that human sins can be forgiven in this life, that our natural death will someday be overcome, and that a life, or a world, not in place yet will be given us by God.[27]

None of these mythopoetic declarations are subject to empirical verification, but their connection to the historical reality of Jesus of Nazareth (grounded as that is in the equally historical experience of the people Israel) means that one who confesses Jesus as God's Son and our Lord on the basis of his story (the gospel) has grounds for professing belief in the earlier biblical affirmation of creation and in the yet-to-be-revealed elements that link the historical community of the church to an unseen but expected future state of creation.

Christian creedal confession began as a doxological act historically related to Eucharist, or "giving thanks" to God; only secondarily did it gave rise to teaching (doctrine) and conduct (ethos).[28] But this ordinary setting of worship, or doxological encounter between God and the believing community, has been obscured by the use of creeds in both doctrinal and interconfessional squabbles. These disputes also allowed the historical elements in the creed to be the model for understanding the mythopoetic ones. The result for teaching and for conduct has been severe. For decontextualizing the creed from worship has lent credence to an approach that reduces the creed (the data of revelation) to a series of *facts* or *events* understood to be historical in the same way that the events of the crucifixion, death, and burial of Jesus of Nazareth are affirmed to have taken place with specific space-time coordinates. Thus a one-dimensional doctrinal approach to the doxological confession of faith has led official teaching about revelation to adopt a literalist interpretation of the mysteries of revelation. In the area of Catholic morality, the same reductive attitude has established a necessary relationship between the facts of biology, physics, and history and the declared will of God. The resulting notion of natural law that I will examine shortly is the prime example of an abstracted myth that has become rigid and determinist in its meaning and application.

This approach is the opposite of Cardinal Newman's understanding of the relationship between doctrinal propositions and the substance of revelation. He affirmed that "Catholic dogmas are, after all, but symbols of a divine fact, which far from being compassed by those very propositions, would not be exhausted, nor fathomed by a thousand." What Newman refers to as "a divine fact" available to us in symbols keeps getting reduced to contingent facts that are somehow presented as the substance of the mystery of redemption.

Naive belief spontaneously and immediately appropriates symbols because it takes for granted that revelation is extraordinary in the same way that much of what we cannot see or validate stems from extraordinary realms beyond our immediate experience. This form of belief still exists in many informal ways among the Catholic populace, as it does in the way many people accept extraordinary coincidences, unexpected sickness, and surprises as somehow ordained by a higher power. But when these symbolic affirmations are made virtually identical with the terms of their doctrinal definition, then the magisterialists are substituting their own concepts for the proper object of revelation. Symbolic affirmations are one thing; the constant inflation of these symbols makes them less true, not more.

The Doctrine of Creation

Regarding creation, Pius XII as late as 1950 (in *Humanae Generis*) expressed alarm over those who did not take the first eleven chapters of Genesis to be a historical account. Abandoning a strictly historical understanding seemed to threaten the doctrine of original sin, which was based on "the sin truly committed by one Adam." Though not a condemnatory document itself (the same pope had advocated scriptural investigations in his 1943 letter *Divino Afflante Spiritu*), the disapproval it expressed was used by censorious officials to sack Henri de Lubac and others from their teaching positions in France and to blackball professors at the Pontifical Biblical Institute through 1964. This reactionary position on the truth of the first five books of the Bible had earlier been pegged to their historical authorship by Moses. In 1906, the Pontifical Biblical Commission issued its diktat that Moses was "substantially" the author of the Pentateuch, thus elevating a naive, traditional notion of the origin of the Pentateuch to a doctrinal standard of orthodoxy. When this short-sighted decree was followed, in 1907, by the Holy Office's decree *Lamentabili* and Pius X's encyclical *Pascendi Dominici Gregis,* the stage was set for the witch hunt that deprived many talented Catholic professors of their positions and the church of their erudition. Pius X denounced the "modernist" theory of authorship as dependent on a "philosophy borrowed from the negation of God"; he enforced an orthodoxy based purely on the traditional attribution of the books of the Bible "to the authors whose names they bear." Even though other members of the Curia did not favor such harshly narrow standards of orthodoxy, it seems clear that the papal magisterium in this case was guilty of inflating what it knew, how it knew it, and its right to hold honest inquirers to its own naive standards of what constitutes orthodoxy.[29]

This example shows that when the symbolic elements of the scriptural narrative are naively historicized, the content of Catholic doctrine expands in an unwarranted fashion. Alternately, the narrative symbols of the Bible are treated literalistically on the presumption that what is narrated has been directly willed by God. The following are examples of doctrines commonly, but uncritically, asserted to represent the truth of Catholic teaching. In fact, they are "abstracted myths." They result, by and large, from a literal reading of mythopoetic material, a habit that has had significant effects on how Catholics have been asked to appropriate the truth of their faith in their everyday lives.

Historical Original Sin

We have already seen how Pius XII was concerned that a nonhistorical reading of Genesis 1–11 would impugn the veracity of the concept of original sin as it depended on a historical sin committed by "one Adam." Of course, the doctrine of original sin has a more complex history. No one read Genesis 3 and concluded from it that humankind was guilty of an inherited sin until Paul in Romans sought to illumine the universal scope of Christ's death and resurrection through recourse to a comparison/contrast with Adam, whom he (perhaps) labels "a type of the one to come" (5:14). Paul's notion of type is rather ambiguous, since the offense of Adam has the exact opposite effect from the gift of the "one man Jesus Christ" (v. 15). His argument is metaphorical and illustrative, but it has been understood as a definitive history of original sin and its removal. Its rhetorical force was such that, once Jerome mistranslated a phrase in 5:12 that seemed to say that in Adam "all" sinned and Augustine took sexual generation as the exact way that Adam's unique sin was passed down to all his physical descendants, the stage was set for a literal doctrine to emerge that presumed that all children were born into the world with a stain on their soul. Unless that stain were removed by being washed away in baptism, those human beings were doomed to hellfire in the hereafter. While this predestination of the majority of humanity to perdition was defended from Augustine through Calvin to Cotton Mather (in his Puritan classic "Sinners in the Hands of an Angry God"), it was so offensive to modern sensibilities that none other than Pius IX began to move away from a doctrinaire understanding of the fate of the unbaptized (and many of the baptized as well). He allowed that most people who do not receive baptism are afflicted by "invincible ignorance" and so not hell-bound by definition.[30] We can conclude that this represents a case of a doctrine becoming so hypertrophied that it imploded; it was seen for the logical absurdity that it was.

The problem with naive faith affirmation does not arise from the mythopoetic imagination of the scriptures or even from the tendency to historicize myth that began with the fathers. Rather it arises from the later habit of theologians to define and delimit doctrine on the basis of inflated, literal readings of the basically symbolic tradition. Since Orthodox Christianity has never accepted the Western church's schematized understanding of original sin and since this difference in interpretation of the biblical material has never entered into the disputes that have kept Orthodoxy and Western Christianity apart, one can presume that, at one level, the doctrine of original sin (as it attributes death to an original act of disobedience that is inherited) represents, not a necessary conclusion, but a narrowed conceptualization of the biblical datum. Naive believers have no problem with the portrayal of the world as fallen and are generally anxious to have some prophylactic recourse against death, bad luck, or evil spirits (as baptism has become in Catholic folk cultures). Philosophically inclined individuals have tended to accept the Augustinian understanding that humanity suffers from some kind of aboriginal dislocation of consciousness, one that even Freud thought traceable to a specific event that he labeled "the murder of the primal father." But more importantly, the symbolic tradition of Christianity has resisted any definition of original sin as a literal or actual historical event and interpreted the fault that crosses our relationship with God as a *felix culpa,* an event whose real meaning only appears in the light of the resurrection of Jesus.

Natural Law and Procreation

A second example again illustrates how blowing up a symbolic narrative creates the conceptual fantasy of a fact whose acceptance is equated with orthodox belief. It arose from Paul's argument about the universal nature of unrighteousness before the law of Moses (later original sin), which was inflated into a doctrine of natural law. In Romans 1:18–23, Paul argued in defense of his gospel as "the power of God for salvation to everyone who has faith, to the Jew first and also to the Greek" (vv. 1:16–17). His point was to persuade his readers that "there is no distinction [between Jews and Greeks], since all have sinned and fall short of the glory of God" (3:22–23). In order to make this scandalous argument, he brings certain traditional apocalyptic and anti-Gentile Jewish missionary traditions together in this way:

For the wrath of God is revealed from heaven against all ungodliness and wickedness of those who by their wickedness suppress the truth. For what can be known about God is plain to them, because God has shown it to them. Ever since the creation of the world his eternal power and divine nature, invisible though they are, have been understood and seen through the things he has made. So they are without excuse; for though they knew God, they did not honor him as God or give thanks to him, but they became futile in their thinking, and their senseless minds were darkened. Claiming to be wise, they became fools; and they exchanged the glory of the immortal God for images resembling a mortal human being or birds or four-footed animals or reptiles.

In v. 20 ("Ever since the creation of the world his eternal power and divine nature, invisible though they are, have been understood and seen through the things he has made. So they are without excuse"), Paul is echoing "a current Jewish idea of the culpability of pagans in not acknowledging and reverencing God as they should have."[31] Paul is relying on a traditional wisdom argument that held the existence of an actual primal revelation that only Israel accepted. In the face of Gentile taunts and persecution Jews sought, by this heuristic fiction, to explain both their singular monotheism and their election. Paul asserts that all human beings in that primeval era "are the common ancestors of what would later be the Gentiles and Jews," who were to be judged on the basis of the same principle ("each one's deeds," 2:6), because "God shows no partiality" (2:11).[32]

For his part, Paul was adapting a conventional argument for Gentile guilt to a new framework wherein universal human guilt was "in this present critical time" reversed by God's justifying love and manifested as an offer to salvation "to all who believe" (3:21–22). He was not propounding the universal norm for morality into which the "law written on the heart" (2:15) has been inflated. It is not the concept itself that is at fault (see chapter 10), but the way it has been totalized and conceptualized by the voluntaristic apparatus of the magisterium. Arguing from inflated premises, dogmatic and moral theologians (for example, Aquinas who in his *Summa Theologica* cites Romans 1:20 extensively as a proof text for the existence of natural law) have formulated many anthropological positions based on abstracted natural law readings of naively mythopoeic biblical material.

This is certainly the case in matters of sexuality and sexual intercourse, much of which received no definitive treatment in the Bible. Christian attitudes that arose in response to pagan ascetical prejudices — for instance, that sexual intercourse was the "lower" part of human nature — were justified by appeals to texts such as Genesis 38:9 (Onan's spilled semen) and Tobit 8:7 (Tobiah's prenuptial prayer). This led to the doctrine that sexual intercourse was justified only for procreation, a standard teaching for the first millennium of Christianity. As we saw above, though he denied the dualistic view of sex as participating in an evil continuation of fleshly existence, Augustine still read Adam and Eve's shame at their nakedness via the stoical fear of the loss of control during coitus. Hence he understood sexual feeling as a penalty for humanity's disobedience and saw the uncontrollable stirrings of genital sexuality as "the fitting punishment of the crime of disobedience."[33] But whereas Augustine understood chastity as possible by God's gracious assistance, the magisterium has turned his teaching on grace into a moralistic demand that what God obliges must be done. Pius XI's *On Chaste Marriage* (1930), Paul VI's *Humanae Vitae*, and John Paul II's *Familiaris Consortio* (1980) all transmute Augustine's principle that grace will suffice (compare 2 Cor 13:13) and assert that "no difficulties can arise that reduce the obligation of God's commandment." Hence the command (against artificial contraception) should be obeyed "with serene confidence in God's grace and in [each person's] own will."[34] From Paul's mythological argument that righteous Gentiles prove the existence of a "law written on the heart" (Rom 2:15) to the magisterium's moral demands requires a critical treatment that will follow in chapter 9.

Biblical Sexuality and Virginity

These examples of inflationary expansion of doctrine have shown that an originally naive reading of the way humanity became guilty or fell from grace was turned, through a negative sexual anthropology, into sexual prohibitions said to be willed by God. We have yet to take into account how the Bible's unsophisticated first reading of the facts of human sexual differentiation, especially as these are subjected to an objectivist reading, have provided fodder for misanthropic and misogynist readings of the facts of revelation. Another example, then, will expand my argument that narrow conceptualism has led to a misappropriation of the symbolic tradition of Catholicism.

In the Bible, "woman" is understood to have been taken from the side of "man" (Gen 2:22), and hence is subordinate to him (1 Cor 11:8; 1 Tim 2:13–14). Female sexual desire and the pain of childbearing are said to be women's punishment, the male "seed" is taken to be the equivalent of offspring (Gen 38:9), and the menstrual flow is understood to be ritually defiling, as is (accidental?) seminal emission (15:18–19). This last act along with male homosexual relations, male and female incest, bestiality, and adultery, is punishable by death. When these prohibitions were filtered through the magisterium's notion of natural law that is said to incline rational beings "to their due act and end" and that is equated with "the eternal reason of God the creator who governs the whole universe," the connection between intercourse and reproduction became determinate and necessary. For every human being's every sexual act is said to be naturally predetermined by God, who has imposed on it a goal or purpose that limits its own (natural) tendency to pleasure (which was understood as disordered). In this moralistic straitjacket, universalizing statements about the purpose of "each and every martial act" are not only possible, but necessary, to make. Therefore the magisterium sees itself as obliged to impose obligations willed by God with the finality of an eternal law! More recently, magisterial statements have sought to overlay this totalistic perspective with personalist categories to ground sexuality in human dignity, but any real respect for individual subjects within this generalized understanding of human acts and their necessary end is genuinely hard to come by given the objectivism inherent in it.

Most Catholics have not followed these natural law principles to their logical ends (as racist and fascist ideologies have done) not only because of their natural good sense but also because of a countervailing tradition that, because of its own excesses, has left most of the faithful in the virtuous middle. This countermovement occurred under the influence of the ascetic tradition of the superiority of virginity. Like natural law, it grew out of a reading of biblical material that froze the idea about the coming of the end of the temporal world. In place of a world-to-come that was expected to arrive soon, later Hellenistic Christianity substituted a vertical universe of higher and lower orders of being. At the top of this hierarchy of being was God, pure spirit. Toward the bottom was the material world, in which spiritual souls had become enmeshed. Pure materiality was evil; only the spiritual was the realm of salvation. Hence, sexuality was the antipode of spirituality and virginity the surest way to escape unspiritual flesh.[35] The biblical evidence for the spiritual tradition that defined virginity as superior to married sexuality is sparse, but not insignificant. Its inflation into a full-blown complex of doctrine will spell out how rationalist conceptualization has turned symbolic affirmations into abstracted myths and imposed naive belief on faith affirmation.

The Complex of Marian Doctrines

Ironically, the articulated doctrine of virginity as a superior state began in the narrative traditions of the births of the patriarchs and was fed by other birth stories and promises about the dynastic line of David until it failed after the exile. The mainspring of this mythopoetic tradition is what J. R. R. Tolkien called a "eucatastrophe...the sudden happy turn in a story that gives sudden relief to nature's material chain of cause and effect."[36] The major eucatastrophe of the first half of Genesis is the unexpected birth of a son and heir to Abraham and Sarah (Gen 21:2), then, less dramatically, to Isaac and Rebecca (25:21). These stories became complemented by the tradition of Moses' birth and salvation from Pharaoh's murderous decree (Exod 2:1–10) and with yet more birth stories of Israel's heroes: both the mother of Samson (Judg 13:5) and the mother of Samuel (1 Sam 1:2) were barren. In a society where polygamy was practiced because the perils of childbirth made wives expendable and a people's future precarious, these narratives of providential birth kept alive a sense of good news.

After David's dynasty had ruled for three centuries in Jerusalem, it seemed to one royal-watcher, Isaiah, son of Amoz, that petty politics and dynastic intrigue were destabilizing the monarchy (see the play on words in Isaiah 7:9: "If you do not stand firm in faith, you shall not stand at all"). Though almost despairing of staving off disaster in his own time (6:11–13; 8:11–15), Isaiah constantly saw his children (and their symbolic names) as "signs and portents in Israel from the Lord of hosts" (8:18). In much the same way, he sought to assure a scheming and unfaithful King Ahaz that, in the birth and early years of another child, whose name would be Immanuel, he would have a sign from the Lord of God's faithfulness (7:1–14).

Isaiah's predictions of disaster eventually came true, and Jerusalem fell to foreign armies in 587 B.C.E. Despite the restoration of the nation under Nehemiah and Ezra the scribe, most of the Jewish people continued to live in exile. Eventually, one thriving community of Jews dwelt in Alexandria on the Nile River delta in Egypt. There a Greek translation of the Torah, the Prophets, and many of the Writings was undertaken, and more books were composed that eventually entered, not the Jewish, but the Christian Bible. Known as the Septuagint, this Greek version of the scriptures sought to show how the ancient text still had resonance with the exiles' lives and still possessed secrets that had yet to be revealed. In this context, when the translators rendered the sign that Isaiah the prophet gave to Ahaz, they transposed Emmanuel's birth from one that might have been surprising (the context is not clear in 7:14) to one that was truly portentous: the young woman (*almah* in Hebrew) of the promise became a virgin (*parthenos* in Greek). Looking forward to the eventual restoration of David's line, they saw the one who was to be born (according to another prophecy in 9:1–7) as an "angel of great counsel," a demigodlike figure, perhaps such as their pagan neighbors affirmed about their deified pharaohs and Alexander. As one virgin-born, he would be godlike and would restore Israel to its rightful place.

Though virginity had played no positive theological role in the scriptures of the First Testament (cf. Judg 11:37; Jer 16:1–4), its use in a birth promise parallel to pagan mythology merged with the more ancient tradition of salvation-births in the interpretive world that produced the New Testament. In both places where this tradition is explicit, the birth narratives of Matthew (1:18–25) and Luke (1:26–38), the virgin birth of Jesus is part of the writers' portrayal of the finality or end-of-the-ages significance of Jesus. He is presented, from birth, as the Messiah (Matt 1:17–18) and "the Son of the Most High" who will "reign over the house of Jacob forever and of his kingdom there will be no end" (Luke 1:33). Though Jesus' virgin birth (a detail that neither Mark, nor the fourth gospel, nor any other New Testament writings attest) originally proclaimed his unique status as God's "Son," that status became known only in the church's experience of his resurrection and in its expectation that he would return "on the clouds of heaven." The virgin motherhood of Mary in both gospels is completely in the service of this gospel proclamation. It was retrojected into the birth narratives to signal that ancient prophecy had been fulfilled and that the era of the Messiah had arrived. In their original shape, they are symbolic of the uniquely divine initiative in the historical person of Jesus of Nazareth as that initiative arose in Israel's history (Matthew) and was extended to the whole (Roman) world (Luke). The virgin birth of Jesus is specifically a rehearsal of Jesus' death and resurrection retrojected into his birth and infancy. The narratives are cast in terms that do not confine themselves to what really happened, preferring, as all mythopoetry does, to reveal the overarching significance of the events by weaving together the wondrous and the ordinary. In its plain, mythopoetic reference, then, the virgin birth seeks to transcend the facts of Jesus' birth, not relate them historically.

The end-of-the-ages significance of virginity (but not the virgin birth) is also attested in the writings of Paul the apostle. While it does not engage his attention frequently, in his first letter to the Corinthians he presents a case, first, for the superiority of virginity and, second, to defend his own missionary practice of not having a wife "as do the other apostles and the brothers of the Lord and Cephas" (1 Cor 9:5). But the context of his presentation of virginity is important. His advice, clearly not a "command of the Lord," (7:12) is given "in view of the impending crisis" (v. 26) and reads this way:

Are you bound to a wife? Do not seek to be free. Are you free from a wife? Do not seek a wife. But if you marry, you do not sin, and if a virgin marries, she does not sin. Yet those who marry will experience distress in this life, and I would spare you that. I mean, brothers and sisters, the appointed time has grown short; from now on, let even those who have wives be as though they had none, and those who mourn as though they were not mourning, and those who rejoice as though they were not rejoicing, and those who buy as though they had no possessions, and those who deal with the world as though they had no dealings with it. For the present form of this world is passing away. I want you to be free from anxieties. The unmarried man is anxious about the affairs of the Lord, how to please the Lord; but the married man is anxious about the affairs of the world, how to please his wife, and his interests are divided. And the unmarried woman and the virgin are anxious about the affairs of the Lord, so that they may be holy in body and spirit; but the married woman is anxious about the affairs of the world, how to please her husband. (1 Cor 7:27–34)

Thus Paul's recommendation of virginity has to be read in the context of the proximity of the end. But, as we have seen, because the world did not pass away, Christian communities began to root themselves in Hellenistic society. When they did, the end-of-the-ages significance of virginity began to be seen as a more spiritual way to live in this world. It allowed one not be "of this world," as Jesus testified of himself in the most "spiritual" of the gospels (John 18:36).

At the same time, Christianity was not the only spiritual force at work in the world of the late empire. It was profoundly influenced by a revival of Platonic thought through the writings of Ammonius Saccus and Porphyry's portrait of Plotinus. As the fourth century ground on, it took on the character of "an ascetic age, where the sensitive man already felt humiliated by his body." Ascetical and spiritual forms of Christianity grew dominant and challenged earlier biblical and Hebraic understandings of how God was present to his creation. These new forms of spirituality often created conflicts between those who clung to a more simple, even anthropomorphic, notion of God and proponents of the newer spiritual ideals that professed a radical nonidentity of this world and the spiritual realm.[37]

Within this changed context for biblical symbols, the virginity of Mary changed, becoming the model of the ascetical life, and she herself became the model of the life-long ascetic. The doctrine of the perpetual virginity of Mary, to which Joseph's own celibacy in marriage was then attached, emerged in the writings of Jerome and others. Mary's other children, the gospels' "brothers and sisters" of Jesus, particularly James, whom Paul knew as "the brother of the Lord" (Gal 1:19), all became assimilated into a hypothetical extended family of Jesus or were understood to be the children of Joseph by a former marriage.[38]

Once the end that was already present (1 Cor 10:11) became a spiritual world vertically fixed above this world, the virgin birth was frozen in the past and became a doctrine necessary to Jesus' divine identity, undergirding a doctrine of salvation from this world of change and decay. The late Roman Empire witnessed a culture of spiritual athleticism (*askesis*) that would make our late twentieth-century Olympics or the Superbowl pale by comparison. Again, the root metaphors of spiritual contest were present in Paul's "racing for the finish line" (Phil 3:12–14) and in the stadium images of 1 Corinthians 9:24–27 and Hebrews 12:1. But they became transposed into a wholly different key when monks became pole-sitters or anchorites or moved under the stairs and stayed there for years as a sign of their holy *apatheia*. In this transposition, the sexual images of the Song of Songs were applied to Mary, who became *tota pulchra* because she was a mother who never had sexual intercourse, labor pains, or natural birth. The perpetual virginity of Mary eventually became almost anti-incarnational: her hymen was miraculously preserved, so that Christ was born in the same way that he emerged from the tomb—miraculously! Mary, it was claimed, never aged in her life on earth and, in her exalted state, she was no longer the lowly one of the gospel narrative, but the Virgin Most Powerful. To her, monks pledged their fealty in the same way knights adopted a noble Lady as their patron.

But this inflation of Mary's identity could occur only at the price of deflating or ignoring those aspects of the gospel in which she is not idealized. For example, in Mark 3:21, 31–35, she and Jesus' family seek to "snatch" him (and presumably bring him home). The scriptural tradition not only remembered that there were siblings of Jesus, but also that they were not with the program during Jesus' ministry (John 7:3, 10). None of these counterindications were allowed to mar the ideal Virgin Mother, which took on a symbolic life of its own. Only with the Renaissance did other idealized females emerge to contest Mary's symbolic hegemony. Venus once again emerged, as in Botticelli's famous painting, and other females from the Bible and pagan legend found a place in the artistic and the popular imagination. This partly accounted for Protestantism's rejection of Mary's (and the saints') intercession: all of them clearly had merged with other imaginative sources and so interfered with that process of literalism or desynonymizing that, first, the Reformation and, then, the Enlightenment championed.

But by the nineteenth century, the figure of Mary once again emerged as a countercultural religious symbol of importance in the Romantic reaction to rationalism and to the collapse of rural life through industrialization. Bernadette Soubirous's vision of a woman calling herself the Immaculate Conception (following the papal definition of that doctrine in 1854) was an example of the desire for eucatastrophic events, an anti-scientific miracle-seeking that continues unabated into the late twentieth century. Bernadette's sanctuary at Lourdes expressed a readjustment in

the "feel" of Catholic spirituality from an ascetic, defensive, and elitist cult of perfection to a warm, popular, penitential, but practical religious sense — aesthetically crude, liturgically unsophisticated, but realistic, hopeful and immensely resilient. It was the "Lourdes type" of Catholicism which carried the Catholic people through the intellectual and psychological demoralization of Christianity which followed the scientific ascendancy and the rise of the technological culture. Catholic religious conviction came through, not by confronting the challenges of science and the new humanism but by ignoring them. (When the Church tried to confront them, as in its dealings with the Modernist movement, it only further destroyed its own credibility.) The Catholic religious sense could afford to ignore them because it was, if narrow, basically satisfying, and realistic about life as experienced by the poor and uneducated and exploited.[39]

This passage sums up the ongoing appeal and shape of much naive Catholic belief into this century, a naivete that peaked in the papal definition of Mary's uniqueness in the Christian drama of salvation, her bodily assumption into heaven. In the Apostolic Constitution *Munificentissimus Deus*, by which Pius XII solemnly defined the Assumption as a dogma of the faith, he took aim explicitly at those who had strayed from "truth and virtue" and who were affected by the "illusory teachings of materialism and the corruption of morals" (read Communism). Hence he defined the doctrine to shore up traditional Christian eschatology, the belief that human beings have a "lofty goal" to which both their bodies and their souls were destined and that the faithful should be confirmed in their own resurrection, which belief could then be made more effective.[40]

Aside from its explicit pastoral orientation, the definition relied upon a mythopoetic formulation to express the content of the doctrine. When the pope proclaimed that, though she "fell asleep" in death, Mary's body was kept free from all corruption and that she was "assumed body and soul into heavenly glory," he used mythological language as if it had properly literal meaning. The entire idiom of the definition retained an unapologetic countercritical sense, seeking to comfort all those who "throughout the course of [their] earthly pilgrimage" are resigned to leading a "life troubled by cares, hardships, and sorrows" until they die. Pius made no attempt to define the precise meaning of "body and soul" or of "heavenly glory" but took for granted that these traditional symbols had a clear meaning for his audience. His claim that the doctrine is "in wonderful accord with those divine truths given us in Holy Scripture" is equally naive and uncritical.[41]

While the language of the definition remained imprecisely mythopoetic and the reasons for making a solemn definition drew upon the doctrine's being "fitting and right," the teaching is understood to have the same force as the defined dogmas of the early councils and to enjoy the character of certainty and infallibility defined by Vatican I. In the next chapter, I will seek to scrutinize more exactly the adequacy of these categories. But here I am seeking only to put forth the basic shape of naive Catholic belief, how it has come to be that way, and how it has led to exaggerated factual and ontological claims. Because the traditional symbols of the faith have been conceptually inflated, they are presumed to yield a determinate reference that neither the symbols nor the language of the creed justifies. The declaration of the Assumption, while materially naive, presumes that it is formally factual and that the factual content of its mythopoetic expression is what constitutes a doctrine of the faith. This combination has created the greatest problems for any modern epistemology of belief, as a philosophy professor illustrated in 1966 when he presented the content of the doctrine (and the resurrection) in these terms: "if one traveled throughout the universe in concentric circles — and God did not withhold your sight — you would have to encounter the bodies of Jesus and Mary." Such are the intellectual absurdities brought on by abstracted or conceptualized myths when they are logically extended into objective descriptions of factual events.

Peter's Primacy, Infallibility, and the Magisterium

A final example of the inflation of a biblical symbol demonstrates how a naive presumption of historicity (with significant overlays of legalism) has created the most neuralgic of the modern Catholic doctrines, papal infallibility. Since the Middle Ages, the text of Matthew 16:16–19 (with some support from Luke 22:31–32) has been consistently inflated until it became a doctrine known by its shorthand title, the power of the keys. Matthew's narrative is as follows:

Simon Peter answered, "You are the Messiah, the Son of the living God." And Jesus answered him, "Blessed are you, Simon son of Jonah! For flesh and blood has not revealed this to you, but my Father in heaven. And I tell you, you are Peter, and on this rock I will build my church, and the gates of Hades will not prevail against it. I will give you the keys of the kingdom of heaven, and whatever you bind on earth will be bound in heaven, and whatever you loose on earth will be loosed in heaven."

While Simon's name change to "Peter" (*Cephas* in Aramaic) affirms his special status among the disciples, Jesus' bestowing the "keys of the kingdom of heaven" symbolized an authority whose extent is not at all clear. We know the idiom of "binding and loosing," which seems to be the purpose of the keys from rabbinic parallels. The same task is bestowed upon all the disciples in 18:18, in the context of excommunicating an unrepentant wrongdoer from the community (18:17). Hence, the keys do bestow authority in the community.[42]

On the historical level, there can be no reasonable doubt that Simon the fisherman "came to be known as Cephas (Peter), probably because Jesus himself gave him the name."[43] On the level of symbolic naming, Jesus' action seems to be both comedic and proleptic. "Cephas" is best understood as a nickname and probably combines, as do most nicknames, elements of the obvious (Simon's strong-headedness) with a note of whimsy or rebuke (his likely cowardice). When Matthew placed the name-giving between Peter's confession of Jesus as Messiah and the first prediction of the passion (rather than just noting the name change, as other gospels do), he clearly reflected a postresurrectional state of affairs when there already was a "gathered community" (*ekklesia,* or church) and Peter was a leader with real authority. This much is clear from the mythopoetic meaning of the scene: just before Jesus related his coming passion and death in Jerusalem, he assured the uncomprehending disciples, through his bestowal of a new identity on Simon, that Simon's risking belief in him would paradoxically prevail. Any failure to see Simon's new identity as foundational to the community of faith (such as in the song, "Jesus built the church on the rock of our faith") misreads the literally poetic sense of the text. Minimally, in Matthew, Peter functions not only as a model of discipleship in general, "but beyond this Matthew gives him a prominence that the others do not get."[44]

Yet, by enshrining that prominence in paradox, Matthew roots the "rockness" of Peter in grace, in God's gift, not in an objective power ontologically bestowed. This means that the keys and the binding and loosing of 16:19 do not represent any material instruments of coercive power, either moral or physical. The proleptic role given to Peter in Matthew's portrait of the ministry of Jesus, in its purely symbolic sense, retains in it an element of "Can you believe that?" Only by retaining the element of nonidentity between literal keys and the authority that Jesus gave to Peter can we avoid the illegitimate objectification of that authority that makes it like that of any other royal or political figure. Mythopoetically, the ever-present "whispered no" that preserves the tension between the obvious, literal meaning of "keys" and its hidden meaning (a nonliteral kingdom) alone allows this story to be read as a revelation of how marvelous it is that "God...had given such authority to human beings" (Matt 9:8 on the power to forgive sins).

The problem arises when the mythopoetic sense of the text is supplanted by a literal understanding, namely, that the kind of authority or power given is the same as that which kings and those who "lord it over their own" take for granted. When the authority of Peter's successor took the place of the power that Caesar wielded in Rome, the same power that princes exercised over their subjects — coercive, legal at best, but often tyrannical, a power over life and death — it became something other than Jesus bestowed. In Matthew 20:26 ("It is not to be that way with you"), the disciples are explicitly forbidden that kind of power. In the previous chapter we saw how grandiose the claims of the medieval popes to absolute power had become, allowing them, hypothetically, to depose emperors. Since then, the imperial claims of the papacy have been dropped, but the naive historicizing of what actually occurred in the ministry of Jesus has given the papacy a dysfunctional self-understanding. Claims such as were made at the Council of Florence (c. 1440), that "the Holy Apostolic See and the Roman Pontiff have primacy in the whole world, and...that to [the Roman Pontiff] in blessed Peter was given by our Lord Jesus Christ the full power of feeding, ruling, and governing the universal Church" (DS 1307), have imposed a medieval reading on texts that cannot bear such inflationary dishonesty.

This fullness of power (*plenitudo potestatis*) is said to be, as regards faith and morals and the discipline and governing of the church, a direct legal (ordinary and immediate) jurisdiction "over each and all the Churches and all the pastors and the faithful" (Vatican I, DS 3064). The papacy's juridical conceptualizing of this power, of course, peaked at Vatican I with its definition that the Roman Pontiff "is possessed of that infallibility with which the divine Redeemer willed that his Church should be endowed." One does not need, "God forbid, to presume to contradict" the definition and thus occur a formal anathema (DS 3075), but one can question whether the gospels allow us to conceptualize so naively the prerogative Jesus bestowed when he nicknamed Simon

"Peter." Even granting that Jesus bestowed a certain authority on him, we have to question whether Jesus could have made a bestowal of authority in the conceptual categories in which these definitions have been proposed and by which the papacy has arrogated authority to itself.

Here I cannot resolve the problems that the conceptual objectification of the mythopoetic affirmations of the Bible have created for creedal affirmation. I am, of course, presuming that there are problems and that the centralizing of all teaching, sanctifying, and governing in the papal magisterium is at the heart of them. But I am seeking to show that naive, precritical faith affirmation can easily be distorted when multivalent symbols like keys become transformed into ontological bestowals of power.

The Preexistence of the Universal Church

A final example of the difference between the mythopoetical presentation of how this gift is given and how the magisterium has grandiosely appropriated it by declaring symbols to be historical events or metaphysical truths will round out this chapter on the first form of faith that belief takes. In June 1992, there appeared the *Letter to the Bishops of the Catholic Church on Some Aspects of the Church Understood as Communion*, issued by the Congregation for the Doctrine of the Faith. The letter took the position that the only theologically correct understanding that does not distort the mystery of the church is one that the "universal Church.... is not the result of the communion of Churches, but... is a reality *ontologically and temporally* prior to every *individual* particular Church" (9, italics original). What the letter wants to protect is the "mystery" of the church, lest the church be understood as similar to other "purely human" groups or societies and the way their parts interact with their totality.

The evidence offered for the priority of the universal church over the particular churches is meant to preempt further theological reflection that might jeopardize the papal magisterium's ability to define the terms of debate about unity and diversity among Catholics and other Christian theologians. It illustrates the extent to which the Vatican has sought to become a centrifugal authority that would make it arbiter of all faith affirmation. To be successful, one might expect the CDF's argument to adopt critical historical tools so as to convince the skeptical that, from the beginning, the church has existed with substantially the same constitution that it historically developed. But instead, the letter presents a series of naive, precritical statements that are presented, not as mythopoetical symbols, but as literal, ontological, and historical truths of fact.

On the level of ontology, the letter refers to claims in "the fathers" (the Second Epistle of Clement and the *Shepherd* of Hermas) that the

Church "precedes creation." As we saw in chapter 2, the notion has a certain poetic force and, metaphorically, describes the society of those who profess Christ Risen as responding to God's prevenient initiative for our salvation. The church can be said to preexist Christ's resurrection in the sense that God's call of the people Israel, though a particular one, had an intended universal extension (cf. Isa 42:6, 49:6). But to identify the church with an actual preexistent, real thing or body of believers grounds the argument in the realm of Platonic ideas that cast their shadows on the world. To claim that there is any literal truth to the notion that the church precedes creation is to make it semidivine, beyond the human and historical. It ignores the "whispered no" that characterizes all metaphorical or symbolic ways of speaking and that must be respected in any truthful effort to speak of the church's antiquity.

What is more, theological tradition no more accepts the preexistence of the church than it does the preexistence of human souls who must wait to be born. Like all those predestined for salvation whose lives begin in a moment of time, the church had a beginning in history and is subject to the vicissitudes of change and development. The effort to claim preexistence for the church, except as a heuristic fiction that reveals the provident love of God at work even before creation, represents an attempt to idealize the church out of reality, to contradict Vatican II's recognition that the church is *semper reformanda,* always in need of reform and change. Here again, the metaphorical truth of the preexistent *ekklesia* is a literal falsity. It is a metaphor that has never been very significant in the church's self-understanding. To make it so now would once again reduce historical Israel to a victim of God's plan to choose the church and reject the synagogue — a piece of bad typology we have only just jettisoned.

The letter's second claim about the priority of the universal church again manages to confuse mythopoetic events and literal, historical ones. It claims that "on the day of Pentecost" the universal church was manifested "in the community of the one hundred and twenty gathered around Mary and the Twelve apostles." It presents Mary as "the representation of the one unique Church" and the apostles as "the founders-to-be of the local Churches, who have a mission directed to the world. From the first the Church *speaks all languages*" (9). The universal church was real before anyone ever set foot outside Jerusalem!

But to claim that the scene in Acts 2 actually records a unique historical event is to treat Acts as if it recorded events the way photographers record actual happenings. Worse still, the letter's claim treats the bestowal of the Spirit as if it were a discrete space-time occurrence like the arrival of an airplane. It quietly ignores the fourth gospel's alternate account of the giving of the Spirit on Easter night (John 20:22–23). More importantly, it nullifies the teaching of the recent council on interpreting scripture by attending "to the customary and characteristic patterns of perception, speech and narrative that prevailed at the age of the sacred writer" (*Dei Verbum* 12). The picture of Mary surrounded by the apostles (cf. Acts 1:14 where she is with Jesus' *brothers,* but they are edited out of the CDF's letter) is precisely that: a picture, an idealized and archetypical representation, a symbolic portrait of the early community, not an actual, constitutive, valid-for-all-time, frozen, and timeless snapshot of what the church was at one moment in time. If it were, we would have to ask why we have not had a vicar of Mary in the church to preside over ecumenical councils, which would be run by the vicar of Peter! Literalism cuts both ways, but the congregation doesn't seem to realize that. Most tragically, its whole conception of the bestowal of the Spirit ignores the fact that, as an event, it is as transcendent of time and space as is the resurrection. It cannot be presented as a legally constitutive moment that justifies magisterial centralism over the church universal.

The historicity that is present in the gospels and in Acts and that Vatican II affirmed (*Dei Verbum* 19) never requires us to adopt a standard of mere facticity or literal representation. The CDF's naive and precritical approach to the temporal priority of the universal church flagrantly ignores the entire modern struggle over the interpretation of the Bible. Its pre-Spinozan approach is not a naive first reading of the symbolic elements that Luke wove into his account of the primitive community but an authoritarian attempt to ignore that the church too has a history and to read a predetermined sense of what God intended into a mythopoetic text. Luke produced a sophisticated theological text in its own right, but one couched completely "according to the customary and characteristic patterns of perceptions, speech, and narrative which prevailed" in his age, not according to the need of a late twentieth-century ultramontanist program for dampening investigations that threaten Roman control of theological dialogue.

Authority and Naive Belief

The truths of Catholic faith and morals are transmitted primarily through the symbols of the Bible, the creeds, and the liturgy before they are shaped (or misshaped) by self-consciously theological discourse. When rationalist and empiricist criticism of the Bible and theology began to impugn the sufficiency of both the early symbols and the later theological concepts of faith affirmation, theologians defended their conceptualized version of the truth with an equally rational, univocal discourse. In turn, this put primarily naive belief in the difficult position of defending itself on rationalist rather than on symbolic grounds. A conceptualist theology, cut off from its mythopoetic roots, narrows the broad range of meaning available in the symbolic discourse of the

Bible and theology. Its narrow rationality then inflates a partial interpretation and makes it stand for the whole truth. When this is accompanied by an appeal to the authority of the magisterium, belief increasingly becomes an act of the will responding to voluntaristic concepts of authority and obedience.[45] This narrowing, in turn, reduces living faith to an ideology that, for all its rational pretensions, is both antirational and antitraditional as well.

Naive believers often accept authoritarian, patriarchal structures because they seem to reflect the pictures of the way things are in the Bible and in traditional societies. This tendency perhaps stems from the habit, in early stages of their development, to accept the word of others who play important roles in their personal world. But just as the original shape of encounter with the world expands and develops as individuals grow and change, for many believers today authoritarian religious authority has become personally inappropriate and socially dysfunctional. In an increasingly complex world of both cultural pluralism and historical ambiguity, the religious equivalent of advanced latency is no longer adequate for adult believers. Latency is a stage when believers can entertain concepts and interiorize certain moral norms, but it cannot explain the whys and wherefores that undermine the conceptualized form of faith affirmation that authority in the Catholic Church continues to promote.

When this stage passes, a person enters upon a journey into critical un/belief. How one is encouraged to weather the crisis of criticism will make all the difference. Some people regress permanently rather than lose the security of primary naivete. Some angrily refuse to admit there's anything inadequate with their ideas and become the scourge of the believing community today: religious ideologues. Others remain angry for a very long time, furious over the credulity they showed for too long, disgusted with persons and institutions who they sense have deceived them. Some others will struggle and fight with themselves and with their tradition to get through the eye of the needle to the uncertain land beyond. The next chapter will seek to show what the vicissitudes of the critical stage of the journey might be like today. Risking it makes great demands for personal and spiritual autonomy. Not doing so makes maturity a distant dream.

Bibliographical Essay

On the character of theology: Dennis Cunningham ("Theology as Rhetoric," *Theological Studies* 52 [1991]: 411–15) distinguishes between Aristotle's notion of analytic argument (comprising such areas as physics, metaphysics, and logic) and his notion of dialectic (which takes in politics, ethics, and poetics), specifically of "rhetoric," the counterpart of dialectic moving in the direction not of theory but of praxis. Whereas dialectical argument may change a person's mind, it does not necessarily lead to action. As Cunningham succinctly puts it: "People are induced to action not by dialectic but by rhetoric." He also notes the predominance of interpretation as central to theology, thereby relativizing claims to objectification. He argues that theologians "should undertake a postcritical appropriation of a distinctly precritical method: namely, the ancient faculty of rhetoric." F. J. van Beeck (*God Encountered: A Contemporary Catholic Systematic Theology,* vol. 1, *Understanding the Christian Faith* [San Francisco: HarperSanFrancisco, 1989], 294 et passim) calls for a theological method to practice "an appreciative hermeneutic across space and time," one that avoids the extremes of dogmatic "integralism" or subjectivist "modernism" (69). To avoid these extremes, not unlike the poles of "necessity" and "possibility" that I have employed, van Beeck calls for "a real hermeneutic of the doctrinal and magisterial Tradition [which] is still largely outstanding." In his earlier study *Christ Proclaimed: Christology as Rhetoric* (New York: Paulist Press, 1979), he traces the roots of "conceptualism," the understanding "that language does not come into its own until it has been made univocal, unambiguous, and as totally denotative as possible." Accordingly, language becomes more geared to the truth according as the elements of dialogue and persuasion (the old *dialectica* and *rhetorica*) recede into the furthest background.

Chapter 9

Believing and Critical Negation

In the last years of the twentieth century, many believers instinctively accommodate their intellectual views to traditional religious ideas about God's will, plan, or design. By definition, accommodations are temporary holding actions, not long-term solutions. They work only while one can balance the stable elements of a worldview with its labile features; if the world changes more radically and worldviews undergo tectonic shift, the pressure to move beyond accommodation builds.

In the Catholic Church today, the magisterium's conceptualized form of naive belief relies on accommodations that are wearing thin. At an earlier stage, doctrinal definitions like that of papal infallibility secured the reliability of the biblical and traditional picture of God and the world. But because they depend on a literal reading of complex symbols, they cannot survive critical examination unchanged. The risk of submitting such formulations to the critical eye of the needle requires more than balancing a mythopoetic worldview with critical perspectives (as Vatican II spontaneously did). A generation after the council, growth requires the painful task of shedding baggage, facing the limitations of our dogmatic formulations, and confessing the self-serving nature of many of our seemingly spiritual notions.

In this chapter, I will engage in a purposefully reductionist critical interpretation of elements of the Catholic tradition of faith and morals. To some, this critique may well skirt blasphemy. But if the eye of the needle has any spiritual potential, critical negation will actually corroborate what the apophatic tradition in theology has long known: the surest truths of faith are composed of what we do not know about God. Equivalently, any serious attempt to encounter God must brave the dark night of the soul, the *nada* (nothing) that believers risk when desiring the all. This perspective has survived Catholicism's rationalism and authoritarianism because the magisterium approves the *via negativa* for individuals (souls). Today it must make the same journey itself.

Religious authority renders itself suspect if it ignores or undersells the discontinuity between the past and the present (the "ugly, wide ditch"). No longer can the magisterium pretend to occupy a place of unambiguous immediacy, unaffected by its own historical shaping. In reality, it has taken a countercritical stance that has enthroned its most treasured idealizations rather than serve the mystery of God's self-revelation. By contrast, the task for faith affirmation is to recognize that critical negation does not argue for or against belief in itself, but only against inflated claims. Critical attempts to examine the historical tradition require us to bring our best interpretive tools to bear on the ambiguous record of faith affirmation. For the Bible and the dogmatic tradition (as fixed) represent, not the total shape of religious identity, but only its relatively stable elements. Their paradigms of believing and living must interact with the adaptable elements of faith response to shape a postcritical faith affirmation. The accumulated tradition functions as an anchor to the past, helping us avoid injudicious lurches into the future. But even as the *regula fidei,* it does not constitute an absolute norm for the full shape of belief. The only absolute norm is the Spirit of God, guiding faith's development, "writing straight with crooked lines." Discerning that Spirit requires some uncomfortable but necessary streamlining of what the magisterium proposes as the content of Catholic faith today.

The Doctrine of Natural Law

I argued in the last chapter that the creeds are anchored in but not confined to actual historical events. To affirm what they profess requires that faith engage in an honest dialectic with history, avoiding inaccurate historical reconstruction. In its critical stage, then, faith involves a dialogue between believing affirmation and un/believing negation. Critical judgments must be made about what the Bible and the doctrinal tradition say and how they make up the rule of faith. If some doctrinal formulations have inflated the mythopoetic material in the Bible and suppressed historical material when it did not support the way tradition grew, we must engage in a countervailing deflation of such exaggerations. Passing through the eye of the needle helps us affirm only what the Holy Spirit expects or requires — not more and not less.

The creed's first affirmation confesses God as Father almighty, creator of heaven and earth. God's existence is taken for granted, not explicitly professed, and God's relationship to all that exists is the core affirmation. Further, the creed did not choose one of the Bible's creation narratives (1:1–2:4a; 2:4b–25) as a norm for description of how the material world came about. Instead, it characterized the relationship via an element of later Jewish belief (God's fatherhood) that interprets the earlier creation account. Divine paternity arose as part of ancient kingship ideology (cf. Ps 89:26, 2:7). The prophetic tradition extended covenantal privilege of adoption to affirm God's special relationship to the downtrodden (Ps 68:5: "Father of orphans and protector of widows is God in his holy habitation"). In the Second Temple period, it was linked more cosmically to the deity's role as creator (Mal 2:10: "Have we not all one father? Has not one God created us?"; 3 Macc 2:21: "Thereupon God, who oversees all things, the first Father of all"). The gospels witness that Jesus intensified the sense that the God of Abraham, Isaac, and Jacob acted directly upon created things (Matt 7:26), but Jesus combined that sense of God's power with calling God *abba,* or "dear Dad." The creed, then, enshrines more than a simple affirmation of God's paternity. Rather, it adopted an intertextual reading of various biblical images, corresponding with this tensive affirmation that God is both a Father who loves his own and will never abandon them (Isa 49:15) and *El Shaddai,* the one who is mighty and can do whatever he wills (Greek *pantokrator;* Latin *omnipotens*).

Until the beginning of the scientific era, this tensive symbol of divinity leaned more heavily in the direction of God's all-powerful nature. Though Christians always called on God in the way Jesus had taught, Augustinian pessimism and Aquinas's philosophical synthesis of Aristotle's first mover and the Bible's creator could not help but attenuate the end-time immediacy of Jesus' teaching. Distinguishing between God's primary (immediate) causality that created a world of potency and act and a secondary causality by which events had other (instrumental) causes paved the way for modern scientific inquiry into physical causality, but it also laid the groundwork for deism. The unwillingness of fundamentalist Christians to give up the literal understanding of God as Almighty stands today as a protest against this philosophical accommodation. But for the most part, contemporary believers concentrate more on God's loving fatherhood rather than on a divine omnipotence that is hard to see as unlimited. Even though God's ultimate responsibility for things that exist is maintained, most Christians bracket "almighty" in favor of their own varied assumptions about nature's autonomy.

A barebones empiricist critique of the doctrine of creation would scoff at the primitive notion that God made the world in any normal use of the word "make." It would also cast doubt on the way believers credit God with caring for his human children but no longer hold God responsible for earthquakes and other natural disasters or for warfare. The critical perspective of un/belief, while not so narrowly empiricist, recognizes that the question of how the physical universe came to be has become an object of scientific inquiry. To the extent that science too points to a beginning in time of the universe, the biblical symbol of creation and its notion that there is a creator is upheld. But it does not require that we know how the cosmos came to be. More important for the critical perspective is the extent to which the symbol of God's almighty fatherhood can be construed to claim that there is an eternal law by which God means to regulate not only the times and seasons but all human moral activity as well.

We saw in the last chapter that Romans 1:18–32 has been central to the abstracted myth of God's eternal law. In Romans, Paul is influenced by his own Hellenistic Jewish background, particularly when he introduces the Stoic term "conscience" as an equivalent to the Hebraic image of "the law written on their heart" (2:15). Yet it is as incorrect to claim that Paul articulated a doctrine of natural law in Romans as it is to claim that he formally taught a doctrine of original sin. The most that can be claimed is that the violations of the moral order that he lists in 1:24–32 were "the equivalent to that called natural law by the church now."[1] For, once the argument has served his rhetorical premise that "all have sinned" and hence "all are justified by grace" (3:23–24), he leaves it behind. When he returns to the moral activity appropriate for the Christian community ("spiritual worship," 12:1), he cites no natural moral order. Rather, he sums up all God's commandments in one: "Love your neighbor as yourself" (Lev 19:18 in 13:9–10). Similarly, when Paul deals with a host of problems in the church at Corinth (including sexual immorality "of a kind not even found among pagans," 1 Cor 5:1), he operates out of a Jewish sense of lawful and unlawful activity as this was nuanced both by his own application of law "in the Spirit" (chapters 6–7) and by his expectation of the world's imminent end (7:31). In Galatians 6:2, he describes this new, spiritual horizon as fulfilling "the law of Christ." In none of these parenetic sections does he base his teaching on the law written on the heart he had cited in Romans (where it probably referred primarily to the commandment against idolatry, the violation of which leads to immorality).

The rest of the New Testament is devoid of any reference to anything like a natural moral order. In fact, much of the literature's dualistic bias is closer to the fourth gospel's view that the "world" (the natural order, or Paul's "flesh") is the realm of rebellion against God. Only when Christianity adopted strategies similar to those of Alexandrian Judaism (Wisdom of Solomon and Philo) and coopted pagan notions, adapting them to their missionary or apologetic purposes (as Paul did with "conscience"), did an idea of natural law begin to solidify. Justin Martyr explicitly cited Paul's claim that the human race is without excuse before God (Rom 1:20) because, "though they have been born rational and contemplative," they have acted sinfully. A philosopher who continued to wear the toga of his profession after becoming a Christian, Justin introduced the Stoic term "natural law" (*physeōs nomos*) into Christian theology.[2] Even then, it was not until the fifth-century Synod of Arles (c. 475) that Paul's "law written on their hearts" was officially called the "natural law." Both Tertullian's and Augustine's writings may have had some influence on this usage. The bishop of Hippo explicitly taught the existence of an "eternal law, the divine reason or will of God, commanding the natural order to be respected." To act against it was sinful because it was a disruption of the "tranquillity of order" that gave everything in the universe and in human beings "a proper place." But despite the growth of this highly Roman (legal) version of Paul's antipolytheistic Jewish idiom, references to the natural law were not frequent in either conciliar or papal statements from the fifth to the nineteenth centuries.

In those centuries, however, two related developments in canon law and in dogmatic theology erected the stage on which natural law would play its leading role in papal pronouncements from Pius IX to John Paul II.[3] As we saw in chapter 7, significant mischief has been done over the centuries by confusing legal and moral categories. In this review of how natural law has been engrafted onto the biblical doctrine of creation in some uncritical ways, we will see again the extent of this confusion.

Typical of the way in which Aquinas's theological insights have been appropriated in magisterial teachings is the statement of Leo XIII that I cited in the last chapter:

The natural law is written and engraved in the minds of individuals because it is human reasoning itself ordering us to act rightly and forbidding us to sin. But that prescription of human reason can have the force of law only if it is the voice and interpreter of a higher reason to which our mind and freedom should be subject. So the law of nature is the eternal law, to be found in rational beings and inclining them to their due act and end, and that in turn is the eternal reason of God the creator who governs the whole universe. (DS 3247–51)

In the twentieth century, then, the standard Catholic understanding is that the eternal law, the natural law, and positive law (or legal statutes) form "a continuous series that may be compared to a tree. The eternal law is its hidden root; the natural law is its main trunk; and the different systems of positive law are its branches." According to this theory, because "positive law is nothing more than an implementation of the natural law that must vary with the changing circumstances and conditions of social life," all analogous forms of law are identified as ultimately having the same source.[4] The source of this theory is not theological reflection but ecclesiastical jurisprudence (going back to the *Decretum* of Gratian in 1140), which has claimed that natural law is divine in origin and was expressed in the Ten Commandments, in the commands of the gospels, and in the Golden Rule and is the basis of all justice or right action.[5] Though some writers have recognized that natural law theory has been formulated unhistorically, abstractly, and dualistically, their efforts to reformulate the theory fall short of the standards of modern critical reason.

In fact, Catholic theology's ingesting pagan philosophical theory is only now being understood as seriously ambivalent. The natural law tradition has strengths that cannot be dismissed but is also plagued by weaknesses that the authorities who continue to invoke it unambiguously have not faced. First, by swallowing up the end-time demands of New Testament ethics into timeless and naturally reasonable rules of conduct, the natural law tradition blunts the specifically Christlike aspects of moral response. Second, this tradition has inflated Aquinas's much more modest claims for what our practical reason can know with certainty. In the critical evaluation that follows, I do not deny the existence or the knowability of natural law. Rather I wish to examine whether, stripped down to useful size, the idea behind the inflated body of truths upon which the magisterium has pronounced can be appropriated postcritically.

Positively, the natural law tradition stands in the tradition of Aristotelian realism, which — when not exaggerated — is a precious heritage. Its core premise can be expressed in the proposition that "human moral reason is trustworthy because it is in touch with reality" and in the corollary premise that "we ought to act as we think we ought to act." But the key to the realism of this tradition of reasoning is its generality and its modesty. Given all the changes in reasonable human behavior that have occurred in the history of human society, speaking of an eternal law that is the eternal reason of God implanted in human beings is at best a literalism pushed beyond reasonable limits. Natural law wedded to a static notion of teleology — that the rightness or wrongness of actions is given by their predetermined ends — is necessarily totalistic and totalitarian. But a theory of natural law based in open-ended teleonomy — that things change through a process of interaction between their stable and labile elements — will account both for the sameness of human nature over time in different cultural settings and for the variability of human moral response.

Because the magisterium has proposed moral truth in legal categories, it has amalgamated the "law of Christ" with a divine, eternal law, implanted in human beings, impelling them to do good and avoid evil.[6] When this is done, the possibility for humans to act in a naturally moral way (as in following their instincts for survival or to procreate) is changed into the necessity that they act only in a certain way lest God's eternal law be violated. The prohibition of artificial birth control and *in vitro* fertilization is a flawed judgment that flows from the invariability of this inadequate notion of natural law. As noted above, when the possible is collapsed into the necessary, the explicitly "surpassing" demands of Jesus in the Sermon on the Mount (Matt 5:20) are said to be precepts of the natural law knowable by reason! This inflation of natural law to encompass even Jesus' eschatological demands (one of which, celibacy,

was only for those "who can accept it," Matt 19:11–12) took a virulent
turn toward totalism when Pius IX concluded that even something as
naturally unacceptable (and hence unreasonable) as Jesus' teaching on
divorce was based on the natural law (DS 2956, 2967). In reality, a natural law of perpetual monogamy could exist only in a universe where
human beings acted purely on instincts (such as some animal pairs that
mate for life) or in a world controlled by a tyrant whose will was far
more absolute than either history (including that of the patriarchs) or
anthropology allow us to accept!

In the formulations of the magisterium, "law" has become a univocal
term whose source and substance is God's will. In turn, all other categories of mediation — even the sacraments — have been subsumed and
subjected to a legal system for dispensing grace. When Gratian's first
commentator, Rufinus, defined natural law as "the divine power that
nature implants in man, impelling him to do good and avoid evil," he
started a ball rolling that still echoes deafeningly down the corridors
of the Vatican. Despite efforts to present natural law and revelation
as "two parallel currents both of which have their source in God"
(Pius XII) or to keep nature and the supernatural as concomitant, if abstract, elements that make up the Christian moral order, the natural law
tradition has consistently reduced the one to the other. Either it makes
the Easter-Pentecost revelation moot, since human rationality is already
God's power within us (Catholic deism), or it makes obedience to natural law a sufficient principle for salvation, and the experience of grace
the icing on the cake of human nature. Even though Paul taught that
fulfilling the natural law could never accomplish what revelation reveals
(the unmerited love of God experienced as Gift, Grace, Spirit), nature
in magisterial theory is made to subsume grace lest the demon of moral
relativity run riot in the world.[7]

Swallowing up revelation in natural law became inevitable when the
later commentators on Aquinas failed to appreciate the subtlety and the
shifts in his own thinking and overlooked weaknesses in his less-than-
complete synthesis of Platonic, Aristotelian, and biblical categories of
thought. Thomas's notion of analogy predicated that, because God and
humanity do not act on the same plane of being, what we do not know
about God is at least as important as what we know. He rejected Augustine's notion that our knowledge of ideas was a direct participation
in God's knowledge by way of illumination, but he kept a form of participation in his theories of both being and knowing. The difference is
that, for the neo-Platonic thinker, God's knowledge and our knowledge
vary only in degree, not kind. For the Aristotelian Thomas, our knowledge differs in kind from God's way of knowing, as our being differs in
kind as well. We participate in both God's Being and eternal truth only
analogously, on different, but related, planes of reality.[8]

Though Thomas retained the framework that posited a hierarchy of being in which humans were the lowest form of intelligent being (because they had bodies), he broke with neo-Platonism by insisting that the senses were necessary to the mind's knowing anything. He did so by what has been termed a two-level theory of truth, which posited that things existed in themselves outside the divine mind and that we know them through an apprehension of things in themselves, not things as they are eternally, or in the divine mind. In this theory of how things are, and how we know them, truth is necessarily analogous. The eternal truth refers to the way things exist as known by God. Created entities attain truth, then, in an improper, analogous sense inasmuch as they conform to the divine mind. On our human level, we know what is true when our minds conform to the thing itself, not to God's knowledge of it. Hence, "truth exists properly, but secondarily in our minds — human truth." Therefore, human, rational knowledge, though real, is always partial and does not amount to a simple-minded abstractionism that pretends that the human intellect has a direct perception of things as God knows them.[9]

Thomas's theory of analogy departed from the earlier, patristic-medieval sense of God's symbolic presence in the world, but it continued to respect the ancient apophatic tradition of God as ultimately incomprehensible to human reason. It is a long way from the indirect signification of analogy to the inflated reason that knows God and the divine will directly. Thomas's thought liberated the created world to be itself, to have its own integrity as created, and to enjoy its own autonomy. Though nature can become rebellious, it is not the state of rebellion in which Augustine placed the *massa damnata* of God's creatures, nor is it simply the rational order by which the human person is directed by the creator how to make use of his own body.[10]

When Thomas wrote of the eternal law and its relation to the natural law, he followed the same careful course that preserved the negative element (what we cannot know). According to him, law is always an exercise of practical reason (rather than "speculative reason") sharing in a true perception of reality through its first principles. But even with this assurance that our minds deal in what is real and can know what is true, Thomas was careful to say that we know things "by their similitudes, not by their essences" (*S.T.* I–II, q. 87, a. 1). It follows that there are limits to what the practical reason can know, since we cannot know the eternal law of God directly but only what Thomas terms natural law. Just as there is no direct passage from the divine mind to the human mind, so there is no immediate correspondence between eternal law and natural law. Even though as rational creatures we participate in the eternal law, we do so analogously (*S.T.* I–II, q. 91, a. 2), not immediately.

Therefore, just as truth in the human mind is a conformity to the truth of things, so moral action is a conformity to the law of things, *not* to God's will as it is the eternal law itself. For we participate in God's will in a way equivalent to how we participate in God's truth — through following the first principles of practical reason (or moral action), not by adhering to the conclusions that are drawn from these principles. In fact, we lack certainty about our conclusions for two reasons. First, because human acts vary according to the conditioning of persons, times, and other circumstances, the conclusions drawn in specific matters "do not proceed from the first precepts of the natural law so as to be binding in all cases, but only in the majority" (*Supplementum*, q. 65, a. 3). Second, in order to preserve human freedom, Thomas affirmed that "the will does not adhere to God of necessity, nor to those things that are of God" (*S.T.* I, q. 82, a. 3). So there is a paradox at the heart of Aquinas's natural law teaching: on the one hand, only God is the proper object of the human will; on the other hand, we do not have any direct apprehension of God.[11]

Though it seems surprising, Aquinas excluded even the Ten Commandments from the first principles or precepts of the natural law, though "with but slight reflection," he said, they were special secondary precepts. Because certain essential human virtues (Aristotle's prudence, justice, fortitude, and temperance, as well as the virtues of faith, hope, and charity) contain a higher degree of generality, they come closer to being first principals of our practical reason. But in his mature thought, Thomas said that considering murder evil could not be counted as a self-evident precept of the natural law because of the variability of human action. Transgressions of the natural law were always variable conclusions that depended for their cogency as guides to moral action on what he called the "judgments of the wise." Hence, these conclusions can change. The one exception to this high level of generality was in the matter of sexual acts, because those actions seemed to him the most obvious application of the ancient lapidary definition that nature is what is "common to man and other animals." In general, Aquinas taught that the way our practical reason (or conscience) guides us is by the natural law. Yet, the natural law is not a body of secondary precepts. It is an *inclination* by which we serve God by following human reason to discover the truth of things as God created them to have their own intelligibility.

Aquinas's theory seems more modest than the claims made for natural law in the writings of modern popes and magisterial theologians. He posits no direct correspondence between the eternal law and the natural law. There is only an analogy between God's overall disposition of the universe and our ability to direct our will in conformity with the law of things as we can best discern it. Yet in magisterial documents, the premise is almost the opposite, as is obvious from the formal teaching of Leo XIII quoted above:

The natural law is written and engraved in the minds of individuals because it is human reasoning itself ordering us to act rightly and forbidding us to sin. But that prescription of human reason can have the force of law only if it is the voice and interpreter of a higher reason to which our mind and freedom should be subject. So the law of nature is the eternal law, to be found in rational beings and inclining them to their due act and end, and that in turn is the eternal reason of God the creator who governs the whole universe. (DS 3247–51)

The first clue here of the inflation of natural law is the expansion of Paul's "written on their hearts" to the papal "written and engraved in the minds of individuals." The change of idiom is significant. While the scriptural metaphor for a natural moral knowledge lies remotely behind it, and Thomas's "inclination in man toward the good" also echoes there, the dominant chord is Augustine's neo-Platonic notion that the eternal makes a direct impression on us, engraving itself into our nature. Thomas's distinction in kind between the eternal law and our sharing in it analogously disappears in Leo's univocal identification of them as the same thing, at best different in degree. The second inflationary element arises from the voluntaristic notion of law. If natural law is to be a law at all, it must have, in the pope's words, "the force of law" capable of subjecting "our mind and our freedom" to a "higher reason."[12] Gone is Thomas's carefully analogous understanding of how human beings indirectly but really apprehend what God's ordering of reason for the common good requires. In its place is a deterministic view of human nature that removes humanity's free acceptance of our creatureliness (our nature) and substitutes for it a human reason subjected by a higher reason to the eternal will of God.

Clearly, the issue of how the divine and the human are related is crucial. Since Augustine, faith affirmation has been tempted to confuse creatureliness with sinfulness, finitude with punishment. But in Aquinas, nature is not the same as sinful, human nature. It is the reflection in time, and on a different level of existence, of the creator's gift of grace, or supernature. While there is a tendency in nature to absolutize itself, to relate only to its expansiveness and not to its limits, this remains only a tendency, the contraversion of the obediential potency of nature for life in communion with God. Sebastian Moore has argued in a related context that

Aquinas' distinction between nature and nature sinfully absolutized is both beautiful and freeing. For on the one hand our nature, while always involved in the struggle between sin and grace, does not get its shape from that struggle, but only from its Creator, who is, at it were, wooing the beauty that first came from his hand. And on the other hand, grace establishes its character as beyond nature, not as against sin — in other words, as supernatural.[13]

The phrase "wooing the beauty that first came from his hand" is a very different idiom from Leo XIII's subjecting "our mind and freedom" to a "higher reason." In fact, the difference in idiom points up that, if natural law is not taken analogously but univocally, as some kind of inexorable decree, it yields a notion of a tyrant God seeking to bend his obstreperous subjects by the force of his superior will and his inexorable laws. This could not be farther from what Thomas meant, but it is the common stock of patriarchal authoritarianism underlying the papal magisterium's prohibition of artificial birth control as contrary to "laws inscribed in the very being of man and woman" (*Humanae Vitae* 12). Once again, in this papal pronouncement, the possibility that during intercourse a couple may generate new life (though the encyclical itself admits it is not inevitable as "God has wisely arranged," 11) becomes, under the impress of the inexorable norms of the natural law, the necessity to risk conception. Though appealing to the "deeply reasonable and human character" of the principle that the "intimate structure" of the conjugal act inseparably joins the unitive and the procreative aspects, Paul VI still asserted that

an act of mutual love that prejudices the capacity to transmit life that God the Creator, according to particular laws, inserted therein, is in contradiction with the design constitutive of marriage, and the will of the Author of Life. Those who make use of this divine gift while destroying, even if only partially, its significance and its finality, act contrary to the nature of both man and woman and of their most intimate relationship, and therefore contradict also the plan of God and his will. (13)

Accordingly, the magisterium has made natural law not a reasonable (or scientifically accurate) appropriation in the human world of God's overall disposition of the universe, but a univocal and literal body of precepts preexisting in the mind of God and literally applicable to every act of intercourse for all time. Absent is any of the modesty of Aquinas's position that our conclusions, based on the first principles of practical reason (the precepts of natural law), must be evident to natural reason. In its place is a notion of nature that is static and unchanging and a notion of law that repudiates Thomistic analogy in favor of a cosmic positivism: once a law is on the books it is engraved in nature, as in stone.[14]

Aquinas's more modest claims for what our practical reason can know with certainty came from his awareness that human acts vary according to the conditioning of persons, times, and other circumstances (*De Malo*, q. 2, a. 4, ad 13). This meant that the conclusions of the natural law were separable from its first principles. Yet when it comes to human sexuality and fertility, the papal definition of the conjugal act admits no such variability. Along with its univocal concept of law (based on God's immutable will) comes a univocal concept of humanity's sexual nature, one common in Thomas's time and deriving from the pagan jurisconsult Ulpian: the right (or law) "which is called natural in the first sense is common to us and to other animals" (*S.T.* II–II, q. 57, a. 3 resp.). *Humanae Vitae* makes human sexuality part of some invariable metaphysical law that clearly defies what is evidently rational for late twentieth-century biology.

Biologically, it is known as scientifically certain that the great majority of acts of sexual intercourse are not "ordered" by nature to procreation. Even those that result in the fertilization of a female ovum by the male sperm naturally implant in the uterus in fewer than a majority of cases. If God is the designer by whose plan and will there must be an unbroken finality between every act of intercourse and conceptive possibility, then divinity has built an Edsel! Thomas's notion of nature was different and did not need to be interpreted through magisterial eyes of faith. Today our scientific understanding of sexuality and procreation has extended our ability to act according to the norms of right reason in a way that Thomas could not have imagined because sexuality has a natural intelligibility far different from the way medieval society understood it. All of this was, of course, argued extensively in the period leading up to Paul VI's publication of his birth control encyclical, but because curial theologians remained wedded to a static and nonempirical notion of human sexuality as immutably fixed by the arbitrary will of God, no change in the official teaching was permitted. The compromise in favor of natural birth control that had emerged from Pius XI and Pius XII represented the limit of accommodation in natural law thinking. But instead of nature whose laws are known by reason and by analogy it is "nature as in the mind of God" that is disclosed by the magisterium.[15]

Though it has sought to accommodate natural law morality to contemporary society by incorporating insights from philosophical personalism and aspects of biology and psychology, the papal magisterium has refused to abandon its framework of predetermined ends. This is especially true of Pope John Paul II's attempt to reframe the teaching on birth control within the context of respect for human persons and their dignity. When it comes to accepting insights from outside the inductive system of magisterial philosophy, there is a dishonest element of picking and choosing.[16] The result is that official Catholic teaching is stuck in a prolonged latency, willing to think harder about some questions but unwilling to surrender its mythopoetic picture of a God ruling the universe by decrees promulgated and enforced by the hierarchy. Despite protestations that magisterial teaching is based on right reason, its proponents depend upon a voluntarist reading of natural law: there is only one course of action available to right reason because divinely appointed authority has determined that these are the contents of right reason. In reality, the teaching is based on a narrow pessimism that despairs of rational mediation and remains fixated in an earlier age's fear of the indeterminacy of the human body.[17]

Some exceptions to Rome's voluntarism have emerged from the acceptance of current conditions and the way that they affect moral judgments in the fields of economic justice, social questions, human rights, and the like. In matters such as freedom of conscience and of religion, the magisterium has adopted contrary positions to ones that it had long held. But despite these changes, its guardians have refused to move off the dime in areas of sexuality and procreation. Increasingly, its natural law concept of sexual relations totally determined by "the laws of the generative process" that deny human beings "unlimited dominion" over their generative faculties (*Humanae Vitae* 13) is about as convincing a description of sexuality as is the creation of Adam and Eve in Genesis chapter 2. While there is wisdom in the natural law outlook, its inherent voluntarism has infected official Catholic teaching, doing enormous harm to its own credibility and to the consciences of many of the faithful. By being so willfully resistant to change, by protecting its immature idealizations of male and female sexuality, by turning its back on scientific sources of knowledge except as they confirm the natural law, its teaching has become irrelevant to many people looking for wisdom in a society suffering from its own sexualized ideals.

On the other hand, the resistance of historical Christianity to affirming whatever feels good in matters of sexuality is more deeply rooted than in a mere stoic distrust of passion or in Victorian repression. But official acceptance of the sexual dimension of human personality has come so slowly and so haltingly that it has been hard even for those who are still listening to trust its sincerity. For their part, the proponents of critical rationality have tended to stress only personal autonomy and individuality in matters of sex, reducing complex phenomena to simple affective self-gratification. The dominance of hard science that, for years, allowed it to turn its back on long-range consequences and adopt partial solutions at the expense of the health of the whole has produced its own brand of technological totalism fraught with great dangers for human and global ecology. In matters of sexuality, the hybrid science of psychoanalysis and its related soft siblings have, as I argued in chapter 5, made important contributions. But popular culture has not been patient of the more philosophical and moral dimensions of this science of the soul. Instead, it has indulged many adolescent, short-sighted perspectives that lead to unhealthy forms of sexual fetishization (associating happiness with sexual fulfillment, reducing personal identity to sexual preference). In its own way it has reversed the formula for spiritual grandiosity with its own combination of the necessary and the possible: the possibility of sexual ecstasy has become, in our commercialized cults of pleasure, an absolute necessity for personal fulfillment.

Within the scope of this study, it is not possible to undertake a review or recasting of magisterial teaching on sexuality. In no other area of human activity is the clash between the outcome of critical rationality and a biblical/traditional faith so stark. But if I can show how literal readings of the doctrine of creation (via natural law) and of the papacy's modern definitions have been part of an inflationary expansion of the conceptual content of faith and morals that has led to their symbolic impoverishment, then perhaps I can open the door for change. Appropriating sexuality through the metaphorical indeterminacy of the human body may allow us to see bodiliness steeped in paradoxes that are not self-evident nor completely predetermined. At best, the Bible and tradition provide faith affirmation with heuristic fictions and symbolic paradigms to guide our ongoing search for adequate moral norms.

Modern Papal Doctrines

The inflexibility of natural law in matters of sexuality needs to be seen as part of official Catholicism's campaign to stem the impact of modernity. In some ways, the anchors of this campaign were the solemn declarations on the Immaculate Conception (1854), the Assumption (1950), and papal infallibility (at Vatican I, 1870). It is fair to say that up to Vatican II these doctrines and the liturgical and ecclesiastical ethos that flowed from them described what it meant to be Catholic. Therefore, we cannot understand the challenges that face Catholicism at the end of the twentieth century unless we trace the roots of this campaign for the renewal of the ideal of virginity and the promotion of the ultramontanist ideal of the monarchical papacy. Along with the missionary expansion of the Roman Catholic Church beyond its European base in the nineteenth and twentieth centuries, these ideals gave Catholicism its normative antimodern shape before Vatican II. Much of the strength of that ethos lay in the cultural and emotional appeal of the Romantic era's idealized picture of the medieval centuries as the Age of Faith in which the cult of the virgin and the papal monarchy flourished.

In the last chapter, I took exception to the way in which the doctrines associated with these ideals were subject to an inflation of meaning. Here I wish to argue that critical un/belief must negate their inflationary shape in order to recover what they say in spite of themselves. By recognizing the social and political setting of these definitions and the way their contexts impose limits on their being universalized as objects of positive revelation, we can establish some parameters for their retrieval as objects of a mature, secondarily naive faith affirmation.

Papal Infallibility

The doctrine of papal infallibility has held a privileged place in recent Catholic sensibilities, not only in the life of the church, but in the devotional life of individual Catholics. But a critical look at the origins of the doctrine, the circumstances of its formulation and definition, and its subsequent role will give critical un/believers pause. To the extent that the doctrine has led to idealizing the men who have occupied the chair of Peter as bishop of Rome, it has played a negative role in the faith maturation of the hierarchy, the clergy, and the faithful. For believing that the bishop of Rome has a constitutive role in the teaching, life, and worship of the Catholic Church does not commit one to the view that the person of the pope is sacred or to the ideology that papal power is unlimited. The belief that the pope is somehow more inspired than ordinary *Christifideles* is the unhealthy result of both the development and present outcome of a quasi-devotional cult of the papacy. St. John Bosco, the founder of the Salesians, was typical of the lengths to which some believers have gone when he wrote in his *Meditations,* "The Pope is God on earth. Jesus has set the Pope above the prophets, above his precursor, above the angels. Jesus has placed the Pope on a level with God."[18]

A critique of the doctrine of papal infallibility, then, must inquire how it overreaches the evidence. We can start with Vatican I's claim that papal infallibility was part of the "ancient and constant faith of the church," representing a "tradition received from the beginning of the Christian faith," and note that the historical record shows otherwise. Infallibility arose indirectly out of a body of law that stressed the primacy or sovereignty of the bishop of Rome. As sovereign pontiff, the bishop of Rome was said to have received from Christ, as Peter's successor, not only the power of orders (as had all the apostles) but the power of jurisdiction that gave him unique authority to settle both doctrinal and disciplinary disputes in the universal church. At the same time, the canonists who developed this theory of jurisdiction did not argue that an infallible head was necessary to sustain the faith of the church. "Rather, they maintained that, however much the head might err, divine providence would always prevent the church from being led astray."[19] A critical examination of the history of this doctrine also reveals that when in 1324 a teaching that the pope was infallible was first introduced — based on the Petrine power of the keys — it was done so by "anti-papal rebels, not by curial theologians." Pope John XXII "indignantly denounced it as a pernicious novelty."[20]

This papal denunciation of infallibility stemmed from the common belief that infallibility existed in the *consensus ecclesiae,* the mind of the believing community, as a guarantee of indefectibility: the church will never fail to exist as a community believing and professing the gospel of Christ. The major scriptural texts adduced for Peter's primacy (Matt 16:18–19; Luke 22:32; John 21:15–17) imply a special charism upon Peter's successors as bishops of Rome only if they are understood in some wholly mystical sense as conferring a suprahistorical Petrine identity upon otherwise very mundane leaders. In fact, Bonaventure, the Franciscan minister general, an early and fervid supporter of papal infallibility, did just that when he declared, "The Pope stands in place of Peter, nay rather of Jesus Christ."[21] From here to Don Bosco's pious blasphemy is not nearly so far as the medieval transition from "vicar of Peter" to "vicar of Christ." Once an apotheosis has begun, it is perhaps hard to halt. But when this material is passed through the critical eye of the needle, the doctrine comes out the other end trimmed to a more modest shape.

The community of Jesus' disciples that survived his crucifixion and was gathered by the power of his outpoured Spirit became "the church" gradually, through the vicissitudes of historical development. It took the church fully fourteen centuries to develop the conceptual tools whereby infallible definitions could begin to be invoked (and rejected) as part of a debate about papal power and Franciscan poverty. It took another five centuries of crises and problems before a majority of bishops conceded a limited statement of the pope's unique teaching role. Vatican I's statement was itself a triumph of moderation in the face of the efforts of the infallibilists at the council to get a much stronger one.[22] But the definition deconstructs itself because it makes a historical claim that Christ willed something quite impossible for a first-century Jew (even possessed of prophetic insight) even to conceive: infallible definitions of faith and morals. To presume that Jesus of Nazareth (even as exalted Lord of the church inspiring the evangelists) was thinking in terms of infallible definitions is to impose abstract categories of thought as absolute norms of truth and to read events of the first century in terms of medieval power struggles. The 1870 definition emerged from a contingent historical situation: the bishop of Rome was in such a weak political position that the conciliar majority adopted a formula meant to shore up his threatened role in nationalism-crazed Europe. Realistically, the definition represented the last gasp of the medieval ecclesiastical order. As an effort to strengthen Catholicism, in Cardinal Manning's words, "not...by criticism on past history, but by acts of faith in the living voice of the church," it represented the quixotic triumph of a counter-critical faith that saw obedience to the pope as equivalent to submitting to the divine will.

Ironically, no sooner was it defined than "new forms of historical study were beginning to reshape the whole consciousness" of Western thought. In consequence, though papalists have consistently sought to present a precritical, harmonizing view of papal authority as growing directly out of the gospels and recognized through all ages of the church, historical criticism has concluded that papal infallibility "was created at a particular point in time to meet the needs of particular persons and groups in the church."[23] It follows that papal infallibility cannot rank as a true norm of the Catholic faith because it is based on inadequate scriptural evidence and inaccurate historical memory. Whatever it affirms, it can do so only after it has withstood this critically negative judgment of its simple facticity. In the next chapter, I will explore what the shape of this belief might look like on the far side of the eye of the needle.

The Immaculate Conception and the Assumption

The theological and political flaws in the definition of papal infallibility has affinities with the Marian definitions of the Immaculate Conception and the Assumption of the Blessed Virgin Mary. All of them seek to express religious truth in an overly objective factual account of realities that defy such a characterization. A critical account of their content will involve us in a further reflection on the problems that the hierarchical magisterium's voluntarism has created for itself and for critical un/believers. Both Marian doctrines, in their explicit dogmatic form, express a premodern, mythic understanding of origins and endings that, when critically examined, also deconstructs them. They mirror each other very directly in abstracting from the incarnational shape of Christian belief and in privileging certain contingent events as timeless actions of God. They arose by extending the logic of myth and then by extrapolating supposed facts from the mythopoetic shape of the cosmic scenario of redemption, based not on analogy and fittingness, but on God's will to accomplish salvation in defiance of human nature.

The history of the doctrine of the Immaculate Conception is longer and more philosophically complex than that of papal infallibility. With its doctrinal twin, the Assumption, it distantly arose from a reflex impulse for seeing God's work in the beginning as it would be at the end, an apocalyptic impulse already present in the gospels. The earliest of them, Mark, locates the "beginning of the gospel" in the end-time event of the preaching of the Baptist (1:1–3). But Matthew, reflecting historical precedents for the Messiah, begins his narrative earlier than Mark, in the "generations" of Jesus (a reference to the *toledoth* in Genesis) that began in Isaac's birth of Abraham (1:1) and continued in Jesus' more wondrous birth (1:18–25); what began then would culminate "at the end of the age" (28:20). For his part, Luke dated Jesus' birth, while also tracing his lineage even farther back to the beginning of time, to Adam, the son of God (3:38). The fourth gospel, punning as Matthew did on the opening words of Genesis, placed Jesus Christ in the very bosom of the Father (1:18), "in the beginning" (1:1).

This reflex storytelling is grounded in historical time but extends the scope of God's action in Christ backward into preexistence and forward to the end. Like the creeds that grew out of this same impulse toward universalization, or catholicity, the gospels grounded the unobservable and unprovable past and future in an explicit historical experience of encounter with Jesus, both in his mortal life and in his risenness. But in the gospels, where the traces of encounter with Jesus are abundant and constitutive, the figure of Mary has left only ambiguous traces, as also in Acts. Consequently, the Marian doctrines followed a different developmental tangent than the central tenets of christological faith affirmation.

Before she became an explicitly symbolic figure in Luke and in the fourth gospel, Mark portrayed her as uncomprehending and resistant to Jesus' mission (3:21–34; cf. Matt 12:46–50). On the basis of the Marcan texts, Tertullian, though he knew of Irenaeus's parallel between Mary and Eve, interpreted Mary as an "estranged mother" who was a "figure of the synagogue" and, like Jesus' unbelieving brethren, "a figure of the Jews."[24] But Tertullian was, not untypically, swimming against the tide. Other authors wrote apocryphal gospels that patterned the early life of Mary on both canonical and apocryphal gospels about Jesus. Unlike Tertullian's literal reading of the texts, this parallelism increasingly characterized the appropriation of Mary for centuries. Though the historical conditions of her life and death remained unknown, her symbolic identity was moulded by its conformity to God's predestining will, and her fate became a mirror in which arguments over anthropology and eschatology were fought.

The trajectory toward the definitions of the Immaculate Conception and the Assumption began at the prompting of an opponent of orthodoxy. Pelagius, in his quest to identify exemplary human beings in the Bible who validated his program of ascetical obedience, said that faith demanded that Mary be confessed as sinless. Likewise, the Pelagian bishop Julian accused Augustine in his doctrine of original sin of delivering Mary "over to the devil by the condition in which (you affirm) she was born."[25] Augustine's reply to Julian did not articulate a doctrine of sinless conception but stressed that, just as Mary had avoided sin by an exceptional gift of grace, so it was by grace that the sinful condition into which she was born was later changed by God's gift. He insisted that Mary shared the lot of all the children of Adam, but the grace she received from God merited her conceiving and bearing the only sinless one, Christ. Augustine's stress on exceptional grace, though denying Mary escaped from original sin, began to lay the foundation for a teaching of her unique exemption from the penalty of Adam's sin. But this development was a long time coming.

Eastern Christianity, especially after the iconoclast controversy (early ninth century), greatly fostered the veneration of the saints and especially of Mary the *Theotokos*. The patriarch of Constantinople Photius taught that she had been predestined uniquely by God to be Christ's mother, but Orthodox thought never had to reconcile the issue of Mary's conception in sin and her sinlessness, because it had never accepted Augustine's formulation that Adam's sin was passed down through sexual generation. As a consequence, Eastern Christianity's silence on the issue matches the silence of most of the patristic writers concerning Mary's exemption from original sin. No one doubted Mary's personal sanctity, but any notion of sanctity *ab origine* seemed to be ruled out, in the West, by the common teaching of universal original sin. In this teaching, Augustine was joined by, among others, Bernard of Clairvaux, Albert the Great, Thomas Aquinas, and Bonaventure, all of whom denied Mary's exemption from original sin, her immaculate conception.[26]

With such a battery of theological heavies pronouncing against a doctrine, one would think it unlikely to have much chance of being accepted in Catholic theological circles. But this fact alone has led proponents of the doctrine to develop a unique apologia for it: if it came to be defined despite the opposition, God's will must be at work! In fact, the doctrine of the Immaculate Conception would never have become accepted had it not been for the Oxford Franciscan Duns Scotus, a founder of voluntarist theology. Affirming that "everything is possible to God that is not manifestly contradictory in itself and does not necessarily lead to a contradiction," Scotus set aside the millennial view of the universality of redemption because it included Mary among those tainted by original sin. He said that he desired to "err by excess rather than by defect" in order to honor Christ, who was a more perfect redeemer for saving one person, not by remitting her sins, but by preventing her from contracting original sin at her conception.[27] Scotus grounded this theological subtlety in his notion that Christ's incarnation existed in the mind of God before creation and, hence, before Adam existed or sinned. Even had Adam not sinned, Scotus taught, God's Word would have become incarnate so that God could deify human nature. Since God had already determined by eternal decree that Christ should be incarnate, Mary was also included in that same act of God's will, said Scotus, and so her existence was decreed even before Adam's. Chosen before all eternity, she did not contract original sin: neither her soul nor her body was stained because God preserved her parents from lust and preserved her soul from any stain of sin. Hence her entire conception, body and soul, were "immaculate."[28] As a philosophical *tour de force,* Scotus's thought was as grandiose as anything the Middle Ages produced.

Initially, the Immaculate Conception remained a partisan theological position promoted by Franciscans and opposed by Dominicans. Consideration of the doctrine was proposed at the Fifth Lateran Council (1517) and, again, at Trent. At a session in 1546, Trent excluded "the Immaculate Virgin Mary" from its decree on original sin but took no position between those who extended her spotless nature to her conception (immaculists) and those who refused to do so (maculists). Prominent among the latter were the Jansenists, whose stout defense of Augustine's position eventually weakened opposition to the doctrine when they were suppressed in the political and religious intrigues of the seventeenth century. The issue caused such controversy that several popes in the seventeenth century forbade all discussion of it from pulpits. In 1655, Alexander VII approved the use of the title "Immaculate Conception," but he and his immediate successors still preferred the more cautious reference to the "Conception of the Immaculate Virgin." In the atmosphere of nineteenth-century Romanticism, even the Dominicans relaxed their opposition, and the stage was set for Pius IX's solemn definition.

That proclamation affirmed, in terms almost identical with those used by Alexander VII (though dropping *macula* for "stain" and substituting the less controversial *labes*), a tradition that had existed for centuries as a pious idea that Mary was, like the bride of the Song of Songs, "spotless" (4:7: *macula non est in te*) and, like preexistent Wisdom, the "spotless" mirror of God (7:26, *specula sine macula*). It solemnly defined that

the doctrine which holds that the Most Blessed Virgin Mary was preserved from all stain of original sin in the first instant of her Conception, by a singular grace and privilege of Almighty God, in consideration of the merits of Jesus Christ, Savior of the human race has been revealed by God, and must, therefore, firmly and constantly be believed by all the faithful. (DS 2803)

The pope prescinded from presenting anything except a very general historical background of the church's belief in the doctrine, concentrating on, in the words of one dogmatic historian, "the realities which are the objects of faith, and which it is his task to define."[29] From a critical perspective, therefore, it is necessary to inquire about the reality of the "stain of original sin" from which Mary is said to have been uniquely preserved.

The notion that original sin confers a stain on the soul is inseparably bound up with the view that sexual generation is, by nature, stained or impure. We saw above that, although Augustine certainly thought sexual urges to be the result of the Fall, he did not exempt Mary or her parents from the universal lot of humanity. Only Mary's conception of Jesus by the Spirit allowed Jesus to be the spotless or sinless one, hence the savior of humanity. But behind antiquity's attitude about bodily discharges (semen, vaginal fluid, menstrual blood) lies an archaic, premoral, and primitively naive belief that sexuality, in itself, is defiling. For Augustine, who adapted this archaic notion by way of the Christian story of redemption, the only escape from the inherited stain of original sin is the baptismal washing; the only refuge from the lifelong effects of that sin

is the grace by which concupiscence is overcome. Though God had predestined some to share Christ's eternal life, human beings generated in
the heat of irrational passion and born *inter urinam et feces* were mired
in physicality and sensuousness *ab initio*. Before the modern world de-
mystified sexuality's biological rhythms, ancient cultures tended to give
a quasimaterial status to experiences that were thought to defile. The
metaphor of stain linked physical experiences with moral conditions of
unworthiness or uncleanliness. Augustine's explicit identification of sin
with sexual genital activity is just one prominent example of the way
moral or psychological feelings were physically objectified in mythopoetic thought. Whenever sexuality became the problem, virginity and
spotlessness came to be identified.[30]

What Scotus sought in his formulation of the Immaculate Conception was to leap-frog over the baneful physical solidarity humans had
with Adam by stressing God's absolute power to act on our behalf
He taught that human salvation resulted from God's eternal willing o
both Christ's and Mary's redemptive lives, which owed nothing to nor
mal human generation. By a special predestination Mary was preventec
even though she was generated sexually, from contracting original sin,
a singular privilege merited for her by Christ's suffering. What appealed
to Scotus was the unique particularity of God's act and the graced intuition by which the believer could know this exceptional act of God's
salvific will. His intellectual grandiosity paved the way for the theology
in which human rationality was seen as capable of all that belief was.
What remained untouched in his scheme was our stained sexual nature
and the menstruating, seed-spilling, defecating, urinating, bleeding lump
of flesh that we call our bodily nature.

It would perhaps strain the evidence to say that, in the ensuing struggles over the definition of the Immaculate Conception, the maculists
were those who, with Aquinas, sought to retain the connection between
nature and grace and to see the body itself as the soul's very matter,
while the immaculists were those who were anxious to dissociate our
unfortunately corporal bodies from our true selves, our souls. But it
is hard to escape this conclusion completely. In stressing Mary's total
solidarity with God's action in Christ, the Immaculate Conception attenuated her solidarity with human beings, whose nature it is to emit
bodily fluids (when we no longer can, we die). A purely literal reading of the doctrine evidences the same ambivalence and impatience, not
just with our fallenness, but with sexual human nature itself. From a
critical perspective, then, the doctrine of the Immaculate Conception involves us, not just in the exaltation of the mother of Jesus in the plan of
salvation, but in an obsessively negative characterization of human sexuality. To the extent that the Assumption is predicated on the sinless (read
"sexless") nature of the perpetually Virgin Mary, whereby she is exempt

from human limitations, it denigrates the totality of God's salvation in Christ. Critically, we must doubt that this doctrine can be held in the literal and historically factual terms in which it is commonly proposed.

Scotus's concept of God's eternal will as decreeing Mary's immaculate conception pretended to know God's mind directly and immediately, presumably through the kind of graced intuition that earned him the nickname "the Subtle Doctor." Because he himself disputed Thomas's notion of analogy, as well as the concept that we know by abstracting from universals, Scotus taught that our knowledge of particulars shared, at least when our intuitions were graced, in God's own knowledge. What is more, it seems that by defining the doctrine the magisterium has decided that Scotus's intuition was indeed graced and that this grace continues as the assistance promised in Peter to the papal magisterium (as it would be put in the 1870 definition of infallibility).

Hence, what we have is the problem created when magisterial definitions proclaim that things like stains exist in the metaphysical order, but can be known, not by right reason but only by inspired teaching. What is worse, although the stain of original sin from which Mary's humanity (along with Christ's) is said to have been exempt clearly refers to a quality of bodies that have experienced lustful sexual intercourse, the terms in which the doctrine was defined presumes that the physical experience of sexual intercourse results from a morally objective disorder. But this disorder is not understood, as in Orthodox Christianity, as Adam's mortality, our life-unto-death, which all humans have inherited. Rather it is understood as Adam's sin, passed on through the lustful act of passion through which humans are conceived. Therefore, to the extent that the doctrine of the Immaculate Conception presumes that our human sexual nature is the problem alienating us from God and that Mary's singular privilege from God amounted to her immunity from sexuality, it inadequately truncates the mystery of salvation. Because the doctrine has been historically and factually fixed to a biological moment of conception — now demonstrated as specious by the science of embryology — it foreshortens the mystery of prevenient grace and defines it in naive terms, making God tinker with Mary's human nature in order that her Son not be born stained. In critical terms, then, the Immaculate Conception suffers from something of the same problem as Infallibility: It is a positive statement of a privative, affirming a nonevent as objective and historical, in literal terms. Both of the doctrines try to lock into space-time categories events of divine necessity that are, in reality, actions of graced nature that cannot be exempted from historical ambiguity without becoming purely mythical or magical. As graced, both Mary as *Theotokos* and the church (not the popes) as teacher manage to exceed history's natural possibilities. But neither is ontologically preserved from error or from sexual human nature.

The defined doctrine, when understood as Mary's predestination to sexlessness, must alienate psychosocially well-adjusted adults and force critical believers into unbelief. No thoughtful person can ignore how much human sexuality is a complex and even confusing gift or how difficult integrating it into one's full personhood remains. But to exempt sexuality beforehand from what Christ has redeemed must denigrate it *in toto*. To do so renders salvation a Platonic affair of the soul alone.

Instead, the Immaculate Conception (and the Assumption) must be understood as symbolic ideas by which tradition adapted its core beliefs by extending prevenient grace backward to include a specific female, the mother of Jesus, in the story of human salvation, and forward to complement the exultation of Christ and express the fullness of human salvation as still future-oriented. But the magisterium has presented these doctrines (and Infallibility as well) as part of the stable core, pretending that they were somehow part of the stuff of Christian belief from the beginning. Such claims are no longer credible; nor can they demand the loyal assent of the faithful because they raise to the status of the creedal norm subsidiary symbols of belief. In the hierarchy of truths, the Immaculate Conception and the Assumption are auxiliary doctrines, not touchstones of Catholic orthodoxy. They are part of the antimodern, countercritical actions by a papal authority that has inflated itself as the regulator of all faith affirmation.

Sexuality and Procreation

Turning from these explicit cases of critical negation of inflated doctrine back to the issue of sexuality and procreation, we find a similar countercritical perspective at work. Today, a tradition essentially shaped by Augustinian asceticism is seeking to accommodate itself to modernity's consciousness of the natural goodness of sexual expression without admitting how checkered its own record has been in dealing with sexual human nature and without changing its voluntarist notions that sexuality has been predetermined by God to function within highly limited parameters. The precritical worldview of the magisterium does not see an individual's sexuality as it develops according to the vicissitudes of nature and nurture to be one of the labile elements of his or her personality. Rather, human sexuality (in general) is understood to represent a stable and unchangeable element of a God-given biological mechanism prohibited by God's design from functioning except in one particular way. The insights into sexuality and personality that have emerged in this century are either ignored or condemned as violations of the design established by the creator because they do not accord with an ancient philosophical tradition about sexuality. Despite our knowledge that Plato, Aristotle, Galen, Augustine, Thomas, and many other profound thinkers were wrong on the facts of sexuality is not allowed to matter a whit because curial theologians will not admit the contingency and reformability of their inflated definition of faith and morals.

In the face of this resistance to growing beyond precritical understanding, critical un/believers must negate the conclusions of the magisterium. But they should not stop with negation. For critical un/belief is itself an unstable and necessarily labile period during which inquiring pilgrims distance themselves from their initial sources of authorization so as to stand on their own two feet, but it is not the end of the journey. Rather, all critical questing must remain open to more than the questions, to something greater than its own self-authorization. Without risking the loss of initial certainties and blithe continuities, the tragically necessary *causa sui* project, believers remain immature, living in a world constructed by others, moral and spiritual children afraid to grow up and take responsibility for the shape of their own lives, decisions, and faith acts. Without enduring these risks, one is stuck in childhood and, hence, cannot become a little child *again* because that kind of spiritual artistry requires risking the journey outward.

Many chronological adults do not believe in any comprehensive fashion because they come through the eye of the needle with little or no faith-baggage at all. For them, to believe means not to mature, but to accept, in a way accommodated to their aging and their disappointments, what they once accepted as children but dismissed. But if critical negation represents anything except rebellion for its own sake, it leads beyond itself and beyond the pain that the loss of immediacy and innocence bring. It is the prelude to a secondary naivete, a chastened but far more real world of personal and religious meaning. Everything I have written thus far leads to this largely undiscovered country, which the saints of old, says Hebrews, "saluted from afar" (11:13). In the last chapter I will explore the condition of postcritical faith and what it might be like to profess it. It is not perfection, nor sainthood, but the risk of mature believing.

Bibliographical Essay

A picture of nineteenth-century Catholicism is available in *Romance and the Rock: Nineteenth Century Catholics on Faith and Reason*, Fortress Texts in Modern Theology, ed. Joseph Fitzer (Minneapolis: Fortress Press, 1989). In Joseph de Maistres *Du pape* [Lyon, 1819], we read a representative passage of the early ultramontanist picture of the papacy:

If from the question of right we pass to that of facts, which are the touchstone of right, we cannot avoid the conclusion that the Chair of St. Peter, considered in the certainty of its decisions, is naturally an incomprehensible phenomenon. Replying to the whole world for eighteen centuries, how often have the Popes been found to be incontestably wrong? Never. Cavils have been raised, but never has it been found possible to allege anything decisive. (*Romance and the Rock,* 206)

The following excerpt from Orestes Brownson, an American convert from Protestantism with a New England Transcendentalist background who published a review in July 1875 of Msgr. de Ségur's *The Wonders of Lourdes,* expresses a kind of cosmic romanticism about Mary in this way:

The Blessed Virgin is the queen of saints and angels, and, as the mother of God, is exalted above every other creature, and is only below the ineffable Trinity. Whom, then, should God more delight to honor, or more delight to have honored by us? She is the spouse of the Holy Ghost, she is his mother; and nothing seems more in accordance with his love and goodness, and the very design, the very idea, if we may use the term, of his mediatorial kingdom, as revealed in the gospel, than that he should do her the honor of making her his chief agent in his work of love and mercy — the medium through which he dispenses his favors to mortals. (*Romance and the Rock,* 236)

A balanced consideration of the debates and setting of Pius IX's council is offered in Dom Cuthbert Butler's *The Vatican Council 1869–1870* (see chapter 3). He noted the charges of Döllinger and other opponents of the definition that Vatican I lacked the necessary liberty of discussion but argued that the volume of recorded discussion belies that charge and accepted Bishop Ullathorne's contentions that "every condition of a full and free debate was satisfied" (440). But he admits that Pius IX was heavy-handed (based on the same Bishop Ullathorne's reminiscences) and that "certain criticisms might fairly be made." By contrast, Bernard Hasler (*How the Pope Became Infallible: Pius IX and the Politics of Persuasion,* 2d ed. [Garden City, N.Y.: Doubleday, 1981], 145) has argued that Pius manipulated the council majority and pressured bishops unduly and that the "external preconditions for a discussion [of the doctrine] simply were not there." Brian Tierney (*The Origins of Papal Infallibility 1150–1350: A Study on the Concepts of Infallibility, Sovereignty and Tradition in the Middle Ages* [Leiden: E. J. Brill, 1972], 275) researched how papal infallibility was first created to limit papal sovereignty and disallow later pope's wishes to back away from Nicholas III's approval of radical Franciscan poverty as the apostolic ideal. Tierney's investigation reads like an intellectual detective story. The idea of infallibility, as we saw, played no role at Trent, and was revived during the seventeenth century in the papal struggle against nationalism and Gallicanism to assure the supranationalism of the ultramontanist view of the papacy. The preservation of a genuine internationalism for the Catholic Church, when so many Protestant ones were being directly subject to national states, is one of the truths that is symbolized by the papacy's role, not an argument for papal infallibility's literal truthfulness.

Chapter 10

Beyond the Needle's Eye:
Mature Believing

Faith Seeking Understanding Today

We have seen that a properly critical form of believing combines the humility of the apophatic tradition and modernity's critical agnosticism, which refuses to say more than is warranted. It requires that believers endure genuine skepticism about their ability to know God's will, both *in globo* and in their individual lives. Yet this believing stance is not formally skeptical; it doubts neither the subject's ability to know nor the knowability of objects in themselves. Rather, it takes into account the irreducible enchantment of both the object of revelation (which can never be adequately objectified) and of the subject of God's self-revelation (the believing community). In faith, if we believe at all, we believe through the detour of signs, knowing symbolically what can be experienced only indirectly and "through a glass darkly." Postcritical faith builds, then, upon a chastened knowing, but one that is far less unreal than the notional certainties of scholastic theology.

Belief as a detour or a journey that must double back on itself and mourn its introjects means that Catholicism's dogmatic practices must be rethought. Here, the biblical paradigm *errore hominum providentia divina* (God's providence is accomplished even through human error) has great potential to rescue us from inflated affirmations that have resulted from papal and hierarchical willfulness. In brief, it would allow us to affirm that, by God's providence, the church has erred but is God's instrument nonetheless. When in 1992 Pope John Paul II formally exonerated Galileo, he excused Cardinal Bellarmine and his colleagues on the basis that they made judgments according to what they knew at the time, as if such contingency were limited to the seventeenth-century Curia! The official church has still not adequately mourned its complicity in intellectual and social repression, the persecution of minorities, and the suppression of honest inquiry, much less its attempts to maintain a social and ecclesiastical status quo to the detriment of human freedom and justice.

263

As Cardinal Newman argued in 1877, one can expect those exercising the governing task to clash with those doing theology and teaching. But he properly saw that the threefold office of sanctification, proclamation, and governing had to be carried out with the checks and balances a healthy church required. When one of the three offices subsumed the others, an unhealthy situation was bound to result.[1] I have referred to this as the pathogenic magisterial system for controlling Catholic truth, which still pertains today. It is not the motives of the hierarchy that I am impugning but their lack of maturity and their clerically obsessive ways of suppressing alternate approaches, which are so damaging to the Body of Christ.

To the present, pleas for a change and scholarly considerations of the possibility of limiting the pope's supreme ordinary jurisdiction over the universal church have been met by punitive measures, stony silence, or a blithe ignoring of suggestions for a devolution of power. The present effort will likely be as unsuccessful at shaking the foundations of a magisterial mythology that has been building for a millennium and a half. But what is different about believing today and about this effort to puzzle through the operative plurality of forms of believing that already exist can be found in my efforts to link the possibility of a postcritical form of Catholic faith to general rules of human development. My contention is that these have given us very new insights into the unity of the act of knowing and believing. Because we have come to understand human beings as psychosomatic unities, we cannot rest content with Platonic or Cartesian dualisms of spirit and flesh or of mind and matter. *What* we know depends on *how* we know it. Hence, any depth-personal knowledge is neither objective nor subjective but a startling combination of both whose changing shape measures our personal and spiritual wholeness. It follows, then, that what a faith tradition affirms is shaped by how it affirms its belief. If Catholics affirm only the stable elements of their tradition (its fixed ideas), they give it over to petrification and ideology. If they heed only the labile elements or base their self-understanding or capacity for relationships on what is unstable and changing, they are courting identity-diffusion and loss of faith. Only by the interplay of stable and labile elements can genuine orthodoxy be maintained.

Before passing on, then, to a postcritical reading of some of the symbols of faith and morals that I have examined, it will be helpful to spell out how religious truth functions beyond the mentalist world of latent ecclesiastics who are stuck on the other side of the needle's eye. Earlier I spelled out how human knowing is, most basically, a process by which we bridge the gaps between inside and outside through symbolizing. We are related to ourselves, to the world, and to all that is, not by mentally ingesting objective ideas that exist outside us and then pass into our purely receptive minds like so many miniature reproductions of the original. Rather, how we know the world is initially shaped by the images that confront us in the stream of life in which we are swimming and by the way that our selfhood attaches meanings, first preverbally and then conceptually, to its environment. Neurologists speak of a "sculpting" process by which individual minds shape themselves (or are shaped — the process overleaps any neat subjective-objective dualism) by making sets of connections and allowing other connections to die out. While no two mental organizations are ever the same, individuals in similar life-worlds share models or mappings of experience.

As our knowing becomes customary, it is typical that we accept the obvious, literal meanings of familiar terms and well-worn phrases as relative guides to transacting life and to communicating with others. But were we reduced to naming reality with labels in the way that the periodic table of the elements labels the physical building blocks of the universe, our knowledge of ourselves and of the world would be severely impoverished. Humans function differently when they do different tasks—driving a car, hammering a nail, writing a letter, teaching a class, praying, running a race, making love, playing with children, reading a newspaper, watching television, cleaning the floor. Though some activities require less conscious participation than others, all depend on an ability to bridge the gaps between our innermost states of mind and the persons and objects we are interacting with. We do this, but on different levels of intensity, via our ability to connect the sensations of the world that impinge on our minds with mental representations stored either consciously or unconsciously. Unlike Freud's archeology of the psyche's stable strata, modern neurophysiological scientists stress the lability of the uniquely subjective pictures of the self and the world in which "every act of memory, of imagination and understanding, constitutes a new, vital, and dynamic creative event."[2]

When it comes to understanding religious truths whose origin cannot be found in the world of matter, we are still dependent, as Thomas argued, on sense. Religious truth does not pass into the mind (or the soul) through a process of spiritual osmosis or direct, divine illumination. It must take the detour of signs, not because it is mysterious in itself, but because all human knowing has a transcendental dimension not reducible either to the objects perceived or to the subjective receiver. In particular, relational knowledge involves more than instinctual reactions. The interplay between subject and object in the act of knowing simultaneously involves both an enhanced subjectivity and a bestowed objectivity, two sets of relationships that mutually coinhere, even if only momentarily. Humans in the act of knowing represent a privileged playing field on which one's own team of receptors engage and disengage multiple visiting teams in games of understanding and misunderstanding where there are few time-outs and no whistle until death interrupts. When we dream, other players take the field, emerging from the dugout of the unconscious to carry on deeply re-membered conflicts, games, and struggles. The interplay between relatively stable and constantly labile elements of the self and the world means that subjects and objects exist only in constantly reworked relationships.

This model for the way we know, or don't know, reality is my attempt to break down the rigid distinctions that have been made since sensation reentered the world of religious knowledge with Aquinas. When the physical world took center stage as that which could be known though direct, manipulative experience of its component parts, religious knowledge either retreated from the field of knowledge (since it was no longer considered *scientia*) and became affective, emotional truth, or it holed up in a Platonic redoubt in an otherwise Aristotelian world of dematerialized forms. A third alternative held that religious ideas were exempt from criticism because they were willed by God in all their plasticity; hence they were to be understood via acts of the will, not according to normal mental knowing. Only after metaphor and symbol began to be rehabilitated, both in science and religion, could we begin to see again that our constructions of reality are neither totally constructed nor all that there is to reality. There is a *via media,* as it were, along which religious knowledge can proceed both with caution and confidence.[3]

This road, which can go straight only by taking the detour of symbols, is different only in degree, not kind, from the way we know ourselves and the world around us from the earliest moments of awareness. What is different, ultimately, is the nonmateriality of the object of revelation as opposed to the materiality of the world of daily experience. But our knowledge of spirit is not nonmaterial. It occurs via our encounter with the created world as it intuits the excess that cannot be adequately accounted for in materiality alone. The desire to know, which Aristotle wrote at the beginning of his *Metaphysics* was basic to the human species, can be biologically accounted for by the fourfold increase in brain size that humans developed in a brief span of evolutionary time. But this desire, whether caused or occasioned by this evolutionary leap, does not have to have been propelled (from behind, as it were) by the impersonal force of evolution. Rather, the excess, which Aquinas also saw as the basis of human mental activity, may well have arisen as a responsive impulse toward the unknown or the inadequately experienced, the desiring subject and desired object that invites consciousness toward greater self-realization and, ultimately, communion with all that is.[4]

I have argued that the best evidence we have of restless habit of consciousness to know is the organic habit, at the basis of all knowing acts, of bridging gaps between the known and unknown. Like arcs of electricity spanning the brain's synapses, understanding takes place by profligate experimentation with connecting, disconnecting, and re-connecting sets of relationships, a process mirrored in the surplus of meaning at the basis of all metaphor. Metaphors are the basis for both our affective relationships (our personal connectedness) and our intellec-tual curiosity and accumulated knowledge, two foci of knowing that are constantly split off from each other, but that really coinhere much more than is normally credited.

It follows, then, that the road on which religious knowledge travels is built of the sensed heuristic fictions that invite the searcher farther and deeper toward an encounter with the "Love that moves the sun and the others stars" (as Dante called the Beatific Vision at the end of *The Divine Comedy*). Like signposts, as well as building blocks of this highway, the ideas that constitute the biblical and historical tradition of Catholicism operate like the stable elements of a people's journey, consolidating the past so as to point to the next, adaptable steps along the way. When these ideas are understood as propositions that define the fixed and eternal content of the way the divine has interfered in the history of the world, when divine facts are understood literally, requiring us to encase them in a philosophical language ignorant of lability, the path leads via idealization to idolatry, into the *cul de sac* of *autodoxy*, a glorying in our own ideas about ourselves. What is missing in most understandings of how religious faith-knowledge operates is the lively sense of the "whis-pered no" that must accompany every statement of religious truth. I have characterized the asceticism of the "whispered no" as the symboli-cal imagination. With it, a believer knows that the tradition reveals what it knows to be true but does not pretend that all truth has finally been made known in such a way that one contingent age of the church or stage of faith can encompass revelation with even near-to-complete adequacy.

If this view of the way religious faith-knowledge operates is cogent, then a postcritical appropriation of the symbols of faith will not seek to redefine traditional doctrines as much as to trace out from their his-torical shape some parameters for understanding the central ideas or symbols of the Catholic tradition. All contemporary considerations of faith agree that believing is not the equivalent of intellectual assent to creedal formulas or to philosophical conclusions made on the basis of a simple reading of the biblical material that is declared orthodox. This helps us to understand that the only truly orthodox teaching is that which truly gives praise to the source and origin of all that is by inviting us into responsive communion. In this concluding segment of my sketch of the spectrum of faith affirmation, it would be impossible to examine the entire scope of Catholic belief and what its doctrines say today. But I hope to illumine some central areas of dogmatic faith and moral response so as to describe the actual way that the tradition's paradigms might function on this side of the needle's eye of critical inquiry.

Belief beyond Literalism

God's Providence via Heisenberg

A critical reading of the doctrine of creation revealed that latent faith has frozen the doctrine by imposing upon it a static concept of natural law. What is more, because the magisterium has used natural law with a voluntarist spin, it has become a literally prescriptive code, binding consciences in ways that often contradict scientific reason. A postcritical retrieval of the doctrine of creation must deal, then, not only with the creedal statement "We believe in God, the Father Almighty, Creator of heaven and earth" but also with the natural law teaching that has emerged from the doctrine of creation.

Belief, on this side of the needle's eye, encompasses the critical negation of literalness, weathering unbelief, moving then to a further stage. There, it first suspends disbelief before appropriating belief with secondary naivete. The first issue to clarify, then, is the kind of statement that the creed makes about God's creative activity. Like the philosophical tradition, the mature believer does not understand "create" as a physical causation in any sense that would compromise the radical nonidentity of creator and created. Hence, a postcritical interpretation agrees that God created the world *ex nihilo* — all that is depends radically on the divine cause for its existence but does not share directly in God's reality. We believe that there is a transcendent reality or uncaused cause at the beginning of all that is, but we do not know by faith how the material world came to be. Scientific investigation uncovers the *how* to some extent, confirming the universe's finiteness and its metaphysical ("beyond the physical") limits. Both the expanse of macro- or outer-space and the minute vastness of micro- or inner-space reveal that matter is too complex to be understood in terms of a simple matter/ spirit dualism or of pure materiality.

Nevertheless, respect for the achievements and limitations of the scientific endeavor allows postcritical believers to be functionally agnostic when it comes to seeking understanding about the origins of the physical universe. It forces us to accept in a new way the analogous, and even more, the metaphorical nature of the term "creator" when we use it of God. When we call God creator, we are speaking a literal falsity in order to affirm the metaphorical truth of the doctrine of creation. What I mean is that we don't understand that God made heaven and earth in any literal sense of the word "make" or "create." To do so would be to limit God's creativity to operations like those we can accomplish or readily understand. Because artificial intelligence has begun to construct machines that in turn accomplish some independent operations, we would be foolish to understand God's creative activity as similar to even the most sophisticated human production lest God's identity as creator be reduced to a more advanced version of the deist's clockmaker.

An analogous situation exists when we shift our perspective from the physical world to the biological realm. In the mythopoetic world of the Bible, God opened and closed wombs and decided which acts of going in of a man to a woman led to conception (Gen 30:2). In the philosophical world of scholasticism, it was understood that the parents generated the body, but it was reserved to God separately to create the soul (*anima*) that quickened the body at some time in the course of gestation. But neither of those immediate creations is an adequate way of understanding the autonomous human sexual process of procreation in which human parents today are understood to be the immediate *genitores* of the human being that results from a successful gestation. Human beings have within themselves not only the genetic wherewithal but also the spiritual capacity to ensoul their offspring. God cannot be said to intervene in the process at any discrete moment of the ongoing human process. If we retain a separate role for immediate divine causality in the process of procreation, we are only opting for a more intimate version of the God of the gaps whom Newton retained because he couldn't understand how gravity did not pull the universe in on itself. As a result, when scientists discovered the physical causes for such previously unfilled gaps, the role of divinity was further reduced and God was headed for the Enlightenment's version of the unemployment line. In both cases, then — creating the world and the individual soul — God's final causality cannot be literally reduced to any level of divine instrumentality.

At first, abandoning a level of literalness in religious doctrines may seem to sever the link between religious affirmations and reality itself. But it is precisely the literal level of understanding that has to be transcended for religious truth to be revelatory in a postcritical setting. Let me illustrate the distinction between abandoning literalness and transcending it by examining two complexes of doctrine implied by the doctrine of creation, one biblical (providence), the other philosophical (natural law). If they can be understood postcritically, beyond their naive and conceptualized shape, then we can move to reappropriate other doctrines that we have critically negated.

The doctrine of providence emerged from the naive portrait of God in scripture. There it is taken for granted that God sees what no human can see, hence that God (and those seers God inspires) can see into the future. It is the sense of the proverb entwined in the narrative of the binding of Isaac: "On the mountain the Lord sees [or 'it is provided']" (Gen 22:14). "Providence" eventually became a virtual synonym for

God (like "heaven"), but only after the notion had been expressed in more mythopoetic terms. In the Exodus tradition, God's providence led the slaves of Pharaoh out of the land in the most direct way imaginable: "The LORD went in front of them in a pillar of cloud by day, to lead them along the way, and in a pillar of fire by night, to give them light, so that they might travel by day and by night. Neither the pillar of cloud by day nor the pillar of fire by night left its place in front of the people" (Exod 13:21–22). This guidance, of course, culminated in the passage of the Red Sea, hence the whole salvific event was remembered in Israel's sense of their chosenness by God.

Or has any god ever attempted to go and take a nation for himself from the midst of another nation, by trials, by signs and wonders, by war, by a mighty hand and an outstretched arm, and by terrifying displays of power, as the LORD your God did for you in Egypt before your very eyes? (Deut 4:34).

The salvation tradition of the Exodus is explicitly connected later on with the creation tradition itself to justify God's exiling the people he had formerly redeemed, as is evident in these passages from the prophet Jeremiah:

It is I who by my great power and my outstretched arm have made the earth, with the people and animals that are on the earth, and I give it to whomever I please. (27:5)
    Ah, Lord GOD, it is you who made the heavens and the earth by your great power and by your outstretched arm! Nothing is too hard for you. (32:17)

It is again evident in the promise of a second Exodus from Babylon, which both prophets Ezekiel and Second Isaiah foresaw:

As I live, says the Lord GOD, surely with a mighty hand and an outstretched arm, and with wrath poured out, I will be king over you. (Ezek 20:33)

Thus says the LORD: In a time of favor I have answered you, on a day of salvation I have helped you; I have kept you and given you as a covenant to the people, to establish the land, to apportion the desolate heritages, saying to the prisoners, "Come out," to those who are in darkness, "Show yourselves." They shall feed along the ways, on all the bare heights shall be their pasture; they shall not hunger or thirst, neither scorching wind nor sun shall strike them down, for he who has pity on them will lead them, and by springs of water will guide them. (Isa 49:8–10)

Isaiah of Jerusalem himself had prepared the way for conditioning the Davidic covenant promise with his explicit prophecies of the destruction of Jerusalem. His ambiguous threat/promise that "a remnant will return" (Isa 10:21) began what became the reworking of the doctrine of providence in the postexilic period. That period began with a universalizing of the notion of providence. The second Isaian prophet then combined the traditions of creation and salvation, transcending earlier ideas that God's favor was part of a national scheme of salvation:

I made the earth, and created humankind upon it; it was my hands that stretched out the heavens, and I commanded all their host. I have aroused Cyrus in righteousness, and I will make all his paths straight; he shall build my city and set my exiles free, not for price or reward, says the LORD of hosts. (Isa. 45:12–13)

God's providence, in other words, was not limited to Israel but actively coopts powerful kings to do God's will. Even while they remained ignorant of the Lord, they operated as part of an inscrutable design. In the tales of the ongoing exile community found in the books of Esther and Tobit, God's provident care for his people among the nations again witnessed to its universal scope. What was different was the modality: in Esther, it is Queen Hadassah (Esther) herself who is the means by which God preserved the people's lives from the machinations of the imperial vizier Haman, while in Tobit the role of savior was played by the angel Raphael, who rescued the fortunes of the faithful Jews Tobit and Sarah by binding the evil angel and transporting him to Egypt.

This doctrine of God's provident care was not universally held. Some authors in the wisdom tradition took a starker view of God's favor and associated wisdom with having moderate expectations in the face of life's ambiguities:

I have seen the business that God has given to everyone to be busy with. He has made everything suitable for its time; moreover he has put a sense of past and future into their minds, yet they cannot find out what God has done from the beginning to the end. I know that there is nothing better for them than to be happy and enjoy themselves as long as they live; moreover, it is God's gift that all should eat and drink and take pleasure in all their toil. I know that whatever God does endures forever; nothing can be added to it, nor anything taken from it; God has done this, so that all should stand in awe before him. That which is, already has been; that which is to be, already is; and God seeks out what has gone by. Moreover I saw under the sun that in the place of justice, wickedness was there, and in the place of righteousness, wickedness was there as well. (Eccl 3:10–16)

More positively, the authors of the Wisdom of Solomon and the book of Proverbs understood that the Lord created Wisdom "at the beginning of his work, the first of his acts of long ago" (Prov 8:22). She was God's vice-regent for creation and thus an agent of providence, who "protected the first-formed father of the world, when he alone had been created," and delivered him "from his transgression" (Wisd 10:1). Wisdom was, then, Israel's savior, whom the Lord "exalted and glorified" and who never "neglected to help them at all times and in all places" (19:22). But Wisdom was also the human ability to reason and to avoid ignorance (17:12–13).

In other words, there is a strain of natural reason in the wisdom tradition. To help people acquire "understanding and knowledge," Jesus, son of Eleazar son of Sirach of Jerusalem, wrote an entire book, pouring forth wisdom with warnings such as "An undisciplined king ruins his people, but a city becomes fit to live in through the understanding of its rulers" (Sir 10:3). Although another strain of this tradition associates this wisdom specifically with the law of Moses (cf. Sir 24:23; Bar 4:1), the wisdom tradition became an important catalyst that broadened the biblical notion of how God exercised provident care over creation.

In the New Testament we have evidence that Jesus understood God's providence in the light of the imminent restoration of God's rule, or kingdom, that he himself preached. God's proximity to the created order provided that not even one sparrow "will fall to the ground apart from your Father," though two of these birds are sold for next to nothing in the market (Matt 10:29). Teachings such as we find in the Sermon on the Mount give evidence of a heightened wisdom perspective that we associate with apocalyptic writers, for whom the desperate conditions of the average person's life was itself the best evidence that "the present form of this world is passing away" (1 Cor 7:31). One of Jesus' most notorious sayings adopts precisely this irrational wisdom perspective:

Look at the birds of the air; they neither sow nor reap nor gather into barns, and yet your heavenly Father feeds them. Are you not of more value than they? And can any of you by worrying add a single hour to your span of life? And why do you worry about clothing? Consider the lilies of the field, how they grow; they neither toil nor spin, yet I tell you, even Solomon in all his glory was not clothed like one of these. But if God so clothes the grass of the field, which is alive today and tomorrow is thrown into the oven, will he not much more clothe you—you of little faith? (Matt 6:26)

In very similar terms, Paul adopted this apocalyptic or restorationist perspective, seeing in the actual "groaning" and distress of all creation a sign not that God was abandoning what he had made, but that the creation itself would soon "be set free from its bondage to decay and obtain the freedom of the glory of the children of God" (Rom 8:21). This allowed him to make one of the most blatant statements of the Christian doctrine of providence:

We know that all things work together for good for those who love God, who are called according to his purpose. For those whom he foreknew he also predestined to be conformed to the image of his Son, in order that he might be the firstborn within a large family. And those whom he predestined he also called; and those whom he called he also justified; and those whom he justified he also glorified. What then are we to say about these things? If God is for us, who is against us? He who did not withhold his own Son, but gave him up for all of us, will he not with him also give us everything else? Who will bring any charge against God's elect? It is God who justifies. Who is to condemn? It is Christ Jesus, who died, yes, who was raised, who is at the right hand of God, who indeed intercedes for us. Who will separate us from the love of Christ?

Will hardship, or distress, or persecution, or famine, or nakedness, or peril, or sword? As it is written, "For your sake we are being killed all day long; we are accounted as sheep to be slaughtered." No, in all these things we are more than conquerors through him who loved us. For I am convinced that neither death, nor life, nor angels, nor rulers, nor things present, nor things to come, nor powers, nor height, nor depth, nor anything else in all creation, will be able to separate us from the love of God in Christ Jesus our Lord. (Rom 8:28–39)

In a more pictorial fashion, the author of Revelation envisioned the collapse of the imperial Roman social order and the beginning of the new creation in the Christian Bible's culminating image of re-creation:

Then I saw a new heaven and a new earth; for the first heaven and the first earth had passed away, and the sea was no more. And I saw the holy city, the new Jerusalem, coming down out of heaven from God, prepared as a bride adorned for her husband. And I heard a loud voice from the throne saying, "See, the home of God is among mortals. He will dwell with them as their God; they will be his peoples and God himself will be with them; he will wipe every tear from their eyes. Death will be no more; mourning and crying and pain will be no more, for the first things have passed away." And the one who was seated on the throne said, "See, I am making all things new." Also he said, "Write this, for these words are trustworthy and true." (Rev 21:1–5)

The question poses itself, both in terms of this vision and in terms of the doctrine of providence, *How are these words trustworthy and true?* How can believers believe, twenty centuries later, especially in the face of the accumulated evils of those centuries, that God exercises provident care over the world? If critical un/belief, from the Lisbon earthquake to the Armenian genocide and the Jewish Holocaust, has sharpened the age-old question of theodicy and disconnected many thinking people from any explicit form of faith, how can a Christian today affirm God's providence?

Again, postcritical belief begins to sort out its own shape, first, by disbelieving the naive affirmation that God moves causatively in the world in any direct or immediate fashion. Whatever God's creativity is like, it does not function like a physical cause in the universe, which itself operates according to appropriately autonomous laws. After having abandoned what is manifestly unreal about God's governance of the created universe, the believer suspends disbelief that the cosmos is confined to what we can presume to know about it. Postcritical belief acts on the hunch that creation is a more comprehensive reality that is not yet fully manifest. If God can be said to govern the cosmos in any sense, that governance must encompass everything that we know about autonomous causality as well as all the undiscovered expanses and inner depths of the totality of what exists. Scientific cause and effect does not represent a closed system of provable hypotheses and limited outcomes. From the time that critical reason was enthroned in the academy until recently, this empiricist model of causality has been predominant. But if critical reason's picture of how the world operates is not complete, neither does the doctrine of providence, as shaped in the Bible, describe a closed system. As we saw in the biblical citations above, God was understood to cause, in a direct and immediate way, the patterns of weather, the rise and fall of empires, all the events of history, and the shape of future events as well. The creator was not only also the redeemer, but the completer or perfecter as well. The events of the future were already somehow present in those of the past and present because they existed in the mind of God, which was equally present to all time.

But a critical reading of the biblical texts on God's provident care of the world allows us to recognize that they do not denote or literally describe actual events. In one form or other, the texts point beyond themselves to a shape of things not yet in place, a more final state of things that, at best, has begun to unfold. They invite their readers into a plan or scheme of things already in progress, but only partially realized and not yet fully in place. These texts on providence, therefore, are best understood as heuristic fictions, as symbolically revealing a state of affairs that summons or invites, that points the way and partly uncovers a world that God is continuing to create out of the stuff of what already is. Hence, even the doctrine of creation has a significant element of the "whispered no" in it. It is like the silent negative present for the writer, as well as the reader, of Genesis when it affirmed: "God saw everything that he had made, and indeed, it was very good" (1:31). This affirmation is not made in fairy-tale fashion, oblivious to the real shape of the world that has come to be. Its retrospective teaching about the nature of things, as they first came forth from God, is itself a heuristic fiction as well because it evaluates the world of matter and sense, not as they manifestly are, but as they were meant to be. The strength of the mythopoetic images resides in their metaphorical truth and thus transcends the literal falsity that "very good" represents. When the myth of the Fall was factored literally into the overall story of Genesis, then the logic of the combined myths required that creation after the Fall and before Christ's return be understood as totally depraved — a Calvinist doctrine based on an exaggeration of Augustine's own negative anthropology and cosmology. Catholicism, as we have seen, resisted this exaggeration but produced in its place a view of human nature where people were endowed with hypertrophied reason and concupiscent sexuality. The real shape of things can never be so simple as to be revealed adequately by either literalism.

Postcritical belief, then, abandons literalness, not because it is necessarily untrue, but because it is not true enough. A second naivete transcends the literal level of understanding of revelation by factoring into belief the shadows and images of a more comprehensive picture, yet unrevealed, that the scriptures hint at in many and varied ways. The postcritical believer in a provident creator, then, does not remain detached from the unfolding drama of what is coming to be. Such belief does not admit that God is complacently the Alpha and the Omega, in the beginning and at the end, without understanding God as somehow suffering the process that divine love has loosed.

Here the Christian doctrine of creation becomes an explicit doctrine of re-creation via the mystery of the cross of Jesus. Contrary to Scotus's voluntarist notion that God could have saved humanity "either by a stone or by an ass," the doctrine of salvation through the self-emptying incarnation and death of Jesus, the Son of God, means that God's providence is most fully revealed when the one sent by God, who is humanity's true representative ("Son of Man"), bore the curse of a criminal's death. The starkest statement of the self-involvement of the godhead in the ultimate state of humanity is found in 2 Corinthians 5:21: "For our sake God made him to be sin who knew no sin, so that in him we might become the righteousness of God." This passage caps Paul's boldest affirmation of the new state of affairs that has followed Christ's death — his resurrection, or his reconstitution beyond the confines of life as we know it in space-time:

> From now on, therefore, we regard no one from a human point of view; even though we once knew Christ from a human point of view, we know him no longer in that way. So if anyone is in Christ, there is a new creation: everything old has passed away; see, everything has become new! All this is from God, who reconciled us to himself through Christ, and has given us the ministry of reconciliation; that is, in Christ God was reconciling the world to himself, not counting their trespasses against them, and entrusting the message of reconciliation to us. So we are ambassadors for Christ, since God is making his appeal through us; we entreat you on behalf of Christ, be reconciled to God. (2 Cor 5:16–20)

This passage on the new creation flies in the face of any literal understanding of the shape of things in this world after the inbreaking of providence in the human life, ministry, suffering, death, and passage of Christ from death to life as the "first-born of those who have died" (1 Cor 15:20). It also helps us to recognize that any doctrine of God's creative providence, after the cross, has to take into account the paradoxical nature of that providence. God is not provident in the abstract but in situations where the freedom of the created order to be itself is at stake. Neither, then, is God unlimited in power when it comes to the created world. God's providence, as part of the doctrine of creation, necessarily involves God's self-limitation as its counterpart. Human sinfulness, error, hypocrisy, power-lust, and death-dealing (as they are played out in the mythopoetic life of Jesus from the slaughter of the innocents to his death-cry on the cross) are revealed to be, ultimately, not the work of the enemy (played adroitly by Satan in the Bible) but the playing out of autonomy's rebellious instincts. Still, they remain the occasion of salvation via the forgiveness, patience, and persuasion that paradoxically constitutes God's greatest power as creator.

In postcritical terms, then, the doctrine of creation and of God's provident care for creatures is a chastened, as well as a deepened, doctrine of providence. From the side of the divine artificer of the world it means that, once creation has begun to unfold, God is not free to lift the limitations of what is not-God. Divine providence commits God to write straight in crooked lines, to compose symphonic works that employ cacophony, to create free creatures whose autonomous natures necessarily involve the risks of careening off into too much necessity or too much possibility. When this chastened perspective is accepted, the doctrines of creation and redemption are revealed as an asymmetrical coincidence of opposites. They do not merely complement each other: their opposition is subsumed in a union that allows for the freedom of the creator and the freedom of creatures to be ultimately and completely reconciled. As we saw in our treatment of a mature hermeneutic of scripture, the formula reads *errore hominum providentia divina*. God in Christ, though not responsible for evil, suffers all its depredations with and in creatures, who themselves must suffer their creatureliness "in hope." Hence, secondary naivete understands providence in a way that, while making it leaner, shows it possessed of malleable strength and complex truth.

The second question that a postcritical appropriation of the doctrine of creation raises is the status, on the leaner side of the needle's eye, of natural law. Earlier, I juxtaposed two different ways of looking at how we can understand the process of growth or change: the teleological and the teleonomical. Following the philosophy of Aristotle, the scholastic tradition saw all change as a movement from potency to act. All movement was effected by a cause, but causality itself was complex. By examining all of these different aspects of causality (both primary and secondary), one understood the total shape of the real. In Aquinas's analysis, God was the final cause of all change, "the principal cause of all actions performed by his creatures which are nothing but instruments in His hands" (*Cont. Gent.* III, 67). Hence, all actions themselves had a final cause, a predetermined end or purpose that dictated the rightness or wrongness, the reasonableness or irrationality of those actions. God ruled creation by implanting within nature itself the predetermined ends or goals of all natural actions.

But since the dawn of the scientific age, this view of nature has become too static and determinist. Though some scientists have proposed a range of mechanistic and deterministic models that are propelled, not from the finality of organisms, but by laws like natural selection, most today understand development less rigidly. While all organisms operate within given biological, chemical, and physical parameters, the rate and kind of change depends on a process that is essentially open to a range of potential adaptations. Thus natural law should no longer be seen as consisting of predetermined rules of conduct that cannot change. Rather it is a process by which right reason determines in practice the best mode of balancing the stable and adaptable elements of an organism. Change occurs in natural law as the parameters of reasonable action shift within the realm of what is naturally (and technologically) possible.

Because scientific reason has brought to bear new tools for investigation and for the manipulation of natural processes, it has introduced a much higher capacity for lability into this equation. The rate and extent of change in what were formally organismic processes has accelerated. It follows that the moral tradition of reflection upon these changes must also accelerate and catch up so as to maintain some reasonable balance. It is no longer enough to articulate laws that cannot change when behavior no longer approximates the conditions under which the secondary principles of the natural law were formulated. Natural law, as an extension of the doctrine of creation, can make sense postcritically as long as it squeezes through the needle's eye and sheds some of its pretensions to omniscience. It represents an ancient tradition of moral reasoning, maintaining that human moral judgments are in touch with reality and that conscience makes real decisions that make a difference for the shape of society and the rightness of the lives people lead within it.

As such, natural law should propose paradigms of what it means to live, to be free, and to pursue happiness as rational persons, whether religious or not. The attempts by the magisterium to define the precepts of the natural law according to unchanging norms of nature have done immense damage to the attractiveness and the cogency of the natural law tradition. As I sketched above, the way the magisterium employs the tradition does not respect Aquinas's own agnosticism concerning what we can know, trading his high level of generality in reasonable morality for its own need to define right and wrong in objectivist terms. What this objectivism has produced is not a realist morality, but a totalistic system of dos and don'ts that less and less represents the real choices people have to make for themselves.

Natural law stemming from a secondarily naive doctrine of creation will take into account that God's creative power encompasses within it, as it unfolds within the material world, a capacity for indeterminacy, for ambiguity, for patience, and for dynamic randomness. These characteristics defy our ecclesiastical needs for definite answers, for unchanging decisions, and for total predictability. Today, neither physics nor a chastened metaphysics will sustain belief in a totalitarian creator whose unchangeable laws of nature allow for no exceptions. Rather, a secondarily naive theology must be capable of relating order in creation to questions like statistical causality, something beyond the ken of the originators of the theory of natural law.

In a paper entitled "Theology and the Heisenberg Uncertainty Principle," the late Christopher Mooney, S.J., concluded that the discovery of the quantum world of subatomic physics gives us a new way to understand the unpredictable openness of persons (human freedom), on analogy with the "hidden looseness of the unfolding quantum process" in the material world. The planned randomness of quantum physics gives us a way of understanding how God can be "both transcendent to human action and intimately involved in it." In this new equation wherein randomness and predictability coincide, "the God of Jesus is thus neither a maker of clocks nor a thrower of dice, but the one ceaselessly at work bringing overall direction and order to the undetermined realms of matter and spirit." In Mooney's view, God's law expresses itself as a process of sublime improvisations that represents the uniquely "divine milieu" in which order and spontaneity do not ultimately conflict. The idea of indeterminacy, which is central to the uncertainty principle,

does not contradict God's providential care, but somehow deepens it. Wave packets propagate and collapse, sparrows fall to the ground, humans freely decide for good or ill, yet hairs of the head nevertheless get numbered, elusive quantium particles eventually statistically stabilize, and "where sin increased, grace abounded all the more."

If the order that characterizes the natural world is indeterminate, then

...the irreducible uncertainty in the microworld, to which science has long become resigned, should encourage theology to live more easily with the mystery of God's active presence in the lives of free persons. For human reality is clearly rooted in quantum reality, and hence theology's classic inability to speak with any precision to the divine-human relationship at the level of freedom can more easily be extended to our corresponding inability to clarify God's action at the quantum level. This is actually in keeping with theology's ancient apophatic tradition: God is hidden and wholly other; our religious language is radically inadequate to address the divine mystery; the theological task is not so much better to understand this mystery as better to locate it....Finding too much order in the world can be as bad as finding too much novelty. Hence the perennial need to recognize that there are limits to what can be known and that these must be respected and lived with.[5]

Mooney's analysis corroborates the claim that postcritical belief has come through the needle's eye with a chastened view of how much we can know. For a theology that demands too much order will be constrained by necessity to claim too much control over its subject matter, and equivalently, a theology that seeks to manage the mystery completely will be beguiled by its own possibility and believe that its own formulations are the reality itself. After the heyday of rationalism, we can recognize how our own desire to control reality through our intellectual abstractions and oversimplifications represents a malformation — for science as well as for theology. The impact of this recognition should be liberating for both: for as the graced randomness of the natural law of quantum reality demonstrates, wrote Mooney, "Even our failures, instabilities and insecurities can be a form of providence."[6] By now, it should be clear that this is but another way of stating the guiding maxim of mature belief: *errore hominum providentia divina.*

Without elevating indeterminacy into a principle for its own sake, a clearly scientific principle should echo what I have argued is constitutive of religious knowledge: that literal falsity is a necessary component of metaphorical (religious) truth. Indeterminacy stands, not for ignorance or for skepticism, but for a realistic picture of how the real is knowable. In religious terms, indeterminacy calls for humility in both scientific and theological formulations, a humility that itself mirrors the tradition of divine humility or *kenosis* (self-emptying). God's infinite patience with fallible natural and human processes must be matched by a theology equally patient of the fallibility of belief, of theology's own failures and self-aggrandizements. But this necessary humility must be tested: does it help us look again at elements of Catholic teaching that a critical perspective have shown to be inflated in their formulation of orthodox belief?

The Fathers' Fallibility

It remains, then, to look explicitly at how we might reappropriate, if not rehabilitate, the doctrines that criticism has negated. I seek to discover in metaphorical indeterminacy an antidote for the literalism infecting the doctrines of papal infallibility, the Immaculate Conception, and the Assumption. By mining this principle, the result of retrieving the "whispered no" in faith affirmation, I hope to show how postcritical believers can find Catholic teaching revelatory. I will then test my rehabilitated reading of these symbolic doctrines by asking whether an equally postcritical reading of the sacraments upholds or jeopardizes their central place in Catholic faith and life.

As we saw above, papal infallibility was defined as a doctrine of Catholic faith in a historical situation in which the papacy faced a severe challenge to its political position. When the papacy was shorn of all vestiges of medieval political power, its pretensions to religious and moral authority grew disproportionately. The slow, unchecked extension of papal authority over jurisdiction, teaching, and appointment has, in turn, created a countervailing crisis of reception that threatens the cogency of Catholic truth claims for an unprecedented number of educated believers. Although Catholics have been generally loyal to the claim of the bishop of Rome to exercise a unique role in the hierarchy, the ultramontanist pressing of the issue after Vatican II and the suppression of effective collegiality has strained this loyalty to an unprecedented degree. Even before the council, loyalty to papal teaching was selective, but the highly symbolic role of the papacy as a distinguishing factor of Roman Catholicity and the passivity of the laity and clergy muted opposition.

Today that has begun to change as the *sensus fidelium* begins to question efforts to make the faith-symbol of the papacy into something literally and legalistically authoritarian. Catholics have always understood the fittingness of the pope's unique authority — when that authority remained at a high level of generality. When it began to be pressed strictly and the papal magisterium began to define the totality of the faith in a way that flattened distinctions in the hierarchy of truths, the faithful began to demur. To some this change represents the evil influence of secular culture and its creed of pleasure-for-its-own sake. To most Catholics it represents a response to the shape of life in which autonomous choices have become blessedly possible. In the medieval world of strict hierarchy, papal absolutism at least had some intellectual integrity. But in a post-Heisenberg universe in which spontaneous autonomy is the path to orderliness, to state, as the magisterium regularly has since 1968, that God's law requires that "every act of sexual intercourse must remain open to the transmission of life" outruns scientific reason, critical faith, and common sense. Thus *Humanae Vitae* was more than an instance of exaggeration. It is endemic of the attitude enshrined in Vatican I's definition of infallibility, that papal definitions are irreformable *ex sese* ("of themselves") and do not depend on the reception of the church. That definition created for the magisterial party in Rome a penumbra of infallibility that has recently created a category of "definitive" though noninfallible teaching to which loyal Catholics must submit. But the effort is pathogenic to belief because it is the result of a literalist understanding of faith-symbols.

Still, Catholics cannot and will not abandon their faith acceptance of ecclesiastical authority in itself. A postcritical and mature characterization of that authority will insist that it tailor itself more to what is symbolically fitting and metaphorically true in having a "Holy Father" at the church's head. Hence we ask: Having divested ourselves of a literal reading of the meaning of infallibility, does anything remain of the idea of infallibility to build up the Body of Christ? Hans Küng and others have argued that, historically and theologically, there is a role for a renewed Petrine ministry even in a reunited Christianity, and ecumenical treatments of the papacy have cleared new ground for a theological reappropriation of a unique role for the bishop of Rome, minus the claim for juridical powers that presently encumber the papacy. But my point here is somewhat different. Once the papacy has finally confronted its checkered past and mourned its abuse of power (admittedly not easy tasks), is there a special sense in which the infallibility credited to the church can be said to adhere, postcritically, to the bishop of Rome in his unique role as successor to the apostle Peter? I will answer yes, but only if we take into account the metaphorical indeterminacy that characterizes all transferential relationships and if we understand the important task that all those who exercise such leadership have to engage knowingly in responsible countertransference.

These are not just therapeutic techniques: they are spiritual truths that demonstrate the depth reality involved in the metaphorical and symbolic relationships that we engage in throughout life. In other words, the idea of papal infallibility is greater than its juridical definition. The legalistic and literalist reading of the symbol, in fact, lessens the real spiritual potential of its truth. The symbol of the papacy sums up the ability the members of the church have to discover the truth of the gospel message incarnated in the ministry of those entrusted with leadership, and ultimately in the ministry of *the* bishop whose ministry is to confirm the brethren and exercise solicitude (not control) for all the churches. Even as an admittedly hypertrophied understanding of Petrine primacy, infallibility justifies the risks that Catholics take when they trust their ordained leaders to hand on the faith of Jesus, in spite of the flaws, mistakes, arrogance, and narcissism that inevitably infects all leadership structures. Infallibility presumes not absolute dogmatic reliability but, as earlier understandings of indefectability made clear, that the truth will out even despite papal and ecclesiastical failures. The meaning of the doctrine cannot be found in any factual or historical preservation of the person of the bishop of Rome from error (as the hedge around the definition itself made clear). But more important and more truthfully, the doctrine means that postcritical believers can risk belonging to a historically fallible institution because the historical community of believers (ordained and otherwise) reveals God's fidelity in and through its graced fallibility.

The pope, a transferential figure par excellence, embodies the promise that the leadership of the church cannot so mislead the faithful that they will fail the testing of their faith. The promise itself is important, because all the failures that mark the history of the church have severely impugned the naive faith that precritical believers profess. Hence, the actual role of the church as a means of salvation is doubted by many. But to pretend that belief in God, who became incarnate in Christ, is possible outside the visible, historical structure of relationships in which humans depend on one another for everything from biological life to spiritual truth is a chimera. One could wish that the doctrine had never been articulated in the narrow, conceptualist terms in which it was defined. But its meaning is not confined to its legalized ideal or its literal content.

Postcritical believers will learn to depend upon those in authority to the extent that it is appropriate for mature persons to learn from, be challenged by, be taught by, and stand up to those in leadership when they are less than what is needed. The ongoing role of the bishop of Rome as the head of a college of bishops, each of whom heads a presbyterate whose members preside over assemblies of word and sacrament, ties Catholics to a uniquely visible, historical, fallible, but graced community across time and space. The continuity and solidarity that this creates is at the heart of Catholicity. But for that connection to be a mature, postcritical one, papal infallibility and the ecclesial gift that underlies it must be understood as profoundly paradoxical, like the Word of God in the Bible (Rom 9:6). Hence the doctrine needs to be understood in much the same way that we have understood postcritical maturity in general: *errore paparum providentia divina,* that is despite the fallible history of the papacy, it still stands as a sign of grace, of providential interdependency that believers suffer gladly, for it is the way the Word continues to be incarnate in time. The graced interdependency that enacts the solidarity of the community of faith is what calls forth a leadership structure in the church. But the present monarchical form of most of that leadership is not part of the constitution of the church, merely its historical baggage. It must be threaded through the critical eye of the needle and rearranged accordingly to fit appropriately mature ways of choosing leaders for the Body of Christ.

The present hierarchical structure takes refuge in the naive mythology that the Holy Spirit is active in the self-serving intuitions of a committee of bishops and tells them who should join them in their college. But the process lacks any of the checks and balances that both ancient systems of electing bishops and modern democratic processes presume necessary for a healthy authority structure. Rome's total centralization of this process, itself a result of extending the penumbra of infallibility over as many decisions of the pope and the Curia as possible, is not God's will. Nor is it the action of the Spirit or the inevitable consequence of anything but the voluntarism that operates *sub rosa* in much of the latency-bound structure that corresponds to an underdeveloped form of faith. Papal authority deserves to be postcritically reappropriated, but the effort can only be hampered by the ongoing efforts of the magisterial party to control the articulation of Catholic faith and the faithful's response in a universal, totalistic way.

Mary's Life and the Life of Believers

A critical reading of both the Immaculate Conception and the Assumption revealed that they represent naive conceptualizations or abstracted myths. They are not on a par with the affirmations of the Creed because they lack the grounding in historicality that characterize the salvific events of Christ's passion and death and the affirmation that he is risen. Nevertheless, the Marian doctrines can be postcritically appropriated once they have been divested of naive affirmations and naive denials. To do this, it is necessary to examine, at long last, the doctrine of the Virgin Birth of Jesus and the Marian offshoots of that doctrine that underlie the inflated definitions.

Without the doctrine of the Virgin Birth, neither of the later teachings would have achieved much currency, let alone been solemnly defined. As we saw, only two of the gospels affirm that the birth of Jesus took place in this special way. Neither Mark nor the fourth gospel found it necessary to specify this detail of Jesus' origins. Though the latter portrays the Word as preexistent, his birth is not explicitly narrated. Rather, the Word is said to have "come unto his own" (1:11) and "dwelt among us" (1:14); birth is exclusively reserved in the gospel's vocabulary to the spiritual realm of rebirth (3:3–5). When the mother of Jesus appears (2:1, 12; 6:42; 19:25), she is not named. What is more, Jesus is explicitly called "son of Joseph" (1:45, 6:42).[7] All of the epistles are silent on Jesus' earthly parenthood (except for Galatians 4:4, "born of a woman, born under the law," and Romans 1:2, "of the seed of David according to the flesh"). Finally, the reference to the pregnant mother of the Messiah in Revelation 12:4–5 makes no reference to a miracle that resulted in the pregnancy.

Consequently, the weight of the biblical doctrine falls upon the testimony of Matthew and Luke concerning the wonder-birth of Jesus from a virgin-mother. Both these gospels, despite their differences, have in common a physical miracle by which Jesus is conceived without benefit of human father. Matthew correlates the birth of Jesus from a virgin with the Septuagint Greek of Isaiah 7:14 (*parthenos*): "A virgin shall conceive and bear a son and shall call his name Emmanuel." As I argued above, both evangelists were perhaps seeking to match pagan myths about parthenogenesis (virgin birth) with a text about the one to be born as the "angel of great counsel" (LXX Isa 9:5). Matthew did not alter the Hebrew text in order to make a tendentious claim; he adopted a syncretist Jewish tradition in order to show that the birth of the Messiah topped the other scandal-filled births to which his genealogical record alluded.

Unlike Luke's more straightforward typology based on Samuel and Samson's mothers, Matthew emphasized how God continued to write straight with crooked genealogical lines to bring the divine promises to fulfillment. The four other women in the genealogy that heads Matthew's gospel all represent deviations in the normal course of either conception or inheritance: Tamar tricked her father-in-law by playing a prostitute and got pregnant, bearing Judah's heir (Gen 38), Rahab was an actual prostitute whose hospitality to Joshua's spies in Jericho saved her and her household (Josh 2:1). In Matthew's heuristic fiction, she was the mother of Boaz, the great-grandfather of King David. Ruth was a Moabite foreigner who, by marrying the same Boaz, insinuated herself into the line of David (Ruth 4:21). The fourth, Bathsheba, who was taken by David in adultery, later became the mother of Solomon. As Matthew constructed it, the royal line had had some amazing twists and turns. But the most amazing of all occurred when Joseph, a dreamer like his namesake (Gen 37), is instructed to take Mary, pregnant "by the Holy Spirit," into his home as his wife. Matthew made it clear that Joseph and Mary did not have sexual relations before Jesus was born (1:25). So, though Joseph names the boy according to the angel's instructions in his dream (1:21), the point of Matthew's narrative is clear: Jesus is to be Joseph's adoptive son only because of Joseph's lineage as a son of David, a son of Abraham. But Jesus is the Messiah and the Son of God because, from his conception, he has been destined to receive all power and authority as the Son of Man who will be with his church "until the end of the age" (28:18–20).[8]

Luke's narrative of Jesus' birth of a virgin presented his divine sonship in an even broader context than Davidic descent. That descent comes only incidentally from Joseph's being of the house of David (1:27, which Jesus' birth in Bethlehem is meant to reinforce). More directly, his birth as "Son of the Most High" who will give Mary's child the "throne of David his father" bestowed his identity upon him. Mary became pregnant through the Holy Spirit's overshadowing her with "divine power" (Gen 1:2), so that she does not have to "know man" before having this child (1:34). Because God's Spirit is the agent of the pregnancy, the child is "God's Son." Gabriel's answer to Mary's question, "How can this be?" (1:34) cites Elizabeth's pregnancy as a lesser to the greater argument. Since the sterile Elizabeth is now pregnant— "for nothing is impossible with God" (1:37, which answers the question in Gen 18:14)—so Mary too can be pregnant even more wondrously without benefit of husband. Luke's infancy narrative thus spelt out in greater detail the servant/son theme of Mark (1:11; 9:7; 15:39). In the earlier gospel, others proclaimed Jesus the Son of God, but it was a title not properly used by humans until Jesus died on the cross. But in Luke, Jesus is a wonderchild, aware, even before he is legally an adult, that God is his Father (2:49). Although this story is manifestly a legend, it shows that the church's reflection on God's unique relationship to Jesus, which flowered in the fourth gospel and beyond in the definitions of Nicea and Chalcedon, had already taken some serious steps very early in the process of development.

When we look at both Matthew's and Luke's presentation of the virgin birth, it is clear that they both framed their narratives for christological purposes, not for mariological ones. Luke's expansion of the role of Mary is not history; it is narrative theology. As a historical figure, she certainly played a biological role as Jesus' mother, but the earlier, unadorned tradition puts her in the camp of those who did not understand the nature of Jesus' mission in his lifetime (Mk 3:21–34; 10:29). Yet Luke is not just engaging in unhistorical idealization. Rather he has retrojected into Jesus' earthly life the post-Easter involvement of his family that he reflected in Acts 1:14 ("All these were constantly devoting themselves to prayer, together with certain women, including Mary the mother of Jesus, as well as his brothers"). We know of their real involvement from Paul's reference to "the Lord's brother" in Gal 1:19. Luke has enhanced this involvement by expanding Mary's role in order to establish both a historical and theological continuity between the church community and the parent community of Israel. He achieved this by weaving together numerous allusions to wonder-births in the First Testament. These he blended into the fabric of the "orderly account" of the events, as he put it, "just as they were handed on to us by those who from the beginning were eyewitnesses and servants of the word" (1:1–4). But this statement of his purpose does not require us to presume that he depended on eyewitness accounts of the events of Jesus' birth. Rather, depending on exegetical traditions developed by Hellenistic congregations from the Greek version of Israel's Bible, the Septuagint, he has presented Jesus' person and work in the full context of God's plan to save all humanity.

Thus a critical reading of the gospel traditions about the virgin birth has to take into account the general truth that Mary's role is mainly symbolic in the New Testament. She is not singled out as an individual in the same way that Jesus, or even Peter and Paul in Acts, are discreet individuals with particular roles in the drama of salvation. She exists in the narrative to connect Jesus to both his historical roots and to the unique divine initiative that *he* represents. In the fifth century, when the dogmatic disputes over the identity of Jesus continued to rage, Mary once again became a filter through whom christological doctrine was refined when she was declared to be the *Theotokos*, "she who bore the one who, even in his humanity, was divine." But as exalted a title as this is, and as privileged a role as it gives Mary in the communion of saints, the question it answered is essentially a christological one: was Jesus, born of Mary, the incarnation of the preexistent Logos and Son of God as well? The title bestowed on Mary at the Council of Ephesus in 431 C.E. answered the question in the affirmative and closed off any attempts to separate the preexistent Son and the biological son of Mary. Jesus' birth of Mary, without a human father's seed, was thus seen as defending the oneness of his person in both its divinity and its humanity. The doctrine of the divine maternity and the cult of the Virgin Mary that flowed from it are clearly a secondary benefit of the christological doctrine, not the chief reason for or content of the gospel tradition of Jesus' singular birth.

In the context of ancient birth-narratives on which the gospels depend, female barrenness or sterility was not a condition that a male was able to change (the perversity of Onan was great because he refused to implant his seed, Gen 38:9). The male was understood to implant the seed that became the human being, without any contribution by the female other than to provide a fertile womb in which the seed could incubate. Both birth narratives reflect these complementary biases: Matthew overlooked Mary's cooperation, securing Joseph's instead so that he might be a surrogate father for the child of the virgin. Luke ignored this patriarchal bias and made the cooperation of the lowly one whom God had extraordinarily favored the point of his narrative. Yet in both narratives it is taken for granted that a birth without benefit of a human father's seed is an appropriate way to express Jesus' absolute origin in God and God's corresponding act of humility, sending his Son in the likeness of human flesh. In other words, the virgin birth breaks the chain of what we would call biological determinacy, the notion that human identity is determined purely by a serendipitous combination of nature and nurture. By contrast, Jesus' identity represented a unique occasion where the extent of God's favor predetermined both his nature and the character of the one who would nurture him.

In the understanding of fertilization that lasted into this century, the biological stage of fetal development known as quickening was understood as the actual ensoulment or animation of the body, making it the earth composite of body and soul. Therefore, Cyril of Alexandria, the staunchest defender of Mary's title as *Theotokos*, took it for granted that Mary's contribution to Jesus person was his "sacred body," not its perfection "by an intelligent soul, to which the Word of God was hypostatically united and by which he was born according to the flesh." According to Cyril, the "earth composite" of body and soul is *not* completely generated in the womb; yet those with the wombs into which immaterial souls are infused are still properly called mothers.[9] Hence, it is the body alone that is understood to be generated by the seed, not the soul or the integral human person either.

This philosophical tradition, though seen to spell out the content of the biblical narrative, actually contradicts it. The biblical narratives presume the unity of the offspring of Mary's womb, not its division into a human body and a human soul, that are "hypostatically united" to the divine person. In order to preserve the sense of the birth narratives, the metaphysical Christology of the dogmatic tradition substituted its own understanding of hypostatic (or substantial) union of the divine and human natures. It ignored the mythopoetic biology of the virgin birth by which the earth composite was generated in the womb of Mary by a fecundating Spirit. In other words, when the philosophically oriented tradition conceptualized the virgin birth, it adapted it in the light of its understanding of what it presumed constituted human personality.

This means that the doctrine that Mary gave birth to a human being who is also divine does not depend upon the Bible's view of the facts of human biology. God's fatherhood of Jesus prescinds totally from the biological *bruta facta* of Jesus' birth. Hence, the doctrine of the virgin birth really points beyond the biological realities of Jesus' physical conception. It transcends the biological conception and birth of Jesus; it does not literally describe it.

It follows that the Catholic doctrine of the virgin birth, as it is normally interpreted, has confused biological reality and transcendent mystery and, in its literalness, has sought to base the reality of Jesus' identity in an inadequate and scientifically inaccurate understanding of human generation. Prescinding from the existence of the soul as an immaterial entity, embryology has determined that the earthly composite necessary for the generation of a living human being results from the commingling of a pair of genetic codes called chromosomes that are donated, one set apiece, from each of the human parents. This was as true two thousand years ago as it is today, but the gospel writers, like everyone else at that time, did not know this. For Jesus to be truly human (*vere homo*), he has to have had a genetic make-up composed of two sets of chromosomes. A literal understanding of the doctrine of the virgin birth, which presumes that a strictly physical miracle was responsible for generating a male seed in Mary's womb, would now have to claim that God generated directly and immediately a set of male chromosomes that bonded with Mary's genetic material in order to generate the human person Jesus. This in turn would require us to accept in literal terms Luke's picture of the fecund "overshadowing" by the immaterial Spirit providing genetic matter for Jesus' conception. Alternately, it would equate the virgin birth with a physical miracle of primary causality in which Mary hermaphroditically generated both the male as well as female chromosomes that became the person of her son. Now, one might argue that science does know of parthenogenesis in simple organisms. Hence, since "nothing is impossible with God," it might be argued that the Spirit's overshadowing accomplished this once-for-all female donation of the male genetic material.

But such an unnatural physical miracle is not necessary for affirming the truth in the doctrine. We no longer literally accept the fecund overshadowing of the Spirit at the creation of the world (Gen 1:2), on which Mary's fecundation is based, as descriptive of how the physical world was generated — except as mythopoetry. Rather, we accept that the physical realm has its own autonomy, that it was created to be itself. Except for the most determined fundamentalists who seek to maintain a bogus creationism, Christian interpreters distinguish between the doctrine of creation, on the one hand, and the direct creation of the physical universe by God, on the other. We have come to accept the natural developmental process of evolution without its impugning our belief in God as creator. But thus far Catholics, at least, have not squarely faced the implications of this recognition when it comes to what the natural developmental process tells us about human sexual generation. For just as we continue to believe that God is the creator of the universe, that the material cosmos has its origin ultimately in God, although we do not believe in the creation of the world as related in the Bible, so we can continue to profess the doctrine of the virgin birth without literally meaning that God directly and immediately created a set of male chromosomes in the womb of Mary. A literal understanding of the virgin birth that requires believers to accept the physical virginity of Mary in conceiving Jesus (hence, that there were no male chromosomes coming from Joseph) violates both the principle of instrumental causality as well as the laws of embryonic science.

This critical perspective on both the gospel texts and the doctrine of the virgin birth is not seeking to demonstrate on rational grounds that the virginal conception of Jesus is an untruth, merely a fable, or even that it is a statement in the mythopoetic genre that needs to be respected in its own right. Rather, I argue that the critical perspective needs to be filled out with a canonical one in order to be maturely appropriated. As we have seen, canonical criticism builds upon the work of historical critics who seek to establish the meaning of texts in their own terms, but then asks other questions about the manner in which the scriptural texts are authoritative. The authority of the texts of the virgin birth cannot be found by interpreting them literally as the record of a factual, miraculous act of intercourseless conception. Their authority arises from the way they retell ancient traditions of the wondrous births of the patriarchs and prophets, but in a higher key. At least in the case of Matthew, that key came from the exegetical tradition in Septuagint Isaiah 7:14, where an act of parthenogenesis was to be the sign that God was saving his people. For both gospel writers, such a birth was a fitting way to reveal the absolute origin in God of Jesus of Nazareth. They announced not a gospel of the miraculous nativity that saved us, but intertextual variations on the message of the resurrection retrojected into narratives of his conception, birth, and childhood. Though both Paul the apostle and the author of the fourth gospel believed that Jesus the Christ had preexisted with God before his earthly life, neither of them felt it necessary to proclaim that he entered the world through a miraculous, fatherless conception. Perhaps they were both aware of the possible charge that the authority of such a narrative would be too full of pagan derivatives for them to entertain a virgin birth. But Matthew and Luke took the risk that their narratives would sound more biblical than pagan.

In doing so, they met a need for filling out the story of Jesus' earthly origins in a way that set the stage for telling an increasingly Gentile church of the cosmic scope of the mission of the Risen One (Matt 28:18–20 and Luke's second work, the Acts of the Apostles). But they could not have known the extent to which many in the late Hellenistic age would see in their accounts an excuse to denigrate sexual intercourse and see in the virginity of Mary (and the fictive virginity of Joseph) symbols of the inferiority of marital sexuality to an ascetical life that renounced sexuality all together. A postcritical appropriation of the virgin birth must profit from bringing the hermeneutics of suspicion to bear not just on the texts of the gospel, to see whether they can bear the full weight of the tradition based upon them, but on the way the virginity of Mary was inflated by later ecclesiastical tradition to mean something other than what the gospels reveal about Jesus' identity. The symbol of the virgin birth came to be understood, not as a heuristic fiction about Jesus' other-than-earthly origin, but as a statement about the normative sinfulness of sexual concupiscence and the greater dignity of virginity. There has always been a great symbolic value placed on the virgin birth. But it became detached from its biblical base and plunged into the dualistic conflict between flesh and spirit. Later Hellenism did not understand this conflict in the Pauline sense of the apocalyptic conflict between this world and the world-to-come but in the neo-Platonic sense of lower worlds of matter and higher world of immateriality.

As the virgin birth was appropriated as a mariological doctrine, separate from its christological base, it took on its normative Catholic form. The full-blown cult of the Virgin reached its highest levels in the twelfth and thirteenth centuries, when hierarchical policies were dictating clerical celibacy, on the one hand, and fighting the more rabidly ascetical Cathar movement, on the other. Her cult, though not universally accepted — and later repudiated by most Protestants — has had a strong impact in institutional Catholicism. Especially as critical rationality began chipping away at traditional religion, the cult of Mary provided Catholics with enormous affective energy with which to maintain religious belief in the face of modern scientific reductionism. Witness the survival of Marian devotions in formerly Communist countries and in Cuba. But to the extent that the cult of the Virgin Mary is based on an absolutizing of her virginity, on an irreducible dualism that pits immaterial spirit against concupiscent flesh, it has expressed an emotional energy that at best sublimates sexuality but more often represses it with dysfunctional side-effects. What is at stake today in the literal understanding of the virgin birth as a biological miracle is not the truth of the gospel that Jesus is uniquely related to God or that Jesus is divine, but the entire complex of sexual and anthropological views that the Catholic hierarchy associates with the natural law and positive divine law. These are understood in absolutist fashion, impervious to any evolutionary development, supposedly written on the heart so that, if people follow sexual inclinations or sexual mores other than those defined as normative, they are guilty if not of sin then of deformations of an order that God is said to have declared must never be broken.

A postcritical appropriation of the doctrine of the virgin birth does not have to buy all the paraphernalia of the tradition. It gains from what critical perspectives have to offer and then reappropriates what the tradition says about the core revelation, but from this side of the critical needle's eye. In this perspective, we can understand the creedal statement that Jesus was "born of the Virgin Mary" as a symbolic affirmation that preserves a "whispered no" to the earthly origin of Jesus. The doctrine expresses the truth that Jesus was born, as all human beings are in the course of nature — hence, he did not descend as an adult from heaven (a possible reading of the ascent/descent Christologies also in the New Testament). But his birth cannot tell us of his origin any more than his death tells us of his end. His birth "from the *seed* of David according to the flesh" would seem to allow that David's seed (via Joseph) was the instrument of Mary's pregnancy. But it is not enough to state his earthly origin without proclaiming him, as Paul immediately does, to have been "declared to be Son of God with power according to the spirit of holiness by resurrection from the dead, Jesus Christ our Lord" (Rom 1:3–4).

The virgin birth is one way of linking these two affirmations in a mythopoetic heuristic fiction that points beyond itself with metaphorical indeterminacy, not with biological accuracy. It is not a necessary vehicle of the doctrine of Jesus' divinity. It strongly affirms that the one Mary conceived and bore (no matter his human origin — and even if Jesus were a bastard by human standards) is God's love breaking into the world to seek the beloved. In Jesus' birth from a virgin, we find something of both the *errores hominum* (concerning who Jesus' father is) and the *providentia divina* (the favored virgin) that characterize both the rhythm of the biblical revelation and a mature, postcritical faith. With this postcritical reading of the more fundamental doctrine of the virgin birth, what can we say about the derivative Marian doctrines that we earlier critiqued?

In the previous chapter I contended that neither the Immaculate Conception nor the Assumption can be held in the literal and historically factual terms that they are commonly proposed. If this is true, in what sense can they be held or proposed by postcritical belief? As positive doctrines, they proclaim the conviction of believers that God's gracious efforts to overcome the nexus of sin and death extends from "before all ages" to "the age to come." Mary's life (from before birth and after

death) became the prism through which the church professed this belief, in faith affirmations that made the mother of the Lord a symbolic
representation of the whole church's beginning and end. As a symbolic
doctrine, the Immaculate Conception stands for more than a singular
privilege for Mary. It is a Marian encoded belief that God's gracious
movement toward humankind was afoot well before human response
ever entered the picture.

Mary's predestination-to-glory (in light of Christ's redeeming sacrifice) stands for the way divine grace goes before humanity, anticipating
human sinfulness and all the violence it would do, as that culminates
symbolically in the death of her son on the cross. Mary becomes the
"servant of the Lord" (Luke 1:38), the mother of God's anointed who
proclaimed the "year of the Lord's favor" (Luke 4:19). But the doctrine
that she was chosen beforehand does not require the literal reading of
her being "full of grace" (Jerome's translation of Luke's *kecharitomenē*)
to justify it, because Mary stands for more than herself in the whole
drama of salvation. Literalizing the doctrine of the Immaculate Conception, seeing in it a unique privilege that separates Mary from the
company of all those redeemed by Christ, only weakens at its heart the
evangelical tenor of the doctrine of grace. Understood symbolically, the
doctrine makes Mary the first of the "first to hope in Christ," without
her maternal singularity making her a demigod.

In other words, Mary's predestination-to-glory stands for the overwhelming character of grace in the face of the all the ambiguities that
surround human sexual generation and all the inadequate settings into
which children are born into this world. But even here, "predestination" must be interpreted not in any strict determinist way that portrays
God's will as arbitrary. Rather, predestination is an idea replete with
the sense of fittingness that overwhelms lovers who believe their love
for each other seems somehow willed from beyond their own abilities
to foresee or decide. Because the historical Mary left only ambiguous
traces in the New Testament, her discreet personality (which is historically confined to her real motherhood) has been subsumed into her
symbolic role. Both in the New Testament and in the liturgical life of
the church, Mary stands in the image of the redeemed human race
(hence, her metaphorical title "second Eve"), truly a mother-figure for
the church and for believers. Her fittingness for her role in the communion of the saints flows precisely from the metaphorical indeterminacy
of her Magnificat in Luke 1:46–55. Like its intertextual partner, the
Song of Hannah (1 Sam 2:1–10), Mary's song of praise stands for every
experience of sudden justice, for every unexpected vindication of the
lowly and the poor, and for every woman whom history and society
have left aside but who finds her liberation in an answering decision for
faithfulness.

If both Mary's song and her experience of grace were merely *her* privilege, elevating her to the status of coredeemer (as a trend in Catholic
Mariology has tended to do), she could be only an apotheosized idealization, someone whose inclusion in a pantheon of demigods would
render her experience unavailable to the average believer. Neither her
song nor her symbolic witness to God's wooing of humanity would allow for the dynamic equivalency that all mature appropriation of the
canonical tradition must afford. Mary's unavailability for postcritical
faith is absolute if her immaculate conception is tied literally to her
virginal spotlessness.

In the last section, I critiqued the way the tradition identified sexual intercourse with the stain from which Mary's conception preserved
her (so that she could be the spotless virgin-mother of the redeemer).
Postcritically, this equation of sexual intercourse with humanity's fallen
condition yields only a misanthrophic and misogynist thinking that must
be mourned and grown out of. Virginity is not necessarily spotlessness,
nor is purity necessarily godly. We know too much today about the
complex, often unconscious, reasons why some people do not engage
in sexual intercourse — some are highly neurotic reactions to developmental vicissitudes. Therefore, mature belief will not automatically
associate virginal chastity with a greater degree of spiritual perfection.
Mary's predestination-to-glory prescinds from whether she had sexual
intercourse with Joseph either in the conception of Jesus or of other
children whom she seems to have borne. Before Mary was subsumed
into the realm beyond time and space, she was a woman who suffered
the pains of childbirth and the joys and sorrows of motherhood. Grace
became the suitor of her ambiguous humanity and found it, despite its
lowliness, very good. Her perfection reveals the depth and breadth of
God's purposeful and sublime improvisation in the human lives of those
uniquely privileged to be vessels of mercy.

Like the Immaculate Conception, the Assumption can be interpreted
postcritically by allowing it, as *mythos*, to expand beyond its literal reference. As a dogmatic symbol, it does not literally profess that Mary's
body was taken out of the realm of space and time but that her dying
anticipates our final and full redemption body and soul, in a perfected
time-space continuum. The doctrine of the Assumption will only be misunderstood if it singles out Mary's body for a unique relationship to
the physical universe. Rather, it proclaims that she is a symbol, even in
death, of our solidarity with the Risen Christ. This means that the salvation we have in Christ is not just a matter of the soul. In Christ, the
body and material reality are destined for some future fulfillment.

Thus, the Assumption is a secondary affirmation of the resurrection,
not a separate fact or a necessary complement to it. Rather, it is fitting that, after the resurrection, Christ has become a body-person whose

identity is truly corporate. He incorporates not only the baptized who are joined to him explicitly through his body the church, but also the whole of creation that, in Christ, is also predestined-to-glory (Rom 8 and 1 Cor 15). Mary's Assumption was proclaimed in an explicit attempt by Pius XII to combat a view of the world (communist dialectical materialism) that reduced human beings to ciphers in an impersonal struggle. The doctrine proclaimed (in naively literal terms) that matter too is redeemed, that heaven is not an alternative universe where we will one day live without the embarrassment of our bodily selves, but that our whole selves will one day be what we were meant to be. Christian belief in the resurrection (and derivatively, Catholic belief in the Assumption) affirms that we live and we die as part of a mysterious solidarity with all that exists, both seen and unseen. Though Christ has "passed beyond our sight" (as the preface of the feast of the Ascension affirms), he is present in his people the church, in their sacramental encounters, and in "the whole creation" that "groans in labor pains until now" along with the church as we await "the redemption of our bodies" (Rom 8:22–23).

But like the resurrection, the Assumption is symbolic of the "whispered no" about redemption: it has already begun, but it has not yet fully triumphed. We are saved "in hope," yet that hope will not leave us disappointed. The metaphorical indeterminacy of the Assumption keeps hope alive, not because it reveals Mary's *apotheosis* — although this seems to be the way Karl Jung understood it when he proclaimed its declaration the most important religious event of the twentieth century. Rather, it affirms that the resurrection possesses an inherent dynamic equivalency and declares that this most central mystery is still unfolding in the lives of the church and of the world. Neither of these great eschatological doctrines can be reduced to the discreet fate of the bodies of Jesus and Mary. The latent meaning in all their indeterminacy will not allow the obvious meaning of the *anastasis* (rising up from the sleep of death) to predominate. A naive picture of heaven-bound bodies cannot be the basic meaning of what faith affirms. Hence, the meaning of the Assumption of Mary can be discovered only in the tension between the obvious and the latent senses enclosed metaphorically within its symbolic shape. Mature belief in the Assumption begins, then, by suspending disbelief that Mary stands for more than herself in this faith affirmation. She is a figure, as her role in the liturgy has always intuitively portrayed her, of sublime metaphorical indeterminacy; she is not a metaphysical oddity. And it is in the liturgy and the sacraments, to which we finally turn, that postcritical belief finds the final proving ground of its secondary naivete.

The Sacraments as Christ's Risen Life

My attempt to sketch out some parameters for a postcritical form of belief has been an exercise in the symbolical imagination. It has been an effort to go beyond the philosophical appropriation of religious symbols and to take into account a rational critique of their accommodated understandings, in an effort to get beyond the impasse between faith and scientific reason. Ultimately, my effort to reintegrate *mythos* and *logos* must pass the test posed by the most basic level of the praxis of belief: Will it lead believers to worship God in Christ in a way that is faithful to the tradition as well as open to the tradition's further development? Another way of posing this is the question of orthodoxy: Will it help those who risk it to give worthy praise to God and invite them, by doing so, to conform their lives more deeply to the mystery of our communion with God in Christ? By inviting this test of postcritical maturity I am making a final effort to remove my theory from the realm of academic discussion and put it in the service of doxological believers, those not too nervous, as they stand on their own two feet to "call upon the name of the Lord" as a condition of their postcritical faith.

The heartbeat of the Catholic life and faith is the sacraments. In them, those who profess Christ's resurrection and who are incorporated into his body the church, believe that they encounter anew the mercy that created, sustains, and redeems the world. Tridentine Catholicism reacted to the Protestant denial of the antiquity and necessity of the seven sacraments by enveloping them in an aura of timelessness. But this effort collapsed under the weight of historical scholarship in the first half of the twentieth century. Vatican II's reform of the sacraments was my first conscious experience of the effort to reintegrate the *mythos* of sacramental encounter and the *logos* of their historical shaping. What can be learned from this effort?

Because symbolization remains basic to our deepest conscious and unconscious thinking, genuine religious symbols can provide mature adults (those who know how to suspend disbelief and approach them with secondary naivete) with neutral areas of experience impervious to challenge in which to transact their faith in mystery. This is particularly the case with those narratives, cult objects, formulas, songs, and rituals that enjoy canonical authority. As real metaphors they simultaneously stand both for themselves and for something more profound. Churches as sacred space are three-dimensional metaphors, veritable transitional spaces that give mature believers some opportunity for being at-one-with and separate-from God.

Mature adults in prayerful worship symbolically participate in a world beyond their full comprehension. On analogy with children engaging the transitional objects that create the real illusions by which their affective and intellectual lives are integrated, adult believers engage a privileged area of experience that allows them safely to relate inner and outer reality, immanence and transcendence. The words, prayers, sights, smells, sounds — especially musical ones — and the gathered community itself all are part of a privileged adult experience of play, a neutral space (which is why churches are places of sanctuary) where they can simultaneously be in communion and discover themselves. Like children managing the interplay between separation and union, adults worship in symbolic forms in order to open themselves to reality at its deepest level.

As mature worshipers enact and appropriate (make their own) the symbols of the liturgy, reality is playfully transformed. This does not mean postcritical believers *play at* worship. Through traditional forms and symbols, they engage something objectively other whose meaning is vitally affected by the *now* of the worshiping community. The gathering, the proclamation of the scriptures, the songs, the preaching, the intercessory prayers, and the proclamation of thanksgiving in which Jesus' act of self-offering is remembered, and finally the sacramental communion it-self — all these elements heuristically and playfully transform the world of the believing community. Liturgical worship allows adults to let go and be dispossessed of their own narcissistic need for control over the meaning of things precisely because it is far more than a self-consciously intellectual activity. It reveals and makes real for its participants new modes of being, new forms of life, and new capacities for believing, hoping, and loving.

Mature worshipers, then, seek just the opposite of the achievement of mastery either over themselves or over the full meaning of their lives. Instead, worship in spirit and in truth occurs when one is un-done in a genuine encounter with the Word and the Sacrament. Good liturgy allows us to experience a certain loss of self-awareness and self-centeredness and frees up its participants to discover something un-expected because its rules play us as much as we play by them. This is so because the canonical dynamics at work in both Word and Sacrament put before us worlds or horizons of encounter and crisis, of sin and grace, of the paradoxical *errore hominum providentia divina* that, when rightly celebrated, actually remake meaning. Postcritical worshipers al-low the paradigmatic narratives of the Bible and the symbolic actions involving water, bread and wine, oil, prayer, laying on of hands, recon-ciling, (and even marital love, a sacrament that only begins in church) to redescribe reality for them. This allows their own horizons genuinely to fuse with God's unlimited horizon.

Not only the Eucharist but all the sacraments of the church are meant to be what Augustine called visible words, revealing what is be-ing spoken about in the sacramental ritual itself. Yet because they are true symbols, not just visible signs of invisible realities, they do not resolve the tension between their obvious meaning and their latent, hidden, fuller, and divine meaning. They never merely describe in literal terms the objective content of their enactment. They always point beyond themselves to a greater horizon where their fuller meaning remains to be revealed.

This sacramental or symbolic structure says something as well about what we normally call morality. For all the actions of believers are also called upon to be symbolic, to stand not only for themselves but also for something not obvious in the moment, or perhaps even in time itself. Jesus' words in the parable of the sheep and the goats, "Truly, I tell you, just as I did it to one of the least of these who are members of my family, you did it to me" (Matt 25:40), define moral action in just such symbolic terms. Not only the sacraments but the very lives of believers are meant to be visible words, to point beyond themselves to the new creation where believers are reconciled to God by the justice of the cross and resurrection (2 Cor 5:14–21).

The gospel of the resurrection of Jesus basically presents a decentering redescription of the world not validated in everyday life. Without the sacraments as symbolic enactments of the counterintuitive, countercultural, and metarational message of a gratuitous and unmerited reconciliation accomplished by God, the message would sink of its own weight in a sea of disbelief. But because of the sacramental nature of our communication with God's world of meaning and the topsy-turvy divine way of doing things, we have access to this message, not just as a religious idea of the way things should be, but as a living truth. We call the Holy Spirit that which lives and continues to generate its effects through the Word as it becomes visible in the sacramental life of God's people — the "pledge" or "down payment" of something that believers do not see as fully operative but as the ultimate shape of reality.

Paul understood this living reality as both the content and object of what he announced, but even more, as the person of Jesus Christ. In his letters, references to "life" and "living" have a primary analogue: the risen one, God's Son revealed to him in the light of God's glory when he least expected it.[10] First-century Jew that he was, Paul understood the resurrection of the dead as the culminating event of history, which Christ's being raised signaled as near. What we normally call the resurrection Paul did not think of as a discrete historical event in the past; it was still unfolding and would continue to do so until Christ returned to "hand over the kingdom" (1 Cor 15:24). Hence Christ himself remains as much that unfolding event as he is the corporate person whom Paul identified as Christ's physical extension in the world, his Body, the *ekklesia,* those called together in fellowship by the Spirit of the risen Jesus. As much as we, from a later perspective, might think that all our faith problems would be solved if we could, as Paul did, "see the Lord Jesus," the Apostle knew better (2 Cor 12–13). Jesus' resurrection stands for more than an Easter Sunday empty tomb (itself a narrative symbol of something far greater). As risen, Jesus himself stands for more than a once-dead-man-now-known-as-God. Even Jesus' resurrection is but a symbol of something more than its obvious meaning. We see him "in mystery" (1 Cor 2:7), "through a glass darkly" (13:12), reflecting God's glory through the church, which, though alight with that gift, is herself but a dark radiance, a symbol caught in the tension of history between the *already* of our communion with Christ and the *not yet* of its full reality.

Because Christ lives in glory, as a metapersonal body, we cannot see him except as he himself is the sacrament of the resurrection of the dead. This means that we experience his living presence only sacramentally. This is not just God's teasing us, but a gift that makes the church itself a sacramental presence and a sacrament of humanity as God wishes humanity to be, redeemed from death and its terror. Both believers and critics may fail to factor into their reaction to the church the necessary tension in all symbols between the actual manifestation and what is manifested. On the one hand, some believers often identify the church with the body of Christ in literal terms. This leads to their idealizing the church's historical shape and absolutizing its authority. On the other hand, many skeptics see only the gaping distinction between the mythopoetic constitution of the church and the actual historical record and pronounce the connection between the two fraudulent and the authority of the church tyranny.

But the postcritical believer strives for that second naivete that gives criticism its due while understanding that Jesus, the crucified one who lives by the power of God, continues to express the divine self-emptying in the sacramentality of the church, not primarily in its legal constitution. At no time can its obvious, historical form and structure exhaust the meaning or the effectiveness of what God is manifesting. At all times, this manifestation takes place in spite of the church as much as through the church. The paradox still holds for ecclesiology as it did for revelation and doctrine: *Errore ecclesiae providentia divina.*

If even the symbol of the resurrection stands for something more than itself, it follows that all our experiences of grace are mediated ones, not direct communication with the divine depths of God. The nature of our communication with and knowledge of the God revealed in the reconciling grace that undid Christ's death (and our death as well) cannot be of the same order as most human knowledge. But the knowledge that informs our belief (*intellectus quaerens fidem*) seems to be most like that knowing which is common to us but buried in our personal depths — the earliest symbolic experiences that disclose or make manifest a deeper shape of things than we can take in schematically or encompass conceptually. By these symbols we participate in the world through an imaginative reconfiguration of it and how we wish to live in it. The instability or tension present in all symbols, but most centrally in sacramental symbols, cannot help but to undo and decenter the lives of participants. But we engage in this destabilizing only so that we can receive a firmer grounding in what we can see only indirectly.

The whole panoply of liturgical symbols, the seasons, feasts, icons, images, and celebrations, similarly point beyond themselves but insist that what lies beyond them can be glimpsed only via our being dispossessed of our private meanings, unhoused from our individual life-settings, and deprived of escapes (one of which is obsessionally neurotic religion) by participating in disclosure events of God's reconciling love for the ungodly. Thus the whole life of the church must be sacramental, sharing in the here and now, but grounded in the hidden truth that, like Jesus, we live by the power of God. There is no way to experience this gift except by the detour of signs, the route of indirection, the "approach to the mercy seat to find favor and grace" (Heb 4:16), that is, via the symbols and metaphors that find their first expression in the life of true *doxology*, or worship. Here postcritical naivete, having resisted the too easy identification of God's gift of reconciliation with the ecclesiastical instruments of salvation, learns that by celebrating the unresolvable tension between the historical manifestation of grace and the gift of God's self being manifested, it can refuse to idealize the church, identifying the gift with the giver and descending into idolatry. But equivalently, mature secondary naivete lifts the believer beyond all critical reductions that identify complex worlds with their component parts, that see history's traces as nothing but residue, that fail to recognize the cognitive and affective truths lurking in the illusions that sacramentality celebrates and makes real for those who have the eyes to see, the ears to hear, and the heart to understand.

Authority and Postcritical Naivete

Unlike naive forms of faith, mature postcritical belief does not find its authentication either in the infallible Bible nor in the infallible church, as these are simplistically understood. Both biblical and dogmatic fundamentalists respond with a pistic form of belief that needs absolutes close to hand. For its part, the attempt by the magisterium to lock up authoritative tradition by declaring itself the only authentic (authoritative) interpreter of the Word of God remains a defensive position crafted in reaction to the Reformation and escalated in reaction to the Enlightenment. As understandable as it might have been in those historical settings, at present it represents an attempt to freeze at one stage of development a living tradition of faith affirmation. Naive believers tend to accept the authoritative guidance of the magisterium out of a sense that authoritative teachers must be able to define the parameters of belief and make it stick. Today, some sophisticated and well-educated members of society, who hold positions of great influence and wield dispositive authority over thousands of people and millions of dollars, reserve some place in their lives for this kind of religious authority. While in the cognitive realm they function like analytic whiz-kids, psychologically and religiously they function like latent preadolescents. To them the doctrinal propositions of the magisterialists do not function symbolically but literally. The strength of objective conceptualism is its ability to give naive believers a sense of certainty about the object of their belief.

But the postcritical naivete that underlies mature belief does not respond to the magisterium's claims to authority in the rebellious and contrary way that we associate with critical un/belief. The agnosticism of that stage of faith's development is so taken up with the task of autonomy, of standing on its own two feet, of authoring itself, that suspending disbelief remains too risky and too threatening. Sadly the negative reaction of the magisterium to all forms of autonomy has deepened the crisis of criticism for many, because the official church so often makes it seem that coming in from the cold world of autonomous criticism back into the bosom of Holy Mother and under the hand of the Holy Father means surrendering important gains made, abandoning one's authentic self, and accepting a divine plan that has already made decisions for you.

The dawn of postcritical naivete can be detected in several movements within the last two hundred years. As different as they are, they have in common an intuitive response to rational autonomy and the forms of technological reason that have come to predominate in the developed world. The first arose in the Romantic movement, which sensed the loss of immediacy that Western religious culture had undergone. Writers like Chateaubriand, Blake, Herder, Möhler, Newman, and others, artists like Maria and Dante Gabriele Rosetti, and architects who pioneered the Gothic Revival all sought to recover lost elements of religious culture that foreshadowed the ability to entertain new forms of putting together the mythopoetic world and the brave, new world of scientific advancement.

But another source of postcritical belief has arisen in this century from reflection on the experience of social and political oppression. For too often, critical rationality, instead of providing liberation from the constraints of earlier "superstitions," only invented far worse systems of thralldom. Appalled at the ambiguous results of progress (especially in its capitalist-consumer shape) some writers and their communities have sought to reappropriate the Bible's paradigms of liberation from oppression as a powerful political message. Others have reacted to the debates for or against autonomous reason and made liberation a retreat into the mythopoetry of apocalypse. Still others have engaged in powerful feminist and womanist critiques of male domination in the institutions of religion in an effort to redescribe what a journey of faith is like and to find room for formerly excluded members of the human race to make it their own.

These currents of liberation today flow together into the various efforts of believers to escape from the cultural and religious impasse that has held sway for too long. It follows then that the authority of postcritical belief is discovered in the experiences of loss and recovery, of dispossession and rediscovery, of innocence lost and dignity restored that spiritual artists learn to create out of the ambiguous record of history. Such artists learn to suffer, as well, the self-styled magisterium's willful presentation of the tradition. But their postcritical believing does not take its shape from clerical authority or from a critical reaction to it. The authority of postcritical belief arises from its own journey via the detour of signs through the irreducible enchantment of human consciousness back to its origin, which is also its end. Perhaps a few saints among us achieve a lasting secondary naivete and do not have to go back, retrace their steps, and remake stages of the journey.

For most of us, the journey doubles back on itself, leads into blind alleys or away from any goal that seems worth pursuing. Often we regress to earlier stages of personal development and to the way faith shapes itself there. Hopefully regression occurs in the service of further progress and we take up the journey, regrounded in our own stories, so as to bring them to the larger story that the Bible witnesses and that the Spirit has been weaving and reweaving from time immemorial. It is the song-story of the lover and the beloved, courting and pursuing each other in poetry and in song, in symbols and in images, beyond reason yet always coming and going through the portal of the senses, the only entryway to the city where God's glory dwells. This work has tried to open that door, which Hebrews called "the new and living way" of Christ's flesh (10:20). Unlike our ancestors in the faith, for whom the flesh had to be overcome as a condition of salvation, modernity has made it normative for our understanding of the human condition. For the church to be Christ's body beyond the world of modernity, it must encounter anew its own fleshly creatureliness. For in that condition alone men and women today will discover for themselves their identity as the Bride of the Lamb ready to celebrate the marriage feast.

Notes

Chapter 1: In the Beginning Was the Image

1. Hans Urs Von Balthasar (*The Glory of the Lord: A Theological Aesthetics*, vol. 1, *Seeing the Form*, trans. Erasmo Leiva-Merikakis [New York: Crossroad, 1982], 608), speaks of the " 'language of myth' [as] nothing other than the common fund of images understood by every human being." Elizabeth A. Johnson (*She Who Is: The Mystery of God in Feminist Theological Discourse* [New York: Crossroad, 1993], 38) emphasizes that symbols not only "give rise to thought" (from Paul Ricoeur) but shape a host of political and social realities.

2. J. Laplanche and J.-B. Pontalis (*The Language of Psycho-analysis*, trans. D. Nicholson Smith [New York: W. W. Norton, 1973], 256) speak of "inter-uterine existence" as the "prototypical form" of primary narcissism before object-relations are formed. The objection that primary narcissism is a highly problematic state because newborns immediately develop "object-love" in suckling (338) helps us understand it as a continuous state of autoerotic need that undergirds any ability humans develop to connect with objects outside us.

3. Gerald G. May (*Will and Spirit: A Contemplative Psychology* [San Francisco: Harper & Row, 1987], 343 n. 19) describes this stage of "deeply unconscious thought" as a "very primitive, nonrational process in which, for example, opposites can co-exist as synonymous and where relationships between thoughts can be established on the basis or sound or symbolism." May uses Harry Stack Sullivan's term "paleologic" to describe it.

4. Willard Gaylin, M.D. (*Adam and Eve and Pinocchio: On Being and Becoming Human* [New York: Viking, 1990], 38) cites philosopher Ernst Cassirer's definition of the symbolic system as the "third link" unique to humans beyond the receptor system and effector system found in all animal species.

5. Thomas Aquinas, *Summa Theologica,* 1a, 9, resp. bases his defense of the scriptural use of "metaphors taken from bodily things" on the premise *omnis nostra cognitio a sensu initium habet* ("all our knowing begins from the senses"). In 1a, 84, 6, he reconciles Augustine's contention (based on Plato) that intellectual cognition is not to be expected from the senses by interpreting it according to Aristotle's agent intellect, which "by a process of abstraction makes images received from the sense actually intelligible." This allows him to stand by Aristotle's contention that *principium nostrae cognitionis est a sensu* ("the beginning of our knowing is from sense").

6. D. W. Winnicott, *Playing and Reality* (London: Tavistock Publications, 1971), 13.

7. May, *Will and Spirit,* 174: "Western thought — except for [William] Reich and to a much lesser extent Jung — has consistently presupposed that

psychic energy is generated in and limited to the individual human mind and body. In contrast, Eastern thought generally poses the existence of a universal energy."

8. Fergus Kerr (*Theology after Wittgenstein* [Oxford: Basil Blackwell, 1986], 109) stresses Wittgenstein's insistence that "it is our bodiliness that founds our being able, in principle, to learn any language on earth." Instincts, not ratiocination, are the source of language.

9. Ibid., 56–57. Wittgenstein cites Augustine's "mentalist-individualist" account of the way children learn language (*Confessions*, I, vi) as mischaracterizing the essence of human language because it locates meaning within the individual consciousness rather than "in the round of collaborative activity that generates the human way of life" (58). Wittgenstein declared, "Words have meaning only in the stream of life" (134). In a similar vein, Ernst Cassirer (*Language and Myth,* trans. Susanne K. Langer [New York: Dover Publications, 1946], 29–30) cites the early Romantic Johann Gottfried Herder against the theories of the Enlightenment that considered language as self-consciously invented. Rather, Herder maintained, humans achieved speech when they "attained that condition of reflection which is peculiar to [them], and when this reflection first achieved free play."

10. F. W. Dillistone, *The Power of Symbols* (London: SCM Press, 1986), 7–8.

11. S. Schneiders (*The Revelatory Text: Interpreting the New Testament as Sacred Scripture* [San Francisco: HarperSanFrancisco, 1991], 32) characterizes those for whom metaphors have become literalized in this way: "They have ceased to hear the whispered 'is not' that a live metaphor always carries in its affirmation."

12. Norman Perrin (*Jesus and the Language of the Kingdom: Symbol and Metaphor in New Testament Interpretation* [Philadelphia: Fortress Press, 1976], 106) wrote of the kingdom parables that "as parables they no not have a 'message.' They tease the mind into ever new perceptions of reality.... They function like symbols in that they 'give rise to thought.'"

13. David Tracy, *The Analogical Imagination: Christian Theology and the Culture of Pluralism* (New York: Crossroad, 1986), 363. E. A. Johnson (*She Who Is,* 116) records the loss of the negating power of analogy after Thomas and the subsequent temptation of theological language to become idolatrous. Recent Catholic thinkers (such as Tracy) have returned to stressing theology's "movement through negation to mystery."

14. Paul Ricoeur, "The Metaphorical Process," *Semeia* 4 (1975): 86.

15. Aidan Kavanaugh, *On Liturgical Theology* (New York: Pueblo Publishing Co., 1984), 47–48.

16. "Imaging" is used purposefully to avoid the wishful-thinking or negative (in the sense of purely fictitious) connotation that "imaginary" and "imagining" and even "imagination" have acquired in our generally literalist sense of how language functions.

17. See David Tracy, *Plurality and Ambiguity: Hermeneutics, Religion, Hope* (San Francisco: Harper & Row, 1987), 29–30.

18. J. Bowlby, *Attachment and Loss,* vol. 1, *Attachment* (Harmondsworth: Penguin, 1987), 248, 153.

19. Tracy (*Plurality and Ambiguity,* 30): "To grant a primary role to symbol in all discourse, for example, is not necessarily to disparage the need for concepts.... We enrich all thought by the use of concepts faithful to the

originating symbols, metaphors, metonyms. We often need the second-order language of concepts in order to understand first-order discourse."

20. Winnicott, *Playing and Reality*, 96

21. Ibid., 51.

22. See Paul Ricoeur, "Appropriation," in *Paul Ricoeur: Hermeneutics and the Human Sciences*, ed. and trans. John B. Thompson (Cambridge: Cambridge University Press, 1981), 182–92. Tracy, *Analogical Imagination*, 113–14: "I lose myself in the play. I do not passively lose myself. In fact, I actively gain another self by allowing myself fully to enter the game. . . . In every game, I enter the world where I play so fully that finally the game plays me."

Chapter 2: Growth in Thinking and Acting

1. Aristotle, *Poetics* V (G. M. A. Grube, *Aristotle: On Poetry and Style* [Indianapolis: Hackett Publishing Co., 1989], 10). See Gustav Stählin, *"Mythos,"* *Theological Dictionary of the New Testament* (henceforth *TDNT*), 4:773; and George Kennedy, *Classical Rhetoric and Its Christian and Secular Tradition from Ancient to Modern Times* (Chapel Hill: University of North Carolina Press, 1980), 78–79.

2. Stählin, *"Mythos,"* 4:773; Johannes Behm, *"Hermeneia," TDNT*, 2:664. See R. M. Grant with David Tracy, *A Short History of the Interpretation of the Bible*, 2d ed. (London: SCM Press, 1984).

3. Grant, *Short History*, 88.

4. Amos Funkenstein (*Theology and the Scientific Imagination: From the Middle Ages to the Seventeenth Century* [Princeton: Princeton University Press, 1986], 219 n.14) also claims that "Thomas' doctrine of analogy did as much to restrict the medieval sense of God's symbolical presence as it did to promote it."

5. F. C. Copleston, S.J., *Aquinas* (Harmondsworth: Penguin, 1979), 10.

6. Ewert Cousins (*Bonaventure: The Soul's Journey into God, The Tree of Life, The Life of St. Francis*, Classics of Western Spirituality [New York: Paulist Press, 1978], 23) details how Bonaventure begins his journey in the material world, but "he holds that knowledge of God is innate in the soul and does not have to be derived from sense data by a reasoning process."

7. E. P. Sanders (*Paul and Palestinian Judaism: A Comparison of Patterns of Religion* [Philadelphia: Fortress Press, 1977], 422) coined the term "covenantal nomism" in order to provide a more accurate understanding of early rabbinic Judaism than the prejudicial portrayal of Judaism in New Testament scholarship as a legalistic religion.

8. The book of Deuteronomy is interpolated into the Exodus-Joshua material to reinforce the theme of the law-giving on Sinai/Horeb, which is not in the ancient recital.

9. Daniel Boyarin (*Intertextuality and the Reading of Midrash* [Bloomington: University of Indiana Press, 1991], 108) distinguishes between rabbinic midrash, which goes "from abstract to concrete," and Origen's allegory, which "is from the concrete to the abstract." He further distinguishes, "In midrash, emotional and axiological content is released in the process of generating new strings of language out of beads of the old" (110).

10. Paul himself said "keeping the commandments" is more important than whether one was circumcised or not (1 Cor 7:19). He was clearly no longer

concerned with making "a fence around the Torah," but he affirmed the centrality of law-keeping nevertheless. James A. Sanders ("Torah and Christ," *From Sacred Story to Sacred Text* [Philadelphia: Fortress, 1987], 43–45) argues that the element of *mythos* in Judaism survives more prominently in Christianity while *ethos* became predominant in diaspora Judaism.

11. Laplanche and Pontalis, *The Language of Psycho-analysis*, trans. D. Nicholson Smith (New York: W. W. Norton, 1973), 442. In psychoanalytic terms, symbolic behavior has a special significance of its own. It is considered "a type of behaviour revealing the subject's aptitude for discerning an order of reality within the perceived that cannot be accounted for in terms of 'things': in fact this aptitude is precisely what permits the subject's generalised handling of 'things.'"

12. Hans W. Loewald, M.D. (*Psychoanalysis and the History of the Individual* [New Haven: Yale University Press, 1978], 49–50), citing Freud's *Interpretation of Dreams,* affirms: "It is this interplay between unconscious and consciousness, between past and present, between the intense density of undifferentiated, inarticulate experience and the lucidity of conscious articulate experience, that gives meaning to our life. Without such meaning-giving play we have no future of our own. Perhaps what we call man's symbolizing activity is that play."

13. Funkenstein (*Scientific Imagination,* 232) cites Maimonides' notion of the "cunning of God" by which God brings about the divine will even through opposition. In "the principle of accommodation" both Jewish and Christian thinkers of the twelfth century "found a rational interpretation of the trends leading toward the present and beyond it" (264).

14. Ernest Becker (*The Denial of Death* [New York: Free Press, 1973], 182), quoted Otto Rank on "the neurotic type" whom he described as someone "bound up in a kind of magic unity with the wholeness of life" rather than with a part of it. Neurotic activity can look very different, but in the psychoanalytic work of Rank, an early follower who broke with Freud, all neurosis expresses the substituting of "the magical, all-inclusive world of the self for the real, fragmentary world of experience."

15. See Bruce B. Lawrence, *The Defenders of God: The Fundamentalist Revolt against the Modern Age* (San Francisco: Harper & Row, 1989).

16. When italicized, *God* here means the concept of divinity or the word that refers to it; when not italicized, it refers to the divine Person that Christians also call the Father of Jesus Christ. Elizabeth A. Johnson (*She Who Is: The Mystery of God in Feminist Theological Discourse* [New York: Crossroad, 1993], 43) quotes Martin Buber on the ambiguity of the word "God": "Yes, it is the most heavy-laden of all human words. None has become so soiled, so mutilated. Just for this reason I may not abandon it."

17. Peter Gay (*The Enlightenment — An Interpretation: The Rise of Modern Paganism* [New York: Random House, 1966], 99): "Lucretius was to the dying Roman Republic much what Hobbes was to the seventeenth century.... A poet who uses the word *religio* in the pejorative sense in which others used the word *superstitio* was dangerous." Michael J. Buckley, S.J. (*At the Origins of Modern Atheism* [New Haven: Yale University Press, 1987], 46), clarifies that Lucretius, like the leading atomists Epicurus and Democritus, "denied only the providence of God." Lucian wrote a satire in the second century C.E. taking aim "at the old Olympian gods and Christianity."

18. Johannes Quasten, *Patrology* I (Westminster, Md.: Newman Press, 1962), 100.

Chapter 3: The Crisis of Criticism

1. Though Thomas Kuhn's notion of a "paradigm shift" has become a frequently employed category when discussing societal changes, some recent work has questioned the exclusivity of worldviews that would require the replacement of all elements of a worldview when a "shift" occurs. R. Rigby, J. Van Den Hengel, and P. O'Grady ("The Nature of Doctrine and Scientific Progress," *Theological Studies* 52 [1991]: 676) propose that L. Laudan's "normative naturalism" and its network model of piecemeal change more accurately describe the way core elements of a religious tradition are modified while other elements are maintained. Hence, progression in matters of religious belief can be shown to occur because core elements are adjusted rather than totally altered (682).

2. J. Bowlby (*Attachment and Loss,* vol. 1, *Attachment* [Harmondsworth: Penguin, 1987], 39–41) distinguishes between teleology, in which predetermined ends are said to be innate in beings, and teleonomy, in which the way an organism interacts with general laws of development determines the end that the growing being achieves. Aristotelian and Thomistic thought are characterized by teleology and its belief in an innate end for all existents. Scientific thought, without being deterministic or chaotic, accepts teleonomy, wherein given parameters affect change, but the intelligent organism has choices to make. This shift in thinking about how ends are achieved will affect the way we understand what is the core of a religious tradition and how it changes.

3. Erik Erikson, *Identity and the Life Cycle* (New York: W. W. Norton, 1980), 125.

4. Peter Blos, *On Adolescence: A Psychoanalytic Interpretation* (New York: Free Press, 1962), 107, citing Fenichel, *The Psychoanalytic Theory of Neurosis.*

5. Erik Erikson (*Identity, Youth and Crisis* [New York: W. W. Norton, 1968], 129–31) outlines these propensities. In his *Young Man Luther* (New York: W. W. Norton, 1962), 102, he states that in times which threaten identity diffusion, such as adolescence, music "can be a very important means of socializing and yet of communing with one's own emotions." It is a unique "bridge to others, and also a means of creating distance."

6. Cf. Amos Funkenstein (*Theology and the Scientific Imagination: From the Middle Ages to the Seventeenth Century* [Princeton: Princeton University Press, 1986], 356), quoting Kant.

7. Peter Gay, *The Enlightenment — An Interpretation: The Rise of Modern Paganism* (New York: Random House, 1966), 39.

8. Ibid., 58. David Tracy, *The Analogical Imagination: Christian Theology and the Culture of Pluralism* (New York: Crossroad, 1986), 196–97.

9. Richard J. Blackwell (*Galileo, Bellarmine, and the Bible* [Notre Dame: University of Notre Dame Press, 1991], 133–34) shows that there were two phases of Galileo's trial. In the first, the issue of biblical exegesis vs. scientific truth was central (1616); but in 1632, "disputes over truth and falsity gave way to authority disputes over loyalty and disobedience."

10. A. Funkenstein (*Scientific Imagination,* 152) identifies the "patterns of hypothetical reasoning" of the late Middle Ages as an influence in the emer-

gence of modern science. Ockham's stress on the conditions of the subject's knowing combined with the new modes of physical experimentation created the conditions for the "demystification" of the ways of God. Gay (*Enlightenment,* 310) quotes d'Alembert's recognition of the convergence of the ideas of both Descartes and Bacon in "experimental science." Bacon called for a "total reconstruction of sciences, arts, and all human knowledge, raised upon proper foundations."

11. N. Eberhardt, *A Summary of Catholic History* (St. Louis: B. Herder, 1962), 2:257.

12. David Tracy (*Analogical Imagination,* 105) states that it is only when historical distance has been recognized and "the brokenness and ambiguity of every tradition" is factored into understanding does the hermeneutical aspect of comprehending any tradition become conscious.

13. Colman Barry, *Readings in Church History* (Westminster, Md.: Newman, 1965), 2:245.

14. Vatican II, *Dignitatis Humanae,* no. 2 defines "religious freedom" as meaning that all "are to be immune from coercion on the part of individuals or of social groups and of any human power, in such wise that in matters religious no one is to be forced to act in a manner contrary to his own beliefs."

15. James A. Sanders, *From Sacred Story to Sacred Text* (Philadelphia: Fortress, 1987), 5.

16. Quoted from the *Irenicum Irenicorum* of a Unitarian reformer by the name of Zwicker, who published it in 1658.

17. Robert M. Grant with David Tracy, *A Short History of the Interpretation of the Bible,* 2d ed. (Philadelphia: Fortress Press, 1984), 106.

18. On Simon, see Grant, *Short History,* 109; P. E. Auvray, "Richard Simon," *Catholic Encyclopedia,* 13, 226. Werner G. Kümmel (*The New Testament: The History of the Investigation of Its Problems,* 2d ed. [Nashville: Abingdon, 1962], 62) notes that some seventeenth-century scholars knew his work and adopted his critical method. On Bossuet, see Owen Chadwick, *From Bossuet to Newman,* 2d ed. (Cambridge: Cambridge University Press), 11, 199. Peter Gay (*Enlightenment,* 75) calls him "a brilliant and triumphant anachronism."

19. Funkenstein, *Scientific Imagination,* 201.

20. "Canon" refers to "standard" books included in the Bible. Though Jews and Christians, and then after Luther, Catholics and Protestants as well, have different canons or lists of what are considered official works, they all agree on the canonical principle.

21. Albert Schweitzer, *The Quest of the Historical Jesus: A Critical Study of Its Progress from Reimarus to Wrede* (New York: Macmillan, 1969), 15.

22. Ibid., 25. Compare Kümmel, *The New Testament,* 90.

23. Hans Urs von Balthasar (*The Glory of the Lord: A Theological Aesthetics,* vol. 1, *Seeing the Form,* trans. Erasmo Leiva-Merikakis [New York: Crossroad, 1982], 84–85) is a real fan of Herder, but he wonders whether his work involves so many "aesthetic harmonies" that one might prefer the "trenchant antitheses" of Schiller, Marx, or Kierkegaard.

24. Quoted in Schweitzer, *Quest,* 79.

25. Ibid., 51, 55.

26. Kümmel, *History,* 121–24.

27. Cf. Grant, *Short History*, 112; Kümmel, *History*, 131; Schweitzer, *Quest*, 200.

28. Schweitzer, *Quest*, 153.

29. Ibid., 182–90.

30. Kümmel, *The New Testament*, 151. A minority of scholars continue to cling to the Griesbach hypothesis that Mark is a summary of both Matthew and Luke, often for the purposes of impugning the critical consensus about Mark's priority.

31. Paul Ricoeur ("The Task of Hermeneutics," *Paul Ricoeur: Hermeneutics and the Human Sciences*, ed. and trans. John B. Thompson [Cambridge: Cambridge University Press, 1981], 49) says that this era was "characterized by a total rejection of Hegelianism and an apology for experimental knowledge."

32. Harnack in *Marcion, Das Evangelium von Fremden Gott* (1924) degnosticized his subject and made him sound like Luther, thus drawing out a tendency to degrade the First Testament that is as old as Marcion and as recent as Bultmann.

33. Kümmel, *History*, 285; Schweitzer, *Quest*, 403.

34. Kümmel, *History*, 307.

35. Although von Balthasar protests against historical criticism constantly (*Glory*, 1:533–34 et passim), from his dogmatic perspective he appropriates this important truth of our contemporary hermeneutical situation; see 1:31, 544, 591.

36. D. Tracy, *Analogical Imagination*, 198.

37. Cf. R. E. Brown, S.S., "Hermeneutics," *Jerome Biblical Commentary* II, 605–23.

38. Gerald G. May, *Will and Spirit: A Contemplative Psychology* (San Francisco: Harper & Row, 1982), 262. See Sanders, *From Sacred Story to Sacred Text*, 4; Tracy, *Analogical Imagination*, 408.

Chapter 4: The Onset of Maturity

1. Carol Meyers (*Discovering Eve: Ancient Israelite Women in Context* [New York: Oxford University Press, 1988]) speaks of Genesis 2–3 as "a true *mythos*, a parable of the human situation" (79). She also points out that they contain "none of the words that are part of the Hebrew vocabulary of sin and transgression" (87).

2. Arno Gruen, *The Betrayal of the Self: The Fear of Autonomy in Men and Women* (New York: Grove Press, 1988), 46–47.

3. Cf. Paul Ricoeur, "The Task of Hermeneutics," in J. B. Thompson, ed., *Paul Ricoeur: Hermeneutics and the Human Sciences*, (Cambridge: Cambridge University Press, 1981), 46.

4. Erik Erikson (*Identity, Youth and Crisis* (New York: W. W. Norton, 1968), 129.

5. Alice Miller (*Thou Shalt Not be Aware: Society's Betrayal of the Child* [New York: New American Library, 1986], 316): "But the truth about our childhood, though present only in scraps of memory or unconscious traces, is stored up in our body, and although we can repress it, we can never alter it. Our intellect can be deceived, our feelings manipulated, our perceptions confused, and our body tricked with medication. But someday the body will present its

bill, for it is as incorruptible as a child who, still whole in spirit, will accept no compromises or excuses, and it will not stop tormenting us until we stop evading the truth."

6. As Alex Haley detailed it in *The Autobiography of Malcolm X* (New York: Grove Press, 1965), from which Spike Lee made the film *X*, Malcolm's childhood traumas and abuse led to his adolescent and young adult delinquency. His search for a lost self-esteem led to his intense filial devotion to Elijah Muhammad, a paternal religious figure. Only when he was forced to deidealize this parental substitute did he genuinely begin to achieve a mature self-awareness. It was accompanied by a new universalist religious awareness that began to be spelled out politically when he was brutally assassinated.

7. Alice Miller (*Thou Shalt Not Be Aware*, 182) avers that "an unacknowledged trauma is like a wound that never heals over and may start to bleed again at any time."

8. David Tracy (*Plurality and Ambiguity: Hermeneutics, Religion, Hope* [San Francisco: Harper & Row, 1987], 70) says we have to confront the ambiguous truth that "a once seemingly clear historical narrative of progressive Western enlightenment and emancipation has now become a montage of... startling beauty and revolting cruelty, of partial emancipation and ever-subtler forms of entrapment."

9. Cf. Peter Gay, *Freud: A Life for Our Time* (New York: W. W. Norton, 1988), 27–28; Ernest Becker, *The Denial of Death* (New York: Free Press, 1973), 151; Sigmund Freud, "The Future of an Illusion," *Pelican Freud Library* (Harmondsworth: Penguin Books), 12:227; hereafter *PFL*.

10. Freud, *PFL* 12:240–41.

11. Gay, *Freud*, 29, 326.

12. *The Standard Edition of the Complete Psychological Works of Sigmund Freud* (London: Hogarth Press and the Institute of Psycho-Analysis, 1948), 4:99; hereafter *SE*.

13. Quoted in Gay, *Freud*, 46 fn.

14. Quoted from "A Difficulty in the Path of Psychoanalysis," in Paul Ricoeur, *Freud and Philosophy: An Essay on Interpretation*, trans. Denis Savage (New Haven: Yale University Press, 1970), 427.

15. Sigmund Freud, "Civilization and Its Discontents," *PFL* 12:296, quoting Augustine. The comparison is explicit in Peter Brown, *Augustine of Hippo* (Berkeley: University of California Press, 1969), *Augustine*, 261; Ricoeur, *Freud and Philosophy*, 427, Becker, *The Denial of Death*, 33.

16. Quoted in Ricoeur, *Freud and Philosophy*, 277.

17. Brown, *Augustine*, 261.

18. Paul Ricoeur, "Proofs," *Paul Ricoeur: Hermeneutics and the Human Sciences*, ed. and trans. John B. Thompson (Cambridge: Cambridge University Press, 1981), 263–67.

19. Letter of May 25, 1895, to Fliess, quoted in Ricoeur, *Freud and Philosophy*, 71.

20. Introduction to the "Project" of 1895, in Ricoeur, *Freud and Philosophy*, 71.

21. W. W. Meissner, *Psychoanalysis, and Religious Experience* (New Haven: Yale University Press, 1984), 4.

22. J. Laplanche and J.-B. Pontalis (*The Language of Psycho-analysis*, trans. D. Nicholson Smith (New York: W. W. Norton, 1973), 64.

23. Gay, *Freud*, 93.
24. Miller, *Thou Shalt Not Be Aware*, 107–57.

Chapter 5: Freud and the Crisis of Modernity

1. Ernest Becker, *The Denial of Death* (New York: Free Press, 1973), 198: "The modern condition is one in which convincing dramas of heroic apotheosis, of creative play, or of cultural illusion are in eclipse."

2. *SE*, 4:28: "Psycho-analysis is founded upon the analysis of dreams," which Freud understands as "the residue of the day's mental work, now become active again" but in a disguised or distorted fashion.

3. Peter Gay's characterization of the unconscious in *Freud: A Life for Our Time* (New York: W. W. Norton, 1988), 128.

4. C. G. Jung, *Psychology and Religion* (New Haven: Yale University Press, 1938), 41.

5. E. Kurtz (*Not-God: A History of Alcoholics Anonymous* [Center City, Minn.: Hazelden, 1979], 167) affirms this reversal when he writes: "Symbolically, in a space of less than eighteen months, Roentgen's discovery of the 'x-ray' and Freud's first published claim for the determinism of the 'unconscious' joined to proclaim the ultimate result of 'enlightened' methods of investigation. . . . Descartes' criterion of the 'clear and distinct' thus became the hallmark of falsehood rather than the guarantee of truth. . . . Such direct correlation of ultimate hiddenness with ultimate reality was hardly what Enlightenment thinkers had in mind when they set their definition of 'modern.'" Paul Ricoeur (*Freud and Philosophy: An Essay on Interpretation*, trans. Denis Savage [New Haven: Yale University Press, 1970], 56): "But in its turn reflection will no longer be the positing . . . of the *I think, I am*: it will have become concrete reflection; and its concreteness will be due to the harsh hermeneutic discipline."

6. *SE*, 4:46–48.

7. E. Becker, *The Denial of Death*, 3–4.

8. Quoted in Peter Gay, *Freud: A Life for Our Time* (New York: W. W. Norton, 1988), 393.

9. In "Civilization and Its Discontents" (*PFL* 12:316) he defines it this way: "Civilization, therefore, obtains mastery over the individual's dangerous desire for aggression by weakening and disarming it and by setting up an agency within him to watch over it, like a garrison in a conquered city."

10. Barbara Tuchman's *The Proud Tower: A Portrait of the World before the War, 1890–1914* (New York: Macmillan, 1966) is a fascinating and sobering portrait of England, Germany, France, and the United States on the eve of World War I. Her *The Zimmerman Telegram* (New York: Random House, 1958) explores another aspect of the human foibles that do their greatest damage when combined with war-making potential. Freud ("Thoughts for the Times on War and Death," *SE* IV:288–317), after a brief bout with Austrian patriotism, sobered up quickly and wrote about the disillusionment of the war and the vagueness of the future.

11. S. Freud, *Ego and Id*, *SE* 19:50–52, quoted in Gay, *Freud*, 415.

12. K. Horney (*New Ways in Psychoanalysis* [New York: W. W. Norton, 1939], 185, 189) prominently accuses Freud of substituting neurotic develop-

ment for normal development. Becker (*The Denial of Death*, 98) has observed that the "fusion of truthful insight with fallacious explanation makes it difficult to untangle Freud."

13. Cf. Erik Erikson ("Womanhood and Inner Space," *Identity: Youth and Crisis* [New York: W. W. Norton, 1968], 267, 275–80) for a description and critique.

14. Gay (*Freud*, 88–89) points out the discrepancies in Freud's self-analysis: He felt guilty for surpassing his father but "was unconsciously eager to leave some of his ambivalence about his mother unanalyzed." In 1921 he wrote that while every lasting, intimate relationship conceals a sediment of hostile feelings, there is perhaps "one single exception," the "relation of mother to son which, founded on narcissism, is undisturbed by later rivalry" (505). Alice Miller's "Oedipus: The Guilty Victim" (*Thou Shalt Not be Aware: Society's Betrayal of the Child* [New York: New American Library, 1986], 143–57), shows how prejudicial society has tended to be toward the victim and prints an account from *Centuries of Childhood: A Social History of Family Life,* by Philippe Ariès of the court sex play into which Louis XIII was introduced as a child. After his seventh year, he was taught decency in language and behavior, but by then a lot of damage had been done!

15. K. Horney ("The Oedipus Complex," *New Ways,* 79–87) says that what Freud calls the Oedipal complex in all children, Horney sees as "an early manifestation of neurotic attachments" in *some* children. Arno Gruen, (*The Betrayal of the Self: The Fear of Autonomy in Men and Women* [New York: Grove Press, 1988], 25–26) claims that "the true source of the Oedipal situation . . . lies in the oppression of women and the consequent attempt of parents to gain importance and power by possessing their children. . . . It is this possessive mentality, the use of children as pawns in a parental power struggle, that creates Oedipal guilt feelings."

16. E. Becker, *The Denial of Death*, 41. Miller (*Thou Shalt Not Be Aware*) opines: "After Adam and Eve ate the apple from the Tree of Knowledge, they became aware for the first time that they were sexual beings and felt ashamed. Not even psychoanalytic theory has been able to set us free from this pattern of knowledge, sexuality, and shame."

17. Gay (*Freud*, 647) comments that Freud's "single-minded Lamarckianism, according to which historical events are transmitted in the unconscious from generation to generation, is no more trustworthy in *Moses and Monotheism* (1938) than in any of his earlier constructions."

18. His thesis was "that at the bottom of every case of hysteria there are one or more occurrences of premature sexual experience, occurrences which belong to the earliest years of childhood but which can be reproduced through the work of psychoanalysis in spite of the intervening decades. I believe that this is an important finding, the discovery of a *caput Nili* [source of the Nile] in neuropathology" (*SE*, 3:202–3).

19. Gay, *Freud*, 148.

20. Quoted in Ricoeur, *Freud and Philosophy,* 196.

21. Ricoeur, *Freud and Philosophy,* 420; Sebastian Moore, O.S.B. (*Let This Mind Be in You: The Quest for Identity through Oedipus to Christ* [San Francisco: Harper & Row, 1985], 6), affirms that Freud corrected the whole philosophical tradition's attention to the sense of lack that humans feel rather than to what Moore will call the "grammar of desire." At the same time,

Freud's estrangements from Alfred Adler, C. G. Jung, Otto Rank, and Sándor Ferenczi (the last three of whom were "son" figures at one time or other) all involved defections from the ranks over his sexual theory. Jung, in particular, not only distanced himself theoretically but later criticized how much the theory and its comprehensiveness meant to Freud personally. Becker (*The Denial of Death*, 95, 123) quotes Jung: "There was no mistaking the fact that Freud was emotionally involved in his sexual theory to an extraordinary degree. When he spoke of it, his tone became urgent, almost anxious.... Freud never asked himself why he was compelled to talk continually of sex, why this idea had taken such possession of him."

22. Becker, *The Denial of Death*, 41–44.

23. Ibid., 231, 237.

24. Ibid., 244–46. K. Horney (*New Ways*, 112) argues that masochism "is not a primarily sexual phenomenon, but is rather the result of certain conflicts in interpersonal relations."

25. Walter Ong, S.J., (*Fighting for Life: Contest, Sexuality and Consciousness* [Amherst: University of Massachusetts Press, 1989], 31) relates male and female not as "complementary" but in a relationship of "asymmetrical opposition" because sexuality is one of those profound truths that says two things that are related to each another "by asymmetrical opposition." Because "masculinity is difficult to interiorize" given its genital structure and since "being human means living from interiority, masculinity is an especially acute problem for human beings" (98), a problem that led to idolizing the phallus and its values.

26. *SE*, 4:174.

27. *SE*, 11:97.

28. Ricoeur, *Freud and Philosophy*, 521.

29. Becker, *The Denial of Death*, 184.

30. After a brilliant early career, the young French poet Arthur Rimbaud, faced with the loneliness of the poet's task, chose the "sanity" of the ordinary and became a trader in gold, rifles, and slaves. See Gruen, *The Betrayal of the Self*, 71, 122–23.

31. "Future," *PFL* 12:184. References in this and the next sections to these three works will appear in the notes only by page: "Group Psychology," 95–178; "The Future of an Illusion," 183–241; "Civilization and Its Discontents," 251–340.

32. Ibid., 274, 302.

33. Ibid., 72, 339.

34. Becker (*The Denial of Death*, 97–98): "The idea of the 'death instinct' was an attempt to patch up the instinct theory or libido theory that he did not want to abandon but that was becoming very cumbersome.... It was becoming difficult to maintain the fundamental assertion of psychoanalysis that man is purely a pleasure-seeking animal."

35. W. W. Meissner, S.J., M.D., *Psychoanalysis and Religious Experience* (New Haven: Yale University Press, 1984), 87.

36. Cf. Becker (*The Denial of Death*, 285): "Rank was not so naive nor so messianic: he saw that the orientation of men has to be always beyond their bodies, has to be grounded in healthy repressions, and toward explicit immortality-ideologies, myths of heroic transcendence."

37. Quoted in Gay, *Freud*, 526. But already in 1905, two years before

he published his first article on the topic, his clinical notes contained the suggestion: "Religion as [ob]sessive neurosis — Private religion."

38. Gay (*Freud*, 334) comments that Freud's "visionary construct" of the killing of the primal father from which humanity's sense of guilt arose did not have its prestige increased by its resembling "of all things, the Christian doctrine of original sin." Freud might be more surprised to find out that his understanding of the genetically inherited sense of guilt paralleled Augustine's understanding of how original sin was passed on — through sexual generation!

39. *PFL* 12:226.

40. Ibid., 239–41.

41. Quoted in Meissner, *Psychoanalysis and Religious Experience*, 97–98.

42. Becker, *The Denial of Death*, 68.

43. Ibid., 96: "Consciousness of death is the primary repression, not sexuality."

44. The history and practice of Alcoholics Anonymous provides experiential confirmation of how "cosmic" vulnerability and healing are related. The first three of the twelve steps are an enactment of Kierkegaardian-psychoanalytic-religious perspective: "1. We admitted that we were powerless over alcohol — that our lives had become unmanageable; 2. Came to believe that a Power greater than ourselves could restore us to sanity. 3. Made a decision to turn our will and our lives over to the care of God as we understood him."

45. Alice Miller (*Thou Shalt Not Be Aware*, 203) points out that the reason most depressed people are suffering from a pervasive malaise is not their present circumstances, but from their introjected self-contempt, whose roots, more than present-day manifestations, have to be unearthed and exposed to the light of day for healing to occur.

46. Becker, *The Denial of Death*, 165–66.

47. Ibid., 259–65.

48. D. W. Winnicott (*Playing and Reality* [London: Tavistock Publications, 1971], 16–17) theorizes: "I am here staking a claim for an intermediate state between a baby's inability and his growing ability to recognize and accept reality. I am therefore studying the substance of illusion, that which is allowed to the infant, and which in adult life is inherent in art and religion, and yet becomes the hallmark of madness when an adult puts too powerful a claim on the credulity of others, forcing them to acknowledge a sharing of illusion that is not their own. We can share a respect for illusory experience, and if we wish we may collect together and form a group on the basis of the similarity of our illusory experiences. This is a natural root of grouping among human beings."

49. W. W. Meissner (*Psychoanalysis and Religious Experience*, 17) formally distinguishes between a derivative of total subjectivity, which he refers to as a delusion, and illusion, which "retains not only its ties to reality but also the capacity to transform reality into something permeated with inner significance." Agreeing with Rank and Becker, he says that human beings "cannot do without illusion, since it gives meaning and sustenance" to their experience of themselves.

50. S. Freud, "Thoughts for the Times on War and Death," *PFL* 12:89.

51. Cited in Becker, *The Denial of Death*, 57. In *Civilization* (*PFL* 12:291) Freud allowed that a "small minority are enabled by their constitution to find happiness, in spite of everything along the path of love.... Perhaps, St. Francis

of Assisi went furthest in thus exploiting love for the benefit of an inner feeling of happiness."

52. Horney, *New Ways*, 305.

53. Miller (*Thou Shalt Not Be Aware*, 102): "The greater the refusal to face the past, the more incomprehensible its neurotic and psychotic manifestations in the next generation. This is true for the children of both the persecutors and the victims."

54. Cf. "The Dynamics of Transference," quoted in Gay, *Freud*, 299.

55. A. Miller (*Thou Shalt Not Be Aware*, 15): "But the experience of one's own truth, and the postambivalent knowledge of it, makes it possible to return to one's own world of feelings on an adult level — without paradise, but with the ability to mourn."

56. Ibid., 104. "These questions are always accompanied by much grief and pain, but the result always is a new authority that is being established in the analysand (like a heritage of the mother who never existed) — a new empathy with his own fate, born out of mourning" (67).

57. Gruen, *Betrayal*, 61: "We struggle to avoid failure and are not even aware that our fear of failure drives us into a nightmare of 'strength.' On the other hand, the strength that grows out of sorrow, distress, helplessness, illness, and bitter pangs has to do with the kind of transcendent experience that brings inner fortitude, which is not contingent upon external power and its constant need for affirmation."

58. Paul Ricoeur, "Proofs," in *Paul Ricoeur: Hermeneutics and the Human Sciences*, ed. and trans. John B. Thompson (Cambridge: Cambridge University Press, 1981), 265–66.

59. Freud to Jung, quoted in Gay, *Freud*, 301.

60. Alice Miller (*The Drama of the Gifted Child: The Search for the True Self* (New York: Basic Books, 1981), 77) relates the interpretive skill of the therapist to his or her own handling of "countertransference," or the bond with the patient felt by the therapist.

61. Becker, *The Denial of Death*, 130. He calls Freud's *Group Psychology and the Analysis of the Ego* (1921) "the single most potentially liberating tract that has ever been fashioned" because of its explanation of an enormous range of human traits from hypnosis to unconscious erotic longings for "strangers" to the psychic cement that binds people in mass movements (133).

62. Ibid., 136.

63. Freud's analysis (*PFL* 12:123) of the illusion of army members' attachment to the commander-in-chief fits with supremely narcissistic leaders such as Napoleon or Patton; it probably applies also to the average soldier in the case of other father-replacements.

64. Ibid., 284–85: "If transference represents the natural heroic striving for a 'beyond' that gives self-validation and if people need this validation in order to live, [Freud's] view of transference as simply unreal projection is destroyed. Projection is necessary and desirable for self-fulfillment.... As Rank so wisely saw, projection is a *necessary unburdening* of the individual" (158).

65. Fergus Kerr, *Theology after Wittgenstein* (Oxford: Basil Blackwell, 1986), 72. George Steiner (*Real Presences* [Chicago: University of Chicago Press, 1989], 93) takes a more negative position when he links Freud, Wittgenstein, and others whom he blames for the "break of the covenant between word and world" that occurred at the end of the nineteenth and the beginning of the

twentieth century. He calls it "one of the very few genuine revolutions of spirit in Western history... which defines modernity itself." My view differs in that I see both as laying the foundation for reintegrating how the word and the world are covenanted.

66. Kerr (*Theology after Wittgenstein,* 10–14) takes Karl Rahner to task for his Cartesian/Kantian notion that we can have immediate nonlinguistic knowledge of our unique inner experience. The experience of pure subjectivity or the subject's "pure openness for absolutely everything" (14) makes everything, including the Incarnation, "natural."

67. Ricoeur, *Freud and Philosophy,* 420–30.

68. David Tracy (*Analogical Imagination: Christian Theology and the Culture of Pluralism* [New York: Crossroad, 1986], 346) adds Nietzsche and Marx to Freud and claims that they "have robbed us of the last illusion of the Enlightenment — the illusion that if we are autonomously conscious and rational we need fear no further illusions."

Chapter 6: Reweaving *Mythos* and *Logos*

1. Gerald G. May (*Will and Spirit: A Contemplative Psychology* [San Francisco: Harper & Row, 1987], 166), quoting Harry Stack Sullivan, argues that in our culture so few contemporary marriages survive because "partners seek other sources of continuing the erotic drama of adolescence or the narcissistic dependency of adulthood."

2. Diogenes Allen (*Christian Belief in a Postmodern World* [Louisville: Westminster/John Knox, 1989], 7) portrays Christianity in the late twentieth century as characterized by theologians who "become modern by getting rid of lots of traditional Christian claims" or by those who seek to "remain premodern" (fideists).

3. See Robert Bellah (citing Erikson), "To Kill and to Survive or to Die and Become: The Active Life and the Contemplative Life as Ways of Being Adult," in *Adulthood,* ed. Erik Erikson (New York: W. W. Norton, 1978), 63.

4. May (*Will and Spirit,* 124): "On a personal level, it is only because we feel separate and self-identified that we are able to appreciate our existence. It is only when we feel distant from our Source that we can experience the joy of reunion. It is only in feeling alone that there is hope for meaning in coming together."

5. Like E. Kurtz, whose history of Alcoholics Anonymous bears the title *Not-God: A History of Alcoholics Anonymous* (Center City, Minn.: Hazelden, 1979), May (*Will and Spirit,* 41) sees addiction as "the sacred disease of the modern world" by which people seek to establish some willful divine "power over destiny" rather than yield willingly to the mystery of being which they cannot control.

6. Raymond Studzinski, O.S.B. (*Spiritual Direction and Mid-Life Development* [Chicago: Loyola University Press, 1985], 37), expresses the "crisis" in this way: "The desire to totally control one's environment and one's future, frequently through a close relationship with God the all-good provider, has proved unrealizable."

7. May (*Will and Spirit,* 241): "It is not as if the masters of the contemplative life have devalued Scripture, revelation, or even knowledge.... But a

perspective is maintained, and the mystery is not lost. Words of Scripture, senses of divine presence, and intellectual ability are no longer things of themselves, no longer even means to an end. They are windows of special clarity into the ever present mystery of creation. They are in fact gifts that expand the even greater gift of not-knowing."

8. Alice Miller (*The Drama of the Gifted Child: The Search for the True Self* [New York: Basic Books, 1981], 100–101) observes that "political action can be fed by the unconscious anger of children who have been so misused, imprisoned, exploited, cramped, drilled. This anger can be partially discharged in fighting our institutions, without having to give up the idealization of one's own mother, as one knew her in childhood. The old dependency can be shifted to a new object."

9. May (*Will and Spirit,* 142) affirms: "It is an historical fact that with rare exceptions the twice born cannot be helped by the once born, but the once born keep trying."

10. Jolande Jacobi (*The Way of Individuation,* trans. R. F. C. Hull [New York: Harcourt, Brace & World, 1967], 134) ends her work with this observation: "For it is not the goal but the striving towards this goal that gives our life content and meaning." The metaphor of circumambulating is Jung's (42).

11. Augustine, *Confessions* I, 1. See Mary T. Clark, *Augustine of Hippo: Selected Writings,* Classics of Western Spirituality (New York: Paulist Press, 1984), 9.

12. Individualism is not the valuing of the individual person (which is called personalism), but the residue of the objectivist and solipsistic premises of the Enlightenment. Like Rousseau's "noble savage," Defoe's Robinson Crusoe, or Swift's Gulliver, today's solo adventurer drives into the jungle to smoke a Camel or hang glides off ocean cliffs.

13. Jacobi (*The Way of Individuation,* 59) notes this idea in Jung's analytic psychology.

14. Jacobi (ibid., 38) cites Jung, who referred to the two opposites to the self as the ego and the shadow, or "the sum of all the qualities... that were neglected or rejected while the ego was being built up."

15. See Gabriel Moran, *Scripture and Tradition: A Survey of the Controversy* (New York: Herder and Herder, 1963), for a summary of the argument in the opening days of the council.

16. J. A. Sanders (*From Sacred Story to Sacred Text* [Philadelphia: Fortress, 1987], 63). This volume has collected Sanders's essays between 1976 and 1982, which will be cited by page number in these notes rather than individually.

17. James A. Sanders, *Torah and Canon* (Minneapolis: Fortress Press, 1986 reprint).

18. Dominique Barthélemy ("La critique canonique," *Revue d'Institut Catholique de Paris* [1991], 211–20) contrasts the work of Brevard Childs, whose "très originales" views risk opposing canon and criticism. The Latin text of *Dei Verbum* 8 defines tradition as that by which *ipsaeque Sacrae Litterae in ea penitus intelliguntur et indesinenter actuosae redduntur* ("... the Holy Scriptures are more profoundly understood and actualized in the church").

19. Sanders, *From Sacred Story to Sacred Text,* 65.

20. Ibid., 172.

21. Ibid., 192. See Sanders, "Canon — Hebrew Bible," *The Anchor Bible Dictionary,* ed. David Noel Freedman (New York: Doubleday, 1992), 1:846.

22. Sanders, *From Sacred Story to Sacred Text,* 142, 144.

23. John P. Meier (*A Marginal Jew: Rethinking the Historical Jesus,* vol. 1, *The Roots of the Problem and the Person,* Anchor Bible Reference Library [New York: Doubleday, 1991], 142 n. 15) defends the distinction between the canonical and the apocryphal gospels against the current fashion that the latter have equal claim to represent sources for reconstructing an image of the historical Jesus. The canon of the gospels was not arrived at by tendentious political decisions but because these books sufficiently balanced the stable and adaptable elements of the message, not falling into either extreme of mythicizing the past of the Messiah or the present of the believer.

24. Sanders, *From Sacred Story to Sacred Text,* 164: "There had been a relationship between tradition, written or oral, and community, a constant, ongoing dialogue, a historical memory passed on from generation to generation, in which the special relationship between canon and community resided. There was a memory that this particular body of tradition had at crucial junctures throughout the centuries of that relationship given life to the communities — just as the communities had given life to it by passing it on and keeping it alive. Torah, and then Christ, was viewed as the way, the truth, and the life. One searched Scripture because in it one found even eternal life (John 5:39). Why? Because in the very conception and birth of canon was the historic event of death and resurrection of the community of faith when it otherwise should have passed from the scene of history like everybody else."

25. Sanders, "Canon — Hebrew Bible," 851: "Understanding canon as having been guided by the Spirit through all its stages of formation permits it to continue functioning for a believing community as paradigm of how that Reality called 'God' impacted the vision and thinking of ancestors in the faith — and how it may continue to do so in the present."

26. Sanders, *From Sacred Story to Sacred Text,* 84.

27. Sanders, "Canon — Hebrew Bible," 849.

28. Ibid., 844: "The God who emerges from the whole can no longer be identified with any one deity of any of the sources but is the God of all life's experiences, what humans would call good as well as what they would call bad — such as defeats and failings."

29. Ibid., 849: "Is it canonically legitimate to read the parts in the light of the whole? The answer is Yes. Most of the prophets did so; Jesus did so. The hermeneutical move is first to theologize in reading all passages, using a theocentric monotheizing view of reality, and then only thereafter to moralize, or ask what it means for the new situation in which it is being read."

30. Ibid., 845: "Such pluralism within a canon provides a self-corrective apparatus within its bounds; no one group of idioms should be absolutized over another. Recognition of this canonical given, or gift, would deter the pervasive tendency to locate the canon within the canon and then to abuse the rest by insisting that it all agrees with the parts chosen."

31. Sanders, *From Sacred Story to Sacred Text,* 180.

32. Ibid., 144–45.

33. Ibid., xi, 163. See also *Canon and Community: A Guide to Canonical Criticism,* Guides to Biblical Scholarship (Philadelphia: Fortress, 1984). In "Canon — Hebrew Bible," 843, Sanders makes the following clarification: "But the Bible is a text in itself. It all hangs together in a larger literary context so that each of the discernible units small and large, including books, may take

on hues and connotations within the whole. Sometimes this resignification of texts may be attributed to an editor, or redactor... but sometimes it is due to the intertextuality of canonical context." The same point is made by liberation theologians who stress that the lives of the people reading the Bible are an essential context that must interact with the work of exegetes. See Carlos Mesters, *Defenseless Flower: A New Reading of the Bible* (Maryknoll, N.Y.: Orbis, 1989), 81.

34. Sanders, *From Sacred Story to Sacred Text*, 167, xi.

35. Ibid., 10.

36. Sanders, "Canon—Hebrew Bible," 849.

37. J. A. Sanders, "From Isaiah 61 to Luke 4," in *Christianity, Judaism, and Other Greco-Roman Cults: Studies for Morton Smith at 60,* part 1: *New Testament,* ed. Jacob Neusner, SJLA 12 (Leiden: E. J. Brill 1975), 75–106.

38. Sanders, *From Sacred Story to Sacred Text,* 70, 190.

39. Ibid., 5.

40. Sanders, "Canon — Hebrew Bible," 850: "But recognition of how a later text 'rings in the changes,' as it were, on earlier traditions and texts by citing, paraphrasing, alluding to them, or imitating their form, is also intertextuality. This means that the original 'intentionality' of individual authors may canonically be overridden in the adaptation of a passage to a new situation."

41. Edward T. Oakes ("The Paradox of the Literal: The Voice of Canon Criticism in Reformation and Counterreformation Polemics," *Reformation and Counterreformation,* ed. John Hawley (Berlin: W. DeGruyter, 1994), 26–27: "Canon criticism... is raising within the world of biblical scholarship questions left unresolved from the time of the Reformation.... Perhaps the paradox of the literal has by now reached its highest pitch, for a full pursuit of the literal has brought us back to insights lost in the heat of the sixteenth-century battle."

42. J. A. Sanders, "Intertextuality and Dialogue" (forthcoming), describes the appropriate interplay in this way: "Whenever an earlier 'text' functions in a later text, whether it be home-grown within 'Israel" or international in scope, the dialogue should be pursued critically and faithfully, that is, with both suspicion and consent."

43. Sanders, "Canon—Hebrew Bible," 850: "It has been recognized, however, that 'inspired' and 'canonical' are not synonymous terms. On the contrary, many in Judaism and Christianity are said to have been 'inspired by God,' yet their writings are not in any community's canon."

44. Werner G. Jeanrond (*Text and Interpretation as Categories of Theological Thinking,* trans. Thomas J. Wilson [New York: Crossroad, 1988], 68–69) complements Ricoeur's analysis of the need for both explanation (of the past) and understanding (for the present) by insisting on the need for assessment. This additional step calls for a "critique of the situation" and corroborates Sanders's threefold scheme for the dynamic appropriation of texts.

45. R. E. Brown, S.S. ("Hermeneutics," *Jerome Biblical Commentary,* 606) was still taking this cautious position in the 1960s: "The principal task of interpretation centers around the author's intended meaning." But more recently (*The Critical Meaning of the Bible* [New York: Paulist, 1981], 19) he contends "that one cannot be satisfied with the literal meaning of Scripture" and adds in a note, "the literal sense is larger than the author's intent." *Dei Verbum* 12 puts a priority on seeking out "the intention of the sacred writers" as part of

our reading and interpreting a text in the light of "the content and unity of the whole of Scripture" and "the living tradition of the whole church." Brown's "biblical meaning" tries to take these other factors into account.

46. See James A. Sanders, *God Has a Story, Too: Sermons in Context* (Philadelphia: Fortress, 1979).

47. Samuel Coleridge, in his *Biographia Literaria* (in *The Portable Coleridge*, ed. I. A. Richards [Harmondsworth: Penguin, 1977], 45–46) called imagination a power that "reveals itself in the balance or reconciliation of opposite or discordant qualities: of sameness, with difference; the individual with the representative." More recently, claims that all truth is perspectival evidence a similar distrust of politically dominant interpretations that claim something universal about themselves.

48. George Steiner, *Real Presences* (Chicago: University of Chicago Press, 1989), 112, 162, 165.

49. Ibid., 181–82, 196–97.

50. Kant is quoted in David Tracy, *The Analogical Imagination: Christian Theology and the Culture of Pluralism* (New York: Crossroad, 1986), 140, n. 37. Sebastian Moore, O.S.B. (*Let This Mind Be in You: The Quest for Identity through Oedipus to Christ* [San Francisco: Harper & Row, 1985], 69) associates "the weakness, the wonkiness, the wobble in one's life" with Paul's experience of the withdrawal of glory (2 Cor 12:10), which is "therefore the place for grace's entry." Equivalently, Steiner (*Real Presences,* 180) speaks of a "wobble in our psychic coordinates of temporality" which brings about "a transient eclipse of the ego" during which "other presences find their luminous or shadowy way."

51. Ricoeur ("Language," *Semeia* 4 [1975]: 145) asserts that these "narratives and symbols...are neither 'within' nor 'without' a rational philosophy" but are paradoxes on the "boundary line."

52. Tracy, *Analogical Imagination,* 145. Sanders (*From Sacred Story to Sacred Text,* 80) passes over Ricoeur's symbolical hermeneutics, but perhaps too quickly. I find Ricoeur and Tracy congenial to Sanders, and, combined with the thinking of Becker, Winnicott, Meissner, and Steiner, very convincing.

53. It is in this sense that Ricoeur ("Appropriation," *Paul Ricoeur: Hermeneutics and the Human Sciences*, ed. and trans. John B. Thompson [Cambridge: Cambridge University Press, 1981], 178) speaks of the necessity of an act of interpretation being complete only when "it culminates in some form of appropriation." The German word for this is *Aneignung,* or "making one's own."

54. Jeanrond (*Text and Interpretation,* 54), quoting Ricoeur: "Reading introduces me to imaginative variation of the ego. The metamorphosis of the world in play is also the metamorphosis of the ego."

Chapter 7: Mourning Lost Innocence

1. J.-H. Walgrave, *Newman the Theologian: The Nature of Belief and Doctrine as Exemplified in His Life and Works,* trans. A. V. Littledale (London: Geoffrey Chapman, 1960), 53–55. Newman's ideas express the "aggregate of the possible aspects of a reality." They normally begin as "intuitions" (95),

but as "living ideas of a community" are expressed in analogy, metaphor, and symbol as their most appropriate vehicles.

2. Amos Funkenstein, *Theology and the Scientific Imagination: From the Middle Ages to the Seventeenth Century* (Princeton: Princeton University Press, 1986), 53.

3. Ibid. 89. Newton the scientist undertook to translate "all symbols and metaphors into unequivocal statements," and Leibniz the philosopher "insisted on the intelligibility of every genuine thing down to its individuality" (101). Claude Geffré (*The Risk of Interpretation: On Being Faithful to the Christian Tradition in a Non-Christian Age,* trans. David Smith [Mahwah, N.J.: Paulist Press, 1987], 62) speaks of scholasticism's overconfidence in the *adequatio* of knower and known as creating "the illusion of truth." In contrast to the resistant Augustinianism of the Jansenists, the "separated theology of nature and grace" had, in its early stages, tried to meet the challenge of critical rationality. But it had become a petrified response that did not benefit from the nineteenth century's further development of critical thinking in more historical directions.

4. Marcellino D'Ambrosio ("Resourcement Theology, Aggiornamento, and the Hermeneutics of Tradition," *Communio* 18 [1991], 554) cites Jaroslav Pelikan's *The Vindication of Tradition* and its general rule that, in theology, "the most creative thinkers have been at the same time the most traditional." "Nor should it be a surprise that these same writers were also connected to Cardinal Suhard whose worker priest movement after World War II was also suppressed by Rome." D'Ambrosio quotes von Balthasar on the need for "creative invention" and Suhard's dictum to his worker priests, "It is not enough to imitate, you must invent."

5. C. Geffré (*The Risk of Interpretation,* 56) cites Pierre Gisel as suggesting that a new form of epistemology that takes up the relationship of history and truth "be called a 'genealogy' in the Nietzschean sense."

6. Peter Brown, *Augustine of Hippo* (Berkeley: University of California Press, 1969), 37.

7. Peter Brown (*The Body and Society: Men, Women, and Sexual Renunciation in Early Christianity* [New York: Columbia University Press, 1988], 394) speaks of the early stage of Augustine's faith in this way: "Through Ambrose and, possibly, through his neo-Platonic readings, Augustine was brushed, for a crucial moment, by the 'wild' Platonism that we have met in the mystical thought of Origen."

8. Brown, *Augustine of Hippo,* 43, 79.

9. Ibid., 140–41, citing *De Consensu Evangelistarum,* IV, x, 20 (400 C.E.).

10. Ibid., 271, citing *De Doctrina Christiana,* Prooem. 6.

11. Ibid., 374–75, citing *Tract. in Joh.* 26, 4. In a late sermon on the fourth gospel, Augustine reached back to a pagan work, quoting Vergil's "Let everyone's pleasure draw them" to speak, not just of the bodily sense pleasures, but of the unique pleasure of the soul to be drawn to the fountain of life (Ps 36).

12. Ibid., 373, citing *Enarr. 8 in Ps 118,* 4.

13. Ibid., 351: In a letter to a rich widow, Augustine warns "I have, however, observed this fact of human behaviour that, with certain people, when sexuality is repressed avarice seems to grow in its place." His biographer also points out that Augustine, in analyzing the slip of the tongue, "anticipates Freud in seeing in this seemingly harmless phenomenon the constant activity of unconscious desires" (366).

14. Cf. Brown, *The Body and Society*, 394.

15. Brown (ibid., 413, 422). Sexuality as a failure of the will made Augustine's diagnosis of fallen human nature much more drastic that simple body-soul antagonism (cf. ibid., 406, 433). In *Augustine* (387), Brown laments the opportunity Augustine missed when he derided the Aristotelianism of Julian, who "anticipates a Christian humanism such as would only be realized 700 years later" in Aquinas (387).

16. Robert Markus (*The End of Ancient Christianity* [Cambridge: Cambridge University Press, 1990], 60) traces a shift in Augustine's thought that involved "the very definite positive re-evaluation of human sexuality...in relation to much of the earlier tradition and, indeed, to the prevailing orientation of Christian thought in his own time. Peter Brown (*The Body and Society*, 433) echoes this difference and summarizes Augustine's "somber doctrine of concupiscence" as bringing to the fore a voluntarism that arose in the biblical tradition of "purity of heart" exacerbated by his negative view of how sexuality "mirrored a failure of the will more drastic" than monastic writers like John Cassian admitted.

17. Geoffrey Barraclough (*The Crucible of Europe: The Ninth and Tenth Centuries in European History* [Berkeley: University of California Press, 1976], 56) speaks of the "myth" of Charlemagne stemming from the second half of the ninth century. Despite its wishful thinking aspect, "it created the idea (or perhaps the ideal) of the unification of Europe."

18. Geoffrey Barraclough (*The Medieval Papacy* [New York: W. W. Norton, 1968], 63) notes that John VIII was murdered in 882, Stephen VI was strangled in prison in 897; the infamous John XII, eighteen when he became pope in 955, died of indulgence in 964; Benedict VI was smothered in 974; and John XIV was killed in the Castel Sant' Angelo in 984. All "were noblemen appointed for reasons of family policy or politics.... But the result was that the papacy, once again, was on the point of losing its moral prestige...and becoming simply the instrument of local Italian factions."

19. Cited in Kenan B. Osborne, O.F.M., *Priesthood: A History of the Ordained Ministry in the Roman Catholic Church* (New York: Paulist Press, 1988), 207.

20. Philip Hughes (*A Popular History of the Catholic Church* [New York: Macmillan, 1966], 109) wrote of him in the 1940s: "Hildebrand stands head and shoulders above all his contemporaries, and this not merely by strength of character or clearness of purpose, but by a realisation that the issues about which the battle was now joined were truly fundamental. He saw that the papacy alone could save the Church."

21. Quoted in Patrick Granfield, *The Limits of the Papacy* (New York: Crossroad, 1990), 34–35.

22. Granfield (ibid., 36) says also that "Boniface VIII, disregarding the facts of history, also asserted that Rome had established all the patriarchal, metropolitan, and episcopal sees" and that a further step was taken by Clement VI (1342–52), who asserted that "the Pope, as Vicar of Christ on earth, possesses the same full power of jurisdiction that Christ himself possessed during his human life."

23. Barraclough, *The Medieval Papacy*, 104.

24. Frederick H. Russell (*The Just War in the Middle Ages*, Cambridge Studies in Medieval Life and Thought, 3d series, vol. 8 [Cambridge: Cambridge

University Press, 1977], 298–99) argues that attempts to extend canonical jurisdiction over various *causae belli* failed because of their dependence on extending papal jurisdictional universally.

25. See Yves M.-J. Congar, *Lay People in the Church*, rev. ed., trans. Donald Attwater (Westminster, Md.: Christian Classics, 1985), 17; also J. Mahoney (*The Making of Moral Theology: A Study of the Roman Catholic Tradition* [Oxford: Clarendon Press, 1987], 104), who says that Thomas's notion of divine law was adduced by his need to fit scripture into his Aristotelian system, not the other way around.

26. Mahoney, "The Language of Law," in *The Making of Moral Theology*, 237.

27. Cf. John Boswell, *Christianity, Social Tolerance, and Homosexuality: Gay People in Western Europe from the Beginning of the Christian Era to the Fourteenth Century* (Chicago: University of Chicago Press, 1980), 277–78.

28. In no uncertain terms, he warned Pope Eugene III (1145–53) in his famous letter *De Consideratione* (IV, 3, 6): "When the Pope, clad in silk, covered with gold and jewels, rides out on his white horse, escorted by soldiers and servants, he looks more like Constantine's successor than St. Peter's" (quoted in Granfield, *The Limits of the Papacy*, 36, from PL 182:776).

29. Erik Erikson, *Identity and the Life Cycle* (New York: W. W. Norton, 1980), 142.

30. Bonaventure, *The Soul's Journey into God, The Tree of Life, The Life of Francis*, trans. Ewert Cousins, The Classics of Western Spirituality (New York: Paulist Press, 1978), 112, 319.

31. Erik Erikson, *Young Man Luther* (New York: W. W. Norton, 1962), 164.

32. Edward T. Oakes ("The Paradox of the Literal: The Voice of Canon Criticism in Reformation and Counterreformation Polemics," *Reformation and Counterreformation*, ed. John Hawley [Berlin: W. DeGruyter, 1994], 20) cites Luther's own disavowal of Augustine in favor of Paul, but Luther's Paul remained an Augustinian.

33. Erikson (*Young Man Luther*, 231) credits Luther's emphasis on individual conscience with preparing "the way for the series of concepts of equality, representation and self-determination which became in successive secular revolutions and wars the foundations not of the dignity of some, but of the liberty of all."

34. Though Richard Simon of the Oratory subverted the Protestant position on the sufficiency of scripture through the historical criticism of the Bible, he was silenced by Bishop Bossuet, Louis XIV's court preacher. Being an ecclesiastical absolutist in the service of a political one, Bossuet could not allow ideas of historical variation to intrude on his ideological presentation of history. He believed in the late seventeenth century what Cardinal Ottaviani's motto read three centuries later: *Semper Idem*, the faith has always been the same.

35. Mahoney (*The Making of Moral Theology*, 124) cites *Exurge, Domine*, the bull excommunicating Luther, as attributing to him the statement that "it is certainly not in the power of the Church or the Pope to lay down articles of faith, or even laws or *mores*, that is, of good works" (DS 1447). Trent's Decree on Sacred Books and the Received Traditions (DS 1501) defended the received canon of scripture and the traditional practices (e.g., praying for the dead) that had arisen in the church (129–32).

36. Mahoney (*The Making of Moral Theology*, 123) says that it is hard to avoid the conclusion that "'*mores*' at Trent would seem to indicate the prac-

tices and customs of the Apostolic Church, some of which touch upon doctrinal matters, others having to do with disciplinary or ceremonial practices." Edmund Hill, O.P. (*Ministry and Authority in the Catholic Church* [London: Geoffrey Chapman, 1988], 69) avers that Trent's "decrees, which were designed to define Catholic doctrine where it had been called into question by the Protestants...nowhere touch on the matter of papal authority, which the Protestants were certainly repudiating." Citing a possible exception in the anathema against those who deny that bishops appointed by the Roman pontiff are not legitimate (DZ 1778), he claims: "The bishops...could not even bring themselves to reaffirm the teaching of the Council of Florence on the subject."

37. Quoted in Mahoney, *The Making of Moral Theology*, 133–34.

38. Funkenstein, *Scientific Imagination*, 28.

39. Mahoney (*The Making of Moral Theology*, 226) contrasts Thomas and Suarez (cf. n. 5).

40. Funkenstein (*Scientific Imagination*, 116) sums up this era in this way: "The medieval sense of God's presence in his creation, and the sense of a universe replete with transcendent meanings and hints, had to recede if not to give way totally to the postulates of univocation and homogeneity in the seventeenth century." According to him Pascal's objections were "the exception, not the rule" (72).

41. Mahoney, *The Making of Moral Theology*, 166: "In more than a century since this extraordinary and infallible moral magisterium of the papacy was solemnly declared it has never once been manifestly exercised."

42. Ibid., 156–63. Hill (*Ministry and Authority*, 102) says: "I am not objecting to the inclusion, but only wondering what an infallible definition about morals would look like." Newman ("Letter to the Duke of Norfolk," 332) wrote that "it is difficult to say what portions of moral teaching in the course of 1800 years actually have proceeded from the Pope, or from the Church, or where to look for such." See Francis Sullivan, *Magisterium: Teaching Authority in the Catholic Church* (Mahwah, N.J.: Paulist Press, 1983), 184. In his authoritative commentary on Vatican II's *Dei Verbum* (1969), theologian Joseph Ratzinger wrote that "to reduce the task of theology to the proof of the presence of the statements of the teaching office in the sources is to threaten the primacy of the sources which...would ultimately destroy the serving character of the teaching office." The future cardinal and head of the Congregation for the Doctrine of the Faith knew that this had been the case and taught, as did Yves Congar, that this was *not* consistent with "what nineteen centuries of the Church's life tell us about the function of the *didaskalos* or doctor."

43. David Tracy (*Plurality and Ambiguity: Hermeneutics, Religion, Hope* [San Francisco: Harper & Row, 1987], 85) speaks of how the claims of the church have been so relativized for nonbelievers who are "unable to consider seriously the intellectual claims of theology because the history of religions also includes such an appalling litany of murder, inquisitions, holy wars, obscuranticisms, and exclusivisms."

44. Attempts such as Elisabeth Schüssler Fiorenza's *In Memory of Her: A Feminist Theological Reconstruction of Christian Origins* (New York: Crossroad, 1983) to reconstruct Christian history in order to recover the forgotten role of women in the church or Ben Witherington's *Women in the Earliest Churches*, SNTS 59 (Cambridge: Cambridge University Press, 1988) are valid and necessary, but they are merely seeking to fill out history so the future can be

built on a broader base. Such reconstruction can aid in the work of mourning but cannot take its place.

45. In the early years of the Reformation an extraordinary group appointed by Paul III mapped a plan for a Catholic reform. Its document *Consilium de emendanda ecclesia* noted that the evils of simony and multiple benefices were the results of the inflation of papal authority. "Thus the will of the pope, of whatever kind it may be, is the rule governing his activities and deeds: whence it can be shown without doubt that whatever is pleasing is also permitted. From this source as from a Trojan horse so many abuses and grave diseases have rushed in upon the Church of God that we now see her afflicted almost to the despair of salvation" (quoted in John C. Olin, *The Catholic Reformation —Savonarola to Ignatius Loyola: Reform in the Church 1495–1540* [New York: Harper & Row, 1969], 187).

46. Ernest Becker, *The Denial of Death* (New York: Free Press, 1973), 145–60.

47. Becker (*The Denial of Death*, 280) questioned Tillich and Jung's ideas on God: "How could the ground of being be as accessible as Jung imagined? It seems to me that this concept would destroy the whole idea of the Fall. How can man have the realm of essence 'on tap,' so to speak; and if he does, doesn't Tillich's understanding of grace lose all its meaning as a pure gift beyond human effort?"

48. J. Laplanche and J.-B. Pontalis, *The Language of Psycho-analysis*, trans. D. Nicholson Smith (New York: W. W. Norton, 1973), 78.

49. Flannery O'Connor (*Letters of Flannery O'Connor: The Habit of Being*, ed. Sally Fitzgerald [New York: Farrar, Straus, Giroux, 1979], 90) wrote: "I write the way I do because (not though) I am a Catholic. This is a fact and nothing covers it like the bald statement. However, I am a Catholic peculiarly possessed of the modern consciousness, that thing Jung describes as unhistorical, solitary and guilty. To possess this *within* the Church is to bear a burden, the necessary burden of the conscious Catholic."

Chapter 8: Primal Faith and Its Misshaping

1. Claude Geffré, *The Risk of Interpretation: On Being Faithful to the Christian Tradition in a Non-Christian Age*, trans. David Smith (Mahwah, N.J.: Paulist Press, 1987), 58. Avery Dulles, S.J. (*The Catholicity of the Church* [Oxford: Clarendon Press, 1985], 121), uses Otto Karrer's term "Catholicist" to express the narrow notion of plenitude that yields "a kind of ecclesiastical totalitarianism" wherein "the machinery of ecclesiastical mediation has been exalted to the point of becoming oppressive. Catholicism has been subject to the extremes of papalism, legalism, dogmatism, ritualism, and sacramentalism. These aberrations, however, are not endemic or inevitable."

2. Avery Dulles, S.J. (*Vatican II and the Extraordinary Synod: An Overview* [Collegeville, Minn.: Liturgical Press, 1986], 31), gives the impression that one of the major purposes of the Synod was to overcome lingering resistance to the council itself. The sharp differences that emerged in the debates have been muted by the secrecy that was imposed on the reports of episcopal conferences and statements of the conference presidents, which "remain unpublished."

3. F. J. van Beeck (*Christ Proclaimed: Christology as Rhetoric,* Theological Inquiries [New York: Paulist Press, 1979], 73) cites J. Verhaar on "conceptualism" and says that the results of gearing language to "truth" is that "the elements of dialogue and persuasion (the old dialectica and rhetorica) recede and "fideistic orthodoxy" advances, proclaiming that "orthodoxy is in the clear-cut dogmatic statements." The act of faith then becomes "increasingly an irrational, fideistic *sacrificium intellectus* allegedly demanded by the 'divine authority' of, say, officially interpreted conciliar tradition or of Scripture literally understood."

4. "On the Introduction of Rationalistic Principles into Revealed Religion" (1835) is cited in F. J. van Beeck (*God Encountered: A Contemporary Catholic Systematic Theology,* vol. 1, *Understanding the Christian Faith* [San Francisco: HarperSanFrancisco, 1989], 47). Owen Chadwick (*From Bossuet to Newman,* 2d ed. [Cambridge: Cambridge University Press], 195) notes that "Newman was a prodigy... because he came to believe in historical development without also believing in liberal philosophies of development."

5. See Karl Rahner, *The Church and the Sacraments* (New York: Herder and Herder, 1963), 39, where he also cites his own more philosophical study, *The Theology of Symbol* (36).

6. Avery Dulles, S.J., in *Models of Revelation* (Garden City, N.Y.: Doubleday, 1983), 131, repeated his earlier formulation in "The Symbolic Structure of Revelation," *Theological Studies* 41, no. 1 (March 1980): 56; see *The Craft of Theology: From Symbol to System* (New York: Crossroad, 1992), 65.

7. See Dulles, "Symbolic Structure," 52–73; *The Craft of Theology,* 3–17.

8. Sandra Schneiders (*The Revelatory Text: Interpreting the New Testament as Sacred Scripture* [San Francisco: HarperSanFrancisco, 1991], 35) tends to take the ontological linguistic analysis of symbol for granted. As a scripture scholar, she seems prejudiced in favor of language as she affirms that "the symbolic mode of revelation... is preeminently realized in language,... the most effective way human beings have of rendering their personhood intersubjectively available" (45). By way of correction or exception, David Tracy (*The Analogical Imagination: Christian Theology and the Culture of Pluralism* [New York: Crossroad, 1986], 205) is more subtle when he cites Eliade on the priority of "manifestation" over "proclamation." He affirms that "in some lives today the experience of sexual love is the last outpost of the power of manifestation in the extraordinary" (384), a reminder that wordless symbolic acts are primordial and, like all symbols, are ambiguous and must be interpreted.

9. Justin J. Kelly ("Knowing by Heart: The Symbolic Structure of Revelation and Faith," in *Faithful Witness: Foundation of Theology for Today's Church,* ed. Leo J. O'Donovan and T. Howland Sanks [New York: Crossroad, 1989], 64) depends uncritically on Durkheim's *participation mystique* by which they "do not merely instruct us but invite us to participate or share a feeling, a perception of reality through the heart." F. W. Dillistone (*The Power of Symbols* [London: SCM Press, 1986], 125) cites Paul Tillich's distinctions between signs and symbols as dependent on symbols' emerging "in some mysterious way" that cannot be fabricated.

10. Schneiders, *Revelatory Text,* 32. Rahner (*Church and the Sacraments,* 38) notes the distinction between two aspects — "the dependence of the actual manifestation on what is manifesting itself, and the difference between the two" — but does not develop this as the mainspring of what triggers the "ex-

cess of meaning" in symbols. Van Beeck (*Christ Proclaimed*, 92) understands metaphors as reflecting both a situation's intelligibility and its strangeness: "Metaphors, therefore, in their very attempt to express meaning, also express, and testify to, the strangeness, the otherness of the object, and to the essential limitations of our cognitive power."

11. Paul's pun in 2 Corinthians 12:4 (*arrheta rhemata*) is difficult to render in English. George Steiner (*Real Presences* [Chicago: University of Chicago Press, 1989], 112) speaks of Joyce's epiphany and Walter Benjamin's aura as "transcendental intuitions [that] have sources deeper than language, and must, if they are to retain their truth claims, remain undeclared." This modern equivalent of the apophatic tradition should temper the claims of our philosophically based tradition, which even Dulles (*The Craft of Theology*, 36) witnesses to when he states: "In consciousness there is no gap between the knower and the known. I am immediately present to myself, without needing any representation to mediate the presence." This "epistemological privilege of the subject" reflects Rahner's idea that "a subject which knows itself to be finite...has already transcended its finiteness" (quoted in Kerr, *Wittgenstein*, 12). Kerr argues: "I discover myself, not in some prelinguistic inner space of self-presence, but in the network of multifarious social and historical relationships in which I am willy-nilly involved" (69). Similarly, Tracy (*Analogical Imagination*, 346) concludes that, when we have shed our Enlightenment illusions, all expressions of consciousness (including self-consciousness) "possess not only their own manifest meanings but conceal and distort a series of latent, overdetermined meanings that demand new modes of analysis."

12. Dulles, "Toward a Postcritical Theology," *The Craft of Theology*, 11, 91, 132. More realistic than Dulles is Newman, who presumed that there had to be a robust dialectic between the several offices in the church lest any one of them become tyrannical. See Ian Ker, *John Henry Newman: A Biography*, Oxford Lives (Oxford: Oxford University Press, 1990), 703. Though Dulles (31) cites Jürgen Habermas's exposure of the "systematic blockages and distortions of communication in modern society," he does not cite Habermas's critique of Gadamer's position on tradition, which can be an instrument of oppression and needs to be critiqued from the perspective of the "hermeneutics of suspicion."

13. Dulles (ibid., 103); see also F. J. van Beeck, *God Encountered*, 1:163. Aidan Kavanaugh (*On Liturgical Theology* [New York: Pueblo Publishing Co., 1984], 145) compares science's attempt to arrive at a knowledge of "things" and what worship does: "The 'thing' about which systematic theology forms propositions is the encounter between God and the world which liturgical rite enacts among those of faith."

14. Dennis Cunningham, "Theology as Rhetoric," *Theological Studies* 52 (1991): 420–24.

15. F. J. van Beeck, S.J. (*God Encountered*, 1:43) locates constructive theology (a form of systematic theology) midway between church dogmatics, or the attempt to present the historical integrity of Christianity's belief, and fundamental theology, the study of the human condition as it is capable of being integrated into the order of grace and remain with its own integrity.

16. Quoted in Avery Dulles, S.J., "From Images to Truth: Newman on Revelation and Faith," *Theological Studies* 51, no. 2 (1990): 255.

17. Van Beeck (*God Encountered*, 1:79) calls for attention "to symptomatic elements in theological systems.... Intelligence and learning, we have discov-

ered, are not the same as self-awareness or mental health; capable theologians have this in common with most other men and women, that they enjoy only limited access to their motives, and, hence, that their insights may be twisted by psychodynamics that are less than entirely sound or constructive." He defines heresy as involving "selective interpretation of the Tradition, replacement of apostolic authority, and factionalism in the community" (231).

18. Ibid., 48.

19. Cunningham ("Theology as Rhetoric," 422) is critical of Tracy's "conversation" model and distinguishes his rhetorical hermeneutics from the former's "truth as disclosure." In addition he takes to task George Lindbeck's *The Nature of Doctrine: Religion and Theology in a Postliberal Age* (Philadelphia: Westminster Press, 1984) for reintroducing a dichotomy of subject and object in his overly analytic view of doctrine.

20. C. S. Lewis, *Surprised by Joy* (New York: Harcourt, Brace, 1955), 228–29.

21. A. N. Wilson, *C. S. Lewis: A Biography* (New York: W. W. Norton, 1990), 220.

22. Ibid., 219.

23. Peter Berger, *A Rumor of Angels: Modern Society and the Rediscovery of the Supernatural* (Garden City, N.Y.: Doubleday, 1969), 68.

24. The word "pistic" (from the Greek *pistis,* faith) is used by van Beeck (*Catholic Identity*, 30–34) to identify believers who have an inappropriate dependency on the clergy, understanding the church to be totalitarian and clerical and to exclude the laity from evangelizing. Generally, the whole pistic structure glorifies an uncritical, revised view of the past.

25. Van Beeck, *God Encountered*, 1:291.

26. Ibid., 1:260–67.

27. The common English translation of *vitam venturi saeculi* as "everlasting life" obscures the cosmic and corporate nature of the promised "new heavens and new earth" and makes it sound as if the creed were affirming personal immortality. Denzinger (*Enchiridion Symbolorum,* 31st ed. [Herder, 1950], 2) cites the older Western form as affirming the "resurrection of the flesh," to which other creeds and the earliest Eastern form add "eternal life."

28. Van Beeck, *God Encountered,* 1:221.

29. Gerald P. Fogarty, S.J. (*American Catholic Biblical Scholarship: A History from the Early Republic to Vatican II* [San Francisco: Harper & Row, 1989], 98–99) affirms that "more recent scholarship indicates that the pope himself was personally responsible for much of the witch hunt against suspected modernists, and that Merry del Val was frequently accused of being too diplomatic."

30. J. Mahoney, *The Making of Moral Theology: A Study of the Roman Catholic Tradition* (Oxford: Clarendon Press, 1987), 196.

31. Joseph Fitzmyer ("Romans," *New Jerome Biblical Commentary,* II, 835, 24) cites Wisdom 13:1–9, Assumption of Moses 1:13 as evidence of its Jewish currency.

32. Normand Bonneau ("Stages of Salvation History in Romans 1:16–3:26," *Église et Théologie* 23 [1992]: 188) demonstrates that Paul's argument is framed around the belief that "each stage of salvation history is characterized by a divine revelation with its attendant human response," a naive and unhistorical fiction that is not to be taken literally.

33. Sermon 151, 8, and *De nupt. et concup.*, I, 24, 27 cited in Peter Brown, *Augustine of Hippo* (Berkeley: University of California Press, 1969), 388.

34. Maloney (*Moral Theology*, 49–53) details how the struggle with Jansenism affected the shift in the teaching from grace to law.

35. Peter Brown (*The Body and Society: Men, Women, and Sexual Renunciation in Early Christianity* [New York: Columbia University Press, 1988], 355–61) details in the writings of men like Ambrose and Jerome the sexualizing of Paul's cosmic term "flesh" and the narrowing of its negative reference to valorize virginity.

36. *The Letters of J. R. R. Tolkien,* ed. Humphrey Carpenter (Boston: Houghton Mifflin, 1981), 100. Affirming that the story of Christ was a true myth that really happened, Tolkien "argued, 'doctrines' which are extracted from the 'myth' are less true than the 'myth' itself. The ideas are too large and all-embracing for the finite mind to absorb them. That is why divine providence revealed himself in story" (Wilson, *C. S. Lewis*, 126).

37. Peter Brown, *Augustine of Hippo* (Berkeley: University of California Press, 1969), 388. Owen Chadwick (*John Cassian*, 2d ed. [Cambridge: Cambridge University Press, 1968], 28) relates that, in 399 C.E., Bishop Theophilus of Alexandria (a follower of Origen) issued a festal letter denouncing the notion that any part of God was material. There were riots as a result, and the bishop was forced to submit to the expulsion of the Origenists, who denied the resurrection of the body.

38. Peter Brown (*The Body and Society,* 352) details Ambrose's inveighing against the "scar of sexuality" and his promotion of the perpetual virginity of Mary as upholding the "perpetual antithesis between the church and the saeculum." John P. Meier (*A Marginal Jew: Rethinking the Historical Jesus,* vol. 1, *The Roots of the Problem and the Person,* Anchor Bible Reference Library [New York: Doubleday, 1991], 324–32) concludes that "the most probable opinion is that the brothers and sisters of Jesus were true siblings" (331).

39. Rosemary Haughton, *The Catholic Thing* (Springfield, Ill.: Templegate, 1979), 37.

40. English text in the *Catholic Mind* (January 1951), 65–78.

41. Aside from the well-known citations in the New Testament that are said to signify Mary's Assumption, the Woman Clothed with the Sun (Rev 12:1) and the angel's greeting to her as "full of grace" (Luke 1:28), the most poetically appealing is from of Psalm 131:8: "Arise, O Lord, into thy resting place: thou and the Ark which you have sanctified."

42. Benedict T. Viviano, O.P., "Matthew," *New Jerome Biblical Commentary* II, 659.

43. *Peter in the New Testament: A Collaborative Assessment by Protestant and Roman Catholic Scholars,* ed. R. E. Brown, Karl P. Donfried, and John Reumann (Minneapolis: Augsburg Publishing House and New York: Paulist Press, 1973), 161.

44. Ibid., 107.

45. Newman lamented this state of affairs after Vatican I when he wrote to a high Anglican clergyman: "There are too many high ecclesiastics in Italy and England, who think that to believe is as easy as to obey — that is, they talk as if they did not know what an act of faith is" (Ker, *John Henry Newman,* 665).

Chapter 9: Believing and Critical Negation

1. Joseph Fuchs, S.J., *Natural Law: A Theological Investigation,* trans. Helmut Reckter, S.J., and John A. Dowling (New York: Sheed and Ward, 1965), 17.

2. *First Apology,* ch. 28, cited in Mahoney, *The Making of Moral Theology: A Study of the Roman Catholic Tradition* (Oxford: Clarendon Press, 1987), 73, n. 6.

3. Fuchs *(Natural Law,* 4–5) cites only a few papal references: Pius II (1359), Innocent XI (1679), and Alexander VIII (1690). Pope John Paul II's *Splendor Veritatis* (46–50) presumes the equivalence of "the law written on their hearts" and "the natural law" that "does not allow for any division between freedom and nature."

4. W. C. H. Wu, "Natural Law (Thomistic Analysis)," *New Catholic Encyclopedia,* 10:256.

5. B. F. Brown, "Natural Law," *New Catholic Encyclopedia,* 10:253.

6. The phrase "law of Christ" represents Paul's play on the law of Moses, which really means the activity of the Spirit; see Galatians 5:25–6:2.

7. Fuchs, *(Natural Law,* 149) cites Pius XII on "two parallel currents." His summation of Catholic teaching on natural law sounds curiously like Paul's analysis of the dilemma of all humanity *before* Christ came: "Although God's grace is therefore co-operating in every salutary fulfillment of the law of nature, this does not imply that man is not able to live such a life by means of a purely natural power. On the other hand it is certain that he would fail to do so because of his actual weakness.... He is unable to express his love for God *super omnia* by acting according to the natural law alone, although this again is exactly what the natural law demands of him" (180).

8. Amos Funkenstein *(Theology and the Scientific Imagination: From the Middle Ages to the Seventeenth Century* [Princeton: Princeton University Press, 1986], 53, n.44) records Aquinas's criticism of Maimonides' theory that the negative attributes of God were all that we know *(S.T.,* I q. 13, a. 2). But the riskiness of Thomas's position and the failure of Catholic thinkers to respect analogy has led Protestant thinkers like Karl Barth to call the "analogy of Being" the "anti-Christ," because it levels the distinction between the creator and created.

9. Anthony Battaglia *(Toward a Reformulation of Natural Law* [New York: Seabury, 1981], 37–38) argues that when this two-tiered theory was misappropriated and the relationship of the natural and the supernatural was misconstrued, what resulted was the two-story theology that I chronicled in chapter 7.

10. Jacques Delumeau *(Sin and Fear: The Emergence of a Western Guilt Culture, 13th–18th Centuries,* trans. Eric Nicholson [New York: St. Martin's Press, 1990], 282) notes that, even while "striving to react against Augustinian pessimism," Aquinas is caught between affirming that while "the majority of men have a sufficient knowledge for the guidance of life," only a minority "attain to a profound knowledge of things intelligible." The result is that "those who are saved are in the minority" *(S.T.* I, q. 23, a. 7). Hence, the magisterium has long claimed a special role for itself in understanding the demands of this not-so-natural law.

11. Battaglia, *Toward a Reformulation of Natural Law,* 60.

12. We should remind ourselves of Suarez's definition of law as "an act of a just and right will, by which a superior wills to oblige an inferior to do this or that" (quoted in Mahoney, *The Making of Moral Theology*, 226, n. 5).

13. Sebastian Moore, "Ratzinger's 'Nature' Isn't Natural: Aquinas, Contraception and Statistics," *Commonweal* (January 26, 1990): 50.

14. Robert Blair Kaiser *(The Encyclical That Never Was: The Story of the Pontifical Commission on Population, Family and Birth, 1964–66* [London: Sheed and Ward, 1987], 164) argues that the legal concept of *possessio juris* (that when a law is "in possession" it is difficult to overturn) swayed Paul VI not to follow his own commission's recommendations for development.

15. Sebastian Moore ("Ratzinger's 'Nature' Isn't Natural," 51) has commented: "In vain...does one point out to the exponents of this position that the relationship between coition and conception is statistical: that the possibility of conception resulting from intercourse has its own intelligibility, not understood in the ancient world, and that this new understanding dissolves the moral difference between "natural" and "artificial" birth control: for both interfere with the probability-shaped relationship between coition and conception. But all this is made irrelevant when we no longer consider nature as subject to "right reason" and consider it understandable only through the eyes of faith, the definitive organ of which is the papal magisterium."

16. The CDF's 1974 *Declaration on Abortion* (13) cites the "valuable confirmation" that modern genetic science brings to the "perpetual evidence" that the fertilized ovum is a human life, but denies to "biological sciences" the ability to make definitive judgments on philosophical and moral questions such as the moment when a human person is constituted.

17. Michael J. Coughlan *(The Vatican, the Law, and the Human Embryo* [Iowa City: University of Iowa Press, 1990], 104–11) argues extensively that the positions of the CDF regarding abortion and fertilization have seriously compromised the Thomistic basis of natural law argumentation. They increasing adopt a more Protestant approach to morality and presume grace supplants nature.

18. Quoted in Patrick Granfield, *The Limits of the Papacy* (New York: Crossroad, 1990), 42, n. 31. By contrast, John Henry Newman reacted to the exaggeration of the pope's infallibility as unlimited (in Cardinal Manning's pastoral letter of October 1870) by bemoaning the deification of the pope as a "a climax of tyranny." See Ian Ker, *John Henry Newman: A Biography*, Oxford Lives (Oxford: Oxford University Press, 1990), 659.

19. Brian Tierney, *The Origins of Papal Infallibility, 1150–1350: A Study on the Concepts of Infallibility, Sovereignty and Tradition in the Middle Ages* (Leiden: E. J. Brill, 1972), 33. Tierney's research also revealed that between "1150 and 1350 the doctrine of papal infallibility was not taught by any considerable number of theologians; nor was it proclaimed by pope and bishops in the discharge of their ordinary teaching office" (274).

20. Ibid., 187.

21. Ibid., 85.

22. See Dom Cuthbert Butler, *The Vatican Council 1869–1870* (London: Collins and Harvill Press, 1930), 249.

23. Tierney, *The Origins of Papal Infallibility*, 8, 272.

24. Georges Joussard, "The Fathers of the Church and the Immaculate Conception," in *The Dogma of the Immaculate Conception: History and Signif-*

icance, ed. Edward Dennis O'Connor, C.S.C., (Notre Dame, Ind.: University of Notre Dame Press, 1958), 65, quoting *De Carne Christi* 7 (PL 2, 766A–768C).

25. Ibid., 69, 71.

26. Carlo Balic, "The Mediaeval Controversy over the Immaculate Conception up to the Death of Scotus," in O'Connor, *The Dogma of the Immaculate Conception,* 183–91.

27. Ibid., 206–7.

28. Hugolinus Storff, O.F.M., *The Immaculate Conception: The Teaching of St. Thomas, St. Bonaventure and Bl. J. Duns Scotus on the Immaculate Conception of the Blessed Virgin Mary* (San Francisco: St. Francis Press, 1925), 197–200.

29. The precis is taken from René Laurentin ("The Role of the Papal Magisterium in the Development of the Dogma of the Immaculate Conception," in O'Connor, *The Dogma of the Immaculate Conception,* 271–324), who defended the form of the definition.

30. P. Ricoeur *(The Symbolism of Evil,* trans. Emerson Buchanan [Boston: Beacon Press, 1969], 28) attests that "an indissoluble complicity between sexuality and defilement seems to have been formed from time immemorial."

Chapter 10: Beyond the Needle's Eye: Mature Believing

1. Ian Ker *(John Henry Newman: A Biography* Oxford Lives [Oxford: Oxford University Press, 1990], 701) calls the preface to the republished *Lectures on the Prophetical Office* Newman's "last great contribution towards a theology of the Church."

2. John Cornwell, "Mind in Nature" (review of Gerald Edelman, *Bright Air, Brilliant Fire*), *The Tablet* (October 24, 1992): 325.

3. Janet Martin Soskice *(Metaphor and Religious Language* [Oxford: Clarendon, 1985], 137) offers to find analogies between the way metaphorical language is reality depicting in science and "the admittedly very different task of reality depiction in theology." In this latter effort, by speaking metaphorically "we do not claim to describe God but to point through His effects, beyond His effects, to Him." She concludes: "And, as we have argued, this separation of referring and defining is at the very heart of metaphorical speaking and is what makes it not only possible but necessary that in our stammering after a transcendent God we must speak, for the most part, metaphorically or not at all" (140).

4. Jaroslav Pelikan *(Christianity and Classical Culture: The Metamorphosis of Natural Theology in the Christian Encounter with Hellenism* [New Haven: Yale University Press, 1993], 41) notes how apophatic theology as early as the fourth century was accused of defying Aristotle's principle of the universal desire to know. In the face of this accusation, Gregory of Nyssa insisted on the "whispered no" that prevented symbolic theology from becoming either a nihilism or a claim to know God directly: "The divine being is to be known only in the impossibility of perceiving it."

5. Christopher F. Mooney, S.J., "Theology and the Heisenberg Uncertainty Principle," paper delivered at the Catholic Theological Society of America, Pittsburgh, Pa., June 1992, 61, 65.

6. Ibid., 66, citing Holmes Rolston III, *Science and Religion* (New York: Random House, 1987), 334.

7. Luke's use of "son of Joseph," with the parenthetical "as it was thought" (3:23) means to cast doubt about Joseph's real fatherhood. But the reference in John 6:42 casts equal doubt on Jesus' birth from any human parents. The unbelieving crowd affirms it knew "where he comes from," but the point is that they do not know of Jesus' heavenly origin.

8. Both Peter (Matt 16:16) and the High Priest (26:63) put the two titles together, and in both places their "royal" Christology is complemented by Jesus' teaching about the suffering and exalted Son of Man.

9. Quoted in Mansi (Graz: Akademische Druck-u Verlaganstalt, 1960–61), 4:891.

10. See Romans 6:23; 8:10; 14:11; Galatians 2:20; 2 Corinthians 4:10–12.

Index of Biblical Citations

Index of Names

337

Index of Subjects